# The 50 Greatest Players in Dodgers History

### Robert W. Cohen

**BLUE RIVER PRESS**

Indianapolis, Indiana

**The 50 Greatest Players in Dodgers History**
Copyright © 2017 by Robert W. Cohen

Published by **Blue River Press**
Indianapolis, Indiana
www.brpressbooks.com

Distributed by **Cardinal Publishers Group**
Tom Doherty Company, Inc.
www.cardinalpub.com

ISBN: 978-1-68157-057-0

Cover Design by Scott Lohr
Cover Photos:
    Sandy Koufax courtesy of Legendary Auctions,
    Jackie Robinson courtesy of RMYAuctions,
    Vintage Baseball Background by Yobro/Dreamstime
Editor: Dani McCormick
Book design by Dave Reed

Printed in the United States of America

10 9 8 7 6 5 4 3 2 1

# CONTENTS

# FOREWORD

Early in the summer of 2016, Bob Cohen contacted me about his latest project, *The 50 Greatest Players in Dodgers History*, and asked me for permission to use a couple of photos of myself that I had posted to Flickr. At that time, I told him, "If I own the rights, you can use them." I remembered that Bob had previously used photos from my site for earlier books on the 50 Greatest Players of the Yankees, Red Sox and Cardinals, and how proud I was to see my work published. I also recalled the time and effort that it took me to secure the rights to the photos that I ended up including in my 2014 autobiography entitled, *Bring In the Right-Hander!* It made a huge difference when someone lent a helping hand. As Willie Stargell once said, "What goes around comes around."

Bob also asked if I would be interested in writing the forward to the book. Now, that's an honor and I was flattered to be considered. I also knew that it meant reading the manuscript carefully prior to its release since I felt a sense of obligation to his readers. After reading Bob's three previous books on the Yankees, Red Sox and Cardinals, I had an idea of what to expect. But this project had a more personal flavor for me.

Considering that this book focuses on many of the Brooklyn and Los Angeles players that I knew personally as teammates, from Dodger events and numerous Fantasy Camps, this would be a chance to separate the personal from the professional and see how they stacked up against one another. This could be and would be fun!

Before I read the manuscript, I was aware of two facts. First, the rankings are subjective to Bob's criteria, which he discusses in the Introduction. I'll leave that to him. Now, you may not agree entirely with him (truth be told—I had my own opinions), but looking at the big picture, isn't that what this book is about? Opinions. Bob states his, backed by his own criteria, and opens the door for the reader to express his or her own, using whatever metrics they wish. That's what makes an entertaining read.

Second, I knew that I was going to learn several things about many former Dodger players that I didn't already know. Who knew how Edwin Snider earned the nickname the *Duke*? How a late-night poker game led to a pain-free pitching elbow for Dazzy Vance? Who encouraged Maury Wills to switch-hit? What foreign substance did Burleigh Grimes use on his spitter? To whom was the quote "Hit 'em where they ain't" attributed? All of these trivia bits are in this book. And there are many more. The trivia alone is worth the price of the book.

Now, for the question many of you are waiting for me to answer: How do I feel about being rated number 56? That's easy! The numbers warrant it. I put an ice bag on my ego and got over it.

If you're a Dodgers fan, *The 50 Greatest Players in Dodgers History* is a must-have book. Grab a chair, kick back and enjoy the stories about the best to wear a Brooklyn or Los Angeles uniform.

Jerry Reuss
Dodgers Pitcher 1979–1987

# ACKNOWLEDGMENTS

I would like to express my gratitude to the grandchildren of Leslie Jones, who, through the Trustees of the Boston Public Library, Print Department, supplied many of the photos included in this book.

I also wish to thank Troy R. Kinunen of MEARS Online Auctions. com, Kate of RMYauctions.com, Pristineauction.com, Bradley Park of ICCsports.com, Jerry Reuss, George A. Kitrinos, Keith Allison, Will Liu, and Griffin Lauerman, each of whom generously contributed to the photographic content of this work.

# INTRODUCTION

## The Dodger Legacy

Originally founded in 1883 by real estate magnate and baseball enthusiast Charles Byrne and his brother-in-law Joseph Doyle, the team that later became known as the Brooklyn Dodgers spent the first year of their existence playing in the minor Inter-State League under the name of the Brooklyn Atlantics. Taking their initial moniker from a defunct team that had played in that New York borough more than a decade earlier, the Atlantics entered the Major Leagues the following year, experiencing very little success in the American Association the next few seasons after changing their name to the Brooklyn Grays. However, they gradually developed into a contender under Manager William "Gunner" McGunnigle, capturing the double-A championship in 1889, after having the moniker "Bridegrooms" affixed to them one year earlier following the nearly simultaneous marriages of seven of their members. Invited to join the more prestigious National League prior to the start of the ensuing campaign, the Bridegrooms won the pennant in their first year in the senior circuit, posting a league-best mark of 86-43 in 1890.

The Brooklyn franchise spent its first several seasons playing in Washington Park, situated on Brooklyn's Fifth Avenue, between third and fourth Streets, before moving into nearby "New" Washington Park, which opened on April 30, 1898. Known legally as the "Brooklyn Base Ball Club" throughout the period despite having nicknames such as the "Grays" and "Bridegrooms" affixed to it at different times, the team was also commonly referred to as the "Trolley Dodgers" due to the complex maze of trolley cars that weaved through the borough of Brooklyn at that time.

McGunnigle and the Bridegrooms parted ways following the conclusion of the 1890 campaign, after which the team entered into a period of mediocrity while being directed by five different managers. Yet, even though they finished as high as third in just one of the next eight seasons, the Bridegrooms featured several outstanding players, including outfielders Mike Griffin and Tommy "Oyster" Burns, shortstop Tommy Corcoran, first baseman Dan Brouthers, and pitchers Tom Lovett and William "Brickyard" Kennedy.

Following the passing of Brooklyn principal owner Charles Byrne in 1897, Harry Von der Horst and Ned Hanlon—co-owners of the Baltimore Orioles—purchased a half interest in the Bridegrooms. Although Hanlon retained his Baltimore presidency, he assumed the managerial reins in Brooklyn in 1899, bringing along with him many of the Orioles' most talented players, including future Hall of Famers "Wee" Willie Keeler, Joe Kelley, and Hughie Jennings. Subsequently dubbed the "Superbas" after a traveling acrobatic troupe popular at the time, Brooklyn captured the next two NL pennants, winning their first world championship in 1900, when they defeated second-place Pittsburgh in a series played for the elegant Chronicle-Telegraph Cup.

The success the Superbas experienced at the turn of the century proved to be short-lived, though, since they ended up losing most of their best players to the newly-formed American League over the course of the next few seasons. Bereft of talent, Brooklyn posted a winning record in just three of the next 14 seasons, finishing higher than fifth only twice during that period.

However, Charles Ebbets, who started out as a ticket seller at Washington Park before he eventually became majority owner of the Superbas by purchasing Von der Horst's stock in the club, helped restore the team to respectability. After constructing Ebbets Field, which opened in 1913 and remained home to the club until it moved to Los Angeles in 1958, Ebbets hired former big-league catcher Wilbert Robinson to manage his team one year later. Following a pair of mediocre finishes, the "Robins," so named because of the overall impact that "Uncle Robbie" made on the Brooklyn franchise and the city as a whole, returned to the top of the National League standings in 1916, capturing their fourth pennant, before losing to the Boston Red Sox in the World Series in five games. After three more subpar seasons, the Robins gained another berth in the fall classic in 1920, only to lose to the Cleveland Indians, this time, five-games-to-two. Standout players for the Robins during Robinson's first several years at the helm included first baseman Jake Daubert and future Hall of Fame outfielder Zack Wheat, who starred for the team for nearly two decades.

Robinson remained manager in Brooklyn another eleven years, with the Robins finishing higher than fourth just once during that time. Finding it particularly difficult to focus on his managerial duties after taking over as team president as well following the passing of Charles Ebbets in 1925, Robinson ended up piloting a squad that subsequently became known as the "Daffiness Boys" for their often puzzling, and always colorful, style of play. Yet, the Brooklyn squads of the 1920s and early 1930s featured a pair of truly exceptional players—right-handed pitcher Dazzy Vance, who captured league MVP honors in 1924, and hard-hitting outfielder Babe Herman, who, in spite of his brilliance at the plate, came to epitomize the team's unpredictable play in the field and on the base paths.

The Brooklyn franchise continued to struggle after Robinson resigned following the conclusion of the 1931 campaign, placing higher than fifth in the NL standings in just one of the next seven seasons, as leadership of the team passed from Max Carey, to Casey Stengel, to Burleigh Grimes. It was during this period, though, that the team became officially known as the "Dodgers," with that name appearing on both home and road jerseys for the first time in 1933.

The hiring of Larry MacPhail as Executive Vice President and General Manager in 1938 brought about dramatic changes in Brooklyn. The innovative MacPhail, who earlier had introduced night baseball to the Major Leagues while serving as GM in Cincinnati, did the same in Brooklyn. He also made improvements to Ebbets Field, appointed Leo Durocher as manager, and bolstered the Dodgers' roster by acquiring veteran sluggers Dolph Camilli and Joe Medwick. The new-look Dodgers ended up capturing the NL pennant in 1941, with Camilli earning league MVP honors and sophomore sensation Pete Reiser finishing second to him in the balloting. However, they once again came up short in the World Series, losing to the Yankees in five games.

After a close second-place finish in 1942, the Dodgers fell out of contention during the war years of 1943-1945. They also lost MacPhail to military service during that time, although they found a suitable replacement for him in longtime Cardinals GM Branch Rickey. Rickey, a master talent-evaluator who excelled at signing and developing young players, quickly built up the Dodgers farm system, making it the deepest in both leagues. Yet, his greatest achievement proved to be the 1946 signing of Jackie Robinson, who integrated the Major Leagues one year later.

The signing of Robinson and the subsequent additions of several other young stars enabled the Dodgers to enter into the greatest period in franchise history. After losing to the Cardinals in a three-game play-off to determine the NL pennant-winner in 1946, the Dodgers won six of the next 10 league championships, finishing a close second on three other occasions. Led by Robinson, slugging first baseman Gil Hodges, short-stop Pee Wee Reese, outfielders Duke Snider and Carl Furillo, three-time league MVP Roy Campanella, and star pitcher Don Newcombe, the Dodgers emerged as a perennial contender, capturing the NL pennant in 1947, 1949, 1952, 1953, 1955, and 1956. They also came within an eyelash of winning the title in both 1950 and 1951, dropping a three-game playoff to the arch-rival New York Giants in the second of those campaigns when Giants outfielder Bobby Thomson hit his historic "Shot Heard 'Round the World." Unfortunately, "The Boys of Summer," as they came to be known, came out on top in just one of their six World Series appearances, defeat-ing the Yankees in the 1955 fall classic in seven games, but losing to them the other five times.

Still, in spite of the success the Dodgers experienced on the field, they found themselves unable to draw large crowds to antiquated Ebbets Field, leaving team President and chief stockholder Walter O'Malley, who as-sumed both positions in 1950, to seek a more modern stadium for his ball club. Unable to reach a suitable agreement with New York City officials, O'Malley ultimately decided to move his team to the West Coast, announc-ing on October 8, 1957 that, after 68 seasons in Brooklyn, the Dodgers intended to relocate to the city of Los Angeles. O'Malley also convinced New York Giants owner Horace Stoneham to join him on the West Coast, with Stoneham subsequently announcing his intention to move his team to San Francisco. The Brooklyn Dodgers played their final game at Ebbets Field on September 24, 1957, when they defeated the Pittsburgh Pirates by a score of 2-0.

While Brooklyn fans lamented the loss of their beloved Dodgers, the fans of Los Angeles welcomed the "Boys of Summer" with open arms. The Dodgers called the Los Angeles Memorial Coliseum home until 1962, when they moved into brand-new Dodger Stadium, an aesthetically pleasing ball park situated at 1000 Elysian Park Avenue, in the hills above Los Angeles.

With the Dodgers moving to California, much of the team's nucleus aging, and Roy Campanella's career tragically ending as the result of an off-season car crash that left him partially paralyzed, the 1958 campaign proved to be a season of adjustment, with the club posting its first losing record in 14 years. However, led by manager Walter Alston, who assumed control of the team in 1954, the Dodgers re-established themselves as perennial contenders the following season, winning the pennant by sweeping the Milwaukee Braves in a best-of-three playoff, before defeating the Chicago White Sox in six games in the World Series. After strong showings in each of the next two seasons as well, the Dodgers barely missed returning to the fall classic in 1962, failing to do so when they lost a three-game playoff to the rival Giants. But, led by co-staff aces Sandy Koufax and Don Drysdale, speedsters Maury Wills and Willie Davis, and two-time batting champion Tommy Davis, the Dodgers captured three of the next four NL flags, finishing first in the senior circuit in 1963, 1965, and 1966. They also won the World Series in two of those years, sweeping the Yankees in four straight games in 1963 and edging out Minnesota in seven games in 1965, before being swept themselves by Baltimore in 1966.

Following the premature retirement of Sandy Koufax due to an arthritic elbow prior to the start of the 1967 campaign, the Dodgers experienced a precipitous fall from grace, finishing well out of contention in each of the next two seasons. They eventually regrouped, though, posting four consecutive second-place finishes in the newly-formed NL West, before finally capturing their first division title in 1974. However, after defeating the Pittsburgh Pirates three-games-to-one in the NLCS, the Dodgers came up short against the Oakland Athletics in the World Series, losing to their American League counterparts in five games.

Alston managed the Dodgers to another pair of second-place finishes before choosing to announce his retirement towards the end of the 1976 campaign. He ended his twenty-three-year managerial career with a total of 2,040 regular-season wins, four world championships, seven National League pennants, six NL Manager of the Year selections, and a plaque waiting for him in Cooperstown.

The Dodgers continued their winning ways following Alston's retirement, capturing the next two National League pennants under new manager, Tommy Lasorda, who remained at the helm nearly as long as his predecessor, serving as skipper in L.A. for nearly 20 years. But, after disposing of Philadelphia in the 1977 and 1978 NLCS, the Dodgers fell victim to their old nemesis, the Yankees, losing both fall classics to New York in six games. Yet, even though they failed to win a World Series during the

1970s, the Dodgers remained one of baseball's most consistent teams, averaging 91 victories per season over that ten-year span. Outstanding performers during the period included infielders Steve Garvey, Davey Lopes, and Ron Cey, outfielders Dusty Baker and Reggie Smith, and pitchers Don Sutton and Tommy John.

After failing to make the playoffs in either 1979 or 1980, the Dodgers gained a measure of revenge against the Yankees in the 1981 World Series, defeating them in six games behind an excellent pitching staff that included NL Rookie of the Year and Cy Young Award winner Fernando Valenzuela. Los Angeles advanced to the postseason three more times during the 1980s, losing to Philadelphia in the 1983 NLCS and St. Louis in the 1985 NLCS, before upsetting the heavily-favored New York Mets in the 1988 Championship Series. The Dodgers subsequently defeated Oakland in the World Series, riding the pitching arm of NL Cy Young Award winner Orel Hershiser and a memorable game-winning home run by league MVP Kirk Gibson to a five-game victory over the powerful Athletics.

The Dodgers did not return to the playoffs for another seven years, finally advancing to the postseason tournament again in 1995, when they lost to the Cincinnati Reds in three straight games in the NLDS. A similar fate awaited them the following year after Tommy Lasorda turned over his managerial duties to longtime Dodger shortstop Bill Russell, who led his team into the playoffs only to be eliminated in the opening round in three straight games by the Atlanta Braves. Yet, even though the Dodgers failed to advance beyond the first round of the postseason tournament at any time during the 1990s, their farm system continued to produce some of the game's best young players, at one point turning out five consecutive NL Rookie of the Year Award winners—Eric Karros (1992), Mike Piazza (1993), Raul Mondesi (1994), Hideo Nomo (1995), and Todd Hollandsworth (1996).

Although the Dodgers remained a solid ball club the next several years as leadership of the team passed from Russell, to Davey Johnson, and, finally, to Jim Tracy, they failed to advance to the postseason again until 2004, when they once again came up short in the NLDS, this time losing to the St. Louis Cardinals in four games. Since that time, the Dodgers have made seven more playoff appearances, finishing first in the NL West on six separate occasions, including four straight times, from 2013 to 2016. But they have been unable to make it back to the World Series, losing in the NLDS three times and the NLCS the other four times. Still, with outstanding players such as Adrian Gonzalez, Corey Seager, Kenley Jansen, and baseball's best pitcher, Clayton Kershaw, gracing their roster, it appears to be only a matter of time before the Dodgers return to the fall classic. Their next World Series appearance will be their 19$^{th}$, with their 21 National League pennants representing the second-highest total in the history of the senior circuit (the Giants have won 23). The Dodgers have also won 15 NL West titles and six World Series.

In addition to the level of success the Dodgers have reached as a team over the years, a significant number of players have attained notable individual honors while wearing a Dodger uniform. The franchise boasts 11 MVP winners and holds major-league records for the most Cy Young Award winners (12) and Rookie of the Year Award winners (16). The Dodgers have also featured 10 home run champions and 11 batting champions. Noted for their exceptional pitching through the years, the Dodgers have also had 17 pitchers lead the National League in ERA and 22 hurlers top the senior circuit in strikeouts. Meanwhile, 40 members of the Baseball Hall of Fame spent at least one full season playing for the Dodgers, 13 of whom had several of their finest seasons as a member of the team.

# FACTORS USED TO DETERMINE RANKINGS

It should come as no surprise that selecting the 50 greatest players ever to perform for a team with the rich history of the Dodgers presented a difficult and daunting task. Even after I narrowed the field down to a mere fifty men, I found myself faced with the challenge of ranking the elite players that remained. Certainly, the names of Sandy Koufax, Don Drysdale, Jackie Robinson, Duke Snider, Roy Campanella, and Clayton Kershaw would appear at, or near, the top of virtually everyone's list, although the order might vary somewhat from one person to the next. Several other outstanding performers have gained general recognition through the years as being among the greatest players ever to wear a Dodger uniform. Gil Hodges, Pee Wee Reese, Don Sutton, Steve Garvey, and Mike Piazza head the list of other Dodger icons. But, how does one differentiate between the all-around excellence of Jackie Robinson and the extraordinary hitting ability of Mike Piazza; or the pitching greatness of Sandy Koufax and the outstanding offensive skills displayed by Duke Snider? After initially deciding who to include on my list, I then needed to determine what criteria to use when formulating my final rankings.

The first thing I decided to examine was the level of dominance a player attained during his time in Brooklyn or Los Angeles. How often did he lead the National League in some major offensive or pitching statistical category? How did he fare in the annual MVP and/or Cy Young voting? How many times did he make the All-Star Team?

I also needed to weigh the level of statistical compilation a player achieved while wearing a Dodger uniform. Where does a batter rank in team annals in the major offensive categories? How high on the all-time list of Dodger hurlers does a pitcher rank in wins, ERA, complete games, innings pitched, shutouts, and saves? Of course, I also needed to consider the era in which the player performed when evaluating his overall numbers. For example, a modern-day starting pitcher such as Clayton Kershaw is not likely to throw nearly as many complete games or shutouts as either Dazzy Vance or Sandy Koufax, who anchored the Dodgers' starting rotation during the 1920s and 1960s, respectively. Meanwhile, Babe Herman had a distinct advantage over Carl Furillo in that he competed during an era that was far more conducive to posting huge offensive numbers. And Dead Ball Era stars such as Jake Daubert and Zack Wheat were not likely to hit nearly as many home runs as the players who performed for the team after the Major Leagues began using a livelier ball.

Other important factors I needed to consider were the overall contributions a player made to the success of the team, the degree to which he improved the fortunes of the ball club during his time in Brooklyn or Los Angeles, the manner in which he impacted the team, both on and off the field, and the degree to which he added to the Dodger legacy of winning. While the number of pennants the Dodgers won during a particular player's years with the ball club certainly entered into the equation, I chose not to deny a top performer his rightful place on the list if his years in Brooklyn or Los Angeles happened to coincide with a lack of overall success by the team. As a result, the names of players such as Eric Karros and Ramon Martinez will appear in these rankings.

There are two other things I wish to mention. Firstly, I only considered a player's performance while playing for the Dodgers when formulating my rankings. That being the case, the names of exceptional players such as Tommy John and Gary Sheffield, both of whom had many of their best years while playing for other teams, may appear lower on this list than one might expect. In addition, since several of the rules that governed nineteenth-century baseball (including permitting batters to dictate the location of pitches until 1887, situating the pitcher's mound only fifty feet from home plate until 1893, and crediting a stolen base to a runner any time he advanced from first to third base on a hit) differed dramatically from those to which we have become accustomed, I elected to include only those players who competed after 1900, which is generally considered to be the beginning of baseball's "modern era." Doing so eliminated from consideration nineteenth-century standouts such as Bob Caruthers, Dan Brouthers, and Mike Griffin.

Having established the guidelines to be used throughout this book, we are ready to take a look at the 50 greatest players in Dodgers history, starting with number one and working our way down to number fifty.

# The 50 Greatest Players
# in Dodgers History

Courtesy of MEARS Online Auctions

The most dominant pitcher of his time, Sandy Koufax won three Cy Young Awards and one NL MVP trophy over a four-year period during the mid-1960's

# 1

# SANDY KOUFAX

In spite of the greatness of Duke Snider and Roy Campanella, Jackie Robinson proved to be the only serious challenger to Sandy Koufax for the number one spot in these rankings. Yet, even though Robinson excelled for the Dodgers at the bat and on the base paths for nearly a decade, overcoming numerous obstacles along the way, it was the manner in which he impacted the game and society as a whole by integrating the Major Leagues that truly made him such a legendary figure. Meanwhile, although some baseball historians object to the idea of Koufax being included among the very greatest pitchers of all time since he spent his first six seasons toiling in mediocrity, even his harshest critics tend to agree with the general consensus that the Brooklyn-born left-hander may well have been the most dominant pitcher in baseball history over the second half of his Hall of Fame career. Between 1961 and 1966, Koufax led all National League hurlers in wins three times, earned run average five times, strikeouts four times, shutouts three times, WHIP four times, and complete games and innings pitched two times each. He also tossed four no-hitters and one perfect game, won three pitching Triple Crowns, claimed three Cy Young Awards, and garnered league MVP honors once during that period, finishing second in the balloting two other times. Koufax's brilliant pitching led the Dodgers to three pennants and two world championships. Here, it earns him the top spot on this list.

Born in Brooklyn, New York on December 30, 1935, young Sanford Braun lived in a single-parent household for six years until his divorced mother decided to remarry after her son turned nine years of age. Taking the name of his stepfather, Irving Koufax, Sandy moved with his parents to Long Island shortly thereafter, before the family chose to return to the borough of Brooklyn some five years later. Koufax attended Brooklyn's

Lafayette High School, where he developed a reputation for excelling in both basketball and baseball. Although basketball remained Koufax's first love throughout most of his teenage years, he gradually began gravitating more towards baseball after the Coney Island Sports League's Parkviews recruited him to pitch for them.

Koufax continued to play both sports while attending the University of Cincinnati, making both the freshman basketball and the varsity baseball teams. However, the young hurler's attention turned primarily to baseball after he received tryouts with the New York Giants at the Polo Grounds and the Pittsburgh Pirates at Forbes Field. During his tryout with the Pirates, Koufax made enough of an impression on then-Pittsburgh GM Branch Rickey that the legendary general manager told his scout Clyde Sukeforth that the left-hander had the "greatest arm [he had] ever seen." Nevertheless, the Pirates failed to offer Koufax a contract until he had already committed himself to the Brooklyn Dodgers, whose scout, Al Campanis, later said, "There are two times in my life the hair on my arms has stood up: The first time I saw the ceiling of the Sistine Chapel, and the first time I saw Sandy Koufax throw a fastball."

After the Dodgers signed Koufax to a huge bonus in 1954, they found themselves unable to send him to the minor leagues since his status as a "bonus baby" forced them to keep him on their major-league roster for at least two years. Unable to either hone his skills in the minors or earn a spot in the Brooklyn starting rotation, the nineteen-year-old Koufax ended up spending most of 1955 languishing in the Dodger bullpen, appearing in only 12 games, making just 5 starts, and compiling a record of 2-2 and an ERA of 3.02, in 41⅔ total innings of work.

Although it became apparent from the outset that the 6'2", 210-pound Koufax had tremendous velocity on his fastball, it soon became equally evident that he had yet to master control of any of his pitches. Duke Snider, already a star in Brooklyn by the time Koufax arrived on the scene, later recalled, "When he [Koufax] first came up, he couldn't throw a ball inside the batting cage."

Koufax continued to see little action over the course of the next two seasons, when, working primarily out of the Dodgers bullpen, he posted a combined record of just 7-8, along with ERAs of 4.91 and 3.88. The struggling southpaw also failed to gain better command of his pitches during that time, averaging about one walk for every two innings pitched. However, he also displayed an ability to throw the ball by opposing batters, averaging nearly a strikeout for every inning of work.

Koufax began to show occasional flashes of brilliance after the Dodgers moved to Los Angeles following the conclusion of the 1957 campaign, striking out 16 batters in a June 1959 contest, before tying Bob Feller's major-league mark a little over one month later by fanning 18 batters in one game. Nevertheless, his overall performance remained extremely inconsistent. In addition to compiling a composite record of 27-30 between 1958 and 1960, Koufax posted an ERA near or above 4.00 in each of those three seasons.

Koufax eventually became so frustrated with his lack of success that he seriously considered leaving the game before he even turned twenty-five years of age. But everything began to come together for him during spring training in 1961, when Dodger catcher Norm Sherry advised him to soften his grip on the baseball and relax his body before releasing it. Koufax later noted, "I became a good pitcher when I stopped trying to make them miss the ball and started trying to make them hit it."

Employing his new technique, Koufax became a completely different pitcher in 1961. En route to earning the first of his six straight All-Star selections, Koufax compiled a record of 18-13 and an ERA of 3.52, threw 255 innings and 15 complete games, walked only 96 batters, and recorded a league-leading 269 strikeouts, breaking in the process Christy Mathewson's fifty-eight-year-old NL mark of 267. The twenty-six-year-old southpaw continued his ascension towards stardom the following year, when, despite being limited by an injured pitching hand to only 26 starts and 184 innings, he went 14-7, with 215 strikeouts and a league-leading 2.54 ERA.

Koufax subsequently established himself as baseball's dominant pitcher in 1963, beginning an extraordinary four-year run during which he compiled an amazing overall record of 97-27. Here are the numbers he posted over the course of those four seasons:

1963: **25**-5, **1.88** ERA, **306** Strikeouts, **0.875** WHIP, **11** Shutouts, 20 CG, 311 IP*

1964: 19-5, **1.74** ERA, 223 Strikeouts, **0.928** WHIP, **7** Shutouts, 15 CG, 223 IP

1965: **26**-8, **2.04** ERA, **382** Strikeouts, **0.855** WHIP, 8 Shutouts, **27** CG, **335.2** IP

1966: **27**-9, **1.73** ERA, **317** Strikeouts, 0.985 WHIP, **5** Shutouts, **27** CG, **323** IP

*Please note that any numbers printed in bold throughout this book signify that the player led the National League in that particular statistical category that year.

With an arsenal that included an explosive fastball and the sharpest-breaking curveball in the sport, Koufax proved to be practically unhittable. In addition to capturing the pitcher's version of the triple crown in three of those four years by leading all NL hurlers in wins, ERA, and strikeouts, Koufax finished first in WHIP and shutouts three times each, while also topping the senior circuit in complete games and innings pitched twice each. At a time when only one Cy Young Award was presented to the best pitcher in both leagues combined, Koufax earned Cy Young honors in 1963, 1965, and 1966. He likely would have won the award in 1964 as well had he not been limited to 28 starts by pain in his pitching arm. Koufax also was named NL MVP in 1963, and he finished second in the balloting in both 1965 and 1966. The Dodgers captured the NL pennant in three of those four years, winning the World Series in 1963 and 1965 as well, with Koufax posting a composite record of 4-1 in those two fall classics, en route to earning Series MVP honors both times. .

The degree to which Koufax dominated the baseball world over the course of those four seasons earned him the admiration and respect of opponents and teammates alike, with pundits often referring to him as "The Left Arm of God."

Hall of Fame outfielder Richie Ashburn stated, "Either he throws the fastest ball I've ever seen, or I'm going blind."

Philadelphia Phillies Manager Gene Mauch commented, "He [Koufax] throws a 'radio ball,' a pitch you hear, but you don't see."

Willie Stargell expressed his admiration for the left-hander by saying, "Trying to hit Koufax was like trying to drink coffee with a fork."

John Roseboro, who served as the Dodgers' primary receiver during Koufax's peak seasons, recalled, "Catching him [Koufax] was like, 'Well, we're gonna kick someone's ass tonight.'"

Duke Snider, who saw Koufax close-up during the various stages of the left-hander's career, said of his former teammate, "He was a fantastic pitcher...the best I've seen."

Unfortunately, Koufax began experiencing pain in his pitching arm in 1964 that grew increasingly worse over the course of the next two seasons. Plagued by a growing arthritic condition in his left elbow, Koufax had to resort to taking pain-killers and anti-inflammatories regularly, and to soaking his arm in a tub of ice after every start. Warned by doctors that he would eventually lose the use of his left arm if he continued to pitch, Koufax elected to announce his retirement at only thirty years of age shortly after the Dodgers lost the 1966 World Series to the Baltimore Orioles. Standing before the assembled media, Koufax explained, "I've been getting cortisone shots pretty regularly, and I don't want to take a chance on completely disabling myself…I've got a lot of years to live after baseball, and I would like to live them with the complete use of my body."

Koufax ended his playing career with a record of 165-87 that gave him an outstanding winning percentage of .655. He also compiled an ERA of 2.76 and a WHIP of 1.106, struck out 2,396 batters in 2,324⅓ innings of work, threw 137 complete games, and tossed 40 shutouts. Many experts consider Koufax, at his peak, to be the greatest pitcher who ever lived.

After retiring from baseball, the always guarded Koufax continued to protect his privacy. Shunning the spotlight, he relocated frequently, changing his address whenever he felt the general public had become too familiar with his whereabouts. Shortly after leaving the game, Koufax signed a ten-year contract with NBC to be a color commentator on the television station's weekly telecasts. However, uncomfortable in front of the camera, he quit before the start of the 1973 season, one year after he became the youngest man ever elected to the Baseball Hall of Fame. Koufax subsequently remained close to the game by serving as a guest pitching coach in various training camps, including those of the Dodgers and New York Mets. He also spent 11 years working as a roving minor league pitching instructor in the Los Angeles farm system, before accepting, in 2013, the position of Special Advisor to Dodgers Chairman Mark Walter. He also currently serves as a member of the advisory board of the Baseball Assistance Team, which is dedicated to helping former Major League, Minor League, and Negro League players through financial and medical difficulties.

In discussing Koufax's life and career, Tom Verducci of *Sports Illustrated* wrote, "Koufax was the kind of man boys idolized, men envied, women swooned over, and rabbis thanked, especially when he refused to pitch Game One of the 1965 World Series because it fell on Yom Kippur.

And, when he was suddenly, tragically done with baseball, he slipped into a life nearly monastic in its privacy."

## Career Highlights:

**Best Season:** Koufax pitched magnificently in all three of his Cy Young campaigns, any of which would have made an excellent choice. Yet, even though he posted a sub-2.00 in both 1963 and 1966, I ultimately settled on 1965 due to the slight superiority of his overall numbers. En route to earning a runner-up finish to Willie Mays in the NL MVP voting, Koufax won 26 games, compiled a 2.04 ERA, tossed 8 shutouts, and posted career-best marks in complete games (27), innings pitched (335 ⅔), WHIP (0.855), and strikeouts (382), establishing a new major-league record in the last category in the process.

**Memorable Moments/Greatest Performances:** Koufax made his first win in the majors a memorable one, allowing just 2 hits and recording 14 strikeouts during a 7-0 victory over the Cincinnati Reds on August 27, 1955.

Koufax tied Bob Feller's major-league record by striking out 18 batters during a 5-2 victory over the Giants on August 31, 1959. Dodger outfielder Wally Moon made a winner out of Koufax when he hit a three-run walk-off homer off Giants reliever Al Worthington in the bottom of the ninth.

Koufax tossed the first of his two career one-hitters on May 23, 1960, when he walked 6 batters, struck out 10, and allowed just a second-inning single to Pittsburgh pitcher Bernie Daniels, in defeating the Pirates by a score of 1-0.

Koufax turned in another dominant performance later in the year, on August 11, 1960, when he struck out 13 batters and allowed just 1 walk during a 3-0, two-hit shutout of the Cincinnati Reds.

Koufax posted nearly identical numbers on June 20, 1961, when he shut out the Cubs by a score of 3-0, surrendering just 2 hits and 2 walks, while recording 14 strikeouts in the process.

Koufax turned in another superb effort against the Cubs three months later, on September 20, 1961, earning a 3-2 victory over them by working a career-high 13 innings, allowing 7 hits, and striking out 15 batters.

Continuing to torment Chicago batsmen the following year, Koufax equaled his career high in strikeouts on April 24, 1962, when he fanned 18 batters during a 10-2 win over the Cubs.

Koufax threw his first no-hitter a little over two months later, on June 30, 1962, when he surrendered 5 walks and struck out 13, in defeating the overmatched Mets by a score of 5-0.

Koufax turned in one of his most dominant performances of the 1963 campaign on April 19, when he allowed just 2 hits and recorded 14 strike-outs during a 2-0 victory over Houston.

Koufax topped that effort the following month, though, when, on May 11, 1963, he tossed his second no-hitter, allowing just a pair of walks during an 8-0 win over the Giants.

Koufax threw the third no-hitter of his career a little over one year later, on June 4, 1964, when he struck out 12 and surrendered just a fourth-inning walk to Dick Allen during a 3-0 victory over the Phillies.

Koufax nearly duplicated that effort on June 20, 1965, when he recorded 12 strikeouts and allowed just 2 walks and a home run by Jim Hickman, in defeating the Mets by a score of 2-1.

Koufax finally attained perfection on September 9, 1965, when he struck out 14 batters and did not permit anyone to reach base during a 1-0 victory over the Cubs.

Koufax hurled another gem some three weeks later, on September 29, 1965, when he tossed a two-hit shutout against Cincinnati, walking 1 and striking out 13, in defeating the Reds by a score of 5-0.

Koufax turned in arguably the most dominant performance of his final big-league season on July 27, 1966, when he allowed 4 hits, 3 walks, and struck out 16 batters during a 2-1, 12-inning Dodgers victory over the Phillies. Koufax worked the first 11 innings, before being relieved in the final frame by Phil Regan, who got the win.

As great as Koufax pitched during the regular season, he proved to be equally effective in postseason play, compiling a lifetime ERA of 0.95 and WHIP of 0.825 in World Series competition, while also striking out 61 batters and surrendering only 36 hits in 57 total innings of work. Particularly effective in the 1963 and 1965 fall classics, Koufax captured Series MVP honors both years, setting the tone for the Dodgers' four-game sweep of the Yankees in the '63 Series by striking out a then-record 15 New York batters during the Dodgers' 5-2 victory in Game One. After Los Angeles won the next two contests, Koufax returned to the mound in Game Four to complete the sweep by recording another 8 strikeouts during his team's 2-1 victory. Following Koufax's win in the Series finale, Yankees Manager Yogi Berra commented, "I can see how he won twenty-five games. What I don't understand is how he lost five."

Koufax provided similar heroics in the 1965 fall classic, when, after making headlines by refusing to start Game One since it coincided with Yom Kippur, the holiest of all Jewish holidays, he took over the Series after the Dodgers and Twins split the first four contests. After tossing a four-hit shutout in Game Five, Koufax took the mound again in Game Seven. Working on only two days' rest, Koufax went the distance, surrendering just 3 hits, in giving the Dodgers a 2-0 victory that made them world champions for the second time in three years. He finished the Series with a record of 2-1, an ERA of 0.38, and 2 complete games, having allowed only one earned run and 13 hits in 24 innings of work, while recording 29 strikeouts.

## Notable Achievements:

- Won at least 25 games three times.
- Topped 18 wins two other times.
- Posted winning percentage in excess of .700 four times, topping the .800-mark once.
- Compiled ERA below 3.00 five times, posting mark under 2.00 on three occasions.
- Posted WHIP under 1.000 four times.
- Struck out more than 300 batters three times, recording more than 200 strikeouts three other times.
- Threw more than 300 innings three times, tossing more than 250 innings one other time.
- Threw more than 20 complete games three times.
- Tossed 11 shutouts in 1963.
- Led NL pitchers in: wins three times, winning percentage twice, ERA five times, WHIP four times, complete games twice, innings pitched twice, shutouts three times, strikeouts-to-walks ratio three times, and starts once.

- Holds Dodgers single-season records for most strikeouts (382 in 1965) and most shutouts (11 in 1963).
- Ranks among Dodgers career leaders in: wins (fifth), winning percentage (eighth), strikeouts (third), shutouts (third), innings pitched ($10^{th}$), WHIP (fifth), games started (seventh), and pitching appearances (seventh).
- Set new major-league record (since broken) with 382 strikeouts in 1965.
- Threw perfect game vs. Chicago Cubs on September 9, 1965.
- Threw three other no-hitters (vs. Mets on June 30, 1962; vs. Giants on May 11, 1963; vs. Phillies on June 4, 1964).
- Three-time NL Triple Crown winner for pitchers (1963, 1965 & 1966).
- June, 1962 NL Player of the Month.
- Two-time World Series MVP (1963 & 1965).
- 1963 NL MVP.
- Finished second in NL MVP voting twice (1965 & 1966).
- Three-time Cy Young Award winner (1963, 1965 & 1966).
- Two-time *Sporting News* Major League Player of the Year (1963 & 1965).
- Four-time NL *Sporting News* Pitcher of the Year (1963, 1964, 1965 & 1966).
- Four-time *Sporting News* All-Star selection (1963, 1964, 1965 & 1966).
- Six-time NL All-Star (1961, 1962, 1963, 1964, 1965 & 1966).
- Member of Major League Baseball's All-Century Team.
- Number 26 on *The Sporting News'* 1999 list of Baseball's 100 Greatest Players.
- Six-time NL champion (1955, 1956, 1959, 1963, 1965 & 1966).
- Four-time world champion (1955, 1959, 1963 & 1965).
- Elected to Baseball Hall of Fame by members of BBWAA in 1972.

# 2

# JACKIE ROBINSON

Rivaling Babe Ruth as the most historically significant baseball player ever, Jackie Robinson may well be the most important figure in American sports history. In addition to being the first man of African American descent to take the field alongside white major-leaguers in the twentieth century, Robinson changed the social consciousness of an entire nation, forcing Americans to reevaluate their views on life, liberty, and the pursuit of happiness. Referred to as "a legend and a symbol in his own time" by Martin Luther King Jr., Robinson also drew praise from historian and longtime Brooklyn Dodgers fan Doris Kearns Goodwin, who suggested that his "efforts were a monumental step in the civil-rights revolution in America…His accomplishments allowed black and white Americans to be more respectful and open to one another, and more appreciative of everyone's abilities."

More than just a symbol of change, Robinson also proved to be an exceptional performer on the playing field over the course of his 10 seasons in Brooklyn, helping to lead the Dodgers to six pennants and one world championship during that time. A pioneer in many ways, Robinson became the first black player in the Major Leagues to win a batting title, the first to be named his league's Most Valuable Player, and the first to be inducted into the Baseball Hall of Fame. Also the winner of baseball's inaugural Rookie of the Year Award, Robinson excelled as a hitter, compiling a batting average well in excess of .300 and an on-base percentage well over .400 six times each, en route to posting lifetime marks of .311 and .409, respectively. An outstanding base-runner as well, Robinson scored more than 100 runs in a season six times and reintroduced the stolen base to the majors as an offensive weapon, intimidating opponents with his daring and aggressiveness on the base paths. One of the fiercest competitors ever to take the field, Robinson inspired the following words from Leo Durocher, his first big-league manager, who later became one of his most bitter rivals:

> *"You want a guy that comes to play. But Robinson didn't just come to play. He came to beat you. He came to stuff the damn bat right up your ass."*

Born into a family of sharecroppers in Cairo, Georgia on January 31, 1919, Jack Roosevelt Robinson grew up in a single-parent household after his father deserted the family less than one year later. Moving to Pasadena, California shortly thereafter, the Robinsons purchased a home in a predominantly white neighborhood, where young Jackie and his brothers had to learn to defend themselves against those who objected to their presence merely because of the color of their skin. Developing a reputation as an outstanding all-around athlete during his teenage years, Robinson lettered in baseball, football, basketball, and track at Muir Technical High School, before doing the same at Pasadena Junior College. Following his graduation from PJC in 1939, Robinson transferred to UCLA, where he became the school's first athlete to earn varsity letters in all four sports, prompting many to refer to him as the "Jim Thorpe of his race." Yet, after averaging more than 11 yards per carry on the gridiron as a junior and leading the Pacific Coast Conference in scoring on the basketball court in both his junior and senior years, Robinson chose to drop out of college just a few credits shy of his graduation requirements to help support his family. He subsequently took a job as an athletic coach for the National Youth Administration and played semi-pro football for the Los Angeles Bulldogs, before signing on to play pro football with the Honolulu Bears in the fall of 1941.

Drafted into the Army early in 1942, Robinson initially encountered resistance when he attempted to enter Officer Candidate School. However, after fellow soldier and boxing legend Joe Louis interceded on his behalf, Robinson eventually earned his stripes, although the military continued to treat him very much as a second-class citizen. Things finally came to a head for the confrontational Robinson on July 6, 1944, when, while serving in Fort Hood, Texas, he refused to follow a white bus driver's directive to move to the back of the bus "where the coloreds belonged." Subjected to court-martial at a subsequent hearing, Robinson triumphed over the charges. Nevertheless, with the Army growing increasingly impatient with him, it granted him an honorable discharge shortly thereafter.

Courtesy of the Look Magazine Collection at the Library of Congress

Jackie Robinson led the Dodgers to six pennants and one world
championship in his 10 seasons in Brooklyn

After leaving the military, Robinson spent one year serving as athletic director at Sam Houston College in Austin, Texas, before he received an offer to play professional baseball in the Negro Leagues with the Kansas City Monarchs. Arriving in Kansas City early in 1945, Robinson ended up appearing in only 47 games for the Monarchs, batting .387 and earning Negro-League All-Star honors, before Brooklyn club president and general manager Branch Rickey approached him with the idea of joining the Dodger organization.

Rickey met with Robinson on August 28, 1945 to pose a series of questions to him that would reveal whether or not the young infielder had the qualities he sought in someone to carry out his "Noble Experiment." When asked if he had the ability not to react violently under the torrents of racial abuse that would undoubtedly be directed towards him, Robinson responded by asking Rickey, "Are you looking for a Negro who is afraid to fight back?" In return, Rickey suggested that he needed someone "with guts enough not to fight back." After Robinson agreed to control his temper for his first two years in Brooklyn, Rickey signed him to a contract, making him the first black player in nearly sixty years to be part of any major-league organization.

Subsequently assigned to Brooklyn's top farm team in Montreal, Robinson ended up leading the International League with a .349 batting average and a .985 fielding percentage in 1946, en route to earning league MVP honors. Yet, in spite of the success he experienced north of the border, several Dodger players expressed their dissatisfaction when the team summoned the twenty-eight-year-old infielder to the majors six days prior to the start of the ensuing campaign. In fact, a group of Southerners reportedly began circulating a petition objecting to his promotion to the big club. However, Rickey and manager Leo Durocher soon quelled the uprising, with the latter telling his troops, "I do not care if the guy is yellow or black, or if he has stripes like a fuckin' zebra. I'm the manager of this team, and I say he plays. What's more, I say he can make us all rich. And, if any of you cannot use the money, I will see that you are all traded."

For his part, Robinson told his new teammates upon his arrival in 1947, "I'm not concerned with your liking or disliking me…All I ask is that you respect me as a human being."

It took some time for most of Robinson's Dodger teammates to warm up to him after he made his historic debut with the club on April 15, 1947, with noted sportswriter Jimmy Cannon observing, "Jackie Robinson is the loneliest man I have ever seen in sports." But, after taking note of the abuse he had to endure from fans and opposing players, virtually everyone on the team rallied around Robinson, causing them to become closer than ever before.

Robinson received his worst treatment from the Phillies and their insufferable manager Ben Chapman, who hurled such cruel racial obscenities at him that the rookie infielder later admitted, "It brought me nearer to cracking up than I had ever been." But the Chapman episode actually strengthened the bond between Robinson and his teammates, with second baseman Eddie Stanky, one of his earlier detractors, challenging the Phillies to pick on someone who had the ability to fight back. Branch Rickey later noted that Chapman "did more than anybody to unite the Dodgers. When he poured out that string of unconscionable abuse, he solidified and united thirty men." Meanwhile, public reaction against Chapman became so severe that he had to ask Robinson to pose for a photo with him to save his job, which Jackie graciously agreed to do.

Triumphing against tremendous adversity, Robinson, who spent his first season in Brooklyn playing the unfamiliar position of first base, ended up earning Rookie of the Year honors and a fifth-place finish in the NL MVP voting by batting .297, finishing second in the league with 125 runs scored, and topping the senior circuit with 29 stolen bases and 28 sacrifice bunts. Robinson's outstanding performance, which helped lead the Dodgers to the pennant, prompted Cardinals second baseman Red Schoendienst to comment, "If it wasn't for him, the Dodgers would be in the second division."

Robinson had another good year in 1948, concluding the campaign with 12 homers, 85 RBIs, 108 runs scored, 22 steals, and a .296 batting average, before beginning an exceptional five-year run during which he compiled the following numbers:

1949: 16 HR, 124 RBIs, 122 Runs Scored, **.342** AVG, .432 OBP, .528 SLG, .960 OPS

1950: 14 HR, 81 RBIs, 99 Runs Scored, .328 AVG, .423 OBP, .500 SLG, .923 OPS

1951: 19 HR, 88 RBIs, 106 Runs Scored, .338 AVG, .429 OBP, .527 SLG, .957 OPS

1952: 19 HR, 75 RBIs, 104 Runs Scored, .308 AVG, **.440** OBP, .465 SLG, .904 OPS

1953: 12 HR, 95 RBIs, 109 Runs Scored, .329 AVG, .425 OBP, .502 SLG, .927 OPS

Freed of his earlier promise to Branch Rickey to control his temper for two years, and ably assisted by Hall of Famer and Dodger advisor George Sisler, who worked with him on hitting the ball to right field and improving his mechanics at the plate, Robinson thrived as never before. En route to earning NL MVP honors in 1949, Robinson led the league in batting average, stolen bases (37), and sacrifice bunts (17). He also finished among the league leaders in nine other offensive categories, placing second in runs batted in, hits (203), and on-base percentage, while finishing third in runs scored, doubles (38), triples (12), slugging percentage, and OPS. Robinson placed near the top of the league rankings in batting average, on-base percentage, runs scored, and stolen bases in each of the next four seasons as well, earning two more top-10 finishes in the NL MVP balloting in the process. He also did an excellent job in the field after being shifted to his more natural position of second base prior to the start of the 1948 campaign. Displaying sure hands, good range, and excellent instincts, Robinson led all NL second sackers in double plays four times, fielding percentage three times, and putouts and assists one time each. The Dodgers won the pennant in 1949, 1952, and 1953, narrowly missing advancing to the World Series in the other two years as well.

During that time, Robinson became known for his fierce competitive spirit, which he defended by saying, "It kills me to lose. If I'm a trouble-maker, and I don't think that my temper makes me one, then it's because I can't stand losing. That's the way I am about winning; all I ever wanted to do was finish first."

Crowding the plate from his spot in the batter's box, the right-handed hitting Robinson dared opposing pitcher's to throw inside to him—a challenge they often accepted. Although not known as a home-run hitter, he had good line-drive power to all fields, a keen batting eye, and rarely struck out. Robinson also excelled as a bunter, twice leading the league in sacrifice hits.

However, Robinson perhaps made his greatest impact on the base paths, creating havoc for the opposition by taking excessively long leads and jockeying back and forth as if he intended to steal on every pitch. Revitalizing the stolen base as an offensive weapon, Robinson drove opposing pitchers to the point of distraction and often embarrassed opposing infielders with his base-running skills. Former teammate Bobby Bragan, one of those who initially expressed an unwillingness to play alongside Robinson, claimed, "He was the only player I ever saw in a rundown who could be safe more often than out. He ran as if his head was on a swizzle, back and forth, back and forth, until he could get out of it." Robinson also revived the art of stealing home, accomplishing the feat 19 times over the course of his career, tying him with Frankie Frisch for the most steals of home since World War I.

Robinson's varied skill-set prompted Dodgers manager Chuck Dressen to proclaim, "Give me five players like Robinson and a pitcher, and I'll beat any nine-man team in baseball."

Pirates Hall of Fame outfielder Ralph Kiner stated, "Jackie Robinson was the best athlete ever to play Major League Baseball."

Branch Rickey expressed his admiration for Robinson by saying, "There was never a man in the game who could put mind and muscle together quicker, and with better judgment, than Robinson."

Meanwhile, longtime teammate Duke Snider commented on the totality of Robinson's game when he said, "He was the greatest competitor I've ever seen. I've seen him beat a team with his bat, his glove, his feet, and, in a game in Chicago one time, with his mouth."

The 1953 campaign proved to be Robinson's last as a full-time starter. After surrendering his second-base duties to Jim Gilliam that year, Robinson spent his last few seasons in Brooklyn splitting his time between third base and left field, never again appearing in more than 124 games or accumulating as many as 400 official at-bats. He hit .300 for the last time in 1954, when he posted a mark of .311, hit 15 homers, and drove in 59 runs for a Dodger team that finished second in the senior circuit. Although Brooklyn won the pennant in each of the next two seasons, Robinson served as a complementary player, seeing both his playing time and offensive production continue to diminish as he grew older and began to suffer from the effects of diabetes, an illness that plagued him for the rest of his life. Traded to the hated Giants following the conclusion of the 1956 campaign, Robinson instead announced his retirement, having previously reached an agreement to become an executive with Chock Full O'Nuts. He ended his career with 137 home runs, 734 RBIs, 947 runs scored, 1,518 hits, 273 doubles, 54 triples, 197 stolen bases, a .311 batting average, a .409 on-base percentage, a .474 slugging percentage, and only 291 strikeouts in just over 5,800 total plate appearances. In addition to his four top-10 finishes in the NL MVP voting, Robinson earned six All-Star selections.

Aside from his position with Chock Full O'Nuts, Robinson spent much of his retirement serving as chairman of the Board of Freedom National Bank, which provided loans and banking services for minority members previously snubbed by establishment banks. He also remained an unofficial spokesman for African Americans and a relentless crusader for civil rights, continuing to champion the cause of racial equality after throwing out the ceremonial first pitch prior to the start of Game Two of the 1972 World Series. Presented a plaque to commemorate the twenty-fifth anniversary of his MLB debut, a nearly blind Robinson accepted the honor graciously, but then added, "I'm going to be tremendously more pleased and more proud when I look at that third base coaching line one day and see a black face managing in baseball."

Jackie Robinson passed away just nine days later, dying at the age of fifty-three, on October 24, 1972, after suffering a fatal heart attack following a lengthy battle with diabetes. In discussing the many trials and tribulations he experienced over the course of his life, Robinson once suggested, "A life is not important except in the impact it has on other lives."

Major League Baseball acknowledged the huge impact that Robinson made on the lives of so many others in 1997, when it "universally" retired his uniform number 42 across all major-league teams, making him the first professional athlete to be so honored. In 2004, MLB also adopted a new annual tradition, declaring April 15 to be "Jackie Robinson Day"—a day on which every player on every team wears number 42.

Looking back at the obstacles his former teammate faced, Duke Snider commented, "He knew he had to do well. He knew that the future of blacks in baseball depended on it. The pressure was enormous, overwhelming, and unbearable at times. I don't know how he held up. I know I never could have."

Speaking of Robinson in his classic 1970 book entitled *The Boys of Summer*, Roger Kahn wrote, "Thinking about the things that happened, I don't know any other ball player who could have done what he did. To be able to hit with everybody yelling at him; he had to block all that out, block out everything but this ball that is coming in at a hundred miles an hour, and he's got a split second to make up his mind if it's in or out, or down, or coming at his head; a split second to swing. To do what he did has got to be the most tremendous thing I've ever seen in sports."

## Career Highlights:

**Best Season:** Although Robinson performed extremely well for the Dodgers from 1947 to 1953, he clearly had the best season of his career in 1949, when he earned NL MVP honors by hitting 16 homers, topping the circuit with 37 stolen bases and a .342 batting average, and finishing either second or third in the league in RBIs (124), runs scored (122), hits (203), triples (12), doubles (38), on-base percentage (.432), slugging percentage (.528), and OPS (.960).

**Memorable Moments/Greatest Performances:** Robinson had one of his finest days at the plate on August 29, 1948, when he helped lead the Dodgers to a 12-7 victory over the Cardinals by hitting for the cycle. He also drove in 2 runs and scored 3 times during the contest.

Robinson had another huge game against St. Louis on May 21, 1949, leading the Dodgers to a 15-6 win over the Cardinals by collecting 3 hits, stealing a base, scoring 3 times, and knocking in a career-high 6 runs.

Just three days later, on May 24, Robinson homered twice and drove in 4 runs during a 6-1 victory over the Pirates.

Robinson continued his assault against Pittsburgh pitching the following year, going 4-for-6, with a homer, 4 RBIs, and 3 runs scored, during a 21-12 mauling of the Pirates on June 24, 1950.

Robinson again torched Pittsburgh's pitching staff nearly one month later, when, during an 11-6 win over the Pirates on July 23, 1950, he went 5-for-6, with a homer, a pair of doubles, 4 RBIs, and 3 runs scored.

Robinson came up big in the clutch for the Dodgers on August 22, 1951, when he led them to an 8-7 come-from-behind victory over the Cardinals in 10 innings. After bringing the Dodgers to within one run of St. Louis with an RBI double in the bottom of the ninth inning, Robinson won the game with a run-scoring single in the ensuing frame. He finished the day 5-for-6, with 3 RBIs and 1 run scored.

Although the Dodgers ended up losing a three-game playoff to the Giants at the end of the 1951 campaign, Robinson performed heroically during a 14-inning, 9-8 win over the Phillies on the final day of the regular season. After preventing Philadelphia from scoring the winning run in the bottom of the ninth inning by making a sensational diving catch, the Dodger second baseman forced the playoff series with the Giants by hitting a game-winning homer in the top of the 14th.

Despite being well past his prime, a thirty-six-year-old Robinson provided fans of the game with a memorable moment in Game One of the 1955 World Series, when, during a 6-5 loss to the Yankees, he recorded an eighth-inning steal of home on a play that Yankee catcher Yogi Berra maintained through the years the home-plate umpire called incorrectly.

Yet, in spite of his many in-game accomplishments, Robinson experienced his most historic moment on April 15, 1947, when he took the field in a Dodgers uniform for the first time, ending in the process MLB's six-decade ban on black players.

## Notable Achievements:

- Batted over .300 six times, topping the .320-mark on four occasions.
- Knocked in more than 100 runs once (124 in 1949).
- Scored more than 100 runs six times, surpassing 120 runs scored twice.
- Topped 200 hits once (203 in 1949).
- Finished in double-digits in triples once (12 in 1949).
- Surpassed 30 doubles six times.
- Stole more than 20 bases five times, swiping more than 30 bags once (37 in 1949).
- Stole home 19 times.
- Drew more than 100 bases on balls once (106 in 1952).
- Compiled on-base percentage in excess of .400 six times.
- Posted slugging percentage in excess of .500 five times.
- Led NL in: batting average once, on-base percentage once, stolen bases twice, and sacrifice hits twice.
- Led NL second basemen in: putouts once, assists once, fielding percentage three times, and double plays turned four times.
- Ranks among Dodgers career leaders in: runs scored (seventh), bases on balls (sixth), on-base percentage (fourth), and OPS (ninth).
- Hit for cycle vs. St. Louis Cardinals on August 29, 1948.

- 1947 MLB Rookie of the Year.
- 1949 NL MVP.
- Four-time *Sporting News* All-Star selection (1949, 1950, 1951 & 1952).
- Six-time NL All-Star (1949, 1950, 1951, 1952, 1953 & 1954).
- Number 44 on *The Sporting News'* 1999 list of Baseball's 100 Greatest Players.
- Six-time NL champion (1947, 1949, 1952, 1953, 1955 & 1956).
- 1955 world champion.
- Elected to Baseball Hall of Fame by members of BBWAA in 1962.

# 3

# DUKE SNIDER

His name immortalized by the phrase "Willie, Mickey, and the Duke" from the song *Baseball*, Duke Snider served as Brooklyn's entry into one of the most passionate debates in baseball history, with New York sportswriter Red Smith once writing, "[Duke] Snider, [Mickey] Mantle, and [Willie] Mays. You could get a fat lip in any saloon by starting an argument as to which was the best." Sharing the big city spotlight with fellow future Hall of Fame center-fielders Willie Mays and Mickey Mantle, Snider proved to be an integral part of a magical period in New York baseball that saw a team from the nation's largest city win the World Series in nine out of 10 seasons between 1949 and 1958. The Dodgers appeared in the fall classic five times over that ten-year stretch, capturing their only world championship in Brooklyn in 1955. Although their lineup featured several other outstanding performers such as Jackie Robinson, Roy Campanella, and Gil Hodges throughout the period, no one on the team wielded a more potent bat than Snider. And, even though the Dodger center-fielder usually came out third-best in comparisons to Mays and Mantle, he hit more home runs (326) and knocked in more runs (1,031) than any other player in baseball during the 1950s.

Born in Los Angeles, California on September 19, 1926, Edwin Donald Snider had the nickname "Duke" assigned to him as a young boy by his father, who, after watching his son strut around the house one day, said, "Here comes the Duke." An exceptional all-around athlete who starred in both baseball and football at Compton High School in Southern California, Snider signed with the Brooklyn Dodgers shortly after he graduated from Compton in 1943. He subsequently split the 1944 campaign between two Dodger farm teams, before enlisting in the United States Navy in 1945. Returning to the States in 1946, Snider spent the entire year playing

Courtesy of MEARS Online Auctionss

Duke Snider hit more homers and knocked in more runs than
any other player in the majors during the 1950's

in the minor leagues, before earning a spot on Brooklyn's roster in spring training of 1947. However, after the free-swinging outfielder struggled at the plate during the early stages of the campaign, the Dodgers sent him back down to the minors, where he spent most of the next two seasons mastering the strike zone. Snider returned to the Dodgers for good during the second half of 1948, batting .244, hitting 5 homers, and driving in 21 runs, in 53 games and 160 official at-bats.

Snider earned the starting centerfield job in Brooklyn in 1949, helping the Dodgers capture the National League pennant by hitting 23 homers, knocking in 92 runs, scoring 100 times, and batting .292. Although the Dodgers failed to repeat as NL champions the following year, Snider emerged as a star, earning the first of seven consecutive All-Star selections and a ninth-place finish in the MVP voting by placing among the league leaders with 31 homers, 107 RBIs, 109 runs scored, 10 triples, 16 stolen bases, a .321 batting average, a .379 on-base percentage, and a .553 slugging percentage, while also topping the senior circuit with 199 hits and 343 total bases.

Despite seeing his batting average slip to .277 in 1951, Snider again posted outstanding overall numbers, concluding the campaign with 29 home runs, 101 RBIs, and 96 runs scored. Nevertheless, with the Dodgers squandering a seemingly insurmountable 13-game lead to the Giants during the season's final two months, eventually losing the pennant to their arch-rivals in a three-game playoff series, Snider received much of the blame for his team's failures in the New York newspapers, prompting the disgruntled outfielder to request a trade. Snider later recalled, "I went to Walter O'Malley and told him I couldn't take the pressure. I told him I'd just as soon be traded. I told him I figured I could do the Dodgers no good."

Snider's temperamental outburst did not sit well with his Dodger teammates, who considered him to be a crybaby, a pouter with a personality problem, and a spoiled mama's boy. However, after being chastised by team captain Pee Wee Reese, who told him to grow up and stop his whining, Snider began to display a level of maturity he previously lacked.

Snider subsequently started off the 1952 campaign slowly, but he caught fire in mid-August, enabling him to finish the season with 21 homers, 92 RBIs, 80 runs scored, and a .303 batting average. He then performed brilliantly against the Yankees in the World Series, nearly leading the Dodgers to their first world championship by hitting 4 homers, driving in 8 runs, and batting .345 during their seven-game loss to their old nemesis in the fall classic. Snider followed that up by beginning an exceptional four-year run during which he established himself as one of the game's elite players. Here are the numbers he compiled over the course of those four seasons:

> 1953: 42 HR, 126 RBIs, **132** Runs Scored, .336 AVG, .419 OBP, **.627** SLG, **1.046** OPS
> 1954: 40 HR, 130 RBIs, **120** Runs Scored, .341 AVG, .423 OBP, .647 SLG, 1.071 OPS
> 1955: 42 HR, **136** RBIs, **126** Runs Scored, .309 AVG, .418 OBP, .628 SLG, 1.046 OPS
> 1956: **43** HR, 101 RBIs, 112 Runs Scored, .292 AVG, **.399** OBP, **.598** SLG, **.997** OPS

In addition to leading the National League in home runs, RBIs, runs scored, on-base percentage, slugging percentage, and OPS at different times during the period, Snider topped the senior circuit in walks once and total bases twice. He finished in the league's top five in each offensive category all four years, with the only exception being batting average, which he finished fourth in once and third another time. The Dodgers won the pennant in three of those four seasons, failing to do so only in 1954, when they finished a relatively close second to the Giants. Snider earned a top-10 finish in the league MVP voting all four years, placing second once, third once, and fourth another time. The "Duke of Flatbush," as he came to be known, also continued to excel in the World Series, performing particularly well in the 1955 fall classic, when he led the Dodgers to a seven-game victory over the Yankees by hitting 4 homers, knocking in 7 runs, and batting .320.

There is little doubt that playing in Ebbets Field aided Snider immeasurably during his time in Brooklyn. A noted bandbox, the Dodgers' home ballpark perfectly suited Snider's left-handed power stroke. He also benefited greatly from batting third in Brooklyn's predominantly right-handed hitting lineup. Surrounded by players such as Jackie Robinson, Roy Campanella, Gil Hodges, Carl Furillo, and Pee Wee Reese, each of whom swung from the opposite side of the plate, Snider rarely faced southpaw pitching, against which he struggled for much of his career. Nevertheless, Snider's contributions to the dominant Dodger teams of the period cannot be overstated. More than just a home run hitter, he proved to be an exceptional five-tool player who also possessed good speed and an outstanding throwing arm in the outfield. In discussing Snider's fielding prowess, Hall of Famer Ralph Kiner once noted, "I'd say Duke covers more ground, wastes less motion, and is more consistent than anyone since DiMaggio." Meanwhile, Stan Musial named Snider, Willie Mays, and Hank Aaron as his all-time National League outfield.

Although Snider hit 40 home runs in 1957, making him one of a select few to reach the 40-homer plateau for five straight seasons, his overall offensive numbers fell off somewhat, as he knocked in 92 runs, scored 91 times, and batted just .274. Snider's offensive production continued to decline after the Dodgers moved to Los Angeles the following year, with the combination of the Los Angeles Coliseum's distant right-field fence and an assortment of injuries bringing to an end his days as a dominant home run hitter. Despite returning to his original hometown, Snider later expressed regret over leaving Brooklyn, telling *The New York Times* in 1980, "We wept. Brooklyn was a lovely place to hit. If you got a ball in the air, you had a chance to get it out. When they tore down Ebbets Field, they tore down a little piece of me."

Appearing in only 106 games his first year on the West Coast, Snider batted .312, hit 15 homers, and drove in 58 runs. He rebounded somewhat in 1959, helping the Dodgers capture the NL pennant by hitting 23 homers, knocking in 88 runs, and batting .308. But, after injuring his knee against Chicago during the 1959 World Series, Snider batted just .243 in 101 games the following year. Limited to only 85 games by a broken elbow in 1961, Snider served as a part-time player his last two seasons in Los Angeles, totaling just 21 home runs and 86 RBIs over the course of those two campaigns, before being sold to the New York Mets prior to the start of the 1963 season. Snider left Los Angeles with career totals of 389 home runs, 1,271 RBIs, 1,199 runs scored, 1,995 hits, 343 doubles, 82 triples, and 99 stolen bases, a lifetime batting average of .300, a .384 on-base percentage, and a .553 slugging percentage. He continues to hold franchise records for most career home runs and RBIs. In addition to his seven All-Star selections as a member of the Dodgers, Snider earned three *Sporting News* All-Star nominations and six top-10 finishes in the NL MVP voting.

Snider spent just one season back in New York, hitting 14 homers, knocking in 45 runs, and batting .243 for the Mets in 1963, before finishing out his career with the San Francisco Giants the following year. He announced his retirement following the conclusion of the 1964 campaign, ending his career with 407 home runs, 1,333 RBIs, 1,259 runs scored, 2,116 hits, 358 doubles, 85 triples, a .295 batting average, a .380 on-base percentage, and a .540 slugging percentage.

Following his playing days, Snider scouted for both the Dodgers and the San Diego Padres, and he also briefly managed in the minor leagues before becoming an announcer for the Montreal Expos from 1973 to 1986. During his time in Montreal, Snider gained induction into the Baseball Hall of Fame, being elected by the members of the BBWAA in 1980. He lived another thirty-one years, passing away at the age of eighty-four, on February 27, 2011, after suffering for years with diabetes, hypertension, and other illnesses.

Upon learning of Snider's passing, Willie Mays said, "Duke was a fine man, a terrific hitter, and a great friend, even though he was a Dodger.... Today I feel that I have lost a dear friend. He was a hero to the fans in Brooklyn and a great Dodger."

Former Dodger teammate Don Zimmer added, "Willie, Duke and Mickey. They were great players in one city, one town. Duke never got the credit of being the outfielder that Mays and Mantle were. But Duke was a great outfielder. He was a great player."

Remembering his longtime friend, legendary Dodgers broadcaster Vin Scully stated, "He had the grace and the abilities of DiMaggio and Mays and, of course, he was a World Series hero that will forever be remembered in the borough of Brooklyn. Although it's ironic to say it, we have lost a giant."

## Dodger Career Highlights:

**Best Season:** It could certainly be argued that Snider had his finest all-around season in 1955, when he placed an extremely close second to teammate Roy Campanella in the NL MVP voting. En route to earning recognition as *The Sporting News* Major League Player of the Year, Snider batted .309, placed among the league leaders with 42 home runs, 104 bases on balls, 338 total bases, a .418 on-base percentage, a .628 slugging percentage, and a 1.046 OPS, and topped the senior circuit with 136 RBIs and 126 runs scored. He also performed brilliantly in 1953, when he earned a third-place finish in the MVP balloting by placing near the top of the league rankings with 42 home runs, 126 RBIs, 198 hits, 38 doubles, 16 stolen bases, a .336 batting average, and a .419 on-base percentage, while finishing first in runs scored (132), total bases (370), slugging percentage (.627), and OPS (1.046). Nevertheless, the feeling here is that Snider had the best year of his career in 1954, when he finished fourth in the league MVP voting. In addition to leading the NL with 120 runs scored and 378 total bases, the "Duke of Flatbush" ranked among the league leaders with 40 homers, 130 RBIs, 199 hits, 39 doubles, 10 triples, a .341 batting average, a .423 on-base percentage, a .647 slugging percentage, and an OPS of 1.071, establishing in the process career-high marks in each of the last seven categories.

**Memorable Moments/Greatest Performances:** Snider put together the third-longest hitting streak in franchise history in 1953, hitting safely in 27 consecutive games from August 19 to September 13 of that year.

Although Snider received far more recognition for his hitting, he excelled in the outfield as well, making perhaps his most memorable defensive play in Philadelphia on May 31, 1954, when he preserved a 5-4 victory over the Phillies by making a brilliant leaping catch against the left-centerfield wall with two men out and two men on in the bottom of the 12th inning. Recalling the play, Pee Wee Reese said, "The greatest catch I ever saw was one made by Snider in 1954, when he climbed the wall of Connie Mack Stadium like a mountain goat to take an extra-base hit away from Willie Jones of the Phillies."

Snider had the first huge game of his career on May 2, 1948, when he went 4-for-5, with a pair of homers, a triple, and 4 RBIs, during a 9-6 win over the Phillies.

Snider helped the Dodgers clinch the pennant on the final day of the 1949 regular season by driving in Pee Wee Reese with an RBI single in the top of the 10th inning that put Brooklyn ahead of Philadelphia by a score of 8-7. The Dodgers pushed across another run shortly thereafter, giving them a two-run lead they protected in the bottom of the frame, thereby enabling them to finish just one game ahead of the second-place Cardinals.

Snider had the only 5-for-5 day of his career on July 16, 1950, when he homered, tripled, singled three times, stole a base, knocked in 3 runs, and scored 3 times during a lopsided 10-2 victory over the Cardinals.

Snider had another big day at the plate a little over two months later, on September 19, 1950, when he led the Dodgers to a 14-3 mauling of the Pirates by going 3-for-5, with a pair of homers, a double, 5 RBIs, and 3 runs scored.

After hitting a home run in the first game of Brooklyn's doubleheader sweep of Pittsburgh on August 23, 1953, Snider homered again, doubled twice, singled, and knocked in 5 runs in the nightcap, in leading the Dodgers to a 9-7 victory over the Pirates.

En route to winning *Sporting News* Major League Player of the Year honors in 1955, Snider turned in a number of exceptional performances, with one of those coming on May 14, when he went 4-for-6, with a homer, double, 3 RBIs, and 3 runs scored, during a 13-2 pasting of the Reds.

Snider had another huge game on June 3, 1955, when he led the Dodgers to a 12-5 win over the Cardinals by going 4-for-5, with a homer, double, and 5 RBIs.

A little over one month later, on July 4, 1955, Snider celebrated Independence Day by hitting a pair of homers, driving in 5 runs, and scoring 4 times during an 11-2 victory over the Phillies.

The Dodgers ended up edging out the Milwaukee Braves for the NL pennant by just one game in 1956, with Snider coming up big on the final day of the regular season, hitting a pair of homers, knocking in 4 runs, and making a spectacular catch in the outfield during an 8-6 pennant-clinching win over Pittsburgh.

Snider hit 3 home runs in one game twice during his career, accomplishing the feat for the first time on May 30, 1950, when, in the second game of a doubleheader sweep of Philadelphia, he went deep three times, in leading the Dodgers to a 6-4 victory over the Phillies. Snider nearly homered for a fourth time in his final trip to the plate, hitting a rising line drive that struck one foot below the top of the right-field screen at Ebbets Field. The ball was hit so hard that he had to stop at first base with a single. Snider duplicated his earlier effort on June 1, 1955, when he went 4-for-5, with 3 homers and a career-high 6 RBIs, during an 11-8 win over the Braves.

An outstanding postseason performer over the course of his career, Snider hit 11 homers, knocked in 26 runs, and batted .286 in his six World Series appearances, establishing himself in the process as the only player to hit at least 4 home runs in two different fall classics. He also holds National League records for most home runs and RBIs in World Series play.

Particularly effective in the 1952 and 1955 fall classics, Snider homered four times in each of those World Series, with his performance in

Game Five of the 1952 Series being perhaps his most memorable. After homering, singling, and making a great defensive play earlier in the contest, Snider drove in the game's winning run with an RBI double in the top of the 11$^{th}$ inning, giving the Dodgers a 6-5 victory and a 3-2 lead in the Series. He followed that up by hitting a pair of homers during the Dodgers' 3-2 loss to the Yankees in Game Six.

Snider again performed brilliantly in the 1955 World Series, hitting 4 homers, knocking in 7 runs, and batting .320, in leading the Dodgers to a seven-game victory over the Yankees. Snider turned in his finest effort of that Series in Game Five as well, homering twice against Yankees starter Bob Grim during a 5-3 Dodgers win.

## Notable Achievements:

- Surpassed 40 home runs five times, topping 30 homers one other time.
- Knocked in more than 100 runs six times, topping 120 RBIs on three occasions.
- Scored more than 100 runs six times, surpassing 120 runs scored on three occasions.
- Batted over .300 seven times, topping the .320-mark on three occasions.
- Finished in double-digits in triples twice.
- Surpassed 30 doubles five times.
- Drew more than 100 bases on balls once (104 in 1955).
- Compiled on-base percentage in excess of .400 five times.
- Posted slugging percentage in excess of .500 ten times, topping the .600-mark three times.
- Compiled OPS in excess of 1.000 three times.
- Led NL in: home runs once, RBIs once, runs scored three times, hits once, total bases three times, walks once, on-base percentage once, slugging percentage twice, and OPS twice.
- Led NL center-fielders in fielding percentage three times.
- Holds Dodgers career records for most: home runs (389), RBIs (1,271), and extra-base hits (814).
- Ranks among Dodgers career leaders in: runs scored (third), hits (fourth), doubles (second), triples (tied-sixth), total bases (second),

bases on balls (fourth), slugging percentage (fourth), OPS (fifth), games played (seventh), plate appearances (seventh), and at-bats (seventh).

- Hit more home runs (326) and knocked in more runs (1,031) during 1950s than any other player in Major Leagues.
- Hit three home runs in one game twice (vs. Philadelphia on May 30, 1950 & vs. Milwaukee on June 1, 1955).
- Ranks fourth all-time in World Series play with 11 home runs.
- Only player to hit at least four home runs in two different World Series (1952 & 1955).
- Finished in top five of NL MVP voting three times, placing as high as second in 1955.
- 1955 *Sporting News* Major League Player of the Year.
- Three-time *Sporting News* All-Star selection (1953, 1954 & 1955).
- Eight-time NL All-Star (1950, 1951, 1952, 1953, 1954, 1955, 1956 & 1963).
- Number 84 on *The Sporting News'* 1999 list of Baseball's 100 Greatest Players.
- Seven-time NL champion (1947, 1949, 1952, 1953, 1955, 1956 & 1959).
- Two-time world champion (1955 & 1959).
- Elected to Baseball Hall of Fame by members of BBWAA in 1980.

# 4

# ROY CAMPANELLA

Generally considered to be one of the greatest catchers in baseball history, Roy Campanella served as the cornerstone of a legendary Brooklyn Dodgers team that won five National League pennants and one World Series between 1949 and 1956. Joining the Dodgers in 1948 after spending his first several seasons in organized ball starring in the Negro Leagues, Campanella went on to capture NL MVP honors three times, helping to establish the Dodgers in many ways as "America's Team." Along the way, the burly receiver hit more than 30 home runs four times, becoming, in 1953, the first catcher in major-league history to reach the 40-homer plateau. Campanella also knocked in more than 100 runs and batted over .300 three times each, earning in the process eight All-Star selections and four *Sporting News* All-Star nominations. Unfortunately, Campanella's time in the Major Leagues proved to be all too brief since his career tragically ended when an automobile accident left him paralyzed from the neck down. Yet, even though he never walked again, Campanella became even more of a hero to millions of Americans, providing inspiration to everyone he touched with his courage, perseverance, and positive outlook on life.

Born in Philadelphia, Pennsylvania on November 19, 1921, Roy Campanella had quite an unusual childhood for someone growing up in the United States during the 1920s and 1930s. The son of an African American mother and an Italian father, Campanella came to view life from a rather unique perspective—one to which few others of segregated America could undoubtedly relate. While Campanella's mixed heritage gained him somewhat greater acceptance within the white community than most other African Americans of his time, it nevertheless caused him to be viewed very much as a second-class citizen.

After starring in the Negro Leagues for several seasons,
Roy Campanella went on to win three MVP Awards
while playing for the Dodgers during the 1950's

Unable to consider a career in the white Major Leagues a viable option during his formative years, Campanella began playing organized ball in 1936 with a local semi-pro team called the Bacharach Giants. Despite being only fifteen years old at the time, Campanella excelled to such a degree that the Washington Elite Giants of the Negro National League extended him an offer to join them early in 1937. Still in high school when he became a member of the Giants, Campanella initially played only on weekends, occasionally substituting behind the plate for Negro League Hall of Famer Biz Mackey, who he later credited with teaching him everything he knew about catching. However, after he celebrated his sixteenth birthday following the conclusion of the campaign, Campanella dropped out of school to play for the team full-time.

Campanella followed the Giants when they moved to Baltimore in 1938, earning the team's starting catching job the following year. Over the course of the next few seasons, he established himself as one of the Negro Leagues' finest players, eventually challenging the aging Josh Gibson for supremacy among all league receivers. However, after quarreling with Baltimore owner Tom Wilson, the twenty-year-old Campanella elected to jump to the Mexican League in 1942. He spent the next two seasons playing south of the border, before returning to Baltimore in 1944.

Even though Campanella remained one of black baseball's greatest stars after he rejoined the Giants, he continued to possess a burning desire to play in the Major Leagues. The young catcher's dream came closer to becoming a reality in 1946, when he became one of five black players signed by Brooklyn general manager Branch Rickey. Campanella spent the next two years in the minor leagues, patiently awaiting his promotion to the Dodgers, while Jackie Robinson paved the way for him and other talented young African American players at the major-league level.

Campanella finally arrived in Brooklyn in 1948, earning a spot on the Dodgers' roster in spring training, before being sent down to St. Paul after struggling during the early stages of the campaign. However, after integrating the American Association, where he batted .325 and hit 13 home runs over the next couple of months, Campanella returned to the Dodgers, for whom he spent the remainder of the year hitting 9 home runs, driving in 45 runs, and batting .258, in 83 games and 279 official at-bats.

Far more comfortable in his second big-league season, Campanella helped the Dodgers capture the 1949 National League pennant by hitting

22 homers, driving in 82 runs, batting .287, and leading all NL receivers in putouts for the first of six times. Campanella's outstanding all-around play earned him All-Star honors for the first of eight straight times. He followed that up by hitting 31 homers, knocking in 89 runs, and batting .281 for a Dodger team that fell just short of winning the league championship again in 1950.

Having already established himself as the senior circuit's top receiver, Campanella laid claim in 1951 to being one of the NL's dominant players by scoring 90 runs and placing among the league leaders with 33 home runs, 108 RBIs, a .325 batting average, 33 doubles, a .393 on-base percentage, and a .590 slugging percentage. Although the Dodgers once again barely missed advancing to the World Series, losing a three-game playoff series to the hated New York Giants on Bobby Thomson's famous "Shot Heard 'Round the World," Campanella ended up being named the league's Most Valuable Player.

The Dodgers captured the league championship in each of the next two seasons, with Campanella proving to be a huge contributor to both pennant-winning teams. After hitting 22 homers, driving in 97 runs, and batting .269 in 1952, the Dodger catcher earned NL MVP honors for the second time the following year by hitting 41 homers, scoring 103 runs, batting .312, and topping the senior circuit with 142 RBIs.

Hampered by a damaged nerve caused by a chipped bone in the heel of his left hand, Campanella appeared in only 111 games in 1954, limiting him to just 19 home runs, 51 RBIs, and an anemic .207 batting average. But he bounced back the following year to lead the Dodgers to the pennant, earning his third MVP Award in the process by hitting 32 homers, driving in 107 runs, and batting .318. Campanella subsequently homered twice and knocked in four runs against the Yankees in the World Series, in helping the Dodgers capture their only world championship while playing in Brooklyn.

Campanella's potent bat certainly made him an integral part of the success Brooklyn's "Boys of Summer" experienced between 1949 and 1956. However, the 5'9", 195-pound receiver contributed to the Dodgers in many other ways as well, most notably with his calm demeanor, exceptional defensive skills, and outstanding ability to handle a pitching staff. An extremely intelligent player, Campanella excelled as a signal-caller, and, as the Major Leagues' first black catcher, he did a superb job of handling Brooklyn's predominantly white pitching staff. And, in spite of his stocky build, he possessed unusual mobility, quickness, and grace for a man of his proportions. Furthermore, Campanella had a strong and accurate throwing arm that enabled him to throw out a major-league record 57 percent of the base-runners who attempted to steal a base against him over the course of his career.

A recurrence of Campanella's earlier hand injury led to a disappointing 1956 campaign in which he hit 20 homers, knocked in 73 runs, batted just .219, and scored only 39 runs. Injuries continued to plague the thirty-five-year-old catcher the following year, limiting him to just 103 games, 13 homers, 62 RBIs, and a .242 batting average. However, as Campanella mended during the subsequent offseason, he anticipated a bounce-back year in 1958, even though he and the rest of the Dodgers regretted leaving the friendly confines of Brooklyn's Ebbets Field for the Los Angeles Coliseum. Campanella failed to play a single game in the Dodgers' new home, though, as his career, and nearly his life, came to a sudden end on a cold wintery night.

On the evening of January 28, 1958, after doing a double-shift at the liquor store he owned in Harlem, Campanella began the long drive back to his home on Long Island. With his car traveling approximately 30 mph, Campanella lost control of his vehicle when it hit a patch of ice. Skidding along the road's slick surface, the car crashed into a telephone pole and flipped over onto its side, pinning Campanella behind the steering wheel and breaking his neck. Suffering from a compressed spinal cord and fractures to his fifth and sixth cervical vertebrae, Campanella never walked again, emerging from the accident paralyzed from the shoulders down.

A little over fifteen months later, on May 7, 1959, the Dodgers honored Campanella with *Roy Campanella Night* at the Los Angeles Memorial Coliseum. The New York Yankees agreed to make a special trip to California to play the Dodgers in an exhibition game, the proceeds of which were used to defray the cost of Campanella's medical bills. A major-league record 93,103 fans attended the festivities, with the evening's most chilling moment taking place when the stadium's lights dimmed for several minutes, allowing everyone in the stands to pay tribute to the former Dodger great by lighting a match.

Campanella spent the rest of his life being confined to a wheelchair. Yet, after initially suffering through a period of deep depression, "Campy," as he became affectionately known to everyone, eventually resigned himself to his condition. Following years of physical therapy, he even regained substantial use of his arms and hands, making it possible for him to feed himself, shake hands, and gesture while speaking. Although Campanella never walked again, he became an inspiration to millions of Americans, giving motivational speeches to youngsters around the nation. Campanella lived far beyond the normal span for quadriplegics, surviving long after being elected to the Baseball Hall of Fame by the members of the BBWAA in 1969. He eventually died of a heart attack on June 26, 1993, in his Woodland Hills, California home at the age of seventy-one.

Upon learning of Campanella's passing, Tommy Lasorda said, "Now he won't be suffering anymore. I loved Roy Campanella, I loved him like a brother. I'm going to miss him very much. As well as being a great baseball player, he was a great human being."

The quality of Roy Campanella's character is perhaps best exemplified by the following words he spoke during one of the many motivational speeches he delivered through the years:

"I asked God for strength, that I might achieve. I was made weak, that I might learn humbly to obey. I asked for health, that I might do great things. I was given infirmity, that I might do better things. I asked for riches, that I might be happy. I was given poverty, that I might be wise. I asked for power, that I might have the praise of men. I was given weakness, that I might feel the need of God. I asked for all things, that I might enjoy life. I was given life, that I might enjoy all things... I got nothing I asked for but everything I hoped for. Almost despite myself, my unspoken prayers were answered. I am, among men, most richly blessed!"

## Career Highlights:

**Best Season:** Campanella performed exceptionally well in all three of his MVP seasons, any of which would make a good choice here. Nevertheless, the 1953 campaign would have to be considered the finest of his career. In addition to batting .312, Campanella posted career-high marks in home runs (41), RBIs (142), runs scored (103), on-base percentage (.395), slugging percentage (.611), OPS (1.006), and total bases (317). His 40 home runs as a catcher remained the single-season record for major-league receivers until 1996, when Todd Hundley homered 42 times for the Mets. Meanwhile, Campanella's 142 RBIs remain the second-highest single-season total in Dodgers franchise history, trailing only the 153 RBIs Tommy Davis compiled in 1962.

**Memorable Moments/Greatest Performances:** Serving as the signal-caller for three no-hitters during his career, Campanella experienced some of his most memorable moments behind home plate. After catching a pair of no-hitters by Carl Erskine, one on June 19, 1952, and another on May 12, 1956, Campanella collaborated with Sal Maglie on the latter's no-no on September 25, 1956.

Campanella had his first big offensive day for the Dodgers on July 4, 1948, when he went 3-for-5, with a pair of homers and 4 RBIs, during a come-from-behind 13-12 win over the Giants.

Campanella had a number of huge days at the plate over the course of his first MVP campaign of 1951, with one of those coming on July 27, when he led the Dodgers to a 12-9 win over the Cardinals by going 3-for-5, with a homer, double, 5 RBIs, and 2 runs scored. Campy's three-run blast in the top of the ninth inning provided the margin of victory.

Campanella went on a hitting spree in early August of 1951, leading the Dodgers to seven wins over an eight-day period with his prolific slugging. After homering twice and knocking in 5 runs during a 9-8 victory over Cincinnati on August 5, Campanella went 3-for-4, with another pair of homers, 3 RBIs, and 3 runs scored, during a 6-5 win over the Giants four days later. He concluded his power surge by hitting 2 more homers and driving in 5 runs, in leading the Dodgers to a 7-2 victory over the Braves on August 12.

Campanella continued to perform well the following month, going 4-for-4, with a pair of homers, a double, and 5 RBIs, during a 7-2 win over the Braves on September 3, 1951.

Campanella defeated Philadelphia almost single-handedly on May 23, 1952, hitting a pair of homers and knocking in all 5 Dodger runs during a 5-1 victory over the Phillies.

On July 18 of his second MVP campaign of 1953, Campanella paced the Dodgers to a 14-6 victory over St. Louis by going 4-for-5, with a homer and 5 RBIs.

Campanella proved to be a one-man wrecking crew against Cincinnati on August 8, 1953, hitting a pair of three-run homers and driving in a career-high 6 runs, in leading the Dodgers to a 7-4 win over the Reds.

Campanella came up big in the clutch for the Dodgers on August 13, 1953, hitting a solo home run against Giants knuckleballer Hoyt Wilhelm with two men out in the top of the ninth inning, to tie the score at 8 runs apiece. Carl Furillo's homer in the ensuing frame gave the Dodgers a 9-8 victory over their bitter rivals. Campanella finished the game 3-for-4, with a pair of homers and 4 RBIs.

Campanella provided similar heroics on June 21, 1956, when his two-out, three-run homer in the bottom of the ninth inning tied the score with St. Louis at 8-8. The Dodgers pushed across another run later in the frame, giving them a 9-8 win over the Cardinals. Campanella concluded the day with a pair of homers and 6 runs batted in.

However, Campanella had the biggest day of his career on August 26, 1950, when he hit 3 home runs and knocked in 6 runs, in leading the Dodgers to a 7-5 victory over Cincinnati.

## Notable Achievements:

- Hit more than 30 home runs four times, topping 40 homers once (41 in 1953).
- Knocked in more than 100 runs three times, topping 140 RBIs once.
- Scored more than 100 runs once (103 in 1953).
- Batted over .300 three times.
- Surpassed 30 doubles once (33 in 1951).
- Posted slugging percentage in excess of .500 four times, topping the .600-mark once (.611 in 1953).
- Compiled OPS in excess of 1.000 once (1.006 in 1953).
- Led NL with 142 RBIs in 1953.
- Led NL catchers in: putouts six times, assists once, double plays turned twice, fielding percentage twice, and caught-stealing percentage five times.
- Ranks among Dodgers career leaders in: home runs (fourth), RBIs (eighth), and slugging percentage (10th).
- Holds MLB record among catchers for highest career caught-stealing percentage (57.4%).
- Hit three home runs in one game vs. Cincinnati Reds on August 26, 1950.

- 1953 *Sporting News* NL Player of the Year.
- Three-time NL MVP (1951, 1953 & 1955).
- Four-time *Sporting News* All-Star selection (1949, 1951, 1953 & 1955).
- Eight-time NL All-Star (1949, 1950, 1951, 1952, 1953, 1954, 1955 & 1956).
- Number 50 on *The Sporting News'* 1999 list of Baseball's 100 Greatest Players.
- Five-time NL champion (1949, 1952, 1953, 1955 & 1956).
- 1955 world champion.
- Elected to Baseball Hall of Fame by members of BBWAA in 1969.

# 5

# CLAYTON KERSHAW

The finest pitcher in the game today, Clayton Kershaw has spent the last nine seasons in Los Angeles, excelling to such a degree during that time that he has evoked in Dodger fans memories of the great Sandy Koufax. A six-time NL All Star, three-time Cy Young Award winner, and one-time league MVP, Kershaw has posted more than 20 victories twice, compiled an ERA under 2.00 three times, and struck out more than 300 batters once, leading all NL hurlers in each of those categories on multiple occasions. The 6'4", 225-pound southpaw has also finished first in the league in WHIP four times, en route to compiling a lifetime mark of 1.007 that ranks as the best in franchise history and the fourth-lowest of any pitcher to ever toe the rubber. Meanwhile, Kershaw's feat of leading all MLB hurlers in ERA four straight times is unprecedented, with only Hall of Fame pitchers Lefty Grove and Greg Maddux previously finishing first in that category as many as three times in succession. In addition to earning numerous individual accolades with his fabulous mound work, Kershaw has helped the Dodgers capture six NL West titles and advance to the NLCS on four separate occasions.

Born in Dallas, Texas on March 19, 1988, Clayton Edward Kershaw attended Highland Park High School in nearby University Park, where he starred on the diamond and also served as the starting center for future NFL quarterback Matthew Stafford on the school's football team. Establishing himself as a top pitching prospect in his senior year at Highland Park by compiling a record of 13-0 and an ERA of 0.77, while also recording 139 strikeouts in only 64 innings of work, Kershaw turned in his most dominant performance in a playoff game against Northwest High School of Justin, Texas, when he struck out all 15 batters he faced in a contest shortened by the "mercy rule." Subsequently named *USA Today's* High

School Baseball Player of the Year and the Gatorade National Player of the Year, Kershaw elected to renege on his earlier commitment to Texas A&M University when the Dodgers offered him a $2.3 million bonus to sign with them after they selected him with the seventh overall pick of the 2006 MLB Draft.

Advancing rapidly through the Los Angeles farm system, Kershaw spent less than two full seasons in the minors before earning a promotion to the big leagues in late May of 2008. Struggling somewhat in two tours of duty with the Dodgers the remainder of the year, the twenty-year-old rookie made 21 starts, compiling a record of 5-5 and an ERA of 4.26, while recording 100 strikeouts and yielding 109 hits and 52 bases on balls in 107⅔ innings of work. Although Kershaw continued to display a lack of control at times the following season, surrendering 91 walks over 171 innings, he ended up posting solid overall numbers, going 8-8, with a 2.79 ERA, 185 strikeouts, and only 119 hits allowed. He followed that up with another strong performance in 2010, finishing the year with a record of 13-10, an ERA of 2.91, and 212 strikeouts, which placed him fifth in the league rankings.

Having gained better command of his pitches and perfected his rather unique delivery to home plate, Kershaw emerged as the senior circuit's top hurler in 2011, capturing the pitcher's version of the Triple Crown by leading the league with 21 victories, an ERA of 2.28, and 248 strikeouts, while also finishing first in WHIP (0.977) and fewest hits allowed per nine innings pitched (6.711), placing second in winning percentage (.808—he went 21-5), strikeouts per nine innings pitched (9.566), and shutouts (2), and ranking third in innings pitched (233⅓) and complete games (5). The twenty-three-year-old left-hander's exceptional performance earned him NL Cy Young and *Sporting News* NL Pitcher of the Year honors, the first of his six consecutive All-Star selections, and praise from former Dodger great and current Special Advisor to the Chairman, Don Newcombe, who commented, "As the winner of the first Cy Young Award, I am so very proud of Clayton Kershaw and his outstanding performances that led to his receiving the 2011 Cy Young Award. I am reminded of Sandy Koufax whenever I see Clayton pitch and feel that there is a deep comparison be-tween the two. Clayton has an outstanding work ethic, as did Sandy, which will show itself through Clayton's baseball career."

Although Kershaw proved to be somewhat less spectacular in 2012, compiling a modest 14-9 record, he nevertheless pitched well enough to

Like his Dodger predecessor Sandy Koufax, Clayton Kershaw has earned Cy Young honors three times and NL MVP recognition once during his time in Los Angeles

Courtesy of Keith Allison

lead the league with an ERA of 2.53, a WHIP of 1.023, and a mark of 6.720 hits allowed per nine innings pitched, while also placing second with 229 strikeouts and 227⅔ innings pitched, en route to earning a runner-up finish in the Cy Young voting. Kershaw captured NL Cy Young and *Sporting News* NL Pitcher of the Year honors for the second time the following year, when he finished 16-9, with a league-leading 1.83 ERA, 232 strikeouts, 0.915 WHIP, and 2 shutouts. His extraordinary effort, which helped lead the Dodgers to the first of their four consecutive division titles, also earned him a seventh-place finish in the league MVP voting. Despite spending most of April on the DL after complaining of back pain, Kershaw clearly established himself as baseball's best pitcher in 2014, when he earned NL MVP and Cy Young honors by finishing first in the senior circuit with a record of 21-3, a 1.77 ERA, a 0.857 WHIP, 6 complete games, a strikeouts-to-walks ratio of 7.710, and a mark of 10.845 strikeouts per nine innings pitched. By leading both leagues in ERA for the fourth straight time, Kershaw became the first pitcher in MLB history to accomplish the feat.

Kershaw's dominance of opposing hitters can be attributed in large part to his outstanding repertoire of pitches, which includes a four-seam fastball with late movement that typically registers close to 95 mph on the radar gun, an 84-87 mph slider, a 12-6 curveball that generally approaches home plate at somewhere between 72-76 mph, a seldom-thrown change-up, and a cutter that he began using in 2015. He also is an excellent fielder who possesses one of the sport's best pick-off moves—one that helps to negate the opposing team's running game. Kershaw complements his other assets by relying heavily on the art of deception, making it difficult for the batter to pick up his offering by keeping the ball hidden from his view until just before he releases it. Employing a consistent overhand delivery on all his pitches, Kershaw lowers his right foot vertically with a slight pause coming out of his windup, before moving it forward towards home plate. When working out of the stretch, he uses a slide step that makes it difficult for the opposing base runner to accurately read his delivery. A noted perfectionist, Kershaw has stated on numerous occasions that he modeled his pitching mechanics after his boyhood hero, Roger Clemens. In discussing Kershaw's cerebral approach to his craft, former Dodger relief ace Mike Marshall, who won the NL Cy Young Award in 1974, stated, "He understands it's a game of pitching, not power. I haven't had a chance to see many of his games, but, from what I've seen, I like his pitch sequences. He challenges himself, not the hitters. It's a matter of keeping the game under control. It's not easy to throw a non-fastball on a 2-and-0 or full count. He does a nice job of keeping the hitters uncomfortable."

Yet, in spite of the overall level of dominance Kershaw has attained, he has been criticized by some for failing to establish himself as an exceptional big-game pitcher. Saddled with a record of just 4-7 and an ERA of 4.55 in postseason play, Kershaw has been average, at best, in the playoffs to this point, detracting somewhat from his reputation as the game's top hurler. He likely will need to alter the opinion held towards him in that regard at some point in the future if he is ever to be viewed as one of the all-time greats.

Kershaw had another exceptional year in 2015, earning a third-place finish in the Cy Young voting and a 10th-place finish in the NL MVP balloting by going 16-7, with an ERA of 2.13 ERA, a WHIP of 0.881, and a league-leading 301 strikeouts, 3 shutouts, 4 complete games, 232⅔ innings pitched, and 11.643 strikeouts per nine innings pitched. After performing brilliantly during the first half of 2016, Kershaw spent most of the season's second half on the disabled list recovering from a mild herniated disc in his back, preventing him from likely winning his fourth Cy Young Award. Rejoining the Dodger starting rotation in mid-September, Kershaw finished the season with a record of 12-4, an ERA of 1.69, a WHIP of 0.725, and a magnificent strikeouts-to-walks-ratio of 15.636. He subsequently helped lead the Dodgers to a five-game victory over Washington in the NLDS by posting a win and a save, before making further strides towards exorcising his earlier playoff demons by yielding just 2 hits and 1 walk over 7 innings, in earning a 1-0 win over the Cubs in Game Two of the NLCS. However, Kershaw faltered in the decisive Game Six, dropping a 5-0 decision to the NL champions.

Heading into the 2017 season, Kershaw boasts a career record of 126-60 that gives him an excellent winning percentage of .677. He also has compiled a lifetime ERA of 2.37, a WHIP of 1.007, 1,918 strikeouts in 1,760 total innings of work, and 15 shutouts. Only twenty-eight years old as of this writing, Kershaw figures to have several more outstanding seasons for the Dodgers, as long as the back issues that cropped up this past season do not prove to be a recurring problem. As to how high a spot on this list he eventually rises, the answer likely lies with how well he performs in his future postseason appearances.

# Career Highlights:

**Best Season:** Kershaw performed brilliantly this past season, establishing career-best marks in ERA (1.69), WHIP (0.725), and strikeouts-to-walks ratio (15.636), setting single-season franchise records in each of the last two categories in the process. However, an injured back forced him to sit out two months, limiting him to only 21 starts, 12 wins, and 149 innings pitched. Kershaw also pitched magnificently in 2011, 2013, and 2015, capturing the pitcher's version of the Triple Crown in the first of those campaigns, compiling a league-leading 1.83 ERA, 0.915 WHIP, and 232 strikeouts in the second, and leading all NL hurlers in five different categories in the third, including amassing a career-high 301 strikeouts. Nevertheless, Kershaw's extraordinary 2014 season would have to be considered his best to-date. En route to earning NL MVP, Cy Young, and *Sporting News* Major League Player of the Year honors, Kershaw recorded 239 strikeouts and led all NL pitchers with 21 victories, an .875 winning percentage, an ERA of 1.77, a WHIP of 0.857, 6 complete games, and an average of 10.8 strikeouts per nine innings pitched. Particularly effective during the month of June, Kershaw compiled a record of 6-0 and an ERA of 0.82, at one point putting together a 42 consecutive scoreless innings streak that lasted into July.

**Memorable Moments/Greatest Performances:** Kershaw turned in his first truly dominant performance for the Dodgers on April 15, 2009, when he recorded 13 strikeouts and yielded just 1 run, 1 hit, and 1 walk over the first seven innings of a contest the Dodgers eventually won by a score of 5-4 over the Giants.

Kershaw again dominated the opposition a little over one month later, throwing 7 hitless innings against the Florida Marlins on May 17, 2009, before surrendering a lead-off double to Cody Ross in the bottom of the eighth. Exiting the game at that point, Kershaw ended up being credited with the 12-5 victory, being charged with 1 run and just that 1 hit, while recording 9 strikeouts.

Kershaw tossed his first career shutout on September 14, 2010, when he defeated the Giants by a score of 1-0, allowing just 4 hits and no walks, while striking out 4 along the way.

Kershaw proved to be even more dominant on May 29, 2011, when he recorded 10 strikeouts and surrendered just 2 hits and 1 walk during an 8-0 shutout of the Florida Marlins.

Kershaw turned in a similarly brilliant effort three weeks later, yielding just 2 hits and 1 walk, while striking out 11, during a 4-0 shutout of the Detroit Tigers on June 20, 2011.

Exactly one month later, on July 20, 2011, Kershaw allowed just 3 hits and recorded 12 strikeouts in 8 innings of work, en route to defeating the Giants by a score of 1-0.

Kershaw experienced one of his greatest thrills on Opening Day of 2013, when he hit the only home run of his career and yielded just 4 hits during a 4-0 complete-game shutout of the Giants.

Kershaw tossed another four-hit shutout later in the year, surrendering just 4 harmless singles and recording 8 strikeouts during an 8-0 win over the Colorado Rockies on July 2, 2013.

Kershaw earned his first postseason victory in Game One of the 2013 NLDS, working 7 strong innings en route to defeating the Braves by a score of 6-1. In addition to yielding just 3 hits and 1 run during the contest, Kershaw struck out 12 Atlanta batters.

Kershaw turned in a number of memorable pitching performances over the course of his personal-best 42 consecutive scoreless innings streak that lasted from June 13 to July 10, 2014, with his most notable effort being his 8-0, no-hit victory over the Colorado Rockies on June 18. Recording a career-high 15 strikeouts during the contest, Kershaw allowed just one base runner the entire game, with Colorado left-fielder Corey Dickerson reaching base in the top of the seventh inning on an error by Dodger short-stop Hanley Ramirez.

Kershaw continued his extraordinary pitching after his streak ended, surrendering just 3 hits and 1 walk, in earning a complete-game 5-0 win over the Giants on July 26, 2014.

Kershaw fashioned another extremely impressive scoreless innings streak the following year, preventing the opposition from crossing the plate for 37⅔ consecutive frames. The streak, which lasted from July 3 to August 1, 2015, featured an exceptional effort against the Washington Nationals on July 18 in which Kershaw led the Dodgers to a 4-2 victory by yielding just 3 hits and recording 14 strikeouts in 8 innings of work. He followed that up by tossing a three-hit shutout against the Mets in his very next start, striking out 11 during the 3-0 win.

Kershaw turned in several other dominant performances later in the year, with the first of those coming on August 28, 2015, when he surrendered 3 hits, 1 run, and recorded 14 strikeouts over the first 8 innings of a 4-1 victory over the Chicago Cubs. Kershaw tied his career-high for strikeouts in his next start, fanning 15 batters during a 2-1 complete-game win over the Giants on September 2. Kershaw again dominated San Francisco's lineup on September 29, 2015, when he recorded 13 strikeouts and yielded just 1 hit and 1 walk during an 8-0 shutout of the Giants, who got their only hit of the game when first baseman Kevin Frandsen singled to right field off Kershaw in the bottom of the third inning.

Kershaw turned in his finest effort this past season on May 12, 2016, when he defeated the Mets by a score of 5-0, surrendering just 3 hits and recording 13 strikeouts, in going the distance.

## Notable Achievements:

- Has won more than 20 games twice.
- Has posted 16 victories twice.
- Has posted winning percentage in excess of .700 three times, topping .800-mark twice.
- Has compiled ERA under 3.00 in each of last eight seasons, posting mark below 2.00 three times.
- Has compiled WHIP under 1.000 five times.
- Has struck out more than 200 batters six times, topping 300 strikeouts once (301 in 2015).
- Has thrown more than 200 innings five times.
- Has led NL pitchers in: wins twice, winning pct. once, ERA four times, WHIP four times, strikeouts three times, shutouts three times, complete games twice, and innings pitched once.
- Holds Dodgers single-season records for: best WHIP (0.725 in 2016), most strikeouts per nine innings pitched (11.643 in 2015), and best strikeouts-to-walks ratio (15.636 in 2016).
- Holds Dodgers career records for best WHIP (1.007) and fewest hits allowed per nine innings pitched (6.622).
- Ranks among Dodgers career leaders in: winning percentage (fifth), ERA (third), strikeouts per nine innings pitched (second), strikeouts (tied-fourth), and strikeouts-to-walks ratio (second).

- Ranks first among active pitchers in career: winning percentage (.677), ERA (2.37), WHIP (1.007), shutouts (15), and fewest hits allowed per nine innings pitched (6.622).
- Ranks among MLB all-time leaders in career: winning percentage (ninth), WHIP (fourth), fewest hits allowed per nine innings pitched (second), and most strikeouts per nine innings pitched (sixth).
- Only pitcher in MLB history to lead both leagues in ERA four straight times (2011-14).
- Threw no-hitter vs. Colorado on June 18, 2014.
- 2011 NL Pitching Triple Crown winner.
- Six-time NL Pitcher of the Month.
- 2011 Gold Glove winner.
- 2012 Roberto Clemente Award winner.
- 2013 Branch Rickey Award winner.
- 2014 *Sporting News* Major League Player of the Year.
- 2014 NL MVP.
- Finished in top 10 in NL MVP voting two other times (2013 & 2015).
- Three-time NL Cy Young Award winner (2011, 2013 & 2014).
- Finished in top three in NL Cy Young voting two other times (2012 & 2015).
- Three-time *Sporting News* NL Pitcher of the Year (2011, 2013 & 2014).
- Three-time *Sporting News* All-Star selection (2011, 2013 & 2014).
- Six-time NL All-Star (2011, 2012, 2013, 2014, 2015 & 2016).

# 6

# DAZZY VANCE

The National League's dominant pitcher for much of the 1920s, Charles "Dazzy" Vance won a total of 190 games as a member of the Dodgers, even though he didn't notch his first victory for them until after he celebrated his thirty-first birthday. Plagued by a sore arm throughout the early stages of his career, the hard-throwing right-hander compiled an overall record in the Major Leagues of 0-8 prior to joining the Dodgers in 1922. However, after having surgery performed on his ailing elbow, Vance developed into one of the game's great pitchers, winning 187 games over the course of the next 11 seasons, despite pitching for mostly mediocre Dodger teams. Leading all NL hurlers in numerous statistical categories during his time in Brooklyn, Vance topped the senior circuit in victories twice, winning in excess of 20 games on three separate occasions. He also led the league in ERA three times, complete games twice, shutouts four times, WHIP three times, and strikeouts a record seven straight times, earning in the process one NL MVP Award and a place in Cooperstown.

Born in Orient, Iowa on March 4, 1891, Charles Arthur Vance spent most of his childhood in Nebraska, moving with his family to a farm in Pleasant Hill Township, near the Kansas state line, while still a young boy. It was in his new home that Vance acquired the nickname "Dazzy," as he explained years later:

> *"Back in Nebraska, I knew a cowboy who, when he saw a horse, a gun, or a dog that he liked, would say, 'Ain't that a daisy,' only he would pronounce 'daisy' as 'dazzy.' I got to saying, 'Ain't that a dazzy,' and before I was eleven years old, the nickname was tacked on me."*

After getting his start in organized baseball by pitching for a semi-pro team in nearby Hastings, Vance signed on with a minor league team

Courtesy of RMYauctions.com

Dazzy Vance proved to be the National League's
most dominant pitcher for much of the 1920's

situated in Red Cloud, Nebraska in 1912. He spent the next two years
pitching for three different teams in the Class-D Nebraska State League,
before advancing to St. Joseph of the Class A Western League midway
through the 1914 campaign. Despite winning a total of 26 games in 1914,
Vance suffered an injury that ended up setting back his career nearly a
decade. Straining his arm by pitching four games in six days, Vance subsequently found himself unable to throw with the same velocity, his performance on the mound further compromised by a constantly-aching elbow.
Vance later revealed, "Something went wrong with my right arm. I no
longer could throw hard, and it hurt like the dickens every time I threw."

With the Pittsburgh Pirates purchasing his contract prior to the start of the 1915 season, Vance made one start for the Pirates, failing miserably in his major-league debut, before being sold to the Yankees. After failing to distinguish himself in eight appearances with the Yankees, going 0-3 with a 3.54 ERA, Vance found himself back in the minors, where he spent the next several seasons continuing to struggle with arm problems, although he did return to New York briefly in 1918. Sold by the Yankees to Sacramento in the Pacific Coast League following the conclusion of the 1919 season, Vance began the ensuing campaign in New Orleans, where fate finally smiled down on him.

Engaged in a late-night poker game with some of his Pelicans teammates, Vance won a hand, after which, in attempting to gather his winnings, he banged his pitching arm on the edge of the table. Feeling a pain in his elbow sharper than anything he had previously experienced, Vance subsequently underwent emergency surgery that ended up relieving the discomfort that had plagued him for years. Although no one actually knows the exact procedure that doctors performed on him, Bill James speculated in his *Historical Baseball Abstract* that they likely removed bone chips and debris from the elbow. In any case, Vance found himself free of pain for the first time in years, later commenting, "My arm came back just as quickly as it went sore on me in 1915. I awoke one morning and learned I could throw without pain again."

After Vance won 21 games for New Orleans the following year, the Dodgers purchased his contract prior to the start of the 1922 campaign. Arriving in Brooklyn shortly after he turned thirty-one years of age, the 6'2", 200-pound Vance joined veterans Burleigh Grimes and Dutch Ruether at the top of the Dodgers' starting rotation, finishing his first full major-league season with a record of 18-12, an ERA of 3.70, 17 complete games, 245⅔ innings pitched, and a league-leading 5 shutouts and 134 strikeouts. He followed that up by going 18-15 with a 3.50 ERA in 1923, while also leading the league with 197 strikeouts and placing among the leaders with 21 complete games and 280⅓ innings pitched.

Just hitting his stride at the age of thirty-three, Vance pitched magnificently in 1924, earning NL MVP honors by winning the pitcher's version of the Triple Crown with a record of 28-6, an ERA of 2.16, and 262 strikeouts. His brilliant performance enabled the Dodgers to finish a close second to the pennant-winning Giants in the National League, with a record of 92-62. Although Vance's ERA rose to 3.53 the following year, he again topped the senior circuit in wins (22) and strikeouts (221), en route to earning a fifth-place finish in the MVP voting.

The fire-balling Vance had the ability to throw the ball by most opposing hitters, with former Brooklyn teammate Johnny Frederick once commenting, "Dazzy Vance could throw a cream puff through a battleship." Yet, even though he is remembered primarily as a fastball pitcher, Vance had an outstanding curve that he often used as his "out" pitch, with Jack Kavanagh and Norman Macht writing in *Uncle Robbie*, "Dazzy's pitching style was simple. He reared back, kicked his left foot high and catapulted the ball overhand. It exploded past the batter or swerved away. Although his speed excited the fans, it was his control of the curve that delighted his manager."

Vance also became noted for his ability to use the elements at Ebbets Field to his advantage. Former Brooklyn teammate Rube Bressler, who also hit against Vance as a member of the Cincinnati Reds, elaborated in Ken Burns' *Baseball* documentary, stating:

"You couldn't hit him on a Monday. He cut the sleeve of his undershirt to the elbow and, on that part of it, he used lye to make it white, and the rest he didn't care how dirty it was. Then he'd pitch overhand out of the apartment houses in the background at Ebbets Field. Between the bleached sleeve of his undershirt waving and the Monday wash hanging out to dry—the diapers, and undies, and sheets flapping on the Clothesline—you lost the ball entirely. He threw balls by I never even saw."

Hampered by injuries, Vance finished just 9-10 with a 3.89 ERA in 1926, although he led the league in strikeouts for the fifth straight time, with 140. With the Dodgers finishing sixth in the National League with a record of just 65-88 in 1927, Vance ended up winning only 16 of his 31 decisions. Nevertheless, he had an excellent year on the mound, ranking among the NL leaders with an ERA of 2.70 and 273⅓ innings pitched, while topping the circuit with 25 complete games and 184 strikeouts. Vance performed even better the following season, concluding the 1928 campaign with a record of 22-10, 24 complete games, 280⅓ innings pitched, and a league-leading 2.09 ERA, 4 shutouts, and 200 strikeouts.

Despite turning thirty-eight years of age shortly before the 1929 season got underway, Vance continued to pitch well for the Dodgers, going 14-13 with a 3.89 ERA and 17 complete games, before posting 17 victories, 173 strikeouts, 20 complete games, and a league-leading 2.61 ERA and 4 shutouts the following year. Vance finally began to show signs of aging, though, in 1931, when he finished just 11-13 with a 3.38 ERA. After compiling a record of 12-11, a 4.20 ERA, and only 9 complete games and 103 strikeouts in 1932, Vance found himself headed for St. Louis when the Dodgers included him in a four-player trade they completed with the Cardinals on February 8, 1933.

The forty-two-year-old right-hander spent just one full season in St. Louis, going 6-2 with a 3.55 ERA in 1933 while working primarily out of the bullpen, before splitting the ensuing campaign between the Cardinals and Cincinnati Reds. After being released prior to the start of the 1935 season, Vance signed with the Dodgers, with whom he ended his career by going 3-2 with a 4.41 ERA in his 20 appearances with the club. Vance announced his retirement at season's end, concluding his major-league career with a record of 197-140 that gave him a winning percentage of .585. He also compiled an ERA of 3.24, struck out 2,045 batters in 2,966⅔ innings of work, threw 217 complete games and 29 shutouts, and posted a WHIP of 1.230. Over parts of 12 seasons in Brooklyn, Vance went 190-131, with a 3.17 ERA, 1,918 strikeouts in 2,757⅔ innings pitched, 213 complete games, 29 shutouts, and a WHIP of 1.212. He continues to rank among the Dodgers' all-time leaders in most statistical categories for pitchers.

The members of the BBWAA elected Vance to the Baseball Hall of Fame in 1955, six years before he died of a heart attack at his home in Homosassa Springs, Florida on February 16, 1961, just two weeks before he turned seventy years of age. Upon learning of Vance's passing, Casey Stengel said, "I hit against Dazzy when I was with the Giants from 1921 to 1923, and I can say he was a great one. I recall a four-game series between the Giants and the Dodgers when Vance struck out eleven men in one game and fourteen in another. I'll always remember his getting out there on the mound with his shirt flapping. It used to bother the opposing hitters, but it wasn't the undershirt that made them swing and miss like they claimed, but the stuff he had on the ball."

## Dodger Career Highlights:

**Best Season:** Although Vance pitched exceptionally well for the Dodgers in 1928, posting 22 victories, throwing 24 complete games and 280⅓ innings, and leading all National League hurlers with a 2.09 ERA, 4 shutouts, 200 strikeouts, and a WHIP of 1.063, he clearly had the greatest season of his career in 1924. In addition to winning the pitcher's version of the Triple Crown by leading the league in wins (28), ERA (2.16), and strikeouts (262), Vance established career-best marks in innings pitched (308⅓), complete games (30), and WHIP (1.022), topping the senior circuit in each of the last two categories. Vance proved to be so dominant over the course of that 1924 campaign that he struck out more batters than the second and third-place pitchers combined. Posting 15 consecutive victories at one point during the season, Vance earned NL MVP honors in spite of the fact that Rogers Hornsby, who finished second in the balloting, batted .424 for the St. Louis Cardinals.

**Memorable Moments/Greatest Performances**: A pretty fair hitter over the course of his career, Vance had a number of outstanding days at the plate for the Dodgers, with the first of those coming on May 30, 1923, when he hit the first of his 7 career home runs during a 5-2 victory over the Giants.

Vance proved to be too much for Philadelphia to handle on June 28, 1924, when, in addition to recording 9 strikeouts during a complete-game 9-1 victory over the Phillies, he homered, singled, and knocked in a pair of runs.

Vance defeated Chicago almost single-handedly on July 9, 1925, hitting a homer, driving in 3 runs, and allowing 6 hits during a complete-game 4-2 victory over the Cubs.

Vance had another tremendous all-around game less than two weeks later, when, during a July 20, 1925 10-inning, 4-3 win over the St. Louis Cardinals, he struck out a career-high 17 batters and went 3-for-4, with a homer and 3 runs batted in.

Vance, though, had arguably his finest day at the plate on May 12, 1927, when, during a complete-game 6-3 victory over the Cincinnati Reds, he went 4-for-4, with a double and 2 runs scored.

Vance tossed a pair of one-hitters during his career, accomplishing the feat for the first time on June 17, 1923, when he allowed just a single and three walks during a lopsided 9-0 victory over Cincinnati. He topped that performance, though, on September 8, 1925, when he carried a perfect game into the ninth inning before surrendering a one-out single to Philadelphia first baseman "Chicken" Hawks. With Hawks subsequently being thrown out attempting to steal second base, Vance ended up pitching to the minimum 27 batters, in defeating the Phillies by a score of 1-0.

However, Vance's crowning achievement came in his very next start, on September 13, 1925, when he no-hit the Phillies, 10-1, allowing just a walk and an unearned run during the contest, while recording 9 strikeouts.

Vance also threw four two-hitters during his time in Brooklyn, with two of those coming against the Cubs—one a 6-0 victory on August 23, 1925 in which he walked 2 and struck out 9, and the other a 2-1 win on September 21, 1928 in which he walked 2 and struck out 11. Vance also tossed two-hit shutouts against the Giants on May 26, 1920 and the Phillies on April 16, 1932, recording 7-0 and 5-0 victories in the process.

Particularly rough on Chicago through the years, Vance surrendered just 3 hits and struck out 14 batters during a 4-0 win over the Cubs on August 1, 1924. He threw another three-hitter against Chicago on September 26, 1926, when he struck out 15 batters during a 3-1 Dodgers victory. Vance again allowed the Cubs just 3 hits and struck out 15, in defeating them by a score of 4-0 on June 17, 1928.

## Notable Achievements:

- Won more than 20 games three times, surpassing 17 victories on three other occasions.
- Posted winning percentage in excess of .700 twice.
- Compiled ERA under 3.00 four times.
- Struck out more than 200 batters three times.
- Threw more than 300 innings once (308$\frac{1}{3}$ in 1924).
- Threw more than 20 complete games six times, topping the 30-mark once (30 in 1924).
- Led NL pitchers in: wins twice, ERA three times, WHIP three times, strikeouts seven times, shutouts four times, and complete games twice.
- Ranks among Dodgers career leaders in: wins (third), strikeouts (tied-fourth', shutouts (tied-sixth), complete games (third), innings pitched (fourth), games started (fifth), and pitching appearances (10th).
- Threw no-hitter vs. Philadelphia Phillies on September 13, 1925.
- Only pitcher in NL history to lead league in strikeouts seven straight years.
- 1924 NL pitching Triple Crown winner.

- 1924 NL MVP.
- Finished fifth in 1925 NL MVP voting.
- 1925 *Sporting News* All-Star selection.
- Elected to Baseball Hall of Fame by members of BBWAA in 1955.

# 7

# ZACK WHEAT

Although the vast majority of Dodger fans have probably never even heard of Zack Wheat, the Hall of Fame outfielder clearly established himself as one of the greatest players in franchise history over the course of his career, which he spent almost entirely in Brooklyn. The club's all-time leader in hits, doubles, triples, and total bases, Wheat also appeared in more games and accumulated more at-bats than anyone else in a Dodger uniform. Over parts of 18 seasons in Brooklyn, Wheat batted over .300 13 times, surpassing the .350-mark on three separate occasions. Starring in the Dodger outfield mostly during the Deadball Era, Wheat also knocked in more than 100 runs twice, scored more than 100 runs once, amassed more than 200 hits three times, and finished in double-digits in triples 11 times, establishing himself in the process as one of the National League's top sluggers and run-producers of the period. An exceptional fielder as well, Wheat led all NL left-fielders in putouts six times, double plays three times, and fielding percentage twice, with his outstanding defensive play earning him a top-10 ranking all-time among players at his position in assists (fifth), putouts (ninth), and double plays (second).

Born in Hamilton, Missouri on May 23, 1888, Zachariah Davis Wheat grew up on his family's farm, some 60 miles northeast of Kansas City, Missouri. The son of an English father and a full-blooded Cherokee mother, young Zack got his start in organized baseball at the age of sixteen, when his family moved to Kansas City, Kansas following the death of his father. After beginning his semi-pro career as a second baseman with the Union club, Wheat traveled to Enterprise, Kansas, where he earned $60 per month playing for an independent team. He subsequently played for minor-league clubs in Fort Worth, Shreveport, and Mobile, earning a repu-

Zack Wheat holds franchise records for most hits,
doubles, triples, and total bases

tation at each stop as an elite defensive outfielder, although he struggled at the plate after contracting malaria while traveling through the South.

Purchased by Brooklyn during the latter stages of the 1909 campaign on the advice of scout Larry Sutton, who saw him playing at Mobile, Wheat joined the Superbas in early September, after which he batted .304 in 26 games over the season's final month. Perhaps revealing the attitude of the times, Wheat drew intended praise from one local newspaper shortly after he arrived in Brooklyn, with the periodical's reporter writing, "He is an Indian, but you would hardly guess it except from his dark complexion. He is a very fine fellow and a quiet and refined gentleman."

Establishing himself as Brooklyn's starting left-fielder the following year, Wheat had a solid rookie season, concluding the 1910 campaign with

2 homers, 55 RBIs, 78 runs scored, 15 triples, 36 doubles, and a .284 batting average. He also finished third among all NL outfielders with a career-high 354 putouts. After batting .287, driving in 76 runs, and stealing 21 bases in 1911, Wheat began a string of three straight seasons in which he topped the .300-mark in hitting, posting averages of .305, .301, and .319 from 1912 to 1914. Particularly effective in the last of those campaigns, Wheat earned a ninth-place finish in the 1914 NL MVP balloting by placing among the league leaders with 9 homers, 89 RBIs, 170 hits, 241 total bases, and an OPS of .830, while also leading all NL outfielders with 331 putouts.

In explaining his increased offensive production at the major-league level, Wheat later revealed, "I was young and inexperienced [in the minors]. The fellows that I played with encouraged me to bunt and beat the ball out. I was anxious to make good and did as I was told. When I came to Brooklyn, I adopted an altogether different style of hitting. I stood flat-footed at the plate and slugged. That was my natural style."

The left-handed swinging Wheat differed from most other Deadball Era hitters in that he held his hands way down by the knob of the bat, refusing to choke up. Corkscrewing his spikes into the dirt with a wiggle that became his trademark, the 5'10," 170-pound outfielder often swung from the heels, eschewing the scientific approach to hitting that prevailed at the time. "There is no chop-hitting with Wheat, but a smashing swipe which, if it connects, means work for the outfielders," wrote one reporter. "The beauty of Wheat's hitting is that many of his drives go for extra bases," offered another member of the press corps.

An outstanding first-pitch hitter who excelled at hitting the curveball, Wheat sometimes drew criticism for his reluctance to bunt. He responded, though, by suggesting that he had more value to his team by swinging away. Using a lighter bat than most of his contemporaries, Wheat explained, "I am an arm hitter. When you snap the bat with your wrists just as you meet the ball, you give the bat tremendous speed for a few inches of its course. The speed with which the bat meets the ball is the thing that counts."

Casey Stengel, Wheat's boyhood friend who played alongside him in the Brooklyn outfield for six seasons, stated years later, "He [Wheat] was the most graceful left-handed hitter I ever saw. With the dead ball, many of his line drives were caught, but they were just shot out of a cannon almost every time up."

In addition to his hitting ability, Wheat became renowned for his graceful and stylish defense, with *Baseball Magazine* suggesting in 1917, "What [Napoleon] Lajoie was to infielders, Zack Wheat is to outfielders— the finest mechanical craftsman of them all. Wheat is the easiest, most graceful of outfielders, with no close rivals."

After a subpar 1915 campaign in which he batted a career-low .258, Wheat helped lead Brooklyn to the NL pennant in 1916 by placing among the league leaders with 9 homers, 73 RBIs, 76 runs scored, 177 hits, 13 triples, 32 doubles, and a .312 batting average, while topping the circuit with a .461 slugging percentage and 262 total bases. With the Dodgers involved in an extremely close pennant race in the closing weeks of the season, Wheat became so excited that he found himself unable to sleep at night, recalling years later, "I was thinking and dreaming and eating pennants. I used to get up in the middle of the night and smoke a cigar so that I could calm down a little and get some sleep." Although the Dodgers edged out Philadelphia for the flag by 2½ games, they, unfortunately, ended up losing the World Series to Boston in five games.

Despite being limited to only 109 games by a series of nagging ankle injuries that plagued him for much of his career, Wheat again performed well in 1917, compiling a batting average of .312. He followed that up by leading the league with a mark of .335 in the war-shortened 1918 season, before returning home to his Missouri farm, where he spent the rest of World War I selling mules to the Army to serve as pack animals on the battlefields of Europe.

Wheat, who spent each offseason raising stock, often used his second occupation as leverage in his contract negotiations with the Dodgers, stating on one occasion, "I am a ball player in the summer and a farmer in the winter time, and I aim to be a success at both professions." Unless Brooklyn met his salary demands each spring, Wheat threatened to remain on his farm the entire year, often causing team management to consider trading him to another club. However, Wheat's popularity with the fans of Brooklyn invariably prevented the Dodgers from making such a move, since, as one local newspaper wrote, "They [Dodger fans] regard Zack and his wife and his two children as members of their own families." The mild-mannered Wheat also remained extremely popular with his fellow players, with his longtime friend Casey Stengel stating on one occasion, "I never knew him to refuse help to another player, were he a Dodger or even a Giant. I never saw Wheat really angry, and I never heard him use cuss words."

After being named captain of the Dodgers prior to the start of the 1919 campaign, Wheat closed out the Deadball Era by batting .297, with 5 homers and 62 RBIs. But, even though he compiled more total bases than any other National League player over the course of the previous 10 seasons, Wheat proved to be even more proficient as a hitter after the Major Leagues began using a livelier ball in 1920. Beginning the new decade in fine fashion, Wheat led the Dodgers to the NL pennant by hitting 9 homers, driving in 73 runs, scoring 89 times, collecting 191 hits, and finishing fourth in the league with a batting average of .328 and an OPS of .848. Although the Dodgers subsequently lost the 1920 World Series to the Cleveland Indians in seven games, Wheat acquitted himself extremely well in the fall classic, collecting 9 hits in 27 at-bats, for a .333 batting average.

Wheat then went on a five-year hitting spree during which he posted a composite batting average of .351, while also driving in more than 100 runs twice and finishing in double-digits in homers four times. After batting .320 and establishing a new career-high by hitting 14 home runs in 1921, Wheat batted .335, slugged 16 homers, and knocked in a career-best 112 runs the following year. He then compiled a .375 batting average in each of the next two seasons, earning a third-place finish in the 1924 MVP voting by also hitting 14 homers, driving in 97 runs, scoring 92 times, and amassing 212 hits, en route to helping the Dodgers finish a close second in the senior circuit, just 1 ½ games behind the pennant-winning Giants. Although Brooklyn finished well out of contention the following year, Wheat again performed brilliantly, placing third in the NL batting race with a mark of .359, while also ranking among the league leaders with 14 homers, 103 RBIs, 14 triples, 42 doubles, and a career-high 125 runs scored, 221 hits, and 333 total bases.

After turning 38 during the early stages of the 1926 campaign, Wheat went on to post his poorest numbers in more than a decade, finishing the season with a .290 batting average and only 5 homers and 35 RBIs, in just 111 games. Released by the Dodgers at season's end, Wheat subsequently signed with the Philadelphia Athletics, for whom he batted .324 in a part-time role in 1927, before spending the final year of his playing career with Minneapolis of the American Association. Wheat announced his retirement from baseball early in 1929, ending his major-league career with 132 home runs, 1,248 RBIs, 1,289 runs scored, 2,884 hits, 476 doubles, 172 triples, 205 stolen bases, a .317 batting average, a .367 on-base percentage, and a .450 slugging percentage. His 2,804 hits, 464 doubles, 171 triples, and 4,003 total bases as a member of the Dodgers remain the highest totals compiled by any player in franchise history.

Following his playing days, Wheat briefly returned to Brooklyn as a coach under Wilbert Robinson, before leaving baseball for good after clashing with his former manager. When asked years later why he didn't remain in the game, Wheat replied, "Nobody asked me to." Wheat then returned to farming, before the Great Depression forced him to sell his 160 acres for just $23,000. After moving his family to Kansas City, Missouri, Wheat became a patrolman with the local police department, continuing to serve in that capacity until he nearly lost his life in 1936 when he crashed his patrol car while chasing a fugitive. Following a five-month stay in the hospital, Wheat settled with his family in Sunrise Beach, Missouri, a resort town on the shores of the Lake of the Ozarks, where he spent the rest of his life. He passed away at the age of eighty-three on March 11, 1972, thirteen years after the members of the Veteran's Committee unanimously elected him into the Baseball Hall of Fame. Upon learning of his selection, the seventy-year-old Wheat stated, "That makes me feel mighty proud. I feel a little younger too."

## Dodger Career Highlights:

**Best Season:** Wheat's outstanding 1914 and 1916 campaigns—seasons in which he ranked among the NL leaders in virtually every offensive statistical category—proved to be his best of the Deadball Era. However, he posted significantly better numbers after the Major Leagues began using a livelier ball in 1920, with his two best seasons coming in 1924 and 1925. En route to earning a third-place finish in the NL MVP voting in the first of those campaigns, Wheat finished among the league leaders in 10 different offensive categories, including placing second in batting average (.375), OPS (.978), hits (212), doubles (41), and total bases (311). Although Wheat finished just 15th in the balloting the following year, he compiled equally impressive numbers, hitting the same number of homers (14), driving in more runs (103 to 97), scoring more times (125 to 92), accumulating more hits (221), doubles (42), triples (14), and total bases (333), and posting a comparable batting average (.359) and OPS (.944). It ended up being an extremely close call, but the fact that Wheat received significantly more support for league MVP honors in 1924 after leading the Dodgers to a close second-place finish (they finished 27 games out of first the following year) prompted me to identify that as his greatest season.

**Memorable Moments/Greatest Performances:** Wheat recorded four hitting streaks of at least 20 games during his time in Brooklyn, with the longest of those coming in 1916, when he hit safely in 29 consecutive contests from August 20 to September 16. During the streak, which remains the second-longest in franchise history, Wheat batted .379, with 3 homers, 18 RBIs, 22 runs scored, 4 triples, and 7 doubles. Even though the Dodgers lost their August 23 matchup with the Cubs by a score of 7-6, Wheat turned in arguably his finest performance of that 29-game streak, going 3-for-5, with a pair of doubles and 5 RBIs.

Wheat led the Dodgers to a 9-2 win over Cincinnati on July 29, 1911 by going 4-for-5, with a career-high 4 runs scored.

Wheat had a huge game on August 30, 1925, when, after failing to hit safely in Brooklyn's 4-3 victory over Cincinnati in the first game of a doubleheader, he led the Dodgers to a 10-8 win in the nightcap by going 3-for-5, with a homer, double, 5 RBIs, and 2 runs scored.

Wheat homered twice in one game four times during his career, doing so for the first time on September 9, 1922, when he reached the seats twice and knocked in 4 runs during a 12-inning, 6-5 victory over the Boston Braves. He accomplished the feat again on May 3, 1924, leading the Dodgers to a 7-2 win over the Phillies by going 4-for-4, with a pair of homers and 3 RBIs. Wheat again tormented Philadelphia's pitching staff four months later, when he led the Dodgers to a lopsided 7-0 victory over the Phillies by going 3-for-4, with 2 homers, a double, 3 runs scored, and a career-high 6 RBIs. Wheat homered twice in the same contest for the final time on June 5, 1925, when he left the yard twice and knocked in 4 runs during a 7-6 win over the Chicago Cubs.

Wheat also went 5-for-5 in a game four times during his career, doing so twice in 1924 and another two times in 1925. After collecting 5 hits and driving in 3 runs during an 11-4 win over the Phillies on April 19, 1924, Wheat had another perfect day at the plate some three months later, on July 23, leading the Dodgers to a 4-3 win over the Pirates in 10 innings in the process. Continuing to feast on Philadelphia pitching the following year,

Wheat led the Dodgers to a 10-8 victory over the Phillies on April 24, 1925 by going 5-for-5, with a homer, 2 RBIs, and 3 runs scored. Wheat again collected 5 hits in 5 trips to the plate on August 1, when he doubled twice, knocked in a run, and scored 2 others during a 7-1 win over the Cubs.

## Notable Achievements:

- Batted over .300 13 times, topping the .350-mark on three occasions.
- Knocked in more than 100 runs twice.
- Scored more than 100 runs once (125 in 1925).
- Surpassed 200 hits three times.
- Finished in double-digits in triples 11 times.
- Surpassed 30 doubles six times, topping 40 two-baggers twice.
- Stole at least 20 bases three times.
- Compiled on-base percentage in excess of .400 three times.
- Posted slugging percentage in excess of .500 four times.
- Led NL in: batting average once, slugging percentage once, and total bases once.
- Led NL outfielders in putouts once and fielding percentage once.
- Led NL left-fielders in: putouts six times, double plays turned three times, and fielding percentage twice.
- Holds Dodgers career records for most: hits (2,804), doubles (464), triples (171), total bases (4,003), games played (2,322), plate appearances (9,725), and at-bats (8,859).
- Ranks among Dodgers career leaders in: batting average (tied-sixth), runs scored (second), RBIs (third), extra-base hits (second), and walks (seventh).
- Ranks among MLB career leaders in: putouts (ninth), assists (fifth), and double plays turned (second) by a left-fielder.
- Finished third in 1924 NL MVP voting.
- Two-time NL champion (1916 & 1920).
- Elected to Baseball Hall of Fame by members of Veteran's Committee in 1959.

# 8

# DON DRYSDALE

Intimidating opposing batters with his size, exaggerated sidearm delivery, and nasty temperament on the mound, Don Drysdale teamed up with Sandy Koufax to give the Dodgers baseball's most formidable pitching duo for much of the 1960s. Although the 6'5", 215-pound Drysdale spent much of his time in Los Angeles playing second fiddle to Koufax, the hard-throwing right-hander carved out quite a career for himself as well, eventually gaining induction into Cooperstown by winning more than 200 games and compiling a lifetime ERA of 2.95, en route to establishing himself as one of his era's most dominant hurlers. An eight-time NL All-Star, two-time top-five MVP candidate, and one-time Cy Young Award winner, "Big D", as he came to be affectionately known to his teammates, posted more than 20 victories for the Dodgers twice, while also winning in excess of 17 games on four other occasions. Drysdale also compiled an ERA under 3.00 in nine of his 14 seasons with the club and struck out more than 200 batters six times, topping the senior circuit in the last category on three separate occasions. A true workhorse, Drysdale led all NL hurlers in starts four times and innings pitched twice, garnering more than 40 starts and throwing more than 300 innings four times each, while also tossing more than 20 complete games twice. By the time Drysdale announced his retirement in 1969, he had helped the Dodgers win five National League pennants and three world championships.

Born in Van Nuys, California on July 23, 1936, Donald Scott Drysdale attended local Van Nuys High School, where he excelled on the mound to such a degree that the Dodgers signed him to a contract shortly after he graduated in 1954. Advancing rapidly through Brooklyn's farm system, Drysdale made his major-league debut with the club less than two years later, at the tender age of nineteen. Appearing in 25 games with the Dodg-

Courtesy of MEARS Online Auctions

Don Drysdale (left) combined with Sandy Koufax
to give the Dodgers baseball's most formidable
pitching tandem for much of the 1960's

ers as a rookie in 1956, Drysdale compiled a record of 5-5 and an ERA of 2.64, while serving the team as both a starter and a reliever. After being inserted into the starting rotation the following year, Drysdale had his first big season, going 17-9, with a 2.69 ERA and 221 innings pitched, tossing more than 200 frames for the first of 12 straight times in the process.

The California native pitched less effectively after the club moved out West in 1958, finishing just 12-13 with a 4.17 ERA in his first year in Los Angeles. However, he rebounded in 1959, earning his first All-Star selection by compiling a record of 17-13 and an ERA of 3.46 for the world champion Dodgers, while also throwing 270⅔ innings, tossing 15 complete games, and leading all NL hurlers with 242 strikeouts and 4 shutouts.

Although the Dodgers failed to win the pennant in either of the next two seasons, Drysdale continued to pitch well, going a combined 28-24, finishing among the NL leaders in ERA, shutouts, and innings pitched both years, and topping the senior circuit with 246 strikeouts and a WHIP of 1.063 in 1960. The big right-hander also continued his string of four straight seasons in which he led all NL hurlers in hit-batsmen, furthering his reputation as one of the sport's nastiest and most intimidating pitchers by doing so.

Having learned the importance of keeping opposing hitters off balance from former Brooklyn teammate Sal "The Barber" Maglie during the early stages of his career, Drysdale put those lessons to good use long after Maglie retired, later stating, "What being around Maglie did for me was to confirm this idea in my mind and refine it. It was part of the game. I watched Maglie, I listened to Maglie, and it all sunk in. It just sort of clicked."

Drysdale's approach to pitching made him absolutely relentless in claiming the inside part of the plate for himself, causing him to frequently throw at opposing hitters. On one particular occasion, after Dodger manager Walter Alston instructed him to intentionally walk Frank Robinson, Drysdale responded by knocking down the Cincinnati slugger with four consecutive pitches, the last of which hit Robinson squarely in the ribs.

In discussing Drysdale's penchant for hitting opposing batters, Robinson claimed, "He was mean enough to do it, and he did it continuously. You could count on him doing it. And, when he did it, he just stood there on the mound and glared at you to let you know he meant it."

Drysdale's mean streak reflected the attitude he carried with him to the mound before each start, which he once explained by proclaiming, "I hate all hitters. I start a game mad and I stay that way until it's over."

Drysdale also had two rules that he always followed, which he explained thusly:

> "My own little rule was two for one. If one of my teammates got knocked down, then I knocked down two on the other team….I never hit anybody in the head in my life. But you have to move them off the plate; you have to get them out of there. This was part of the game and everybody accepted it as part of the game."

Further expounding upon his principle of pitching inside, Drysdale said, "When the ball is over the middle of the plate, the batter is hitting it with the sweet part of the bat. When it's inside, he's hitting it with the part of the bat from the handle to the trademark. When it's outside, he's hitting it with the end of the bat. You've got to keep the ball away from the sweet part of the bat. To do that, the pitcher has to move the hitter off the plate."

Opposing batters became all too familiar with Drysdale's aggressive approach to pitching. Orlando Cepeda suggested, "The trick against Drysdale is to hit him before he hits you."

Dick Groat, who faced Drysdale as a member of the Pirates, Cardinals, and Phillies, quipped, "Batting against Don Drysdale is the same as making a date with a dentist."

Mickey Mantle, who faced Drysdale in the 1963 World Series and in numerous All-Star Games, revealed, "I hated to bat against Drysdale. After he hit you he'd come around, look at the bruise on your arm, and say, 'Do you want me to sign it?'"

The Dodgers again failed to earn a berth in the World Series in 1962, narrowly missing winning the pennant by losing a three-game playoff to the Giants. Nevertheless, Drysdale had the finest season of his career, earning Cy Young honors and a fifth-place finish in the NL MVP voting by going 25-9, with a 2.83 ERA, 19 complete games, and a league-leading 232 strikeouts and 314⅓ innings pitched. He followed that up by posting 19 victories for the pennant-winning Dodgers in 1963, while also compiling an ERA of 2.63 and ranking among the league leaders with 251 strikeouts, 17 complete games, and 315⅓ innings pitched. Drysdale then helped the Dodgers sweep the Yankees in the World Series by out-dueling New York starter Jim Bouton in Game Three, surrendering just three hits during a 1-0 complete-game victory.

Despite pitching some of the best ball of his career in 1964, Drysdale finished just 18-16 due to a lack of run support from his teammates. Still, he placed second in the league with an ERA of 2.18, a WHIP of 0.965, 21 complete games, and 5 shutouts, while finishing third among NL hurlers with 237 strikeouts and topping the senior circuit with 321⅓ innings pitched. Drysdale then teamed up with Sandy Koufax the following year to lead the Dodgers to their second pennant in three seasons by going 23-12, with a 2.77 ERA, 210 strikeouts, 7 shutouts, 20 complete games, and 308⅓ innings pitched, finishing either second or third in the league in each of the last three categories. After subsequently faltering against Minnesota in Game One of the World Series, Drysdale returned to the mound in Game Four to earn a complete-game 7-2 victory over the Twins that evened the fall classic at two games apiece.

Koufax and Drysdale proved to be so successful together over the course of that 1965 campaign (they combined to post 49 of their team's 97 regular-season wins) that they decided to conduct a joint holdout at the end of the season. Although the two pitchers ended up settling for less than the original amount they demanded from the Dodgers, they did quite well for themselves, with Koufax eventually signing for $120,000 and Drysdale inking a deal that netted him $105,000.

The Dodgers repeated as National League champions in 1966, but Drysdale suffered through a subpar campaign that saw him finish just 13-16 with a 3.42 ERA. With the early retirement of Koufax the following year, Drysdale assumed the number one spot in the Los Angeles starting rotation. Yet, despite pitching markedly better, compiling an ERA of 2.74 and ranking among the league leaders with 196 strikeouts and 282 innings pitched, "Big D" ended up posting an identical 13-16 record for a weak-hitting Dodgers team.

Even though Drysdale subsequently compiled a record of just 14-12 in 1968, he pitched extremely well for the Dodgers over the course of the season, concluding "The Year of the Pitcher" with an ERA of 2.15, and finishing second among NL hurlers with 8 shutouts—6 of which came in succession as part of a 58⅔ consecutive scoreless innings streak that established a new major-league record (since broken).

Unfortunately, the 1968 campaign ended up being Drysdale's last full season in the big leagues. Limited to just 12 starts the following year by a torn rotator cuff, Drysdale chose to announce his retirement at season's end, saying at the time, "A torn rotator cuff is a cancer for a pitcher. And, if a pitcher gets a badly torn one, he has to face the facts—it's all over baby." Only thirty-three years old at the time of his retirement, Drysdale ended his career with a record of 209-166 that gave him a winning percentage of .557. He also compiled an ERA of 2.95 and a WHIP of 1.148, struck out 2,486 batters in 3,432 innings of work, threw 167 complete games, and tossed 49 shutouts. Drysdale continues to rank second in franchise history in wins, strikeouts, shutouts, and innings pitched.

Following his playing days, Drysdale entered into a career in broadcasting, serving at different times as an announcer for the Montreal Expos, (1970-71), the Texas Rangers (1972), the California Angels (1973-79, 1981), and the Chicago White Sox (1982-87), before spending his final six seasons in the broadcast booth calling Dodger games. Drysdale also spent nearly a decade doing color commentary for ABC's Game of the Week and Playoff coverage. Elected to the Baseball Hall of Fame by the members of the BBWAA in 1984, Drysdale lived another nine years, passing away at only fifty-six years of age, on July 3, 1993, after suffering a heart attack while in Montreal to announce a Dodgers-Expos game. Drysdale's broadcasting colleague, Vin Scully, who received instructions not to say anything on the air until the former's family received notification of his passing, announced the news of his death by saying, "Never have I been asked to make an announcement that hurts me as much as this one. And I say it to you as best I can, with a broken heart."

## Career Highlights:

**Best Season:** It could be argued that Drysdale pitched his best ball for the Dodgers in 1964, when, despite finishing just 18-16, he compiled an exceptional ERA of 2.18, recorded 237 strikeouts, tossed 5 shutouts, and established career-best marks in WHIP (0.965), complete games (21), and innings pitched (321⅓), leading all NL hurlers in the last category. Nevertheless, the 1962 campaign is generally considered to be his signature season. En route to earning Cy Young honors and his lone *Sporting News* All-Star selection, Drysdale led all major-league pitchers with 25 wins, 232 strikeouts, 41 starts, and 314⅓ innings pitched, while also placing among the leaders in ERA (2.83), WHIP (1.113), and complete games (19).

**Memorable Moments/Greatest Performances:** An outstanding hitting pitcher, Drysdale hit 29 homers and knocked in 113 runs over the course of his career, doing much of his damage in 1958 and 1965, when he combined for 14 homers and 31 RBIs. Hitting 7 home runs, driving in 12 runs, and batting .227 in the first of those campaigns, Drysdale turned in his finest performance at the plate on August 23, 1958, when he reached the seats twice and knocked in 4 runs during a 10-1 victory over the Braves in which he allowed only 4 hits to Milwaukee's potent lineup. However, Drysdale had his best year at the bat in 1965, when he hit 7 homers and established career-high marks in RBIs (19), runs scored (18), hits (39), and batting average (.300), making him the only Los Angeles player to top the .300-mark in batting.

Drysdale pitched one of his most memorable games on May 22, 1959, when he worked all 13 innings of a 2-1 victory over the Giants, surrendering just 6 hits and striking out 11 batters along the way.

Drysdale turned in another dominant performance a little over three weeks later, on June 15, 1959, when he allowed only 4 hits and recorded 13 strikeouts during a 4-0 shutout of the Braves.

Drysdale hurled another gem later in the year, surrendering just 3 hits and striking out 11, in defeating the Phillies by a score of 1-0 on September 9, 1959.

Drysdale again dominated Philadelphia's lineup on July 22, 1960, when he allowed just 4 hits and 1 walk during a 2-0 win over the Phillies in which he recorded a career-high 14 strikeouts—a figure he matched on two other occasions.

Drysdale won a pitcher's duel with Milwaukee's Lew Burdette on September 11, 1960, surrendering just 2 hits and striking out 7, in defeating the Braves' right-hander by a score of 2-0.

Drysdale tossed another two-hit shutout on September 4, 1961, this time defeating Juan Marichal and the Giants by a score of 4-0.

Drysdale threw the only one-hitter of his career on May 25, 1965, when he won a 2-0 pitcher's duel with Bob Gibson. After surrendering a leadoff single to Curt Flood in the top of the first inning, Drysdale retired 27 of the next 28 batters, with the only other Cardinals player to reach base doing so on an infield error.

Drysdale came up big for the Dodgers down the stretch in 1965, helping them overcome a 4 ½ game deficit to the first-place Giants in the season's final 2 ½ weeks by winning his last four starts, allowing a total of only 2 runs in the process. Particularly effective in his final two starts, Drysdale tossed a pair of shutouts, surrendering just 8 hits over the course of the two contests.

Drysdale turned in the finest postseason performance of his career in Game Three of the 1963 World Series, when he allowed just 3 hits, 1 walk, and struck out 9, in recording a 1-0 victory over the Yankees.

Still, Drysdale accomplished his most memorable feat in 1968, when he threw six straight shutouts and $58\frac{2}{3}$ consecutive scoreless innings between May 14 and June 8, establishing in the process a new major-league record that stood for another 20 years. Highlights of the streak included a two-hit, 1-0 victory over Ferguson Jenkins and the Cubs on May 14 and a three-hit, 5-0 win over Jim Bunning and the Pirates on June 4.

## Notable Achievements:

- Won more than 20 games twice, posting 25 wins in 1962.
- Surpassed 17 victories four other times.
- Posted winning percentage in excess of .700 once (.735 in 1962).
- Compiled ERA below 3.00 nine times, posting mark under 2.50 twice.
- Posted WHIP under 1.000 once (0.965 in 1964).
- Struck out more than 200 batters six times.
- Threw more than 300 innings four times, tossing more than 250 innings four other times.
- Threw more than 20 complete games twice.
- Led NL pitchers in: wins once, strikeouts three times, shutouts once, innings pitched twice, starts four times, and assists four times.
- Ranks second in Dodgers history in: wins (209), strikeouts (2,486), shutouts (49), innings pitched (3,432), games started (465), and pitching appearances (518).
- Ranks sixth in Dodgers history in complete games (167).
- Set new major-league record (since broken) in 1968 by throwing 58⅔ consecutive scoreless innings.
- Three-time NL Player of the Month.
- Finished fifth in NL MVP voting twice (1962 & 1965).
- 1962 Cy Young Award winner.
- 1962 *Sporting News* Major League Player of the Year.
- 1962 *Sporting News* NL Pitcher of the Year.
- 1962 *Sporting News* All-Star selection.
- Eight-time NL All-Star (1959, 1961, 1962, 1963, 1964, 1965, 1967 & 1968).
- Five-time NL champion (1956, 1959, 1963, 1965 & 1966).
- Three-time world champion (1959, 1963 & 1965).
- Elected to Baseball Hall of Fame by members of BBWAA in 1984.

# 9

# DON SUTTON

Extremely durable and remarkably consistent, Don Sutton posted double-digit wins for the Dodgers 15 straight times between 1966 and 1980, en route to compiling a total of 233 victories as a member of the team that places him first in franchise history. Topping 20 wins once and 15 victories eight other times, the hard-throwing right-hander performed particularly well from 1971 to 1976, posting a composite mark of 110-63 over the course of those six seasons that gained him general recognition as one of the game's elite pitchers. And, after Sutton left the Dodgers following the conclusion of the 1980 campaign, he went on to win nearly 100 more games, giving him a career total of 324 victories that eventually earned him a place in Cooperstown. Sutton, though, pitched his best ball for the Dodgers, compiling an ERA under 3.00 seven times during his time in Los Angeles, while also amassing more than 200 strikeouts five times, tossing more than 200 innings 15 straight times, and posting a WHIP under 1.000 on three separate occasions. By the time Sutton threw his last pitch for the Dodgers, he had established himself as the franchise's all-time leader in six different categories, including wins (233), strikeouts (2,696), shutouts (52), and innings pitched (3,816⅓). He also earned four All-Star selections and five top-five finishes in the NL Cy Young voting as a member of the team, helping the Dodgers capture five league championships in the process.

Born to Southern sharecropper parents in the small town of Clio, Alabama on April 2, 1945, Donald Howard Sutton moved with his family to Molina, Florida as a youngster. After starring in baseball, basketball, and football at Gonzalez Tate High School in nearby Pensacola, where he earned All-County, All-Conference, and All-State honors on the diamond in each of his final two seasons, Sutton attended Gulf Coast

Courtesy of MEARS Online Auctions

Don Sutton won more games for the Dodgers
than anyone else in franchise history

Community College in Panama City, Florida for one year, before signing with the Dodgers as an amateur free agent in 1964.

Sutton subsequently spent just one full season in the minor leagues pitching for the Sioux Falls Packers, before the Dodgers assigned him a regular spot in their starting rotation at the beginning of the 1966 campaign. Performing extremely well in his first big-league season, the twenty-one-year-old rookie helped Los Angeles capture the NL pennant by going 12-12, with a 2.99 ERA and 209 strikeouts. However, with the weak-hitting Dodgers posting a losing record in each of the next two seasons, poor run support relegated Sutton to a mark of just 11-15 in both 1967 and 1968. Sutton failed to establish himself as a consistent winner in the next two seasons as well, compiling an overall record of 32-31 in 1969 and 1970, although he ranked among the league leaders in strikeouts and innings pitched both years.

After pitching fairly well his first five seasons in Los Angeles, Sutton really came into his own in 1971, emerging as one of the senior circuit's top starters. Aided by better command of his pitches and a more potent Dodger lineup, the twenty-six-year-old right-hander began an extremely successful six-year run during which he won no fewer than 16 games. Here are the numbers he posted over the course of those six seasons:

1971: 17-12, 2.54 ERA, 194 Strikeouts, 1.078 WHIP, 4 Shut-outs, 265.1 Innings Pitched
1972: 19-9, 2.08 ERA, 207 Strikeouts, **0.913** WHIP, **9** Shutouts, 272.2 Innings Pitched
1973: 18-10, 2.42 ERA, 200 Strikeouts, 0.983 WHIP, 3 Shut-outs, 256.1 Innings Pitched
1974: 19-9, 3.23 ERA, 179 Strikeouts, 1.163 WHIP, 5 Shutouts, 276.0 Innings Pitched
1975: 16-13, 2.87 ERA, 175 Strikeouts, **1.038** WHIP, 4 Shut-outs, 254.1 Innings Pitched
1976: 21-10, 3.06 ERA, 161 Strikeouts, 1.169 WHIP, 4 Shut-outs, 267.2 Innings Pitched

Although none of those seasons could be considered truly spectacu-lar, Sutton continued to perform at an extremely high level throughout the period, demonstrating the extraordinary consistency that became his trademark. In addition to leading all NL hurlers in WHIP twice and shut-outs once, Sutton finished in the league's top five in the first category two other times and the second category all but once. He also placed near the top of the league rankings in wins and ERA four times each, while finishing among the league leaders in strikeouts, innings pitched, and complete games three times each. Sutton's 21 victories in 1976 placed him second in the league, as did his 2.42 ERA in 1973 and his 4 shutouts in 1970. Sutton earned All-Star honors in 1972, 1973, and 1975, and he placed in the top five in the NL Cy Young voting each year from 1972 to 1976, finishing as high as third in the last of those campaigns.

Sutton enjoyed his first 11 years in Los Angeles, holding in extremely high esteem the Dodgers' soft-spoken manager Walter Alston. However, he began to sour on L.A. after Tommy Lasorda replaced Alston at the helm prior to the start of the 1977 campaign. Sutton did not appreciate Lasorda's gregarious manner and "rah-rah" style of managing, considering both to be somewhat disingenuous. Although the two men got along publicly, they rarely interacted with one another away from the playing field. Yet, Lasorda later expressed his admiration for Sutton as a pitcher when he said, "When you gave him the ball, you knew one thing—your pitcher was going to give you everything he had. You win as many games as he did—to me, that should be automatic Hall of Fame."

Sutton also grew increasingly unhappy during his time in L.A. due to the fact that he had few close friends on the team, finding particularly objectionable Steve Garvey and the importance he placed on his public image. Things finally came to a head between the teammates on August 20, 1978, when Garvey confronted Sutton in the clubhouse after the latter criticized him in a *Washington Post* story, claiming that the Dodger first baseman received far too much media attention, and stating that he considered Reggie Smith to be the true MVP and leader of the team. After Sutton confirmed that he had made the comments, an argument ensued during which Sutton insulted Garvey's wife. The two men then began wrestling on the clubhouse floor, before finally being separated by teammates and team officials.

Still, in spite of his growing level of discontent, Sutton continued to pitch well for the Dodgers, going a combined 29-19 in 1977 and 1978, in helping them capture back-to-back pennants. After a subpar 1979 campaign in which he finished just 12-15 with a 3.82 ERA, Sutton rebounded the following year to go 13-5, with a league-leading 2.20 ERA and 0.989 WHIP, while also continuing his string of 15 straight seasons with more than 200 innings pitched and his streak of 12 straight years with at least 30 starts.

Having spent the previous few seasons longing to pitch in Houston's spacious Astrodome, Sutton signed with the Astros when he became a free agent following the conclusion of the 1980 campaign. However, he ended up spending less than two full seasons in Houston, posting an overall mark of 24-17 for the Astros, before being traded to the AL pennant-winning Milwaukee Brewers during the latter stages of the 1982 campaign. Sutton remained in Milwaukee through the end of 1984, when the Brewers traded him to Oakland for two nondescript players. After posting 13 victories for the A's during the first five months of the 1985 season, Sutton found himself headed back to Southern California when Oakland dealt him to the Angels in early September. He then spent two-plus years with the Angels, having his last big year for them in 1986, when he helped them capture the AL West title by winning 15 games. A free agent again at the end of 1987, the forty-three-year-old Sutton signed with the Dodgers, spending his final big-league season in the same place his career began 23 years earlier. He retired at season's end with a career record of 324-256, an ERA of 3.26, 3,574 strikeouts, 58 shutouts, 5,282⅓ innings pitched, 178 complete games, and a WHIP of 1.142. Sutton currently ranks 14th all-time in wins, seventh in strikeouts and innings pitched, 10th in shutouts, and third in games started. In his years with the Dodgers, he went 233-181, with a 3.09 ERA, 2,696 strikeouts, 52 shutouts, 156 complete games, 3,816⅓ innings pitched, and a WHIP of 1.123.

Following his playing days, Sutton began a lengthy career in broadcasting that has seen him spent nearly three decades serving as a commentator for three different teams, including the Dodgers (1989), Braves (1989-2006, 2009-present), and Washington Nationals (2007-2008). During that time, Sutton received MLB's highest honor, being voted into the Baseball Hall of Fame by the members of the BBWAA in 1998—his fifth year on the ballot. While making his induction speech, Sutton expressed his gratitude to those who influenced him the most during the early stages of his major-league career, stating:

*"I wish Walter Alston could be here. When I joined the Dodgers in '66, I joined the man as a manager who was an extension of my relationship with my dad, in more ways than one. He once told me I was the second most stubborn person he'd ever met. I asked him who was first, and he said, 'I am. And it might do you well to remember that.' But he took a chance on a twenty-year-old when a couple of fairly decent and well-known pitchers were holding out.*

*And my first week in the big leagues, I was named a start-ing pitcher with Koufax, Drysdale, and Osteen because Walter Alston was willing to take a chance. And, speaking of Drysdale, I'd give anything if he could be here. No kid could ever ask for more than to come on to a ball club—it could be pretty scary—that had just won a World Cham-pionship where your three starting pitchers are Drysdale, Koufax, and Osteen. But those are three starting pitchers that taught me a lot about a lot of things. I didn't know you had to tip in the clubhouse. I think I'd only been west of the Mississippi once. And tipping in restaurants, and what to wear, and how to pitch hitters, all three of those guys played a very, very active part.*

*To Claude, thank you. To Sandy, thank you. And I hope I thank 'Big D.'"*

## Dodger Career Highlights:

**Best Season:** Although Sutton topped 20 victories for the only time in his career in 1976, he pitched his best ball for the Dodgers four years ear-lier, concluding the 1972 campaign with a record of 19-9, 207 strikeouts, and career-best marks in ERA (2.08), complete games (18), shutouts (9), and WHIP (0.913), leading all NL hurlers in the last two categories.

**Memorable Moments/Greatest Performances:** Sutton put together a pair of extremely impressive consecutive scoreless innings streaks over the course of his exceptional 1972 season, tossing 30⅔ straight shutout innings from April 25 to May 12, before keeping the opposition off the scoreboard for 36 consecutive frames from September 10 to October 3.

Sutton turned in his finest performance as a rookie on August 16, 1966, when he allowed just 2 hits, walked 1 batter, and struck out 8 during a 2-0 complete-game win over the Cincinnati Reds.

Sutton threw another gem against Cincinnati the following year, al-lowing just a harmless pair of singles and striking out 11, in defeating the Reds by a score of 9-0 on June 27, 1967.

Sutton turned in his most dominant performance of the 1968 campaign on September 4, when he surrendered only 3 hits, walked 4 batters, and recorded a career-high 12 strikeouts during a 3-0 shutout of the Phillies.

Sutton, who threw five one-hitters over the course of his career, ac-complished the feat for the first time on May 1, 1969, when he allowed just

2 walks and a one-out double by Jim Davenport in the bottom of the eighth inning, in defeating the Giants by a score of 5-0.

Sutton equaled his career-high in strikeouts on July 17, 1970, when he struck out 12 batters, walked 3, and surrendered 5 hits during a 10-inning, 1-0 complete-game win over the Mets.

Sutton tossed the second one-hitter of his career on June 19, 1971, allowing just 4 walks and a sixth-inning double to future Dodgers teammate Jim Wynn during a 4-0 win over the Astros.

Sutton got off to a tremendous start in 1972, winning his first eight decisions before suffering his first defeat. Performing brilliantly in his second start of the season, Sutton tossed a two-hit shutout against the Atlanta Braves on April 19, defeating them by a score of 4-0 in the process. Although Sutton failed to get a decision in the Dodgers' 13-inning, 1-0 loss to Montreal on May 7, he turned in arguably his finest performance of the year, allowing just 1 hit and 4 bases on balls in 10 innings of work.

Sutton continued to excel later in the year, surrendering just 2 hits and 2 walks, while striking out 9, in defeating the Astros by a score of 5-0 on June 28, 1972.

Sutton hurled another gem on September 22, 1972, allowing 3 hits, 4 walks and striking out 11 over 11 innings, in earning a 1-0 decision over the Giants.

Sutton turned in his most dominant performance of the 1973 season on June 26, when he yielded just 2 hits and 1 walk during a 7-0 shutout of the San Diego Padres.

Sutton continued to torment the Padres the following year, defeating them by a score of 6-0 on May 9, 1974, surrendering only 2 walks and a second-inning single to John Grub during the contest.

Sutton threw another one-hitter on April 15, 1975, allowing just 1 walk and a seventh-inning home run to Johnny Bench, in defeating the eventual world champion Cincinnati Reds by a score of 3-1.

Sutton turned in a similarly dominant effort against Pittsburgh on August 21, 1976, working seven perfect innings before finally surrendering 2 hits and 1 run to the hard-hitting Pirates in the top of the eighth inning of a 5-1 Dodger victory.

Sutton hurled his fifth and final one-hitter on August 18, 1977, when he yielded just 4 walks and a two-out eighth inning single to catcher Marc Hill during a 7-0 win over the rival Giants.

Sutton performed brilliantly against Pittsburgh in the 1974 NLCS, leading the Dodgers to a four-game victory over the Pirates by winning both his starts, including tossing a 3-0 shutout in Game One. He finished the Series with a record of 2-0 and an ERA of 0.53, surrendering just 7 hits in 17 total innings of work, while striking out 13 and allowing only 2 bases on balls. Although the Dodgers subsequently lost the World Series to Oakland in five games, Sutton gave them their only victory in Game Two, scattering 5 hits over 8 innings, before turning the ball over to Mike Marshall for the save that gave the Dodgers a 3-2 win.

## Notable Achievements:

- Won more than 20 games once (21 in 1976).
- Surpassed 15 victories eight other times, winning 19 games twice.
- Posted double-digit wins 15 straight times (1966-80).
- Posted winning percentage in excess of .700 once (.722 in 1980).
- Compiled ERA below 3.00 seven times, posting mark under 2.50 on three occasions.
- Posted WHIP under 1.000 three times.
- Struck out more than 200 batters five times.
- Threw more than 200 innings 15 times, surpassing 250 innings pitched eight times.
- Led NL pitchers in: ERA once, WHIP three times, shutouts once, strikeouts-to-walks ratio twice, and starts once.
- Holds Dodgers career records for most: wins (233), strikeouts (2,696), shutouts (52), games started (533), innings pitched (3,816⅓), and pitching appearances (550).
- Ranks among Dodgers career leaders in complete games (eighth) and WHIP (seventh).
- 1966 *Sporting News* NL Rookie Pitcher of the Year.
- 1977 All-Star Game MVP.
- 1976 Lou Gehrig Memorial Award winner.
- April 1972 NL Player of the Month.
- Three-time NL Pitcher of the Month.

- Finished in top five in NL Cy Young voting five times.
- 1976 *Sporting News* All-Star selection.
- Four-time NL All-Star (1972, 1973, 1975 & 1977).
- Five-time NL champion (1966, 1974, 1977, 1978 & 1988).
- 1988 world champion.
- Elected to Baseball Hall of Fame by members of BBWAA in 1998.

# 10

# GIL HODGES

Perhaps the most beloved player on a Brooklyn Dodgers team that dominated the National League from 1949 to 1956, Gil Hodges made key contributions to six pennant-winning teams and two world championship clubs during his 15 years with the Dodgers. A power-hitting first baseman who also excelled in the field, Hodges gained general recognition as the senior circuit's finest all-around player at his position for much of the 1950's, earning eight All-Star selections, three top-10 finishes in the league MVP voting, and three Gold Gloves. Ranking second only to teammate Duke Snider among all major-league players in both home runs and RBIs during the decade, Hodges reached the seats 310 times and knocked in 1,001 runs over the course of those 10 seasons, surpassing 30 homers six times and 100 RBIs on seven separate occasions. The powerful first baseman also provided leadership to his Dodger teammates, both on and off the field, with his calm demeanor, quiet strength, and strong sense of decency.

Born in Princeton, Indiana on April 4, 1924, Gilbert Raymond Hodges spent most of his youth in nearby Petersburg after moving there with his family at the age of seven. A four-sport star at Petersburg High School, where he earned a combined seven varsity letters in baseball, football, basketball, and track, Hodges declined a 1941 contract offer he received from the Detroit Tigers shortly after he graduated, choosing instead to attend Saint Joseph's College in the hope that he might eventually become a collegiate coach. However, after starring on the diamond for two years at Saint Joseph's, Hodges elected to sign with the Brooklyn Dodgers in 1943. He made his major-league debut with them in early October, appearing in just one game at third base, before entering the Marine Corps to take part in the war effort. Hodges spent the next 2½ years in the military, serving as an anti-aircraft gunner in the battles of Tinian and Okinawa, and receiving a Bronze Star and a commendation for courage under fire for his actions.

After leaving the service, Hodges spent much of the next two seasons in the minor leagues, before returning to Brooklyn during the latter stages of the 1947 campaign. Appearing in 24 games at catcher for the pennant-winning Dodgers, Hodges homered once, drove in 7 runs, and batted .156. Shifted to first base the following year to make room behind the plate for Roy Campanella, Hodges ended up having a decent rookie season, hitting 11 homers, knocking in 70 runs, and batting .249.

Hodges began to establish himself as one of the National League's most potent batsmen in 1949, helping the Dodgers win the pennant by hitting 23 home runs, driving in 115 runs, scoring 94 times, and batting .285. He also displayed his fielding prowess by leading all NL first base-men in putouts, double plays, and fielding average, while ranking second in assists. Hodges' outstanding all-around play earned him an 11th-place finish in the league MVP voting and All-Star honors for the first of seven straight times.

Although Brooklyn failed to return to the World Series in either 1950 or 1951, finishing an extremely close second in the NL standings both years, Hodges continued his ascension into stardom, ranking among the league leaders in home runs and RBIs both seasons. After hitting 32 hom-ers, driving in 113 runs, scoring 98 times, and batting .283 in 1950, Hodg-es homered 40 times, knocked in 103 runs, scored 118 times, and batted .268 the following year. He had another productive season for the pennant-winning Dodgers in 1952, hitting 32 homers, driving in 102 runs, scoring 87 times, and finishing second in the league with a career-high 107 bases on balls. However, Hodges performed terribly during the Dodgers' seven-game loss to the Yankees in the 1952 World Series, failing to get a hit in 21 official trips to the plate. Nevertheless, his struggles at the plate proved to be a blessing in disguise in some ways, since they helped him realize just how much he meant to the fans of Brooklyn.

The fans that frequented Ebbets Field tended to be a rowdy bunch that didn't hesitate in the least to express their feelings—good or bad—to their beloved Dodgers. Sooner or later, every member of the team incurred their wrath; that is, everyone except Hodges. Immersed in the worst hitting slump of his young career, Hodges drew nothing but words of encourage-ment from the Dodger faithful, who sent him thousands of letters as a way

Courtesy of RMYauctions.com

Gil Hodges ranked second only to teammate Duke Snider
among all Major League players during the 1950's
in both home runs and RBIs

of reaffirming their affection for him. Even the Church showed its support for him when his slump continued into the following spring, with Father Herbert Redmond of the St. Francis Roman Catholic Church in Brooklyn telling his flock one day: "It's far too hot for a homily. Keep the Commandments and say a prayer for Gil Hodges." The Dodger first baseman began hitting again shortly thereafter, with his performance in postseason play never again proving to be so dismal.

Hodges' Dodger teammates also held him in extremely high esteem, expressing to a man their respect and admiration for him. Pitcher Carl Erskine said, "Gil was a quiet and private person, but everybody looked up to him because of his dedication and his strength and character. He never showed emotion. Never saw it on the outside. If a pitcher was in a tough situation, Gil would come over and say a few words, and it really made you calm down and concentrate. He had a real knack for that."

Fellow Dodger hurler Clem Labine suggested, "Not getting booed at Ebbets Field was an amazing thing. Those fans knew their baseball, and Gil was the only player I can remember whom the fans never, I mean never booed."

Hall of Fame catcher Roy Campanella said of Hodges, "He was never booed anyplace. They knew what kind of man he was, so they never booed him. He was a leader of our team. Everybody respected Gil and looked up to him. Gil, of course, went on to become the best first baseman in the league. In fact, he was the best first baseman I ever saw. He was just a great human being whom everybody respected. Everybody liked Gil Hodges."

Dodger captain Pee Wee Reese paid Hodges the ultimate compliment, stating, "If you had a son, it would be a great thing to have him grow up to be just like Gil Hodges."

After starting off the 1953 campaign slowly, Hodges ended up having one of his finest seasons, helping the Dodgers capture the NL pennant by hitting 31 homers, knocking in 122 runs, scoring 101 times, and batting .302. He subsequently redeemed himself for his poor performance in the previous year's World Series, compiling a batting average of .364 during the Dodger's six-game loss to the Yankees in the fall classic.

Although the Dodgers failed to represent the senior circuit in the 1954 World Series, Hodges had another big year, finishing second in the league with 42 homers and 130 RBIs, while also scoring 106 runs and batting .304. Appearing in all 154 games for the Dodgers, Hodges also led all NL first basemen in both putouts and assists, earning a 10th-place finish in the league MVP voting in the process.

Hodges again posted outstanding numbers for the Dodgers in 1955, concluding the campaign with 27 homers, 102 RBIs, 75 runs scored, and a .289 batting average. He then helped them capture their first world championship by homering once, driving in 5 runs, and batting .292 during their seven-game victory over the Yankees in the World Series.

The Dodgers won their last pennant in Brooklyn the following year, with Hodges hitting 32 homers and knocking in 87 runs, before homering once, knocking in 8 runs, and batting .304 during the team's seven-game loss to the Yankees in the 1956 World Series. The thirty-three-year-old first baseman had his last big year in 1957, hitting 27 homers, driving in 98 runs, scoring 94 times, and batting .299, en route to earning his final All-Star selection and a seventh-place finish in the league MVP voting. He also won the first of his three consecutive Gold Glove Awards, claiming the honor in the first year MLB acknowledged defensive excellence in that manner.

Experiencing a decrease in offensive production after the Dodgers moved to Los Angeles in 1958, the aging Hodges hit 22 homers, knocked in 64 runs, and batted .259 in his first year on the West Coast, before mounting something of a comeback the following season, when, despite appearing in only 124 games, he hit 25 home runs, drove in 80 runs, and batted .276 for the eventual world champions.

After totaling only 16 home runs and 61 RBIs over the course of the next two seasons in a part-time role, Hodges found himself left unprotected by the Dodgers in the 1962 expansion draft. Subsequently claimed by the New York Mets, Hodges returned to the city of his greatest triumphs, spending his final two seasons serving as a backup on one of the worst teams in baseball history. He announced his retirement shortly after the Mets traded him to the Washington Senators on May 23, 1963. Hodges ended his career with 370 home runs, 1,274 RBIs, 1,105 runs scored, 1,921 hits, 295 doubles, 48 triples, a .273 batting average, a .359 on-base percentage, and a .487 slugging percentage, compiling virtually all those numbers while playing for the Dodgers.

Beginning a new career in managing immediately after he left New York, Hodges piloted the lowly Senators through the completion of the 1967 campaign, helping them improve their record each year. However after five seasons in Washington, Hodges returned to New York in 1968 to manage the equally woeful Mets, who he amazingly led to the world championship the following year, earning in the process NL Manager of the Year honors.

Unfortunately, Hodges did not live far beyond that 1969 season. After leading the Mets to identical 83-79 third-place finishes in 1970 and 1971, he died suddenly of a heart attack on April 2, 1972, after playing golf earlier in the day with other members of New York's coaching staff in West Palm Beach, Florida. Mets' coach Joe Pignatano later recalled Hodges falling backwards and hitting his head on the sidewalk with a "sickening knock," bleeding profusely and turning blue. Pignatano said, "I put my hand under Gil's head, but, before you knew it, the blood stopped. I knew he was dead. He died in my arms." A lifelong chain smoker, Hodges passed away just two days shy of his forty-eighth birthday.

Upon learning of Hodges' passing, several of his former Dodger teammates expressed their reverence for him, with Duke Snider saying, "Gil was a great player, but an even greater man." Johnny Podres stated, "I'm sick. I've never known a finer man." Don Drysdale later wrote in his autobiography that Hodges' death "absolutely shattered me. I just flew apart. I didn't leave my apartment in Texas for three days. I didn't want to see anybody. I couldn't get myself to go to the funeral. It was like I'd lost a part of my family."

Numerous campaigns have since been waged to get Hodges elected to the Baseball Hall of Fame. His supporters point to his 370 career home runs, 1,274 runs batted in, eight All-Star selections, and sterling defensive record. In fact, the most overlooked aspect of Hodges' all-around game may well have been his fielding ability. Former teammate Carl Erskine called Hodges "…the best at first I ever saw; great footing and range; good hands; made difficult plays look easy."

Longtime Dodger right-fielder Carl Furillo stated, "Gil made everything look easy at first base. He was so smooth that even the hard plays looked easy when Gil made them. In all my years in baseball, I never saw a better first baseman than Gil."

Duke Snider said, "We used to marvel at the way Gil could play defense. Any throw that went over to first base you knew Gil was going to come up with. He was so steady that if he didn't come up with a throw it made you wonder if he wasn't feeling well that day."

Meanwhile, former New York Mets catcher Jerry Grote preferred to focus on his onetime manager's unique personal qualities that he believed earned him a place in Cooperstown:

*"I wasn't set as a ballplayer or a person until Gil Hodges came along. He settled me down and encouraged me to think. Gil stressed fundamentals...basic fundamentals. He always wanted you thinking out there. I don't think any of us realized at the time the kind of effect Gil was having on us as men. But as you get older you realize things, and I know he made me a better individual in a lot of ways. He had an impact on everybody he touched. He got a lot of respect, and he didn't have to work for it because everybody knew what kind of man he was. He was a great baseball man, and a great human being."*

## Dodger Career Highlights:

**Best Season:** Hodges had an outstanding year for the Dodgers in 1953, concluding the campaign with 31 homers, 122 RBIs, 101 runs scored, a .302 batting average, a .393 on-base percentage, and a .550 slugging percentage. However, he performed slightly better the following season, earning a 10th-place finish in the NL MVP balloting by scoring 106 runs and posting career-high marks in home runs (42), RBIs (130), batting average (.304), hits (176), slugging percentage (.579), and OPS (.952). Hodges also led all NL first basemen with 1,381 putouts and 132 assists in 1954, establishing career-best marks in each of those categories as well.

**Memorable Moments/Greatest Performances:** Hodges had a big day at the plate on June 12, 1949, helping the Dodgers record a lopsided 20-7 victory over Cincinnati by going 3-for-4, with a three-run homer, a grand slam, 8 RBIs, and 3 runs scored.

Hodges had another huge game some two weeks later, on June 25, 1949, when he hit for the cycle during a 17-10 win over the Pittsburgh Pirates. He finished the day 5-for-6, with a pair of homers, 4 RBIs, and 4 runs scored.

Hodges keyed a 14-3 victory over Pittsburgh on September 19, 1950 by hitting 2 homers and knocking in 6 runs.

Hodges had a similarly productive afternoon against Pittsburgh's pitching staff on May 22, 1951, when he homered twice, drove in 6 runs, and scored 3 times during a 17-8 win over the Pirates.

A little over three months later, on August 29, 1951, Hodges led the Dodgers to a 13-1 mauling of Cincinnati by going 3-for-5, with a pair of homers, a double, 7 RBIs, and 3 runs scored.

Hodges turned in a pair of outstanding performances against Chicago exactly one week apart in late July 1953, going 4-for-5, with a homer, triple, 4 RBIs, and 3 runs scored during a 15-4 rout of the Cubs on July 21, before having a perfect 4-for-4 day at the plate, with a homer, double, 3 RBIs, and 3 runs scored, in leading the Dodgers to a 13-2 massacre of the Cubs on July 28.

On August 3, 1955, Hodges helped pace the Dodgers to a 9-6 win over the Milwaukee Braves by homering twice and knocking in 6 runs.

Yet, Hodges had the greatest day of his career on August 31, 1950, when he hit 4 home runs, singled, knocked in 9 runs, and scored 5 times, in leading the Dodgers to a lopsided 19-3 victory over the Braves. The slugging first baseman's four round-trippers, which came against four different pitchers, enabled him to join Lou Gehrig as the only twentieth-century players at that time to homer 4 times in a game without the bencfit of extra innings.

After struggling so terribly at the plate in the 1952 World Series, Hodges performed much better in his remaining postseason appearances, coming up particularly big in Game Seven of the 1955 fall classic, when he drove home both runs in the Dodgers' 2-0 win over the Yankees that gave them their first world championship. After knocking in the game's first run with a two-out single in the fourth inning, Hodges gave the Dodgers an insurance run with a sacrifice fly in the sixth.

Hodges also proved to be a key figure in the Dodgers' 1959 World Series triumph over the Chicago White Sox, batting .391 and giving Los Angeles a 5-4 victory in Game Four by hitting a solo homer in the bottom of the eighth inning.

## Notable Achievements:
- Hit more than 30 home runs six times, topping 40 homers twice.
- Knocked in more than 100 runs seven times, topping 120 RBIs twice.
- Scored more than 100 runs three times.
- Batted over .300 twice.

- Walked more than 100 times once (107 in 1952).
- Posted slugging percentage in excess of .500 nine times.
- Led NL in sacrifice flies twice.
- Finished second in NL in: home runs twice, RBIs once, and walks once.
- Led NL first basemen in: putouts three times, assists three times, fielding percentage three times, and double plays turned four times.
- Ranks among Dodgers career leaders in: home runs (second), RBIs (second), runs scored (fifth), hits (ninth), extra-base hits (third), doubles (10th), total bases (third), bases on balls (third), games played (fourth), plate appearances (sixth), and at-bats (sixth).
- Ranked second among MLB players during 1950s in home runs (310) and RBIs (1,001).
- Hit for cycle vs. Pittsburgh Pirates on June 25, 1949.
- Hit 4 home runs in one game vs. Boston Braves on August 31, 1950.
- Three-time Gold Glove winner (1957, 1958 & 1959).
- 1959 Lou Gehrig Memorial Award winner.
- Eight-time NL All-Star (1949, 1950, 1951, 1952, 1953, 1954, 1955 & 1957).
- Seven-time NL champion (1947, 1949, 1952, 1953, 1955, 1956 & 1959).
- Two-time world champion (1955 & 1959).

# 11

# PEE WEE REESE

The unquestioned leader of the legendary "Boys of Summer" team that dominated the National League for nearly a decade, Pee Wee Reese spent his entire sixteen-year major-league career with the Dodgers, establishing himself during that time as one of the finest shortstops in baseball. An outstanding fielder, solid hitter, and extremely intelligent player, Reese earned 10 All-Star selections and 8 top-10 finishes in the league MVP voting during his time in Brooklyn, in helping the Dodgers win seven National League pennants and one world championship. Yet, it is for his sense of justice and fair play that Reese is perhaps best remembered, with his willingness to accept Jackie Robinson as his teammate helping to pave the way for other players of African American descent to enter the Major Leagues.

Born in Ekron, Kentucky on July 23, 1918, Harold Henry Reese grew up some fifty miles northeast in the town of Louisville, where he acquired the nickname "Pee Wee" at the age of fourteen after he won a national marbles tournament, a "pee wee" being a kind of marble. After graduating from DuPont Manual High School, where he spent just one season playing baseball due to the fact that he weighed only 120 pounds as a senior, Reese took a job as a cable splicer for the Louisville phone company. At the same time, though, he remained active on the diamond, playing amateur ball in a local church league and performing so well for the New Covenant Presbyterian Church team that the Louisville Colonels of the minor league American Association signed him to a contract following the conclusion of the 1937 campaign.

"The Little Colonel," as he came to be known while playing for Louisville, continued to excel at the minor-league level, making an extremely favorable impression on all those who saw him perform, including Dodg-

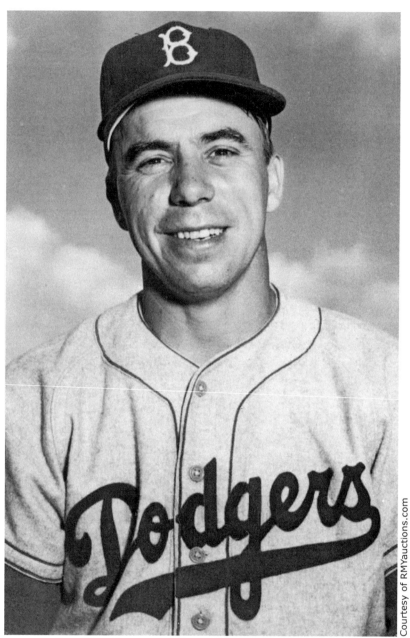

Pee Wee Reese spent most of his time with the
Dodgers serving as team captain

ers general manager Larry MacPhail, who called him "the most instinctive base-runner I've ever seen." Brooklyn scout Ted McGrew added, "What amazes me is how much he's learned in so short a time." Meanwhile, Colonels' manager and former major-league shortstop Donie Bush told *The Sporting News* that he "thinks Reese is the best-fielding shortstop he's seen in his thirty-one years in the game."

After the Boston Red Sox acquired Reese's rights in 1939, the Kentucky native found his path to the Major Leagues blocked by Boston player-manager Joe Cronin, who showed little interest in surrendering his starting shortstop duties to the youngster. As a result, the Dodgers swooped in, obtaining Reese from the Red Sox for three players and the sum of $35,000. Upon learning of the deal, *The Sporting News* wrote, "Bill Meyer, manager of the Kansas City Blues, and Babe Ganzel, St. Paul pilot, when informed of Reese's sale…called him the best infield prospect in the league." The paper also described Reese as "probably the most popular player ever to wear a Louisville uniform."

Unlike Boston, the Dodgers wasted little time in summoning Reese to the big leagues, with the twenty-one-year-old shortstop earning the team's starting shortstop job in spring training of 1940. However, after performing well during the season's first half, Reese had to sit out virtually all of the final three months of the campaign after breaking a bone in the heel of his foot, leaving him with rookie totals of 5 home runs, 28 RBIs, 58 runs scored, and 15 stolen bases, along with a batting average of .272. Upon returning to the Dodgers the following year, Reese struggled both at the bat and in the field, hitting 2 homers, driving in 46 runs, scoring 76 times, batting just .229, and committing a league-leading 47 errors at shortstop, although he also managed to finish first among players at his position with 346 putouts. He rebounded somewhat in 1942, though, earning All-Star honors for the first time by knocking in 53 runs, scoring 87 times, batting .255, placing among the league leaders with 15 stolen bases and 82 walks, and leading all NL shortstops in putouts, assists, and double plays turned.

Reese then enlisted in the Navy to serve his country during World War II, forcing him to miss the next three seasons. However, after rejoining the Dodgers in 1946, "The Little Colonel" showed little, if any, rust, finishing his first year back with 5 home runs, 60 RBIs, 79 runs scored, and a .284 batting average, en route to earning a sixth-place finish in the league MVP voting and the first of nine consecutive All-Star selections. He followed that up by hitting 12 homers, knocking in 73 runs, scoring 81 times, batting .284, and drawing a league-leading 104 bases on balls for the pennant-winning Dodgers in 1947, earning in the process an eighth-place finish in the MVP balloting. Reese, though, made his greatest impact on the Dodgers that year off the field, helping to ease the transition of new teammate Jackie Robinson into the Major Leagues.

Reese, who grew up in the segregated South during the 1920s and 1930s, initially had reservations about Robinson becoming his teammate, admitting years later that he had never shaken the hand of a black man until he greeted the rookie infielder on the first day of spring training. Nevertheless, Reese ended up taking the lead in welcoming Robinson to the Dodgers, eventually becoming his closest friend on the team. The first player to shake Robinson's hand when the latter arrived at the Dodgers' training base, Reese also helped squelch a petition several of his southern teammates began circulating calling for the rookie's dismissal, telling them flatly, "He [Robinson] can play, and he can help us win…that's what counts." And, when the rebellion continued, Reese befriended his beleaguered teammate, prompting the other Dodger players to fall in line. Still, Reese made his greatest statement on Robinson's behalf one April afternoon in 1947, when he displayed for all to see his support of his new teammate.

The incident took place in Cincinnati's Crosley Field, shortly after Reds fans and players began hurling racial epithets at the rookie first baseman. Roger Kahn described the events that subsequently transpired in his book, *The Boys of Summer*:

"Reese raised a hand. Then he walked from shortstop to first base and put an arm around the shoulders of Jackie Robinson. He stood there and looked into the dugout and into the stands, stared into the torrents of hate, a slim white southerner who wore number 1 and just happened to have an arm draped in friendship around a black man who wore number 42. Reese never said a word. The deed was beyond words."

Kahn then shared with readers Robinson's feelings about Reese's act, revealing that Jackie later told him, "After Pee Wee came over like that, I never felt alone on a baseball field."

Pitcher Rex Barney, who started the game for the Dodgers that day in Cincinnati, provided his own personal account of the episode in Peter Golenbock's 1984 book entitled *Bums*, recalling:

"I was warming up on the mound, and I could hear the Cincinnati players screaming at Jackie... and then they started to get on Pee Wee. They were yelling at him, 'How can you play with this nigger?' and all this stuff, and, while Jackie was standing by first base, Pee Wee went over to him and put his arm around him as if to say, 'This is my boy. This is the guy. We're gonna win with him.' Well, it drove the Cincinnati players right through the ceiling, and you could have heard the gasp from the crowd as he did it. That's one reason Pee Wee was such an instrumental person contributing to Jackie's success—Pee Wee more than anyone else, because Pee Wee was from the South.

Pee Wee understood things a little better... They became very close friends, and they understood each other."

Subsequently asked by reporters to explain his actions, Reese stated simply, "You can hate a man for many reasons; his color isn't one of them."

His leadership and strong sense of justice notwithstanding, Reese contributed to the Dodgers in many other ways as well. In addition to being a good hitter and one of the sport's top defensive shortstops, he excelled as a base-runner and did a superb job of working the count, annually finishing among the NL leaders in runs scored, stolen bases, and bases on balls.

Reese continued to perform well for the Dodgers over the course of the next nine seasons, leading them to five more pennants between 1948 and 1956. Averaging 100 runs scored during that period, Reese also stole more than 20 bases five times, leading the NL with 30 thefts in 1952. Reese had one of his finest seasons in 1949, when he hit a career-high 16 homers, knocked in 73 runs, batted .279, finished second in the league with 26 stolen bases and 116 walks, and topped the senior circuit with a career-high 132 runs scored, en route to earning a fifth-place finish in the league MVP voting. He had another big year in 1951, concluding his second season as team captain with a .286 batting average, 94 runs scored, and a career-best 84 RBIs. Two years later, Reese batted .271, scored 108 runs, and finished second in the league with 22 stolen bases. He followed that up by scoring 98 runs and batting a career-high .309 in 1954, before batting .282 and scoring 99 runs for Brooklyn's 1955 world championship team.

After Reese's offensive production fell off somewhat in 1956, he assumed a part-time role on the club the following year, surrendering his starting shortstop job to Charlie Neal, while splitting time at third base with Randy Jackson. Reese remained with the Dodgers one more year, traveling with them to Los Angeles in 1958, before announcing his retirement at season's end after batting just .224 in a backup role. Reese ended his career with 126 home runs, 885 RBIs, 1,338 runs scored, 2,170 hits, 330 doubles, 80 triples, 232 stolen bases, a batting average of .269, an on-base percentage of .366, and a slugging percentage of .377. In addition to his 10 All-Star selections and eight top-10 finishes in the league MVP balloting, Reese earned one *Sporting News* All-Star nomination, being voted onto the team in 1953.

Following his playing days, Reese spent one season on the Dodgers' coaching staff, before beginning a lengthy career as a baseball analyst for both NBC and CBS. He also spent several years serving as a representative for Louisville Slugger, the world's most respected maker of baseball bats. After Reese underwent surgery for prostate cancer during the 1980s, doctors diagnosed him as having lung cancer in 1997. He lived another two years, losing his battle with the dreaded disease on August 14, 1999, just three weeks after he celebrated his eighty-first birthday.

Upon learning of his former teammate's passing, pitcher Carl Erskine told *Jet* magazine, "Think of the guts that [refusing to sign a petition that threatened a boycott if Jackie Robinson joined the team] took. Pee Wee had to go home [to segregated Louisville, Kentucky] and answer to his friends. I told Jackie later that [Reese's gesture] helped my race more than his."

Former Dodger hurler Joe Black, who played with both Reese and Robinson in Brooklyn, spoke these words at Reese's funeral:

> *"When Pee Wee reached out to Jackie, all of us in the Negro League smiled and said it was the first time that a white guy had accepted us. When I finally got to Brooklyn, I went to Pee Wee and said, 'Black people love you. When you touched Jackie, you touched all of us.' With Pee Wee, it was number one on his uniform and number one in our hearts."*

## Career Highlights:

**Best Season:** Reese performed extremely well for the Dodgers in 1953, hitting 13 homers, driving in 61 runs, scoring 108 times, batting .271, and compiling a .374 on-base percentage. He had another big year in 1954, when he knocked in 69 runs, scored 98 times, and established career-high marks in doubles (35), batting average (.309), and OPS (.859). Nevertheless, Reese had his finest all-around season in 1949, when he earned his lone top-five finish in the NL MVP voting by driving in 73 runs, stealing 26 bases, batting .279, compiling an OPS of .806, and reaching career highs in home runs (16), walks (116), total bases (253), and runs scored (132), topping the senior circuit in the last category. Reese also led all league shortstops with 316 putouts and a career-best .977 fielding percentage.

**Memorable Moments/Greatest Performances:** Reese made his first big-league home run a memorable one, giving the Dodgers a 2-1 victory over Philadelphia on May 26, 1940 with his solo blast off future teammate Kirby Higbe in the top of the 10th inning.

Reese provided similar heroics a little over one month later, on July 3, 1940, when he capped a six-run top of the ninth inning by homering with the bases loaded, giving the Dodgers a 7-3 win over the Giants in the process.

Reese came up big in the clutch for the Dodgers again later in the year, on August 4, 1940, when, after bringing the Dodgers to within one run of the Cubs with a two-run single in the sixth inning, he tied the score at six runs apiece with a one-out solo homer in the bottom of the ninth inning. Dolph Camilli won the game for the Dodgers two innings later with a solo blast of his own.

Reese had a big day at the plate on April 19, 1941, leading the Dodgers to an 8-0 win over the Boston Braves by going 4-for-4, with a homer, double, 3 RBIs, and 3 runs scored.

During a lopsided 14-2 victory over the Pittsburgh Pirates on May 9, 1948, Reese went 3-for-5, with a homer, double, and career-high 6 runs batted in.

Reese continued to torment Pittsburgh's pitching staff later in the year, leading the Dodgers to an 8-5 win over the Pirates on September 14, 1948 by homering, doubling, and knocking in 5 runs.

Reese helped pace the Dodgers to a 15-6 victory over the Cardinals on May 21, 1949 by going 4-for-5, with a homer, double, 3 RBIs, and career-high 5 runs scored.

Reese hit 2 home runs in one game for one of four times in his career on July 2, 1949, reaching the seats twice, driving in 4 runs, and scoring 3 times during a 13-8 win over the Giants.

Reese had the only 5-for-5 day of his career on July 12, 1952, when he hit safely in all 5 trips to the plate and scored 3 times during a 12-2 rout of the Cubs in Chicago.

Although the Dodgers lost the 1952 World Series to the Yankees in seven games, Reese performed brilliantly, homering once, knocking in 4 runs, scoring 4 times, and batting .345.

Still, Reese made his greatest contribution to the Dodgers, baseball, and society as a whole on that April 1947 afternoon in Cincinnati, when he showed his support for Jackie Robinson by putting his arm around his new teammate. Dodger pitcher Ralph Branca later said that Reese's gesture communicated to the players in the opposing dugout, "Hey, he's my friend. It says Brooklyn on my uniform and Brooklyn on his, and I respect him." In discussing his feelings at the time, Robinson later revealed, "Pee Wee kind of sensed the sort of hopeless, dead feeling in me and came over and stood beside me for a while. He didn't say a word but he looked over at the chaps who were yelling at me … and just stared. He was standing by me, I could tell you that. I will never forget it." Years later, Reese explained his actions by telling Roger Kahn, "I was just trying to make the world a little better. That's what you're supposed to do with your life, isn't it?"

## Notable Achievements:

- Batted over .300 once (.309 in 1954).
- Scored more than 100 runs twice, surpassing 120 runs scored once (132 in 1949).
- Finished in double-digits in triples once (10 in 1946).
- Topped 30 doubles twice.
- Stole more than 20 bases five times, surpassing 30 steals once (30 in 1952).
- Walked more than 100 times twice.
- Compiled on-base percentage in excess of .400 twice.
- Led NL in: runs scored once, stolen bases once, walks once, and sacrifice hits once.
- Led NL shortstops in: putouts four times, assists once, fielding percentage once, and double plays turned twice.

- Holds Dodgers career records for most runs scored (1,338) and most bases on balls (1,210).
- Ranks among Dodgers career leaders in: RBIs (seventh), hits (second), doubles (fourth), triples (eighth), total bases (fifth), stolen bases ($10^{th}$), games played (third), plated appearances (second), and at-bats (second).
- 1956 Lou Gehrig Memorial Award winner.
- Finished in top 10 of NL MVP voting eight times, placing as high as fifth in 1949.
- 1953 *Sporting News* All-Star selection.
- 10-time NL All-Star (1942 & 1946-54).
- Seven-time NL champion (1941, 1947, 1949, 1952, 1953, 1955 & 1956).
- 1955 world champion.
- Elected to Baseball Hall of Fame by members of Veteran's Committee in 1984.

# 12

# STEVE GARVEY

A model of consistency during his time in Los Angeles, Steve Garvey established himself as one of the National League's most productive hitters while manning first base for the Dodgers from 1974 to 1982. Over the course of those nine seasons, Garvey surpassed 20 home runs and 100 RBIs five times each, while also batting in excess of .300 and amassing more than 200 hits on six separate occasions. Appearing in a National League record 1,207 consecutive games at one point, Garvey earned eight straight All-Star selections and five top-10 finishes in the NL MVP voting as a member of the Dodgers, capturing league MVP honors in 1974, when he led them to the pennant for the first of four times. An outstanding fielder as well, Garvey won four consecutive Gold Gloves for his excellent defensive work at first base. In all, the muscular first baseman earned All-Star honors and MVP consideration in eight of his nine full seasons in Los Angeles, making him one of the most successful and respected players in franchise history.

Born in Tampa, Florida on December 22, 1948, Steven Patrick Garvey spent much of his youth around major-league players, serving, at different times between 1956 and 1961, as bat boy for the Dodgers, Yankees, and Tigers during spring training. After graduating from local Chamberlain High School, Garvey played football and baseball at Michigan State University, starring as a defensive back on the gridiron and as an infielder on the diamond. Choosing to focus exclusively on baseball after the Dodgers selected him with the 13th overall pick of the 1968 amateur draft, Garvey spent most of the next three seasons in the minor leagues, although he made brief appearances at the major-league level in both 1969 and 1970, hitting one homer, driving in 6 runs, and compiling a composite batting average of .271, in 96 total at-bats.

Garvey began to receive more extensive playing time after the Dodgers summoned him to the big leagues in 1971, hitting 7 homers, knocking in 26 runs, and batting .227, in 81 games and 249 total plate appearances. The twenty-three-year-old infielder saw even more action the following year, when, appearing in 85 games at third base, he hit 9 homers, drove in 30 runs, and batted .269. Yet, Garvey's 28 errors at the hot corner convinced team management that it needed to find another position for him.

Moved across the diamond to first base in 1973, Garvey found a new home, with then-Dodgers manager Walter Alston noting, "He began making all the plays, especially digging out low throws." After establishing himself as the team's full-time starter at the position midway through the campaign, Garvey went on to hit 8 homers, knock in 50 runs, and bat .304, topping the .300-mark for the first of four straight times. During that season, he also became part of the most enduring infield in baseball history, joining second baseman Davey Lopes, third baseman Ron Cey, and shortstop Bill Russell on a unit that remained together for the next 8 ½ years.

Garvey really came into his own the following year, leading the Dodgers to the 1974 NL pennant by hitting 21 homers, driving in 111 runs, scoring 95 times, collecting 200 hits, and batting .312, en route to earning league MVP honors and the first of his eight straight All-Star selections. By being voted on to the senior circuit's starting squad as a write-in candidate, Garvey became one of only two players to be so honored. The 5'10", 192-pound first baseman earned the additional distinction of winning his first of four straight Gold Gloves for his excellent work around the bag.

Although the Dodgers failed to repeat as NL champions in either of the next two seasons, Garvey continued to post outstanding numbers, concluding the 1975 campaign with 18 homers, 95 RBIs, a .319 batting average, and 210 hits, before batting .317, hitting 13 homers, driving in 80 runs, and amassing 200 hits the following year. With Los Angeles subsequently capturing the NL flag for the first of two straight times in 1977, Garvey began an outstanding four-year run during which he compiled the following numbers:

1977: 33 HR, 115 RBIs, 91 Runs Scored, 192 Hits, .297 AVG, .335 OBP, .498 SLG PCT

1978: 21 HR, 113 RBIs, 89 Runs Scored, **202** Hits, .316 AVG, .353 OBP, .499 SLG PCT

1979: 28 HR, 110 RBIs, 92 Runs Scored, 204 Hits, .315 AVG, .351 OBP, .497 SLG PCT

Courtesy of Pristine Auction

One of the most consistent hitters of his era, Steve Garvey
surpassed 20 home runs and 100 RBIs five times each
as a member of the Dodgers`

1980: 26 HR, 106 RBIs, 78 Runs Scored, **200** Hits, .304 AVG, .341 OBP, .467 SLG PCT

In addition to leading the NL in hits in two of those years, Garvey finished second in the league in batting in 1978. He also ranked among the leaders in RBIs and total bases all four years, en route to earning three more top-10 finishes in the NL MVP voting, including a runner-up finish to Pittsburgh's Dave Parker in the 1978 balloting. Continuing his NL record-setting string of consecutive games played, Garvey did not miss a single contest over the course of those four seasons.

Aside from his skills on the playing field, Garvey's good looks, clean-cut image, and strong work ethic helped make him one of the most popular players of his time. Manager Tommy Lasorda praised his first baseman by saying, "He comes to the ballpark every day ready to play. He's ready to give you his best, every day. He doesn't make trouble; he doesn't give anyone a headache. He just does his job." Named a starter on the NL All-Star team virtually every year, Garvey gained general recognition as one of the game's top players. Yet, his detractors pointed to his inability to reach base via the walk, which becomes evident when one looks at his rather mediocre lifetime on-base percentage of .329. Furthermore, even though Garvey compiled an excellent fielding percentage over the course of his career, leading all players at his position in that category a total of five times, his critics found fault with his somewhat limited range and weak throwing arm, which generally caused him to make the "safe" play in the field, preventing him from ever placing at the top of the league rankings in assists.

Nevertheless, Garvey continued to be viewed as arguably the National League's premier first baseman during the strike-shortened 1981 campaign, earning his eighth straight All-Star nomination by hitting 10 homers, driving in 64 runs, and batting .283 for a Dodgers team that went on to capture the world championship. He spent one more year in Los Angeles, hitting 16 homers, knocking in 86 runs, and compiling a .282 batting average in 1982, before signing a five-year, $6.6 million free-agent deal with the San Diego Padres. Garvey left the Dodgers with career totals of 211 home runs, 992 RBIs, 852 runs scored, 1,968 hits, 333 doubles, and 35 triples, a .301 batting average, a .337 on-base percentage, and a .459 slugging percentage.

Garvey ended up spending his five remaining big-league seasons in San Diego, earning two more All-Star selections during that time. He had his two best years for the Padres in 1984 and 1985, helping them capture the National League pennant in the first of those campaigns by knocking in 86 runs and batting .284 during the regular season, before earning NLCS MVP honors for the second time in his career by leading San Diego to a five-game victory over Chicago by driving in 7 runs and batting .400, including hitting a two-run walk-off homer off Lee Smith in the bottom of the ninth inning of Game Four. Garvey followed that up by hitting 17 homers, knocking in 81 runs, and batting .281 in 1985. Choosing to announce his retirement during the 1987 campaign after batting just .211 in a part-time role through late May, Garvey ended his career with 272 home runs, 1,308 RBIs, 1,143 runs scored, 2,599 hits, 440 doubles, 43 triples, a .294 batting average, a .329 on-base percentage, and a .446 slugging percentage.

Garvey, who earlier aspired to enter the world of politics following the conclusion of his playing career, found his political ambitions crushed after the sordid details of his personal life began to surface once his playing days ended. Once known as "Mr. Clean" due to the wholesome image he desperately sought to cultivate during his time in Los Angeles, Garvey actually proved to be far less perfect in real life. In addition to engaging in numerous extramarital affairs during his marriage to his first wife, Cyndy, who eventually left him for Marvin Hamlisch after claiming that her husband "gave me away" to the famous composer after a private two-hour conversation, Garvey became involved in a series of overlapping relationships, fathering several children out of wedlock in the process. Having lost numerous business opportunities due to his sullied reputation, Garvey found himself burdened by the millions of dollars he owed in legal fees, as well as the exorbitant amounts he had to pay in child support. Forced to abandon his political aspirations, Garvey had to settle on a different career path to pay off his debts. After founding Garvey Communications, a television production company, he turned to hiring himself out as a motivational speaker, primarily for corporations. Garvey also spent fifteen years in the Dodgers' Community Affairs department, before losing his job in 2011 after publicly criticizing team owner Frank McCourt. Since that time, Garvey has served as a member of the board of the Baseball Assistance Team, a non-profit organization dedicated to helping former Major League, Minor League, and Negro League players through financial and medical hardships.

## Dodger Career Highlights:

**Best Season**: Garvey earned NL MVP honors in 1974, when he hit 21 homers, scored 95 runs, and placed among the league leaders with 111 RBIs, 200 hits, 301 total bases, and a .312 batting average. Yet, he compiled equally impressive numbers from 1977 to 1979. I ultimately elected to go with Garvey's 1978 campaign since it proved to be arguably his most consistent season. En route to earning a runner-up finish in the NL MVP voting by hitting 21 homers, driving in 113 runs, scoring 89 times, batting .316, collecting 9 triples, 36 doubles, and a league-leading 202 hits, and posting a career-high .852 OPS, Garvey put together two long hitting streaks, hitting safely in 21 straight games, from April 7 to May 2, and collecting at least one hit in 20 consecutive games, from September 9 to September 30. Furthermore, in addition to topping the senior circuit in hits, Garvey finished in the league's top five in four other offensive categories, placing second in batting average, third in RBIs and total bases (319), and fourth in triples.

**Memorable Moments/Greatest Performances**: Garvey had a big day at the plate on September 26, 1973, leading the Dodgers to a 9-8 victory over Atlanta by going 4-for-5, with a homer, 4 RBIs, and 3 runs scored.

Garvey helped the Dodgers improve their 1974 record to 9-3 by going 3-for-5, with a pair of homers, 4 RBIs, and 3 runs scored, during a 14-1 rout of Cincinnati on April 17.

Garvey had the first 5-for-5 day of his career later that season, hitting safely in all 5 trips to the plate and scoring 3 times during a 7-6 win over the Cubs on August 28, 1974.

Garvey led the Dodgers to a 14-0 mauling of the San Diego Padres on September 24, 1975 by going 4-for-6, with a pair of homers, a double, 3 runs scored, and a career-high 6 RBIs.

Garvey again homered twice during a 13-7 win over the Braves on June 29, 1977—a game in which he also went 4-for-4 with 3 runs scored.

Garvey had a huge game against the Cardinals some two months later, going 5-for-5, with a pair of homers, 3 doubles, 5 RBIs, and a career-high 5 runs scored, during an 11-0 Dodgers win over St. Louis on August 28, 1977.

An outstanding postseason performer over the course of his career, Garvey compiled a lifetime batting average of .338, with 11 homers and

31 RBIs, in 55 postseason contests. Particularly effective against Pittsburgh in the 1974 NLCS and Philadelphia in the 1978 NLCS, Garvey hit 2 homers, knocked in 5 runs, and batted .389, in leading the Dodgers to a four-game victory over the Pirates in his first foray into postseason play. Doing most of his damage in Game Four, Garvey collected 4 hits, homered twice, drove in 4 runs, and scored 4 times during the 12-1 series clincher. He proved to be even more of a factor against the Phillies in the 1978 NLCS, earning Series MVP honors by hitting 4 homers, driving in 7 runs, scoring 6 times, and batting .389 during the Dodgers' four-game win over Philadelphia. Garvey set the tone for the entire series by hitting a pair of homers, tripling, knocking in 4 runs, and scoring 3 times during the Dodgers' 9-5 win in Game One.

## Notable Achievements:

- Hit more than 20 home runs five times, topping 30 homers once (33 in 1977).
- Knocked in more than 100 runs five times.
- Batted over .300 seven times.
- Surpassed 200 hits six times.
- Topped 30 doubles six times.
- Led NL in hits twice and games played five times.
- Finished second in NL in: batting average once, hits once, and total bases twice.
- Led NL first basemen in putouts five times and fielding percentage four times.
- Ranks among Dodgers career leaders in: home runs (sixth), RBIs (fifth), hits (fifth), extra-base hits (sixth), doubles (third), total bases (sixth), games played (ninth), plate appearances (eighth), and at-bats (eighth).
- September, 1976 NL Player of the Month.
- Four-time Gold Glove winner (1974, 1975, 1976 & 1977).
- 1981 Roberto Clemente Award winner.
- Two-time All-Star Game MVP (1974 & 1978).
- 1974 NL MVP.
- Finished second in 1978 NL MVP voting.
- 1978 NLCS MVP.

- Four-time *Sporting News* All-Star selection (1974, 1975, 1977 & 1978).
- Eight-time NL All-Star (1974, 1975, 1976, 1977, 1978, 1979, 1980 & 1981).
- Four-time NL champion (1974, 1977, 1978 & 1981).
- 1981 world champion.

# 13

# MIKE PIAZZA

Widely considered to be the greatest hitting catcher in major-league history, Mike Piazza compiled some extremely impressive offensive numbers over the course of his Hall of Fame career. En route to hitting more home runs than any other receiver in the history of the game, Piazza surpassed 30 homers nine times, reaching the 40-homer plateau on two separate occasions. He also knocked in more than 100 runs six times, batted over .300 nine times, and compiled an OPS in excess of 1.000 three times, en route to earning 10 Silver Sluggers, 12 All-Star selections, 10 *Sporting News* All-Star nominations, and seven top-10 finishes in the NL MVP voting. Particularly outstanding during his time in Los Angeles, Piazza slugged more than 30 home runs in four of his five full seasons with the Dodgers, failing to do so only in the strike-shortened 1994 campaign. Piazza also topped the 100-RBI mark three times and batted well in excess of .300 in each of his five years in Los Angeles, earning in the process five consecutive top-10 finishes in the league MVP balloting, including runner-up honors two straight times. Although the Dodgers failed to capture the pennant during Piazza's relatively brief stint in L.A., they won a pair NL West titles and finished second in the division two other times, with the hard-hitting catcher proving to be the driving force behind their consistently strong showing.

Born in Norristown, Pennsylvania on September 4, 1968, Michael Joseph Piazza grew up in nearby Phoenixville rooting for the Philadelphia Phillies and his favorite player, Mike Schmidt. A huge baseball fan and outstanding player as a youngster, Piazza had the opportunity to serve as the Dodgers' batboy when they played in Philadelphia one summer due to his father's friendship with Los Angeles manager Tommy Lasorda. Although only thirteen years old at the time, Piazza gave an early indication of his hitting prowess one day by hitting a ball into the seats at Veterans Stadium during batting practice.

Piazza began to pursue his dream of playing in the Major Leagues while attending Phoenixville High School, where he batted .442 and hit 11 home runs as a senior. However, in spite of the excellent numbers he compiled, he received little interest from major universities following his graduation, forcing him to eventually enroll at Miami-Dade Community College. After batting .364 while playing first base in his sophomore year at Miami-Dade, Piazza entered the 1988 Major League Baseball Amateur Draft, where the Dodgers selected him as a favor to Tommy Lasorda in the $62^{nd}$ round, with the $1,390^{th}$ overall pick. With major-league scouts

considering him a long-shot to make the big leagues, Piazza heeded the advice of Lasorda, who suggested to him that he trade in his first base-man's glove for a catcher's mitt, believing that doing so would give him his best chance of eventually making it to the majors. Yet, while Piazza acquiesced to Lasorda's wishes, he began his professional career with a huge chip on his shoulder, recalling years later, "Nobody wanted me. Scouts told me to go to school, to forget baseball. Coaches said, 'You're never going to make it.' I appreciated their honesty because I think when someone tells you something you may not like you have to use that as fuel for motivation."

After attending a special training camp for catchers in the Dominican Republic following his first season in the minors, Piazza spent the next two years in Class A, before being promoted to double-A San Antonio in 1992. Excelling at that level, Piazza soon advanced to triple-A Albuquerque, where he batted .341 with 16 homers, making him a finalist for the *USA Today* and *The Sporting News* Minor League Player of the Year awards.

Called up by the Dodgers for the final month of the 1992 campaign, Piazza began his major-league career by hitting one home run, driving in 7 runs, and batting .232, in 21 games and 69 official at-bats. After being inserted into the starting lineup early the following year, Piazza ended up posting huge offensive numbers, finishing among the league leaders with 35 home runs, 112 RBIs, a .318 batting average, and a .561 slugging per-centage, with his 35 homers representing the highest total ever posted by a rookie receiver. Piazza's fabulous performance earned him NL Rookie of the Year honors, his first of 10 consecutive All-Star selections, and a ninth-place finish in the league MVP voting.

Courtesy of George A. Kitrinos

Mike Piazza hit more than 30 home runs in four
of his five full seasons with the Dodgers

Despite missing a significant amount of playing time in each of the next two seasons, Piazza continued to compile outstanding numbers, earning two more top-10 finishes in the MVP balloting. After hitting 24 homers, driving in 92 runs, and batting .319 during the strike-shortened 1994 campaign, Piazza battled through injuries to hit 32 homers, knock in 93 runs, and finish second in the league with a .346 batting average the following year, even though he started only 110 games behind the plate. Healthy again in 1996, Piazza posted the best numbers of his young career, hitting 36 homers, driving in 105 runs, scoring 87 times, collecting 184 hits, and finishing third in the league with a .336 batting average, en route to earning a runner-up finish to San Diego's Ken Caminiti in the NL MVP voting.

Possessing tremendous power to all fields, the right-handed hitting Piazza, who stood 6'3" and weighed close to 220 pounds, had the ability to drive the ball out of any part of the ballpark, hitting many of his home runs to center and right-center. He also did not strike out a great deal for a slugger, fanning as many as 90 times just once his entire career, and never topping the 100-mark in that category. Meanwhile, Piazza's ability to hit for both power and average made him one of the finest all-around batsmen in all of baseball.

Piazza followed up his exceptional 1996 season with an even stronger performance in 1997, placing in the league's top five in eight different offensive categories, including home runs (40), RBIs (124), batting average (.362), hits (201), and OPS (1.070). Piazza's tremendous year earned him his second consecutive runner-up finish in the league MVP balloting and his fifth straight Silver Slugger.

Poised to be become a free agent following the conclusion of the 1998 campaign, Piazza rejected a six-year, $80 million contract the Dodgers offered him during spring training, prompting teammate Brett Butler to comment, "Mike Piazza is the greatest hitter I have ever been around. But you can't build around Piazza because he's not a leader." However, sportswriter Tim Kurkjian had another take on the situation, later writing, "I also don't think Piazza was very happy being a Dodger by then. If he was, he would have been thrilled to take that deal. So I think he was ready to move on. I don't blame him for that. I don't blame the Dodgers, either. It was time for some new chemistry on that club."

Piazza ended up spending just a little over one month of the 1998 season with the Dodgers, before being included by them in a seven-player trade they completed with the Marlins on May 14 that also sent Todd Zeile to Florida in exchange for Gary Sheffield, Bobby Bonilla, Charles Johnson, Jim Eisenreich, and Manuel Barrios. Piazza didn't remain in Florida for long, though, since the Marlins dealt him to the New York Mets for three prospects just eight days later. Piazza left Los Angeles with career totals of 177 home runs, 563 RBIs, 443 runs scored, 896 hits, 115 doubles, and 3 triples, a batting average of .331, an on-base percentage of .394, and a slugging percentage of .572. He continues to rank among the franchise's all-time leaders in five different offensive categories, including home runs (ninth), batting average (fourth), and slugging percentage (second).

Starting anew in New York, Piazza began the second phase of his career—one that saw him hit 220 homers, drive in 655 runs, and compile a batting average of .296 over the course of the next eight seasons, en route to earning seven more All-Star selections, five more Silver Sluggers, and two more top-10 finishes in the league MVP balloting. Piazza had his two most productive seasons for the Mets in 1999 and 2000, hitting 40 homers, knocking in 124 runs, scoring 100 times, and batting .303 in the first of those campaigns, before earning a third-place finish in the MVP voting the following year by leading New York into the World Series with 38 homers, 113 RBIs, 90 runs scored, and a .324 batting average.

Piazza remained in New York through the end of 2005, when he signed with San Diego as a free agent. After one year with the Padres, Piazza joined the Oakland A's, with whom he spent his final season serving almost exclusively as a part-time designated hitter. Announcing his retirement following the conclusion of the 2007 campaign, Piazza ended his career with 427 home runs, 1,335 RBIs, 1,048 runs scored, 2,127 hits, 344 doubles, 8 triples, a .308 batting average, a .377 on-base percentage, and a .545 slugging percentage. His 396 homers as a catcher represent the highest total in MLB history.

Still, in spite of the exceptional offensive numbers Piazza posted over the course of his career, he constantly found himself being criticized for his defensive shortcomings, which included a weak throwing arm that enabled him to throw out only 23 percent of attempted base-stealers—well below the league average of 31 percent over the same period of time. Piazza, himself, wrote in his 2013 autobiography *Long Shot* that his critics implied he was an "imposter behind the plate" and claimed that he was "clinging to the catcher position" toward the end of his career in order to set offensive records at a position where elite hitting is rare.

However, pitchers who worked with Piazza viewed him far more favorably, claiming that his weak arm overshadowed everything else he did on defense. Hall of Fame pitcher Tom Glavine, who spent three years in New York with Piazza, told NJ Advanced Media in 2014, "He did a lot of things well behind the plate. Yeah, he wasn't the greatest thrower. That unfortunately translated into people thinking that some of his other game wasn't as good as it was. He called a good game. He received the ball fine. He blocked balls fine. But so often catchers are defined defensively on how well they throw, and there's much more that goes into just being a good defensive catcher than being able to throw."

Piazza also found the legitimacy of his offensive numbers being questioned by some due to unsubstantiated rumors about steroid use—rumors that kept him out of the Hall of Fame the first three times his name appeared on the ballot. Glavine, though, called Piazza a "first-ballot Hall of Famer, certainly the best-hitting catcher of our era, and arguably the best-hitting catcher of all time." The members of the BBWAA finally chose to take a similar stance in 2016, electing Piazza into Cooperstown by placing his name on 83 percent of the ballots they cast.

## Dodger Career Highlights:

**Best Season:** Although Piazza posted exceptional numbers in each of his five full seasons with the Dodgers, he clearly had his best year for them in 1997, when he established career-high marks in home runs (40), RBIs (124), runs scored (104), hits (201), total bases (355), batting average (.362), on-base percentage (.431), and slugging percentage (.638), en route to earning his second consecutive runner-up finish in the league MVP voting. The NL Player of the Month in both June and August, Piazza finished in the league's top five in eight different offensive categories, including placing second in total bases, slugging percentage, and OPS. Piazza's 40 homers represent the third-highest total ever compiled by a catcher, with only Javy Lopez (42 in 2003) and Todd Hundley (41 in 1996) hitting more for their respective teams. (Johnny Bench homered 45 times for the Reds in 1970, but he hit only 38 of those as a catcher). Meanwhile, Piazza's .362 batting average established a new league record for receivers, breaking the sixty-year-old mark of .354 previously set by Chicago's Gabby Hartnett in 1937, and tying the major-league record set by Bill

Dickey, who batted .362 for the Yankees in 1936. Minnesota's Joe Mauer later established a new record for catchers by batting .365 in 2009.

**Memorable Moments/Greatest Performances:** Piazza had one of his biggest days as a rookie on June 15, 1993, when he helped lead the Dodgers to a 12-4 win over Colorado by going 4-for-5, with a pair of homers, 5 RBIs, and 3 runs scored.

Piazza had another huge game later in the year, when he went 4-for-4, with a homer, 4 RBIs, and 3 runs scored, during a lopsided 13-4 victory over the Pittsburgh Pirates on August 24, 1993.

Piazza led the Dodgers to a 12-10 win over his future team, the New York Mets, on April 30, 1994 by going 4-for-5, with a homer, double, 4 RBIs, and 2 runs scored. Piazza delivered the game's big blow in the top of the eighth inning, when he tied the score at 10-all by hitting a two-out, three-run homer off New York reliever Josias Manzanillo.

Piazza came up big for the Dodgers in another 12-10 slugfest the following year, collecting 4 hits, including a pair of homers, driving in 6 runs, and scoring 3 times during a May 7, 1995 win over the Colorado Rockies at Coors Field.

Later that year, on August 27, 1995, Piazza proved to be a one-man wrecking crew, leading the Dodgers to a 9-1 victory over the Phillies by going 4-for-4, with 2 homers, 2 doubles, 3 runs scored, and a career-high 7 runs batted in.

Piazza nearly equaled that RBI total on August 27, 1997, when he paced the Dodgers to a 9-5 win over Pittsburgh by hitting a pair of homers, scoring 3 times, and driving in 6 runs.

Piazza displayed his tremendous power nearly one month later, when, during a 10-5 loss to Colorado on September 21, 1997, he became just the third player to hit a ball completely out of Dodger Stadium, driving a Frank Castillo offering over the left-field pavilion, some 478 feet from home plate.

Piazza defeated Arizona almost single-handedly on April 9, 1998, driving in 6 of the Dodgers' 7 runs with a pair of homers, in leading them to a 7-2 victory over the Diamondbacks.

Piazza, though, had the greatest day of his career on June 29, 1996, when he homered 3 times and knocked in 6 runs during a 13-10 win over the Rockies in Colorado.

## Notable Achievements:

- Surpassed 30 home runs four times, topping 40 homers once (40 in 1997).
- Knocked in more than 100 runs three times, topping 120 RBIs once (124 in 1997).
- Scored more than 100 runs once (104 in 1997).
- Batted over .300 five times, topping the .330-mark on three occasions.
- Topped 200 hits once (201 in 1997).
- Surpassed 30 doubles once (32 in 1997).
- Compiled on-base percentage in excess of .400 three times.
- Posted slugging percentage in excess of .500 five times, topping the .600-mark twice.
- Compiled OPS in excess of 1.000 twice.
- Finished in top three in NL in: batting average three times, slugging percentage twice, OPS twice, hits once, and total bases once.
- Ranks among Dodgers career leaders in: home runs (ninth), batting average (fourth), on-base percentage (eighth), slugging percentage (second), and OPS (third).
- Hit three home runs in one game vs. Colorado on June 29, 1996.
- Holds major-league record for most home runs hit by a catcher (396).
- 1993 NL Rookie of the Year.
- 1996 All-Star Game MVP.
- Four-time NL Player of the Month.
- Five-time Silver Slugger winner (1993, 1994, 1995, 1996 & 1997).
- Finished second in NL MVP voting twice (1996 & 1997).
- Five-time *Sporting News* All-Star selection (1993, 1994, 1995, 1996 & 1997).
- Five-time NL All-Star (1993, 1994, 1995, 1996 & 1997).
- Elected to Baseball Hall of Fame by members of BBWAA in 2016.

# 14

# MAURY WILLS

The offensive catalyst of Dodger teams that won three National League pennants and two world championships during the mid-1960s, Maury Wills helped revive the stolen base as part of baseball strategy with his thievery on the base paths. Topping the senior circuit in thefts six straight times, Wills established a new major-league record (since broken) in 1962 by swiping 104 bags, en route to earning NL MVP honors. Wills also stole 94 bases three years later, helping the Dodgers capture their second pennant in three seasons in the process. More than just a base-stealer, Wills batted over .290 for the Dodgers four times, scored more than 100 runs twice, and won two Gold Gloves for his outstanding defensive play at shortstop, earning five All-Star selections and four top-10 finishes in the league MVP balloting along the way.

Born in Washington, DC, on October 2, 1932, Maurice Morning Wills attended local Cardozo High School, where he starred on the mound, once tossing a one-hitter and striking out 17 batters in a game against Phelps. Moving to shortstop after signing with the Dodgers in 1951, Wills spent the next eight years in the minor leagues, before he received advice from a rather unlikely source that helped turn his career around.

Having advanced to the Dodgers' top farm team in Spokane, Washington by 1958, Wills found himself being managed by Bobby Bragan, who, several years earlier, had signed a letter saying that he refused to play alongside Jackie Robinson in Brooklyn. Later realizing the error of his ways, Bragan explained to Wills that his prejudiced-thinking resulted from his ignorance over racial matters, since he had been raised in segregated Birmingham, Alabama. A far more tolerant Bragan took Wills under his wing, suggesting to the right-handed hitting shortstop that he learn how to switch-hit, since he tended to flinch against curveballs thrown by right-handed pitchers.

Bragan's advice ended up making a huge impact on Wills, who not only improved significantly as a hitter, but also found it easier to bunt from the left side of the plate, noting, "To first, you can take it with you. To the left side, you can hit it hard enough to go past the pitcher and third base-man." Wills, who stood 5'11" tall and weighed only 170 pounds, tended to slap at the ball to begin with, estimating that infield hits accounted for an annual increase of 30-40 points in his batting average.

Having improved his offensive performance dramatically, the twenty-six-year-old Wills joined the Dodgers in early June of 1959, compiling a batting average of .260, scoring 27 runs, and stealing 7 bases in his 83 games with the club over the final four months of the campaign. Establishing himself as the Dodgers' starting shortstop and leadoff hitter the following year, Wills played well in his first full season, batting .295, scoring 75 runs, and topping the senior circuit with 50 stolen bases, although he also led all players at his position with 40 errors. Wills subsequently emerged as the National League's top shortstop in 1961, earning his first All-Star nomination, the first of his three *Sporting News* All-Star selections, and a ninth-place finish in the NL MVP voting by batting .282, scoring 105 runs, and stealing a league-leading 35 bases. He also played far more consistently in the field, winning his first of two straight Gold Gloves.

Wills took his game to the next level in 1962, earning NL MVP honors by batting .299, scoring 130 runs, amassing 208 hits and a league-leading 10 triples, and breaking Ty Cobb's forty-seven-year-old major-league record of 96 stolen bases by swiping 104 bags. Although Wills posted a less-impressive stat-line the following year, he helped the Dodgers capture the NL flag by batting a career-high .302, scoring 83 runs, and leading the league with 40 thefts. Wills remained the Dodgers' offensive catalyst in each of the next two seasons, batting .275, scoring 81 runs, and topping the senior circuit with 53 stolen bases in 1964, before earning a third-place finish in the 1965 NL MVP balloting by batting .286, scoring 92 times, and swiping 94 bases.

The Dodger teams of the early and mid-1960s, which, for the most part, lacked offensive firepower, predicated much of their success on their exceptional pitching, outstanding defense, and excellent team speed. And, at the core of whatever success they experienced on offense was Wills,

Courtesy of RMYauctions.com

Maury Wills captured NL MVP honors in 1962,
when he established a new major-league record
by stealing 104 bases

who proved to be easily their biggest threat on the base paths. In describing the Dodgers' offense, Sandy Koufax noted, "That used to be our attack. Maury would get on, get around somehow, come to the dugout, and say, 'There's your run, Sandy.' I had to make it stand up."

Although Wills lacked the blazing speed of teammate Willie Davis, he possessed tremendous acceleration and superb instincts, making him the superior base-stealer of the two. He also studied pitchers relentlessly, watching their pick-off moves even when not on base. And, even when Wills elected not to break for second, he served as a significant distraction to the opposing pitcher, allowing the men who followed him in the Dodgers batting order to get better pitches to hit.

The thirty-three-year-old Wills began to show signs of slowing down in 1966, finishing the season with a .273 batting average, only 60 runs scored, and just 38 stolen bases in 62 attempts. As a result, the Dodgers elected to trade him to the Pittsburgh Pirates for infielders Bob Bailey and Gene Michael following the conclusion of the campaign. Wills spent the next two years in Pittsburgh, batting .302, scoring 92 runs, and stealing 29 bases in 1967, before batting .278, scoring 76 times, and finishing second in the league with 52 steals the following season.

After being left unprotected in the 1969 expansion draft, Wills joined the Montreal Expos, with whom he spent the first two months of the season, before being traded back to the Dodgers in early June. Wills remained in Los Angeles the next 3 ½ years, posting batting averages of .297, .270, and .281 from 1969 to 1971, while stealing a total of 58 bases. However, after Wills batted just .129 while serving as a backup in 1972, the Dodgers released him, bringing his playing career to an end. Wills subsequently announced his retirement with career totals of 20 home runs, 458 RBIs, 1,067 runs scored, 2,134 hits, 177 doubles, 71 triples, and 586 stolen bases, a batting average of .281, an on-base percentage of .330, and a slugging percentage of .331. Over parts of 12 seasons in Los Angeles, he hit 17 homers, drove in 374 runs, scored 876 times, collected 1,732 hits, 150 doubles, 56 triples, and a franchise-record 490 stolen bases, batted .281, compiled a .331 on-base percentage, and posted a .332 slugging percentage.

Following his playing days, Wills managed in the Mexican Pacific League for four seasons and also served as a baseball analyst at NBC from 1973 to 1977. After leaving the broadcast booth, Wills briefly managed the Seattle Mariners, during which time he became noted for his many blunders, which included calling for a relief pitcher when he had no one warming up in the bullpen, holding up a game for 10 minutes while looking for a pinch-hitter, and leaving a spring-training game in the sixth inning to fly to California. Relieved of his duties in Seattle early in 1981, Wills subsequently lapsed into cocaine and alcohol addiction, developing, by his own estimation, a $1,000-a-day drug habit that lasted until 1989, when he finally got sober, with the help of former Dodger pitcher Don Newcombe. Wills later returned to the Dodger organization, where he has served as a representative of the Dodgers Legend Bureau since 2009. He also does radio color commentary for the Fargo-Moorhead RedHawks, a member of the American Association of Independent Professional Baseball Teams situated in Fargo, North Dakota.

Although Wills' name never appeared on more than 41 percent of the ballots cast by the members of the BBWAA for election into the Baseball Hall of Fame during his period of eligibility, Doug Krikorian of the *Long Beach Press-Telegram* is one who believes that the former shortstop is worthy of enshrinement, once writing:

"I look at Maury Wills, and I get the feeling the old shortstop smiles through a wounded heart because he has become the Forgotten Man of his sport, shunted into the shadows in recent years despite his heroic achievements across 14 blazing seasons he spent in the Major Leagues. No one has vocally stood up and railed about the injustice of Wills not having a plaque in Cooperstown. All Wills did was bat .281, collect 2,134 hits, steal 586 bases, play on four NL pennant-winning Dodger teams, and alter forever the contours of his sport."

## Dodger Career Highlights:

**Best Season:** Wills unquestionably had the greatest season of his career in 1962, when he batted .299 and established career-high marks in home runs (6), RBIs (48), runs scored (130), hits (208), triples (10), and stolen bases (104), finishing either first or second in the National League in each of the last four categories. Wills, whose 104 steals in 117 attempts established a new major-league record, swiped more bags by himself than every other team in the majors that year. He also appeared in all 165 regular-season games the Dodgers played (162 plus 3 regular-season playoff games), giving him a single-season MLB record that still stands.

**Memorable Moments/Greatest Performances:** Wills helped the Dodgers defeat the Braves by a score of 8-7 on September 15, 1959 by going 5-for-5, with a triple, an RBI, and 3 runs scored.

During an 11-4 victory over the Chicago Cubs on August 6, 1961, Wills went 3-for-4, with a homer and a career-high 4 runs scored.

Wills turned in a number of exceptional performances during his MVP campaign of 1962, with the first of those coming on May 25, when he helped lead the Dodgers to a 17-8 mauling of the Mets by going 4-for-5, with 3 runs scored and 3 stolen bases.

Wills continued his assault against Mets pitching five days later, on May 30, 1962, when he hit 2 home runs in one game for the only time in his career during a 13-6 victory over New York. He finished the contest 4-for-6, with 2 RBIs and 3 runs scored.

Wills led the Dodgers to a doubleheader sweep of Pittsburgh on June 5, 1962 by going a combined 7-for-10, with a pair of doubles, 4 runs scored, and a stolen base.

Wills sparked an 8-1 victory over the Chicago Cubs on September 10, 1962 by going 4-for-5, with 3 runs scored and 3 stolen bases.

Wills had a big day against Pittsburgh on September 11, 1963, leading the Dodgers to a 9-4 win over the Pirates by going 4-for-5, with 2 RBIs, 3 runs scored, and a pair of stolen bases.

Wills continued to torment Pittsburgh's pitching staff the following year, going 3-for-4, with a homer, 2 RBIs, 3 runs scored, and 3 steals, during a 10-3 pasting of the Pirates on May 30, 1964.

Wills led Los Angeles to a pair of resounding victories over San Francisco in 1965, going 3-for-4, with 3 runs scored and 3 stolen bases, during a 9-0 win over the Dodgers' arch-rivals on May 8, before hitting safely in 4 of his 5 trips to the plate, scoring 3 times, and stealing a base during a 9-3 win over the Giants on June 29.

Although the Dodgers lost to the Giants by a score of 14-13 on July 17, 1969, Wills had another big game, going 3-for-6, with a homer, a pair of triples, 2 runs scored, and a career-high 4 RBIs.

Wills turned in one of his finest offensive performances against Chicago on August 14, 1970, going a perfect 5-for-5, with 1 RBI and 2 runs scored, during a 13-9 win over the Cubs.

Although Wills struggled at the plate in his three other World Series appearances, posting a composite batting average of .167, he performed magnificently in the 1965 fall classic, batting .367, driving in 3 runs, scoring 3 times, and stealing 3 bases, in helping the Dodgers defeat the Minnesota Twins in seven games.

## Notable Achievements:

- Batted over .300 once (.302 in 1963).
- Scored more than 100 runs twice, scoring 130 times in 1962.
- Surpassed 200 hits once (208 in 1962).
- Finished in double-digits in triples twice.
- Stole more than 30 bases seven times, topping 50 thefts four times and 100 steals once.

- Led NL in: stolen bases six times, triples once, and sacrifice hits once.
- Led NL shortstops in assists once.
- Holds Dodgers single-season records for most: stolen bases (104 in 1962), games played (165 in 1962), plate appearances (759 in 1962), and at-bats (695 in 1962).
- Holds Dodgers career record for most stolen bases (490).
- Ranks among Dodgers career leaders in: runs scored (10$^{th}$), hits (10$^{th}$), plate appearances (10$^{th}$), and at-bats (10$^{th}$).
- Set new major-league record (since broken) with 104 stolen bases in 1962.
- Holds single-season major-league record for most games played (165 in 1962).
- Two-time Gold Glove winner (1961 & 1962).
- 1962 NL MVP.
- 1962 *Sporting News* Major League Player of the Year.
- 1962 All-Star Game MVP.
- Finished third in 1965 NL MVP voting.
- Three-time *Sporting News* All-Star selection (1961, 1962 & 1965).
- Five-time NL All-Star (1961, 1962, 1963, 1965 & 1966).
- Four-time NL champion (1959, 1963, 1965 & 1966).
- Three-time world champion (1959, 1963 & 1965).

# 15

# CARL FURILLO

Perhaps the most overlooked and underappreciated member of Brooklyn's "Boys of Summer" team that won six pennants over a ten-year period, Carl Furillo is remembered today primarily for his powerful throwing arm. Yet, even though Furillo did indeed possess one of the strongest throwing arms of any outfielder in baseball history, he contributed to the Dodgers in many other ways over the course of his fifteen-year career. In addition to being an exceptional defensive outfielder who did a superb job of playing the tricky right-field wall at Ebbets Field, Furillo compiled a lifetime batting average of .299 for the Dodgers, hitting over .300 on five separate occasions, including 1953, when he won the National League batting title with a mark of .344. The right-handed hitting Furillo also proved to be an excellent run-producer, surpassing 100 RBIs twice, while knocking in more than 90 runs on four other occasions. Furillo also hit more than 20 homers and scored more than 90 runs three times each, establishing himself in the process as arguably the finest all-around right-fielder of his time.

Born to Italian immigrant parents in the Reading, Pennsylvania suburb of Stony Creek Mills on March 8, 1922, Carl Anthony Furillo dropped out of school after completing the eighth grade and worked at various jobs, before signing with the Reading team in the Interstate League following the death of his mother in 1940. After spending his earliest days in the minor leagues splitting his time between pitching and playing the outfield, Furillo became a full-time outfielder, with Reading manager Fresco Thompson later recalling, "He could certainly throw, but who knew where? He broke four ribs and two wrists before we decided, as an act of public safety, to make him spend all his time in the outfield."

Furillo's powerful throwing arm, which enabled him to amass 25 assists in his first full season as an outfielder, eventually earned him the nickname "The Reading Rifle." He also displayed solid hitting skills, batting .313 and compiling a .490 slugging percentage in 125 games with the Reading Brooks in 1941, before being promoted to Brooklyn's top farm team, the Montreal Royals of the International League, the following year. After batting .281 for the Royals in 1942, Furillo appeared to be on the verge of being call up to the Major Leagues. However, he ended up spending the next three years in the Army, serving in combat in the Pacific Theater, where he received three battle stars for his courage under fire.

After being discharged from the military early in 1946, Furillo received a $3,750 offer from the Dodgers, which he turned down, angering Brooklyn manager Leo Durocher, who told him, "Take it or leave it." Furillo eventually came to terms with the Dodgers, but animosity continued to develop between him and Durocher when rumors began to circulate about Furillo's drinking habits. Although the young outfielder steadfastly denied the accusations, Durocher chose not to believe him, infuriating Furillo, who also became incensed when his manager predicted that he would never be a full-time player because he struggled somewhat against right-handed pitching. In discussing his feelings towards Durocher years later, Furillo said, "He knew his onions. . . . He knew his baseball, and that's about all. . . . He didn't know how to handle young players."

Playing centerfield mostly against left-handed pitching in 1946, Furillo had a decent rookie season, hitting 3 homers, driving in 35 runs, and batting .284, in 117 games and 335 official at-bats. With Durocher suspended the following year for consorting with gamblers, Furillo improved upon his performance considerably under manager Burt Shotten, helping the Dodgers capture the 1947 NL pennant by hitting 8 homers, knocking in 88 runs, and batting .295. However, Furillo didn't truly begin to thrive until the Dodgers replaced Durocher at the helm with Shotten during the latter stages of the ensuing campaign. After hitting just 4 homers, driving in only 44 runs, and batting .297 in a part-time role in 1948, Furillo proved he had the ability to hit right-handed pitching the following year, when he helped lead the Dodgers to the pennant and earned a sixth-place finish in the NL MVP voting by hitting 18 homers, knocking in 106 runs, scoring 95 times, and batting .322, while also leading all players at his position in both putouts and assists in his first full season in right field.

Although the Dodgers failed to repeat as league champions in either 1950 or 1951, Furillo performed extremely well both years, hitting 18 homers, driving in 106 runs, scoring 99 times, and batting .305 in the first of those campaigns, before hitting 16 homers, knocking in 91 runs, scoring 93 times, batting .295, and collecting a career-high 197 hits in the second. Meanwhile, "Skoonj," as he came to be known to his teammates for his love of the Italian dish scungilli, gained widespread acclaim as one of the senior circuit's top defensive outfielders, leading all NL right-fielders with a career-high 325 putouts in 1951, while finishing first among players at his position in assists for the second and third straight times.

In addition to possessing the league's strongest throwing arm, Furillo became quite adept at negotiating balls hit off the high right-field wall at Ebbets Field, with former teammate George Shuba stating, "Other players had trouble with bounces off the wall, but Carl was a magician."

Speaking of Furillo in his book, *The Duke of Flatbush*, Duke Snider wrote, "He played the tricky right-field wall in Ebbets Field with precision. I'd always been told that Dixie Walker played it well, but I don't see how he could have played it any better than Skoonj. And I know Walker never had the arm that Furillo had."

That throwing arm of which Snider spoke intimidated opposing players to such an extent that they simply refused to challenge it. In fact, after amassing a career-high 24 assists in 1951, Furillo never again compiled more than 12 assists in any single season.

Although not considered to be a true home run hitter, Furillo also developed into quite an offensive threat. Powerfully built at 6' tall and 195 pounds, Furillo consistently drove fierce line drives to all parts of the field, making him an excellent run-producer. Perhaps his only weakness as a hitter proved to be his lack of patience at the plate, since he drew more than 50 bases on balls just once his entire career. On the other hand, he rarely struck out, fanning as many as 40 times on just three occasions.

Bothered by cataracts throughout the 1952 campaign, Furillo had his least productive season as a starter, finishing the year with only 8 home runs, 59 RBIs, and a .247 batting average. However, after undergoing surgery during the subsequent offseason, he returned in 1953 to have arguably his finest all-around season, hitting 21 homers, driving in 92 runs, scoring 82 times, winning the batting title with a mark of .344, and placing among the league leaders with 38 doubles and a .580 slugging percent-

Courtesy of RMYauctions.com

Nicknamed 'the Reading Rifle' for his powerful throwing arm,
Carl Furillo also excelled as a hitter,
batting over .300 five times for the Dodgers

age, even though he missed the final three weeks of the campaign after fracturing his knuckle during a fight with Giants manager, and longtime adversary, Leo Durocher.

The aforementioned incident, which took place on September 6, 1953, resulted from the animosity that had existed between Furillo and Durocher for years, as well as the hatred that the Dodgers and Giants had for each other, which Furillo described years later when he said, "We hated them. We just hated the uniforms." Vin Scully later gave the following account of the events that transpired that day:

"Late in the 1953 season, Ruben Gomez, a screwball pitcher for the Giants, hit Furillo. Furillo went down to first and glared at Leo in the dugout. Then he motioned to him with his index finger to come out and fight, sort of saying, 'Come on, come on.' Leo in turn motioned Carl to come in. The two met halfway, and Carl got Leo around the forehead and put a lock on him like you wouldn't believe. If he'd got him around the throat, he would have killed him. And I'm not speaking figuratively. I mean actually killed him....Leo's bald head turned maroon before anybody could get to them. Both benches cleared, and everyone dove on the two of them. Carl ended up on the ground and someone stepped on his hand. That's how he broke it."

Furillo followed up his exceptional 1953 campaign with three more excellent years, averaging 22 home runs and 91 RBIs from 1954 to 1956, while compiling batting averages of .294, .314, and .289. He also played well for the Dodgers in the 1955 World Series, helping them win their only world championship in Brooklyn by homering once, driving in 3 runs, scoring 4 times, and batting .296. Although Furillo remained a productive player in 1957 and 1958, age and injuries limited his playing time somewhat, preventing him from appearing in more than 122 games either year. Nevertheless, after batting .306 in 1957, he hit 18 homers, knocked in 83 runs, and batted .290 the following season.

The 1958 campaign proved to be Furillo's last as a full-time starter. He ended up appearing in only 50 games in 1959, before being released by the Dodgers on May 17, 1960 after suffering a torn calf muscle several days earlier. Furillo ended his playing career with 192 home runs, 1,058 RBIs, 895 runs scored, 1,910 hits, 324 doubles, 56 triples, a .299 batting average, a .355 on-base percentage, and a .458 slugging percentage.

Furillo subsequently sued the Dodgers, disputing the legality of his release since he had a baseball-related injury. Feeling that the team parted ways with him when it did to avoid paying him the $21,000 that remained on his $33,000 annual salary, Furillo continued to hold a grudge against the Dodgers in future years, even though a court eventually awarded him back pay.

Subsequently blackballed from baseball coaching and scouting jobs, Furillo returned to Pennsylvania for a period of time, before opening up a delicatessen in Flushing, Queens during the mid-1960s. He later worked as a night watchman, and he also spent some time installing elevators at the World Trade Center. Unfortunately, Furillo developed leukemia in his later years, dying in his sleep of heart failure at the age of sixty-six, on January 21, 1989.

Although Furillo died believing that baseball had completely forgotten about him and his accomplishments, his former Dodger teammates certainly remembered him. Upon learning of his passing, Roy Campanella said, "He had the best throwing arm of any right-fielder I ever played with or against."

Carl Erskine recalled, "'I remember how tough he was, how strong he was, how consistent he was as a player. When he hit a single, it was a bullet. When he hit a homer, it was a rocket. And his arm portrayed his strength."

Duke Snider wrote in his autobiography, "I always thought he was the most underrated of all the Dodgers, and Buzzie Bavasi, our general manager in those years, told me not long ago that he agreed. Carl did more things to win games for us than he ever got credit for."

Vin Scully said of Furillo, "He was basically a no-nonsense, blue-collar player who played hard and played every day. He was very strong, and I can't stress enough how hard he played."

Meanwhile, Roger Kahn wrote in his classic book, *The Boys of Summer*, "I cannot imagine Carl Furillo in his prime as anything other than a ballplayer. Right field in Brooklyn was his destiny."

## Career Highlights:

**Best Season:** Furillo played extremely well for the Dodgers in 1949, earning a sixth-place finish in the NL MVP voting by hitting 18 homers, scoring 95 times, batting .322, compiling an OPS of .875, and establishing career-high marks in RBIs (106) and triples (10). He posted similar numbers the following year, concluding the 1950 campaign with 18 homers, 106 RBIs, 99 runs scored, and a .305 batting average. Furillo had another big year in 1955, when he hit a career-high 26 homers, knocked in 95 runs, and batted .314. Nevertheless, the 1953 season is generally considered to be his finest. In addition to topping the senior circuit with a batting average of .344, Furillo hit 21 homers, drove in 92 runs, and placed among the league leaders with 38 doubles and an OPS of .973, establishing career-high marks in each of the last two categories.

**Memorable Moments/Greatest Performances:** Furillo put his powerful throwing arm on display for all to see on August 27, 1951, when, during a 5-0 win over Pittsburgh, he threw out Mel Queen by two feet at first base after the Pirates pitcher had apparently singled to right field.

Furillo led the Dodgers to a 9-8 win over Cincinnati on June 22, 1947 by knocking in a career-high 7 runs with a grand slam homer and a pair of singles.

Furillo nearly hit for the cycle on June 26, 1949, when he homered, tripled, and singled three times during a perfect 5-for-5 outing that helped pace the Dodgers to a lopsided 15-3 victory over Pittsburgh. Furillo also drove in 4 runs and scored 4 times during the contest.

Furillo had another huge day at the plate on September 22, 1949, when he led the Dodgers to a 19-6 pounding of St. Louis by going 5-for-6, with 3 doubles and 7 RBIs, matching his single-game high in the last category in the process.

Furillo went on a two-game hitting spree on the 23rd and 24th of June 1950, leading the Dodgers to 15-3 and 21-12 victories over Pittsburgh by going a combined 8-for-10, with a homer, a double, 5 RBIs, and 7 runs scored.

Furillo hit a game-winning home run against the hated New York Giants at the Polo Grounds on April 22, 1951, going deep against Sal Maglie in the top of the 10th inning, to give the Dodgers a 4-3 victory over their arch-rivals.

Furillo provided similar heroics at the Polo Grounds on August 13, 1953, homering off Hoyt Wilhelm in the top of the 10th inning, to give the Dodgers a 9-8 win over the Giants.

Furillo came up big in the clutch again on August 15, 1955, when, after hitting a pair of solo homers earlier in the game, he delivered a two-out run-scoring single in the bottom of the 13th inning that gave the Dodgers a 5-4 victory over the Philadelphia Phillies.

Furillo led the Dodgers to a 10-8 win over the Chicago Cubs on July 15, 1956 by driving in 6 runs with a pair of homers, one of those being a sixth-inning grand slam.

Although the Dodgers ended up losing the 1947 World Series to the Yankees in seven games, Furillo performed exceptionally well, compiling a team-leading .353 batting average. He again played well in the 1953 fall classic, homering once, knocking in 4 runs, scoring 4 times, and batting .333 during the Dodgers' six-game defeat at the hands of their old nemesis. In between, Furillo preserved a 6-5 Brooklyn victory in Game Five of the 1952 World Series when he robbed Johnny Mize of an apparent home run by making a leaping catch at Yankee Stadium's right field wall with one out in the bottom of the 11th inning.

Although the thirty-seven-year-old Furillo garnered only four plate appearances in the 1959 World Series, he made one of them a big one, delivering a two-run pinch-hit single in the bottom of the seventh inning of Game Three that gave the Dodgers a 3-1 win over the Chicago White Sox.

Yet, Furillo considers the Dodgers' victory over the Yankees in the 1955 fall classic to be his greatest thrill in baseball, recalling years later, "Oh God, that was the thrill of all thrills.... I never in my life have seen a town go so wild.... We accomplished something .... You did it for yourself, too, but you did it for the people."

## Notable Achievements:

- Hit more than 20 home runs three times.
- Knocked in more than 100 runs twice.
- Batted over .300 five times, topping the .320-mark twice.
- Finished in double-digits in triples once (10 in 1949).
- Surpassed 30 doubles four times.
- Posted slugging percentage in excess of .500 three times.
- Led NL with a .344 batting average in 1953.
- Led NL outfielders in assists twice and double plays turned once.
- Led NL right-fielders in: putouts three times, assists three times, fielding percentage once, and double plays turned twice.
- Ranks among Dodgers career leaders in: home runs (seventh), RBIs (fourth), runs scored (eighth), hits (seventh), extra-base hits (seventh), doubles (fifth), total bases (seventh), games played (eighth), plate appearances (ninth), and at-bats (ninth).
- Finished in top 10 of NL MVP voting twice (1949 & 1953).
- 1953 NL Comeback Player of the Year.
- 1953 *Sporting News* All-Star selection.
- Two-time NL All-Star (1952 & 1953).
- Seven-time NL champion (1947, 1949, 1952, 1953, 1955, 1956 & 1959).
- Two-time world champion (1955 & 1959).

# 16

# DON NEWCOMBE

One of only two pitchers in baseball history to capture Rookie of the Year, Cy Young, and league MVP honors during his career, Don Newcombe proved to be a pioneer of sorts in his eight seasons with the Dodgers. In addition to winning MLB's inaugural Cy Young Award in 1956, Newcombe earlier became the first pitcher of African American descent to start a World Series game. He also was the first black hurler to win as many as 20 games in a season. A hard-throwing right-hander who intimidated opposing batters with his fastball and imposing 6'4", 220-pound frame, Newcombe posted at least 20 victories for the Dodgers on three separate occasions, including 1956, when his record of 27-7 enabled him to become the first hurler to win the Cy Young and MVP Awards in the same season. An outstanding hitter as well, Newcombe compiled a lifetime batting average of .271 and hit 15 career home runs, prompting the Dodgers to often use him as a pinch-hitter. Unfortunately, Newcombe's period of dominance lasted only a few short seasons due to a two-year stint in the military and a dependence on alcohol he developed largely because of the many racial inequities he had to endure during his time in Brooklyn.

Born in Madison, New Jersey on June 14, 1926, Donald Newcombe grew up in nearby Elizabeth, where he attended Jefferson High School. Although Newcombe did not seriously consider making a career out of baseball in his formative years, he signed a contract with the Newark Eagles of the Negro Leagues in 1943 after both the U.S. Army and Navy rejected him for being underage. Discovered by Dodger scout Clyde Sukeforth two years later while pitching in an exhibition game against white major-leaguers at Brooklyn's Ebbets Field, Newcombe signed with the Dodgers shortly thereafter, being assigned to their Class B farm team at Nashua, New Hampshire, along with catcher Roy Campanella.

Courtesy of RMYauctions.com

Don Newcombe's 27 victories in 1956 earned him
Cy Young and NL MVP honors

The addition of Newcombe and Campanella to Nashua's roster in 1946 marked the first time in the 20th century that black and white players played alongside one another on a baseball team based in the United States. Fully aware of the significance of that last fact, Newcombe told *The Nashua Telegraph* more than fifty years later, "When Roy Campanella and I came to Nashua in 1946 we were embarking on a mission. This was a mission in Nashua that was helping to revolutionize the game of baseball; that was going to impact on black people all over the world...It was in April of 1946, and the graciousness of how we were accepted here really shocked us."

After leading the New England League with 19 wins and 186 strike-outs in his second season at Nashua in 1947, Newcombe advanced only to triple-A Montreal the following year, while Campanella and fellow black hurler Dan Bankhead joined Jackie Robinson in Brooklyn. Disconsolate over the apparent snub, the extremely sensitive Newcombe nearly decided to quit baseball, leaving Montreal briefly, before returning to the team three days later. He ended up spending the entire season with the Royals, later coming to realize that Dodgers GM Branch Rickey held him back one year because he thought it best to gradually integrate the team at the major-league level.

Finally arriving in Brooklyn in 1949, Newcombe took the senior circuit by storm, helping the Dodgers capture the NL pennant by compiling a record of 17-8, finishing among the league leaders with a 3.17 ERA, 149 strikeouts, 19 complete games, 244⅓ innings pitched, and a WHIP of 1.211, and topping the circuit with 5 shutouts, en route to winning Rookie of the Year honors. Newcombe's exceptional performance also earned him the first of his four All-Star selections and an eighth-place finish in the league MVP voting, with his nomination to the All-Star Team making him one of the first four black players to be so honored (teammates Jackie Robinson and Roy Campanella, and Cleveland's Larry Doby being the others). Newcombe subsequently appeared in two games in the 1949 World Series, losing both his starts against the Yankees, although he pitched relatively well, losing Game One by a score of 1-0 on a ninth-inning home run by Tommy Henrich, compiling an ERA of 3.09, and striking out 11 batters in 11⅔ total innings of work.

Reflecting back on the surreal nature of his World Series appearance, Newcombe told Art Rust, Jr. in *Get That Nigger off the Field*,

> *"I was the first black pitcher ever to take the mound in a Major League World Series game. At the time, I remember I had a double set of feelings: a modicum of fear about the Yankee dynasty we were playing, and that I was only a rookie....I didn't have a dream back in 1944 that I would be pitching against the Yankees in the 1949 Series. Back in 1944, there was no way that a kid from the ghetto in Elizabeth, New Jersey, could ever think along those lines."*

Although the Dodgers barely missed winning the pennant in each of the next two seasons, Newcombe continued to excel on the mound, going 19-11, with a 3.70 ERA, 20 complete games, and 267⅓ innings pitched in 1950, before compiling a record of 20-9, an ERA of 3.28, 18 complete games, 272 innings pitched, and a league-leading 164 strikeouts the following year. After being drafted into the Army following the conclusion of the 1951 campaign, Newcombe spent the next two years serving his country in Korea. Struggling upon his return to Brooklyn in 1954, Newcombe went just 9-8 with a 4.55 ERA for a Dodger team that finished second in the National League, five games behind the pennant-winning Giants.

Newcombe regained his earlier form in 1955, concluding the campaign with a record of 20-5 that gave him a league-leading .800 winning percentage. He also finished first among NL hurlers with a WHIP of 1.113, while ranking among the leaders with a 3.20 ERA, 143 strikeouts, 17 complete games, and 233⅔ innings pitched. Newcombe followed that up with a virtuoso performance in 1956, earning Cy Young and NL MVP honors by going 27-7, with an ERA of 3.06, 139 strikeouts, 5 shutouts, 18 complete games, 268 innings pitched, and a league-leading WHIP of 0.989. However, he subsequently faltered during the World Series, losing his only decision, while failing to make it past the fourth inning in either of his two starts.

In spite of the success Newcombe experienced during his first several seasons with the Dodgers, he grew increasingly despondent over the shabby treatment he and the other black players of his day had to endure simply because of the color of their skin. Not allowed to share the same accommodations as their white teammates on road trips, players of African American heritage found themselves being treated as lesser individuals—a fact that weighed heavily on Newcombe, who finally complained to Jackie Robinson, telling his teammate, as reported by Art Rust, Jr. in his aforementioned book, "I've just spent two years in the Army fighting for my flag, for my country. I'm not going to live like a substandard human being anymore unless somebody can tell me why I've got to live like that."

After expressing their feelings to management, Newcombe and Robinson eventually earned the right to stay with their white teammates, with Newcombe telling Rust, "Eventually, Jackie, I, and Roy Campanella moved into all the hotels with the team on a regular basis, and incidents like these became part of baseball lore."

Newcombe also had to deal with the racial stereotypes that existed at that time, particularly about black pitchers, who were generally thought to have less drive, heart, and intelligence than their white counterparts.

However, even though many others considered the big right-hander to be lethargic and unwilling to work hard, Jim Gilliam defended his former teammate, stating, "Everyone thought he was a lazy pitcher, but actually Don was the hardest-working pitcher around."

The prejudice that Newcombe constantly faced placed an undue amount of pressure on him, causing him to finally turn to the bottle for comfort. But, while alcohol provided Newcombe with a temporary source of relief, it also helped bring his career to a premature end. After establishing himself as baseball's best pitcher the previous year, Newcombe finished just 11-12 with a 3.49 ERA in 1957. He followed that up by losing his first six decisions in 1958, prompting the Dodgers to trade him to Cincinnati midway through the campaign. Newcombe remained in Cincinnati for much of the next two seasons, pitching his best ball for the Reds in 1959, when he went 13-8, with a 3.16 ERA and 17 complete games. However, after Newcombe went a combined 6-9 for the Reds and Indians in 1960, Cleveland released him in January 1961, bringing his major-league career to an end. He finished his playing days with a record of 149-90, an ERA of 3.56, 1,129 strikeouts in 2,154⅔ innings of work, 136 complete games, 24 shutouts, and a WHIP of 1.203. Over parts of eight seasons with the Dodgers, Newcombe went 123-66, with a 3.51 ERA, 913 strikeouts in 1,662⅔ innings of work, 111 complete games, 22 shutouts, and a WHIP of 1.191.

Although Newcombe has not come close to making the Hall of Fame, Chicago Cubs slugger Ernie Banks paid tribute to his former opponent when he said, "A lot of fans have asked me who's the toughest pitcher I had to face in the majors. I would say Don Newcombe. He had tremendous drive. He loved competition, was a winning-type pitcher….He had great control, and he could hit like hell; he was the type of man everybody would like to be like."

Following his release by the Indians, Newcombe spent the 1961 season in the minors, before signing with a Japanese team, with whom he ended his playing career one year later. After becoming sober in 1967, Newcombe eventually returned to the Dodger organization, beginning in the late 1970s a lengthy stint as the team's Director of Community Affairs. While serving in that capacity, he also devoted a considerable amount of time to helping others who succumbed to substance abuse, including former Dodger standout Maury Wills, who credited Newcombe with helping him regain sobriety when he told a group of listeners, "I'm standing here with the man [Newcombe] who saved my life. He was a channel for God's love for me because he chased me all over Los Angeles trying to help me, and I just couldn't understand that—but he persevered; he wouldn't give in and my life is wonderful today because of Don Newcombe."

In discussing the role he has assumed for most of the last four decades, Newcombe said, "What I have done after my baseball career—and being able to help people with their lives and getting their lives back on track and they become human beings again—means more to me than all the things I did in baseball."

## Dodger Career Highlights:

**Best Season:** Newcombe pitched exceptionally well for the Dodgers in 1951 and 1955, winning 20 games each season, while placing among the league leaders in numerous statistical categories each year. However, he unquestionably had the greatest season of his career in 1956, when, en route to earning NL MVP honors and MLB's first Cy Young Award (only one recipient was named for both leagues combined from 1956 to 1966), he posted a league-leading 27 victories, .794 winning percentage, and 0.989 WHIP. Newcombe also finished in the league's top five in ERA (3.06), shutouts (5), complete games (18), and innings pitched (268). Commenting on Newcombe's brilliant performance in *Out By A Step: The 100 Best Players Not in the Baseball Hall of Fame*, former Dodgers General Manager Buzzy Bavasi stated, "Throughout his career, Newcombe was a great pitcher. He was consistent, and he was dominating. But, in 1956, he was the best I ever saw."

**Memorable Moments/Greatest Performances:** An outstanding hitter over the course of his career, the left-handed swinging Newcombe performed particularly well at the plate in 1955, batting .359 and totaling 7 home runs and 23 RBIs, in only 117 official at-bats. He homered twice in one game on two separate occasions that year, doing so for the first time during a 10-8 victory over the Giants on April 14, before accomplishing the feat again on May 30, in leading the Dodgers to an 8-3 win over the Pirates. Newcombe went 3-for-4 with 3 RBIs and 3 runs scored in the second contest. He hit 2 home runs in one game for the third and final time in his career during a lopsided 17-2 victory over the Cardinals on September 19, 1956, going 3-for-4 with 3 RBIs and 3 runs scored in that contest as well. Newcombe had the only four-hit game of his career on July 15, 1955, when he went 4-for-5, with a homer, double, 3 RBIs, and 2 runs scored, during a 12-3 win over the Cardinals.

On the mound, Newcombe put together a pair of impressive scoreless innings streaks during his time in Brooklyn, with the first of those coming from August 21, 1949 to September 6, 1949, when he shut out the opposition for 31⅔ consecutive frames. Newcombe compiled an even longer streak seven years later, throwing 39⅔ consecutive scoreless innings from July 25, 1956 to August 11, 1956.

Newcombe threw back-to-back three-hit shutouts in September 1950, blanking the Giants 2-0 on the second of the month, before shutting out the Phillies by the same score just four days later.

Although he also walked seven batters during the contest, Newcombe tossed the first of his two career one-hitters on June 23, 1951, when he defeated the Pirates by a score of 13-1. Newcombe proved to be even more dominant on May 10, 1955, when he allowed just a fourth-inning single to Chicago second baseman Gene Baker during a 3-0 victory over the Cubs. With Baker subsequently being thrown out attempting to steal second base, Newcombe ended up pitching to the minimum number of 27 batters. He also recorded 6 strikeouts during the contest.

Newcombe hurled another gem against Chicago a little over two months later, striking out 8 and surrendering just 2 hits and a pair of walks during a 10-1 win over the Cubs on July 20, 1955.

Newcombe continued to torment the Cubs the following year, tossing a pair of three-hit shutouts against them in 1956, defeating them by scores of 6-0 on May 8 and 3-0 on September 15.

Showing no favoritism, Newcombe surrendered just 4 hits and struck out 10 during a 3-0 win over the Braves on August 2, 1956.

Still, it is for his postseason failures that Newcombe is perhaps remembered most. Featuring a lifetime record of 0-4 and an ERA of 8.59 in World Series play, Newcombe developed a reputation as being someone who had a difficult time winning the "big game." Nevertheless, he often pitched in hard luck, with perhaps the greatest example being Game One of the 1949 fall classic, when he lost a 1-0 pitcher's duel with Yankees right-hander Allie Reynolds on a Tommy Henrich home run in the bottom of the ninth inning. Newcombe also proved to be a victim of ill fortune on October 3, 1951, when he left Game Three of the playoff series between the Dodgers and Giants ahead by a score of 4-2 in the bottom of the ninth inning, before Bobby Thomson won the pennant for the Giants by hitting a three-run homer off Brooklyn reliever Ralph Branca.

## Notable Achievements:

- Won at least 20 games three times, surpassing 25 victories once (27 in 1956).
- Won at least 17 games two other times.
- Compiled winning percentage in excess of .700 twice, topping the .800-mark once.
- Posted WHIP under 1.000 once (0.989 in 1956).
- Threw more than 250 innings three times.
- Threw 20 complete games in 1950.
- Led NL pitchers in: wins once, winning percentage twice, WHIP twice, shutouts once, strikeouts once, and putouts once.
- Ranks ninth in Dodgers history in career winning percentage (.651).
- 1949 NL Rookie of the Year.
- 1956 NL MVP.
- 1956 Cy Young Award winner.
- 1956 *Sporting News* NL Pitcher of the Year.
- Two-time *Sporting News* All-Star selection (1955 & 1956).
- Four-time NL All-Star (1949, 1950, 1951 & 1955).
- Three-time NL champion (1949, 1955 & 1956).
- 1955 world champion.

# 17

# FERNANDO VALENZUELA

Emerging as a cult hero of sorts in his early days with the Dodgers, Fernando Valenzuela gained instant fame by beginning his career in magnificent fashion. Winning his first eight starts, with five of those being shutouts, Valenzuela went on to capture NL Cy Young and Rookie of the Year honors in 1981, becoming in the process the first player to receive both accolades in the same season. Valenzuela's dream season continued in the playoffs and World Series, when he won three of his four decisions, in helping the Dodgers capture their first world championship in 16 years. Although Valenzuela's fabulous rookie campaign proved to be the highlight of his career, the Mexican-born left-hander remained an extremely effective pitcher in the years that followed, topping 20 victories once and 17 wins on two other occasions, en route to earning a total of six All-Star selections and three more top-five finishes in the NL Cy Young balloting. Along the way, Valenzuela led all NL pitchers in wins, strikeouts, and innings pitched once each, while also topping the senior circuit in complete games three times. In all, Valenzuela's outstanding pitching helped the Dodgers win three division titles, two pennants, and two World Series.

Born in Etchohuaquila, a small Mexican town within the municipality of Navojoa, in the state of Sonora, Fernando Valenzuela has an official birth date of November 1, 1960, although the accuracy of that date frequently came into question during his playing days, with many people believing him to be considerably older than his listed age. Valenzuela began his career in professional baseball with the Mexican League's Mayos de Navojoa in 1977, shortly after he graduated from Navajoa High School. After spending the next three seasons pitching for various teams south of the border, Valenzuela became a member of the Dodger organization when

Los Angeles purchased his contract from the Yucatán Lions for $120,000 on July 6, 1979.

After spending the remainder of the 1979 campaign with the Lodi Dodgers of the high-A level California League, Valenzuela advanced to double-A San Antonio the following year, where he learned how to throw the screwball from Dodgers pitcher Bobby Castillo. Armed with his new weapon, the nineteen-year-old southpaw developed into one of the Texas League's best pitchers, compiling a record of 13-9 and an ERA of 3.10, while topping the circuit with 162 strikeouts.

Called up to the Dodgers in mid-September 1980, Valenzuela made an immediate impression on team brass by winning both his decisions, while recording 16 strikeouts in 17⅔ of work and not allowing a single run to score over 10 relief appearances. Having earned a spot in the Dodgers' starting rotation the following spring, Valenzuela replaced an injured Jerry Reuss as the team's opening day starter, after which he went on to shut out the Houston Astros by a score of 2-0. Valenzuela's blanking of Houston began an extraordinary run during which he posted eight straight complete-game victories, five of which were shutouts.

Rapidly developing into a cultural icon due to his magnificent pitching and popularity with the local Latino community, Valenzuela drew huge crowds whenever he started a home game for the Dodgers, with the craze surrounding him commonly being referred to as "Fernandomania." With the PA system at Dodger Stadium playing ABBA's 1976 hit song *Fernando* as Valenzuela warmed up on the mound in between innings, the portly left-hander further entertained the fans in attendance with his unusual, flamboyant windup during which he looked skyward just before delivering the ball to home plate.

After compiling a brilliant 0.50 ERA in his first eight starts, Valenzuela proved to be somewhat less dominant the rest of the year, particularly after play resumed in mid-August following a two-month players' strike. Nevertheless, "El Toro," as he came to be known, ended up compiling a record of 13-7 and an ERA of 2.48, while leading all NL hurlers with 180 strikeouts, 8 shutouts, 11 complete games, and 192⅓ innings pitched. Valenzuela's exceptional pitching, which helped the Dodgers advance to the playoffs, earned him the first of his six consecutive All-Star selections, a fifth-place finish in the league MVP voting, and NL Rookie of the Year and Cy Young honors. Valenzuela continued his outstanding work in the playoffs and World Series, posting a win in each round of the postseason tournament as the Dodgers went on to win the world championship.

Valenzuela followed up his virtuoso performance with an excellent 1982 campaign in which he compiled a record of 19-13 that tied him with Montreal's Steve Rogers for the second most wins in the league (Steve Carlton topped the circuit with 23 victories). Valenzuela also ranked among the NL leaders with a 2.87 ERA, 199 strikeouts, 4 shutouts, 18 complete games, and 285 innings pitched, earning in the process a third-place finish in the Cy Young voting. A somewhat less impressive 1983 season followed in which Valenzuela finished 15-10 with a 3.75 ERA, although he ended up placing among the league leaders with 189 strikeouts, 4 shutouts, 9 complete games, and 257 innings pitched. Valenzuela subsequently posted better overall numbers in 1984, concluding the campaign with a 3.03 ERA and placing near the top of the league rankings in complete games (12), innings pitched (261), and strikeouts (240). However, poor run support from his light-hitting teammates relegated him to a record of just 12-17.

Pitching for a stronger Dodgers team in 1985, Valenzuela had one of his finest seasons, earning a fifth-place finish in the NL Cy Young balloting by compiling a record of 17-10, while ranking among the league leaders with a 2.45 ERA, 208 strikeouts, 5 shutouts, 14 complete games, and 272⅓ innings pitched. He followed that up with an equally impressive 1986 campaign in which he finished 21-11, with a 3.14 ERA, a career-high 242 strikeouts, and a league-leading and career-best 20 complete games.

A true workhorse during his time in Los Angeles, Valenzuela annually placed near the top of the league rankings in complete games and innings pitched, leading all NL hurlers in the first category three times, while tossing more than 250 innings six straight times. Valenzuela also consistently finished among the league leaders in shutouts and strikeouts, with his screwball proving to be a baffling pitch to opposing hitters, particularly those who swung left-handed. In fact, Valenzuela accumulated more strikeouts (1,448) from 1981 to 1987 than any other pitcher in baseball. He also faced more batters (7,413) than anyone else during that time frame, with his 1,788 innings pitched and 111 wins being surpassed only by Jack Morris. Meanwhile, the 3.11 ERA Valenzuela compiled over the course of his first seven seasons placed him second only to Nolan Ryan among major-league pitchers.

Courtesy of MEARS Online Auctions

Fernando Valenzuela captured NL Cy Young
and Rookie of the Year honors in 1981, when he
helped lead the Dodgers to the world championship

Valenzuela's effectiveness and durability helped make him one of the most prominent figures on the Dodgers his first several years in Los Angeles. Adding to his popularity were his unique delivery, charisma, and stout frame, which belied his athletic prowess. While sportswriter H.G. Reza once wrote, "Watching Fernando Valenzuela force himself into a Los Angeles Dodgers uniform is something like seeing Kate Smith struggling to fit into a pair of Brooke Shields' designer jeans," the stocky left-hander actually possessed outstanding athletic ability. In addition to being surprisingly quick on the mound (he won a Gold Glove and twice led NL pitchers in assists), Valenzuela proved to be an excellent hitting pitcher, hitting 10 home runs and batting .200 over the course of his career, including posting a mark of .304 one season. Indeed, in his rookie campaign of 1981, Valenzuela batted .250 and struck out only 9 times in 71 total plate appearances, en route to earning the first of his two Silver Sluggers.

Valenzuela's string of six consecutive All-Star selections ended in 1987, when he suffered through a subpar campaign during which he went just 14-14, with a 3.98 ERA and an uncharacteristically high 1.506 WHIP. Nevertheless, he still managed to record 190 strikeouts and lead the league with 12 complete games.

Valenzuela saw another streak come to an end the following year, when, after taking his turn on the mound 255 straight times to open his career, he missed the final two months of the 1988 campaign with a shoulder injury. Yet, Valenzuela, who finished the year with a record of 5-8 and an ERA of 4.24, expressed a desire to pitch through the pain, refusing to use his sore arm as an excuse for his failures on the mound. In explaining his poor performance, Valenzuela told Sam McManis of the *Los Angeles Times*, "I've had a bad year. It's not my arm. In the beginning of the season, I needed more time to warm up, but I didn't feel anything until the last start." Dodgers manager Tommy Lasorda believed differently, though, telling that same reporter, "I always felt that way, that something was wrong. But he would never tell you because he's such a tremendous competitor. It's good to know, though, that we're able to take care of him. The longer he pitched with it, the more injurious it is to his health."

After returning to the Dodgers at the beginning of the 1989 season, Valenzuela failed to regain his earlier form, finishing the year with a record of just 10-13 and an ERA of 3.43. He followed that up by going 13-13 with an inordinately high ERA of 4.59 in 1990, prompting the Dodgers to release him prior to the start of the ensuing campaign. Valenzuela left Los

Angeles having compiled a career record of 141-116, along with an ERA of 3.31, 1,759 strikeouts in 2,348⅔ innings pitched, 29 shutouts, 107 complete games, and a WHIP of 1.283.

Following his release by the Dodgers, Valenzuela spent the next several seasons trying to recapture his earlier glory, traveling from one team to another, but experiencing very little in the way of success. After appearing in only two games with the California Angels in 1991, Valenzuela spent the 1992 season pitching in Mexico. Returning to the big leagues the following year, Valenzuela split his final five seasons between Baltimore, Philadelphia, San Diego, and St. Louis, pitching his best ball during that time for the Padres in 1996, when he went 13-8 with a 3.62 ERA. Released by the Cardinals on July 15, 1997, Valenzuela chose to announce his retirement, ending his career with a record of 173-153, an ERA of 3.54, 2,074 strikeouts in 2,930 innings of work, 31 shutouts, 113 complete games, and a WHIP of 1.320. After spending the next few years away from baseball, Valenzuela returned to the Dodger organization in 2003 as an analyst on the team's Spanish language radio broadcast. He continued to assume that role until 2015, when he became the color commentator on the Spanish-language feed of SportsNet LA.

## Dodger Career Highlights:

**Best Season:** Valenzuela had a big year for the Dodgers in 1986, posting career-high marks in wins (21), complete games (20), and strikeouts (242), en route to earning a runner-up finish in the NL Cy Young voting. He also performed extremely well in 1982 and 1985, winning 19 games, compiling a 2.87 ERA, tossing 18 complete games, and throwing a career-high 285 innings in the first of those campaigns, before posting 17 victories, recording 208 strikeouts, tossing 272⅓ innings, and compiling a career-best 2.45 ERA in the second. Nevertheless, Valenzuela's rookie year of 1981 is generally considered to be his signature season. Although his overall numbers might seem less impressive due to the player's strike that shortened the season, Valenzuela compiled an ERA of 2.48, finished second in the league with 13 wins and a career-low WHIP of 1.045, and led all NL hurlers with 180 strikeouts, 8 shutouts, 25 starts, 192⅓ innings pitched, and 11 complete games. In addition to earning him NL Rookie of the Year and Cy Young honors, Valenzuela's outstanding pitching prompted *The Sporting News* to name him its NL Pitcher of the Year and Major League Player of the Year.

**Memorable Moments/Greatest Performances:** As noted earlier, Valenzuela began his rookie campaign of 1981 in magnificent fashion, winning his first eight starts and tossing five shutouts. After defeating Houston by a score of 2-0 on opening day, Valenzuela beat the Giants 7-1 in his next start, allowing the Dodgers' chief rival just 4 hits while striking out 10. Valenzuela then reeled off three straight shutouts, blanking San Diego 2-0 on 5 hits while recording 10 strikeouts, outdueling former Dodger Don Sutton in defeating the Astros 1-0, and defeating the Giants again, this time by a score of 5-0. Valenzuela finally surrendered a run in his next start—a 6-1 win over Montreal—before defeating the Mets by a score of 1-0 in his next outing. But, by the time the Expos scored their lone run against him in the eighth inning of their May 3 loss to the Dodgers, Valenzuela had thrown 36 consecutive scoreless innings—a streak that began almost three weeks earlier, on April 14.

Valenzuela turned in his finest performance of the ensuing campaign on August 20, 1982, when he defeated Pittsburgh by a score of 1-0, allowing just a harmless pair of singles and 3 walks to the Pirates, while recording 9 strikeouts.

Valenzuela hurled another gem on May 28, 1983, when he tossed a two-hit shutout against the Giants, defeating them by a score of 5-0. He also walked 2 batters and struck out 5 during the contest.

Nearly one year later, on May 23, 1984, Valenzuela recorded a career-high 15 strikeouts during a three-hit, 1-0 victory over Philadelphia.

Valenzuela tossed back-to-back shutouts in April 1985, defeating the Giants by a score of 1-0 in his second start of the season, before allowing just 2 singles and 3 walks in his next outing, a 5-0 victory over San Diego.

Although Valenzuela suffered a 1-0 defeat at the hands of the Padres 10 days later, on April 28, 1985, he pitched one of his finest games of the season, surrendering just 2 hits and 1 walk, while recording 10 strikeouts.

Although the Dodgers ended up losing their September 6, 1985 matchup with the Mets by a score of 2-0 in 13 innings, Valenzuela performed brilliantly, allowing 6 hits over 11 scoreless innings, before finally being removed for a pinch-hitter in the bottom of the 11th.

Valenzuela tossed a pair of two-hit shutouts just four days apart in 1986, blanking Montreal 4-0 on May 20, before defeating Philadelphia by a score of 6-0 on the 24th of the month, recording a total of 17 strikeouts over the course of the two contests.

Nevertheless, Valenzuela turned in his most memorable performance of the 1986 campaign at the annual All-Star Game, tying a record Carl Hubbell set in the 1934 Midsummer Classic by striking out 5 consecutive American League batters. Entering the contest in the top of the fourth inning, Valenzuela retired the side in order by fanning Don Mattingly, Cal Ripken Jr., and Jesse Barfield. He continued his streak in the ensuing frame by whiffing Lou Whitaker and pitcher Teddy Higuera, before Kirby Puckett ended the string by grounding out to short. Valenzuela worked a scoreless sixth inning as well, completing his three innings of work having allowed just 1 hit, while striking out 5.

Yet, ironically, Valenzuela pitched his greatest game for the Dodgers in his final year with the club—one in which he resembled merely a shell of his former self. Facing St. Louis on June 29, 1990, Valenzuela tossed the only no-hitter of his career, allowing just 3 walks and recording 7 strikeouts during a 6-0 victory over the Cardinals that evened his record at 6-6.

## Notable Achievements:

- Won 21 games in 1986.
- Surpassed 17 victories two other times.
- Compiled ERA below 3.00 three times, posting mark under 2.50 twice.
- Struck out more than 200 batters three times.
- Threw more than 250 innings six times.
- Threw 20 complete games in 1986.
- Led NL pitchers in: wins once, strikeouts once, shutouts once, complete games three times, innings pitched once, games started once, and assists twice.
- Ranks among Dodgers career leaders in: wins (eighth), strikeouts (sixth), shutouts (tied-sixth), innings pitched (ninth), and games started (sixth).
- Threw no-hitter vs. St. Louis on June 29, 1990.
- Three-time NL Pitcher of the Month.
- Two-time Silver Slugger winner (1981 & 1983).

- 1986 Gold Glove winner.
- 1981 NL Rookie of the Year.
- 1981 *Sporting News* Major League Player of the Year.
- 1981 *Sporting News* NL Pitcher of the Year.
- 1981 NL Cy Young Award winner.
- Finished in top five in NL Cy Young voting three other times, placing as high as second in 1986.
- Finished fifth in 1981 NL MVP voting.
- Two-time *Sporting News* All-Star selection (1981 & 1986).
- Six-time NL All-Star (1981, 1982, 1983, 1984, 1985 & 1986).
- Two-time NL champion (1981 & 1988).
- Two-time world champion (1981 & 1988).

# 18

# OREL HERSHISER

The author of the longest consecutive scoreless innings streak in major-league history, Orel Hershiser put together a magical 1988 season in which he not only established the aforementioned mark, but also led the Dodgers to the world championship. Displaying tremendous tenacity and a fierce competitive spirit, the slight-of-build right-hander practically guaranteed the Dodgers victory every time he took the mound the final six weeks of the campaign, winning seven of his last eight decisions, while shutting out the opposition six times. Hershiser subsequently continued his remarkable run in the postseason, leading the Dodgers to unexpected wins over the New York Mets in the NLCS and the Oakland Athletics in the World Series. Yet, even though Hershiser reached his zenith during the latter stages of that 1988 campaign, he proved to be much more than a one-year wonder, compiling a total of 204 victories over the course of his career, with 135 of those coming as a member of the Dodgers. A three-time NL All-Star and one-time Cy Young Award winner, Hershiser finished in the top five of the balloting for that prestigious award three other times, leading all NL hurlers in wins, winning percentage, and complete games once each, shutouts twice, and innings pitched three times. Nevertheless, it is for his brilliant performance in 1988 that Hershiser will always be remembered most fondly by Dodger fans.

Born in Buffalo, New York on September 16, 1958, Orel Leonard Hershiser lived a somewhat nomadic existence as a youngster, moving with his family to Detroit, Michigan at the age of six, before relocating to Toronto, Canada after he turned twelve years of age. Hershiser's family eventually settled in southern New Jersey, where he attended Cherry Hill East High School. After failing to make that institution's varsity baseball team as either a freshman or a sophomore, Hershiser flourished in his final two seasons at Cherry Hill, setting the school record for most strikeouts in a single game as a senior by fanning 15 Deptford batters, en route to earning All-Conference honors.

Awarded only a partial scholarship to Ohio's Bowling Green State University, Hershiser accomplished very little on the playing field and in the classroom his first two years, prompting him to briefly leave school. However, after his parents convinced him to return to college, Hershiser reapplied himself, put on some much-needed weight, which enabled him to gain five miles per hour on his fastball, and ended up making the All-Mid-American Conference All-Star team as a junior. Subsequently selected by Los Angeles in the 17th round of the 1979 amateur draft, Hershiser entered the Dodger organization having received unfavorable reviews from several major-league scouts, who suggested that he lacked velocity on his fastball, criticized his control, and questioned his mental makeup.

After being assigned to the Class A Clinton Dodgers for the remainder of 1979, Hershiser spent the next two seasons working primarily out of the bullpen for the double-A San Antonio Dodgers in the Texas League. Hershiser continued to work mostly in relief after the Dodgers promoted him to their Pacific Coast League triple-A affiliate in Albuquerque in 1982, before finally being called up to the majors during the latter stages of the 1983 campaign. Making eight relief appearances over the season's final month, Hershiser worked a total of eight innings, earning a save and compiling an ERA of 3.38.

After claiming the final spot on the Dodgers' pitching staff the following spring, Hershiser spent the first part of 1984 serving the team primarily as a long reliever. However, after being lambasted by manager Tommy Lasorda, who accused him of being too timid on the mound and giving opposing hitters too much respect, the twenty-three-year-old right-hander eventually earned a regular spot in the starting rotation. Finishing the year strong, Hershiser, who Lasorda nicknamed "Bulldog" in order to toughen him up, went on to compile a record of 11-8, an ERA of 2.66, 150 strikeouts, and a league-leading 4 shutouts in his first full season, earning in the process a third-place finish in the NL Rookie of the Year voting.

Hershiser continued his maturation the following year, concluding the 1985 campaign with a record of 19-3 that gave him a league-leading .864 winning percentage. He also placed among the NL leaders in ERA (2.03), shutouts (5), and WHIP (1.031), en route to earning a third-place finish in

En route to leading the Dodgers to the world championship in 1988, Orel Hershiser established a new major-league record for most consecutive scoreless innings pitched

the Cy Young voting. Hershiser regressed somewhat in 1986, finishing just 14-14 with a 3.85 ERA, before rebounding in 1987 to earn his first All-Star selection and a fourth-place finish in the Cy Young balloting by ranking among the league leaders with a 3.06 ERA, 190 strikeouts, and 10 complete games, topping the circuit with 264⅔ innings pitched, and compiling a record of 16-16 for a Dodger team that finished just 73-89.

Everything truly came together for Hershiser the following season, though, when he emerged as baseball's best pitcher. After having his spring training delayed by an emergency appendectomy, Hershiser nevertheless performed extremely well through the first four-and-a-half months of the campaign, going 16-7 with a sub-3.00 ERA. However, the 6'3", 195-pound right-hander proved to be practically unbeatable from that point on, beginning on August 19 an extraordinary two-month run during which he made 14 starts and one relief appearance, allowing a total of only 11 runs (9 earned) in 124⅔ innings of work, while compiling an ERA of 0.65, recording 89 strikeouts, throwing 11 complete games, and tossing 8 shutouts. Along the way, Hershiser kept the opposition off the scoreboard for 59⅓ consecutive innings at one point, breaking in the process the previous major-league mark of 5⅔ straight scoreless frames set by Don Drysdale twenty years earlier. Hershiser's amazing streak enabled him to conclude the campaign with a record of 23-8, an ERA 2.26, 178 strikeouts, a WHIP of 1.052, and a league-leading 8 shutouts, 15 complete games, and 267 innings pitched. He then punctuated his magnificent performance by going 3-0 with a composite ERA of 1.05 during the postseason, in leading the Dodgers to the world championship.

Although not quite as dominant in 1989, Hershiser continued to pitch extremely well, earning his third straight All-Star nomination and a fourth-place finish in the Cy Young voting by placing among the league leaders with a 2.31 ERA, 4 shutouts, 8 complete games, and 178 strikeouts, while also topping the circuit in innings pitched (256⅔) for the third straight time. However, due to poor run-support, he finished the season just 15-15.

Hershiser excelled on the mound even though he lacked overpowering stuff. Depending primarily on his intelligence, ability to change speeds, and excellent location, Hershiser explained his pitching repertoire and approach to his craft in 1989, stating:

"I have a sinking fastball to either side of the plate, a cutter (which changes the direction of my fastball so it breaks instead of sinking) to either side of the plate, a curveball I throw at three speeds and three angles, a straight change—using the same arm speed and position as a fastball, but with a grip and a release that slows it dramatically, and changeups to different locations that I throw off my sinker, which look like batting practice fastballs. Different locations, different speeds, and slightly different arm angles on all those pitches give me a wide palette of choices."

The 1989 campaign ended up being Hershiser's last year as an elite pitcher. After undergoing shoulder reconstruction surgery to repair a torn rotator cuff early the following year, Hershiser missed much of the next two seasons, although he did return to the Dodgers in time to earn UPI Comeback Player of the Year honors in 1991 by compiling a record of 7-1 over the season's final four months. But, lacking the same velocity on his pitches he possessed prior to his injury, Hershiser failed to regain his earlier form in subsequent seasons, compiling an overall record of just 28-35 from 1992 to 1994. With the Dodgers displaying little interest in retaining his services when he became available as a free agent following the conclusion of the 1994 campaign, Hershiser signed a three-year deal with the Cleveland Indians on April 8, 1995.

Although Hershiser never again attained the same level of success he reached earlier in his career with the Dodgers, he remained an effective pitcher in Cleveland, helping the Indians advance to the 1995 World Series by winning all three of his playoff starts, after compiling a record of 16-6 and an ERA of 3.87 during the regular season. In fact, by defeating Seattle twice in the ALCS, Hershiser earned ALCS MVP honors, making him the first player to be named MVP of the LCS in both leagues.

Hershiser spent two more years in Cleveland, posting a record of 15-9 and an ERA of 4.24 for the Indians in 1996, before going 14-6 with a 4.47 ERA the following season. He then split the next two seasons between the San Francisco Giants and New York Mets, going a combined 24-22 during that time, before rejoining the Dodgers after he became a free agent again following the conclusion of the 1999 campaign. Hershiser's second tour of duty with the Dodgers proved to be quite brief, though, since the team released him on June 27, 2000, after he posted a record of just 1-5 with an embarrassingly high ERA of 13.14 in his 10 appearances with the club. Hershiser subsequently announced his retirement, ending his career with a record of 204-150, an ERA of 3.48, 2,014 strikeouts in 3,130⅓ total innings of work, 68 complete games, 25 shutouts, and a WHIP of 1.261. Over parts of 13 years in Los Angeles, he went 135-107, with a 3.12 ERA, 1,456 strikeouts in 2,180⅔ innings pitched, 65 complete games, 24 shutouts, and a WHIP of 1.212.

Following the conclusion of his playing career, Hershiser remained with the Dodgers briefly as a player-personnel consultant, before accepting a broadcasting position with ESPN and ABC as an analyst for the network's coverage of the Little League World Series and Wednesday Night Baseball. After two years in that post, he joined the Texas Rangers organization, initially as a special assistant to General Manager John Hart, before spending the next four years serving as the Rangers pitching coach. After being assigned the position of Executive Director of the Rangers following the conclusion of the 2005 campaign, Hershiser elected to return to the broadcast booth a few months later, leaving the Rangers to rejoin ESPN as an analyst for Baseball Tonight, Sunday Night Baseball, and the Little League World Series. Hershiser remained with ESPN until 2014, when he accepted a position as an analyst for Dodger telecasts with the team's new regional sports network, SportsNet LA.

# Dodger Career Highlights:

**Best Season**: Even though Hershiser performed brilliantly in 1985, earning a third-place finish in the Cy Young balloting by compiling a record of 19-3 and career-best marks in ERA (2.03) and WHIP (1.031), there can be no doubting that he had his finest overall season in 1988. In addition to leading the league with 23 wins, 8 shutouts, 15 complete games, and 267 innings pitched, he finished third in ERA (2.26) and fourth in WHIP (1.052). Furthermore, Hershiser's record-setting streak of 59⅓ consecutive scoreless innings provided the impetus for the Dodgers to win the world championship. Hershiser's string of scoreless frames, which broke the mark of 58⅔ innings previously set by former Dodger Don Drysdale in 1968, began on August 30, when he worked 4 scoreless frames at the end of a 4-2 victory over Montreal, and ended in his final start of the regular season, when he threw 10 shutout innings during a game the Dodgers eventually lost to San Diego in 16 innings. Hershiser ended up becoming the only player ever to receive the Cy Young Award, the Championship Series MVP Award, and the World Series MVP Award in the same season. He also later received the additional honors of being named *The Sporting News* Pitcher of the Year and *Sports Illustrated* magazine's Sportsman of the Year.

**Memorable Moments/Greatest Performances:** In addition to his record-setting performance in 1988, Hershiser went on another exceptional run four years earlier, when he kept the opposition off the scoreboard for 34⅓ consecutive innings from June 29, 1984 to July 24, 1984. Highlights of the streak, which featured three straight shutouts, included back-to-back two-hit shutouts—one, an 8-0 blanking of the Cubs on July 14, and the other, a 10-0 whitewashing of the Cardinals five days later. And, after Hershiser's streak ended with a 4-2 loss to Atlanta on July 24, he tossed another two-hit shutout in his very next start, defeating Cincinnati by a score of 1-0 on July 29.

Hershiser hurled another gem on April 21, 1885, when he shut out the San Diego Padres by a score of 2-0, surrendering just 2 hits and 2 walks, while recording 8 strikeouts during the contest.

Hershiser threw the first of his two career one-hitters just five days later, allowing just a walk and a fourth-inning single to Tony Gwynn during another 2-0 victory over the Padres.

Hershiser tossed his second one-hitter later in the year, on July 23, 1985, when he surrendered only a leadoff single to Jason Thompson in the top of the second inning, in defeating the Pirates by a score of 6-0. Hershiser also walked 6 batters and struck out 7 during the contest.

Before beginning his record-setting streak later in the year, Hershiser helped the Dodgers even their record at 1-1 on April 5, 1988 by allowing just 3 hits and 2 walks during a 5-0 shutout of the Giants.

Hershiser recorded his second shutout of the 1988 season on June 29, when he blanked the Astros by a score of 2-0, allowing just a pair of singles and a walk during the contest.

Hershiser turned in his finest performance of the ensuing campaign on May 14, 1989, when he tossed a two-hit shutout against Philadelphia, surrendering just a single, double, and 4 walks during the 9-0 victory.

However, Hershiser's amazing streak during the final two months of the 1988 season will always be viewed as his most notable achievement. One of his finest efforts during the string took place on September 5, when he allowed just 4 hits, 1 walk, and struck out 8, in defeating Atlanta by a score of 3-0. He tossed another four-hitter exactly two weeks later, on September 19, when he defeated Houston by a score of 1-0. And, even though Hershiser failed to earn a decision against San Diego on September 28, he concluded his extraordinary run by tossing 10 shutout innings in a game the Dodgers eventually lost by a score of 2-1 in 16 innings.

Continuing his exceptional work in the postseason, Hershiser won his only decision, earned a save, and compiled an ERA of 1.09 against New York in the NLCS, posting his lone victory in the decisive seventh contest, when he defeated the Mets by a score of 6-0. Hershiser then led the Dodgers to the world championship by tossing two complete-game wins over the Oakland A's, defeating them by scores of 6-0 and 5-2. He also collected 3 hits during his Game Two victory, while holding the powerful A's to only 3 safeties. Following Hershiser's Series-clinching win in Game Five, Oakland slugger Jose Canseco marveled, "I couldn't figure out why I was missing his pitches in Game Two. Then I looked at the videos and I saw how much the ball was moving. In Game Five, I got a dose of his curveball, which is in Bert Blyleven's class. Great stuff, great pitcher."

## Notable Achievements:

- Won 23 games in 1988.
- Won 19 games in 1985.
- Posted winning percentage in excess of .700 three times, topping the .800-mark once.
- Compiled ERA below 3.00 four times, posting mark under 2.50 on three occasions.
- Threw more than 200 innings seven times, tossing more than 250 innings three times.
- Led NL pitchers in: wins once, winning percentage once, shutouts twice, complete games once, innings pitched three times, assists twice, and putouts three times.
- Ranks among Dodgers career leaders in: wins (10th), strikeouts (seventh), shutouts (ninth), and games started (ninth).
- Holds major-league record for most consecutive scoreless innings pitched (59⅓ in 1988).
- Four-time NL Pitcher of the Month.
- 1988 Gold Glove winner.
- 1993 Silver Slugger winner.
- 1988 NL Cy Young Award winner.
- Finished in top five in NL Cy Young voting three other times.
- Finished sixth in 1988 NL MVP voting.
- 1988 *Sporting News* Major League Player of the Year.
- 1988 *Sporting News* NL Pitcher of the Year.
- 1988 NLCS MVP.
- 1988 World Series MVP.
- 1988 *Sporting News* All-Star selection.
- Three-time NL All-Star (1987, 1988 & 1989).
- 1988 NL champion.
- 1988 world champion.

# 19

# MATT KEMP

One of baseball's best all-around players his first several years with the Dodgers, Matt Kemp spent parts of nine seasons in Los Angeles, excelling in every facet of the game before being slowed by injuries. En route to earning two Silver Sluggers, two Gold Gloves, a pair of All-Star selections, and a pair of top-10 finishes in the NL MVP voting, Kemp surpassed 25 home runs four times and 30 stolen bases on three occasions, falling one homer short in 2011 of becoming the first player in franchise history to reach the 40-mark in both categories in the same season. The right-handed hitting Kemp also knocked in more than 100 runs twice, scored more than 100 runs once, and compiled a batting average in excess of .300 three times, while simultaneously doing an outstanding job of patrolling centerfield at Chavez Ravine. Unfortunately, Kemp's days as a truly elite player ended after he suffered a series of debilitating injuries from 2012 to 2013, prompting the Dodgers to eventually part ways with him prior to the start of the 2015 campaign.

Born in Midwest City, Oklahoma on September 23, 1984, Matthew Ryan Kemp attended Midwest City High School, where he starred in baseball and basketball, earning All-City honors in the latter sport by averaging 20 points a game as a senior. After being selected by the Dodgers in the sixth round of the 2003 amateur draft, the eighteen-year-old Kemp began his professional career with the Gulf Coast Dodgers that summer, before splitting the next two seasons between the Columbus Catfish and the Vero Beach Dodgers. Gradually improving his power numbers at each minor-league stop, Kemp earned a spot on the Florida State League All-Star team in 2005 by setting Vero Beach franchise records for most home runs (27) and highest slugging percentage (.569).

Promoted to the Dodgers in late May 2006 after getting off to a fast start at double-A Jacksonville, Kemp struggled over the course of the next six weeks, prompting the Dodgers to reassign him to triple-A Las Vegas. But, before being sent down to the minors, the 6'4", 225-pound rookie received the following rave review from columnist Tom Verducci in the July 3, 2006 edition of *Sports Illustrated*:

> *"The guy [Kemp] has the all-around game of Joe DiMaggio, with the instant impact of Chipper Jones [according to Dodger Manager Grady Little], the size and athleticism of Dave Parker [say many scouts], and the talent of Manny Ramirez, but with a better glove [in the estimation of teammate Sandy Alomar Jr.]."*

Returning to Los Angeles when rosters expanded in September, Kemp ended up hitting 7 homers, driving in 23 runs, scoring 30 times, and batting .253, in his first 52 games and 154 official at-bats at the major-league level. Splitting the following year between Las Vegas and Los Angeles, Kemp had an outstanding sophomore campaign, compiling a .342 batting average, hitting 10 homers, knocking in 42 runs, and scoring 47 times in his 98 games with the Dodgers.

After spending most of the previous season in right field, Kemp claimed the Dodgers' starting centerfield job in 2008, displaying his strong throwing arm by leading all NL outfielders with 16 assists. He also had a solid year at the plate, concluding his first full season with 18 home runs, 76 RBIs, 93 runs scored, 35 stolen bases, and a .290 batting average. Improving upon those numbers in 2009, Kemp earned his first Silver Slugger and a 10th-place finish in the NL MVP voting by hitting 26 homers, driving in 101 runs, scoring 97 times, stealing 34 bases, and batting .297. He also did an excellent job in centerfield, finishing third among players at his position in putouts, while placing second among all league outfielders with 14 assists, en route to earning his first Gold Glove. However, Kemp subsequently suffered through a subpar 2010 campaign during which he batted just .249 and struck out 170 times, although he still managed to hit 28 homers and knock in 89 runs.

Bouncing back in a big way from his disappointing 2010 season, Kemp performed magnificently in 2011, earning his first All-Star selection and a runner-up finish to Ryan Braun in the NL MVP voting by topping the senior circuit with 39 home runs, 126 RBIs, 115 runs scored, and 353 total bases, while also placing among the league leaders with a

Matt Kemp came within one home run of joining
the exclusive 40-40 club in 2011

Courtesy of Keith Allison

.324 batting average, 195 hits, 40 stolen bases, a .399 on-base percentage, and a .586 slugging percentage. Kemp's brilliant performance left many observers feeling that he had established himself as the finest all-around player in the game. In explaining his decision to place Kemp third in the NL batting order for the 2011 All-Star Game, Giants' manager Bruce Bochy said, "He's a guy with speed, power; a guy that can beat you with a base hit or a long ball. He's what you call a complete player—tremendous defender, but more so, in the 3-hole, he can do so many things for you. He's so dangerous."

After being rewarded by the Dodgers for his superb play with a franchise record eight-year, $160 million contract extension during the off-season, Kemp continued to excel during the early stages of the 2012 campaign, finishing the month of April with 12 home runs, 25 RBIs, and a .417 batting average. But a strained hamstring he suffered in early May subsequently proved to be the first in a series of injuries that ended up derailing his season. After seeing his streak of 399 consecutive games played come to an end with a brief stint on the disabled list, Kemp re-injured his hamstring while running the bases just two days after he returned to the team, putting him on the DL once again. Kemp suffered a far more serious injury, though, later in the year, when he crashed into the outfield wall at

Coors Field during an August 28 contest against the Colorado Rockies, damaging both his knee and his shoulder. Forced to undergo surgery to repair a torn labrum and some minor damage to his rotator cuff at season's end, Kemp finished the year with 23 home runs, 69 RBIs, and a .303 batting average, in only 106 games.

Kemp's injury woes continued in 2013, when, after missing the first two weeks of June with another pulled hamstring, he found himself back on the disabled list on July 8 after experiencing pain in his surgically repaired shoulder. Kemp returned to action on July 21 but seriously injured his ankle in a play at home plate in his first game back, all but ending his season. Appearing in a total of only 73 games, Kemp concluded the 2013 campaign with just 6 home runs, 33 RBIs, and a .270 batting average. Kemp's defense suffered as well whenever he found himself able to take the field, with him becoming something of a liability in centerfield.

Criticized by the local fans and media for his inability to reach the lofty standards he set for himself the previous few seasons, Kemp accepted his plight, stating, "You have to do that every single year. You've got to be the exact same or even better. Fans, they want to see results. I've been a fan before. I get it. But I see the bigger picture, too. I would never say an athlete sucks after they've been good, because you don't know what they're going through. They might be going through something that they can't shake."

Kemp had a far more difficult time accepting the anguish that he had to go through in October of 2013 when the Dodgers made their first postseason appearance in four years. Having undergone two separate medical procedures in rapid succession, one to clean up the left shoulder he damaged in 2012, and the other a more serious micro fracture surgery on his left ankle, Kemp found himself unable to walk at all. Looking back at his gloomy situation, Kemp recalled, "I think my worst time was having shoulder surgery one week, then the next having ankle surgery. That's when I was like, 'Dang, this is crazy.' I was in a boot, but I couldn't use crutches because I had a sling on. So I was watching the playoff games from a scooter. It was bad."

Returning to action in 2014, Kemp posted solid, if unspectacular, numbers, finishing the campaign with 25 home runs, 89 RBIs, 77 runs scored, and a .287 batting average. Nevertheless, he drew frequent criticism for his diminished defensive skills, a situation he addressed when he stated:

"I don't think people understand what micro fracture surgery is. It's pretty serious. A lot of basketball players get it in their knees, and, if they do bounce back, it takes a while. I was trying to deal with that, and trying to figure out how to be myself with not a bum ankle, but one that was not as explosive. They started talking about my defense. I just couldn't run the way I wanted to run. It's not because I became a terrible defensive player. I just couldn't do some of the things I'm used to doing."

Still, with Kemp displaying glimpses of his old form during the latter stages of the campaign by hitting 19 homers, driving in 54 runs, and batting .309 over the season's final 64 games, he increased his market value enough to draw interest from other teams during the subsequent offseason. With the Dodgers finding a willing trade partner in the San Diego Padres, the two teams worked out a five-player deal on December 18, 2014 that sent Kemp and Tim Federowicz to San Diego for Zach Eflin, Yasmani Grandal, and Joe Wieland. Kemp left Los Angeles with career totals of 182 home runs, 648 RBIs, 650 runs scored, 1,188 hits, 215 doubles, 33 triples, and 170 stolen bases, a .292 batting average, a .349 on-base percentage, and a .495 slugging percentage.

Although Kemp has failed to reestablish himself as one of the game's finest all-around players since leaving the Dodgers, he has performed extremely well over the course of the past two seasons, hitting 23 homers, knocking in 100 runs, and batting .265 in 2015, before hitting 35 home runs, driving in 108 runs, scoring 89 times, and batting .268 while splitting the 2016 campaign between the Padres and Atlanta Braves, who acquired him just prior to the trade deadline. Kemp will enter the 2017 season with career totals of 240 home runs, 856 RBIs, 819 runs scored, 1,513 hits, 285 doubles, 36 triples, and 183 stolen bases, a lifetime batting average of .286, an on-base percentage of .340, and a slugging percentage of .490.

As for why the Dodgers elected to trade him, Kemp speculates, "Maybe they wanted to get younger. They have a younger outfield now. [Yasiel] Puig and Joc [Pederson]; There's a lot of outfielders over there. But I think they just had different plans, and I wasn't in those plans."

## Dodger Career Highlights:

**Best Season:** Kemp unquestionably had his best year for the Dodgers in 2011, when he established career-high marks in virtually every offensive category, placing among the NL leaders in 10 different categories as well. In addition to topping the senior circuit with 39 home runs, 126 RBIs, 115 runs scored, and 353 total bases, Kemp finished third in the league with a .324 batting average, placed second in hits (195), stolen bases (40), slugging percentage (.586), and OPS (.986), and finished fourth in on-base percentage (.399).

**Memorable Moments/Greatest Performances:** Kemp got off to a fast start after joining the Dodgers in late May of 2006, homering in his second Dodger Stadium at-bat during a 7-2 victory over the Phillies on June 1. He followed that up by hitting home runs in each of the next two games as well, before reaching the seats twice during a 6-5 win over Colorado on June 11.

Kemp had another big day against Colorado on April 19, 2009, going 3-for-5, with a pair of homers, a double, 5 RBIs, and 3 runs scored, during a 14-2 rout of the Rockies.

Kemp delivered the first walk-off hit of his career on June 16, 2009, when he drove home Orlando Hudson with an RBI single in the 10th inning, to give the Dodgers a 5-4 win over the Oakland Athletics. Kemp finished the game with 3 hits.

Kemp came up big for the Dodgers again a little over one month later, on July 19, 2009, when his solo homer in the bottom of the eighth inning provided the winning margin in a 4-3 victory over the Houston Astros.

Just two days after leading the Dodgers to a 9-1 win over Atlanta by knocking in 5 runs with a homer and a pair of singles, Kemp paced them to a lopsided 17-4 victory over Milwaukee on August 4, 2009 by going 4-for-5, with a homer, double, 5 RBIs, and 3 runs scored.

Kemp began the 2010 campaign in fine fashion, hitting 7 home runs in the month of April, including a four-game stretch from April 13-16 during which he reached the seats four times.

Although the Dodgers lost their August 2, 2010 matchup with the Giants by a score of 10-5, Kemp had the only 5-for-5 day of his career, collecting a homer, double, 3 singles, and 3 RBIs during the contest.

Kemp finished the 2010 season in very much the same way he began it, homering in each of the final five games, becoming in the process the first major league player to accomplish that feat.

Kemp led the Dodgers to an 11-8, 11-inning victory over Cincinnati on June 4, 2011 by homering twice and driving in a career-high 6 runs.

Kemp delivered the game's big blow in the top of the eighth inning, when he tied the score at 7-7 with a grand slam home run off Reds reliever Logan Ondrusek.

Kemp contributed to a lopsided 10-0 victory over the Giants on July 28, 2012 by going 4-for-5, with a homer, 2 doubles, 4 RBIs, and 3 runs scored.

Kemp earned NL Player of the Week honors for the fifth time in his career the last week of July 2014 by homering five times in six games. He also finished the season strong, earning NL Player of the Month honors for September by hitting 9 homers, driving in 25 runs, and batting .322.

Displaying an ability to perform well under pressure during his time in Los Angeles, Kemp hit four walk-off homers while playing for the Dodgers, delivering his first such blow on June 1, 2010, when he drove home the game's only run with a 10th-inning blast against Arizona reliever J.C. Gutierrez. Kemp provided further heroics in April of 2011, giving the Dodgers a 2-1 victory over St. Louis on the 17th of the month by hitting a two-run homer off Cardinals reliever Ryan Franklin in the bottom of the ninth, before going deep against Atlanta reliever Cristhian Martinez with one man aboard in the bottom of the 12th inning just four days later, to give the Dodgers a 5-3 win over the Braves. Kemp hit his final walk-off homer as a member of the Dodgers on April 28, 2012, when his solo blast off Washington reliever Tom Gorzelanny in the bottom of the 10th gave the Dodgers a 4-3 win over the Nationals.

## Notable Achievements:

- Hit more than 20 home runs five times, topping 30 homers once (39 in 2011).
- Knocked in more than 100 runs twice, surpassing 120 RBIs once (126 in 2011).
- Scored more than 100 runs once (115 in 2011).
- Batted over .300 three times, topping the .320-mark twice.
- Surpassed 30 doubles three times.
- Stole more than 30 bases three times, reaching the 40-mark once (40 in 2011).
- Posted slugging percentage in excess of .500 four times.
- Surpassed 30 home runs and 30 stolen bases in same season once (2011).

- Led NL in: home runs once, RBIs once, runs scored once, total bases once, and games played once.
- Finished second in NL in: hits once, slugging percentage once, and OPS once.
- Led NL outfielders in assists once and double plays once.
- Led NL center-fielders in assists three times and double plays three times.
- Ranks eighth in Dodgers history with 182 career home runs.
- Two-time NL Player of the Month.
- Two-time Silver Slugger winner (2009 & 2011).
- Two-time Gold Glove winner (2009 & 2011).
- 2011 NL Hank Aaron Award winner.
- 2012 NL Wilson Defensive Player of the Year.
- Finished second in 2011 NL MVP voting.
- Two-time *Sporting News* All-Star selection (2009 & 2011).
- Two-time NL All-Star (2011 & 2012).

# 20

# RON CEY

The second member of the Dodgers' longstanding infield of the 1970s and early 1980s to make our list, Ron Cey spent much of his time in Los Angeles being overshadowed by fellow National League third basemen Mike Schmidt and Pete Rose. Nevertheless, the hard-hitting Cey proved to be one of the senior circuit's most productive hitters and adept fielders at the hot corner over the course of his 10 full seasons with the Dodgers, helping to lead them to four pennants and one world championship. In addition to hitting more than 20 home runs seven times as a member of the team, Cey surpassed 100 RBIs twice, en route to earning six All-Star selections and one top-10 finish in the league MVP voting. Meanwhile, Cey annually ranked among the league's top third basemen in most defensive categories, leading all NL third sackers in putouts once, assists once, double plays once, and fielding percentage twice over the course of his career, which continued with a successful four-year stint in Chicago after he left Los Angeles following the conclusion of the 1982 campaign.

Born in Tacoma, Washington on February 15, 1948, Ronald Charles Cey attended local Mount Tacoma High School, where he starred in multiple sports, earning a total of nine varsity letters. Following his graduation in 1966, Cey enrolled at Washington State University, where he excelled on the diamond for two seasons, before being selected by the Dodgers in the third round of the 1968 amateur draft. Cey spent most of the next five years in the minor leagues, reaching the Dodgers' triple-A affiliate in Spokane by 1971. While at Spokane, the right-handed hitting third baseman played alongside several other Dodger prospects that would eventually join him in Los Angeles, including Davey Lopes, Joe Ferguson, Tom Paciorek, Von Joshua, and Bobby Valentine. Cey also played under future

Dodger manager Tommy Lasorda, who nicknamed the 5'10", 185-pound infielder "The Penguin" for his slow, waddling running gait.

After making brief appearances with the Dodgers in both 1971 and 1972, Cey arrived in Los Angeles to stay in 1973. Replacing Steve Garvey, who moved over to play first base, as the team's regular third baseman, Cey appeared in 152 games, hitting 15 home runs, driving in 80 runs, scoring 60 times, batting .245, and leading all NL third sackers with 328 assists and 39 double plays. Cey increased his offensive output the following year, hitting 18 homers, knocking in 97 runs, scoring 88 times, and batting .262, while also compiling a career-high 365 assists and 155 putouts at the hot corner for the National League champions. Cey's strong all-around play earned him All-Star honors for the first of six straight times. Although the Dodgers failed to capture the pennant in either of the next two seasons, Cey continued to post solid offensive numbers, concluding the 1975 campaign with 25 homers, 101 RBIs, and a .283 batting average, before hitting 23 homers, knocking in 80 runs, and batting .277 the following year.

With Tommy Lasorda replacing longtime Dodgers manager Walter Alston as the team's skipper prior to the start of the 1977 season, Cey assumed the cleanup spot in the Los Angeles batting order for the first time. Thriving in his new role, the twenty-nine-year-old third baseman got off to a tremendous start, earning NL Player of the Month honors in April by batting .425, hitting 9 homers, and driving in a major-league record 29 runs during the season's first month. Although Cey failed to maintain the same torrid pace the rest of the season, he still managed to establish career-high marks in home runs (30) and RBIs (110), joining Steve Garvey, Reggie Smith, and Dusty Baker as a member of the first quartet of teammates to reach the 30-homer plateau in the same season. And, even though Cey concluded the campaign with a batting average of just .241, his 93 bases on balls enabled him to compile a very respectable .347 on-base percentage. With the Dodgers capturing the NL West title, Cey's strong performance earned him an eighth-place finish in the league MVP voting. He then homered once, drove in 4 runs, and batted .308 against Philadelphia in the NLCS, in helping the Dodgers dispatch of the Eastern Division champions in four games. Although Cey subsequently batted just .190 against the Yankees in the World Series, he homered once and knocked in 3 runs during the six-game loss to New York.

The Dodgers repeated as National League champs in 1978, with Cey once again making major contributions to the success of the team by

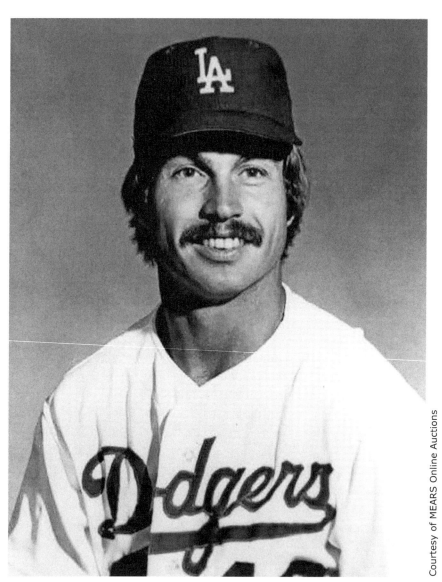

Ron Cey hit more than 20 home runs
seven times for the Dodgers

Courtesy of MEARS Online Auctions

hitting 23 homers, knocking in 84 runs, scoring 84 times, batting .270, and drawing 96 bases on balls. He also hit well during the postseason, homering once, knocking in 3 runs, and batting .313 against the Phillies in the NLCS, before reaching the seats once, driving in 4 runs, and batting .286 against the Yankees in the World Series.

Cey continued to perform well for the Dodgers the next two seasons, hitting 28 home runs in both 1979 and 1980, while knocking in a total of 158 runs and posting batting averages of .281 and .254, respectively. Despite missing three weeks of the strike-shortened 1981 campaign after being struck in the left forearm by a pitch thrown by San Francisco's Tom Griffin, Cey again posted solid numbers, finishing the year with 13 homers, 50 RBIs, and a career-high .288 batting average. He then helped lead the Dodgers to their first world championship in 16 years by knocking in 9 runs and batting .316 during the postseason.

Cey remained in Los Angeles one more year, hitting 24 homers, driving in 79 runs, and batting .254 in 1982, before being traded by the Dodgers to the Chicago Cubs for a pair of minor leaguers at season's end. Over parts of 12 seasons in Los Angeles, Cey hit 228 homers, knocked in 842 runs, scored 715 times, amassed 1,378 hits, 223 doubles, and 18 triples, batted .264, compiled a .359 on-base percentage, and posted a .445 slugging percentage.

Cey spent the next four years in Chicago, averaging 24 homers and 83 RBIs from 1983 to 1985, and helping the Cubs capture the NL East title in 1984 by hitting 25 homers and driving in 97 runs. However, after injuries and advancing age limited him to only 97 games in 1986, Cey found himself headed to Oakland when Chicago traded him to the A's at season's end. After Cey batted just .221 and hit only 4 home runs in his first 45 games with the A's, Oakland elected to release him midway through the 1987 campaign, bringing to an end the career of the thirty-nine-year-old third baseman. Cey subsequently announced his retirement, concluding his seventeen-year big-league career with 316 home runs, 1,139 RBIs, 977 runs scored, 1,868 hits, 328 doubles, 21 triples, a .261 batting average, a .354 on-base percentage, and a .445 slugging percentage. In all, he topped the 20-homer mark 10 times and knocked in at least 90 runs on five separate occasions. Meanwhile, even though Cey lacked superior running speed, his quickness and sure hands enabled him to place among the top three players at his position in putouts seven times and assists 10 times.

Following his retirement, Cey returned to the Dodger organization, where he continues to serve the team as a community relations representative.

## Dodger Career Highlights:

**Best Season:** En route to establishing career-high marks in home runs (30) and RBIs (110) in 1977, Cey performed brilliantly during the month of April. However, he proved to be far more consistent in both 1975 and 1979, compiling better overall numbers in each of those years. Earning the second of his six consecutive All-Star selections in the first of those campaigns, Cey hit 25 homers, knocked in 101 runs, scored 72 times, batted .283, compiled an on-base percentage of .372, and posted a slugging percentage of .473, giving him an OPS of .845. Four years later, Cey hit 28 homers, drove in 81 runs, scored 77 times, batted .281, compiled a career-high .389 on-base percentage, and posted a .499 slugging percentage, giving him an OPS of .888 that represented his highest mark as a member of the Dodgers. It's an extremely close call, but the fact that Cey started 10 more games at third base in 1975 than he did in 1979 (158 to 148) allowed him to have a slightly greater impact on the team, which finished the regular season with 9 more wins than it did four years later. That being the case, 1975 would have to be considered Cey's finest all-around season.

**Memorable Moments/Greatest Performances:** Cey had the first big day of his career on May 13, 1973, when he went 4-for-5, with 5 RBIs and 1 run scored, during a lopsided 15-3 victory over the Giants.

Just three days later, on May 16, 1973, Cey helped lead the Dodgers to an 8-6 win over Cincinnati in 11 innings by going 4-for-6, with a homer, 2 doubles, and 4 RBIs.

Cey led the Dodgers to a 10-0 rout of the Chicago Cubs on June 1, 1974 by hitting a pair of homers, driving in 7 runs, and scoring 3 times.

Cey had another huge day at the plate on July 31, 1974, when he helped pace the Dodgers to a 15-4 win over the San Diego Padres by hitting 2 homers, scoring 3 times, and collecting a career-high 8 RBIs.

Cey proved to be the difference in a 10-8 victory over the Phillies on May 7, 1976, going 4-for-5, with a homer, 5 RBIs, and 2 runs scored during the contest.

Some three weeks later, on May 30, 1976, Cey had the first 5-for-5 day of his career, collecting 3 doubles and a pair of singles, driving in 2 runs, and scoring twice during a 6-5 win over the Reds.

Cey turned in a number of exceptional performances during his fabulous month of April, 1977, performing particularly well over a five-day stretch that lasted from the 23rd to the 27th. Leading the Dodgers to five consecutive wins over the Braves and Padres, Cey went a combined 11-for-16, with 6 walks, 5 home runs, 14 RBIs, and 7 runs scored. He had his two biggest games against Atlanta on the 24th and San Diego on the 25th, hitting a homer, driving in 5 runs, and scoring twice during a 16-6 win over the Braves, before homering twice, knocking in 3 runs, and scoring twice during a 7-3 victory over the Padres.

Later that year, Cey had a huge day against San Francisco, leading the Dodgers to a 10-7 win over the Giants on July 3, 1977 by going 5-for-5, with a pair of doubles, 4 RBIs, and 2 runs scored.

Cey defeated Montreal almost single-handedly on May 12, 1981, going 3-for-4, with 2 homers and 4 RBIs during a 5-0 win over the Expos.

Cey went on to have a memorable 1981 World Series, eventually sharing Series MVP honors with teammates Pedro Guerrero and Steve Yeager after homering once, driving in 6 runs, and batting .350 against New York pitching. After going just 1-for-8 in back-to-back losses to the Yankees in the first two contests, Cey sparked a Dodger comeback by hitting a three-run homer off Dave Righetti in the bottom of the first inning of Game Three. The Dodgers ended up winning that contest by a score of 5-4, before emerging victorious in the next three games as well. Perhaps the most indelible image of Cey in that year's fall classic, though, came out of Game Five, when he suffered a beaning at the hands of Hall of Fame flamethrower Goose Gossage. Forced to leave the game prematurely, Cey later recalled, "I remember falling in slow motion. I wasn't bleeding, and there wasn't anything that happened, other than me having a concussion; and, under today's rules and regulations, I would've been ruled out for the rest of the Series. But they were different at that point in time, and the decision was left up to me after I was cleared…I was given the okay to go back to New York and ready to go." Cey ended up playing in the Series finale, going 2-for-3, with an RBI and a run scored, in helping the Dodgers defeat the Yankees by a score of 9-2.

## Notable Achievements:

- Hit more than 20 home runs seven times, topping 30 homers once (30 in 1977).
- Knocked in more than 100 runs twice.
- Topped 30 doubles once (32 in 1978).
- Led NL third basemen in: putouts once, assists once, double plays turned once, and fielding percentage once.
- Ranks among Dodgers career leaders in: home runs (fifth), RBIs (10th), bases on balls (fifth), and extra-base hits (10th).
- April, 1977 NL Player of the Month.
- 1981 World Series co-MVP.
- 1982 Lou Gehrig Memorial Award winner.
- Six-time NL All-Star (1974, 1975, 1976, 1977, 1978 & 1979).
- Four-time NL champion (1974, 1977, 1978 & 1981).
- 1981 world champion.

# 21

# PEDRO GUERRERO

Once proclaimed by noted baseball historian Bill James to be "the best hitter God had made in a long time," Pedro Guerrero proved to be one of the finest batsmen Dodger fans have seen since the team moved to Los Angeles nearly sixty years ago. Hitting for both power and average, the right-handed swinging Guerrero compiled 171 home runs and a .309 batting average over parts of 11 seasons with the Dodgers, topping 30 homers three times and 100 RBIs twice, while also surpassing the .300-mark in batting on six occasions. Seeing extensive playing time at first base, third base, and all three outfield positions during his time in L.A., Guerrero spent six-plus seasons serving as a member of the Dodgers' everyday starting lineup, establishing himself during that time as one of the senior circuit's most feared sluggers. A four-time NL All-Star as a member of the team, Guerrero also earned three top-five finishes in the league MVP voting while wearing Dodger Blue, placing third in the balloting on two separate occasions. In all, Guerrero's potent bat helped the Dodgers capture three division titles, one pennant, and one world championship.

Born in San Pedro de Macoris, a dense provincial city situated on the east coast of the Dominican Republic, on June 29, 1956, Pedro Guerrero came from humble beginnings. After leaving school as a young teenager to help support his family by working in the local sugar cane fields, Guerrero spent much of his youth earning a few dollars a week cutting cane for the island's rum industry. But, while Guerrero's hard work earned him little financial reward, it allowed him to gradually develop into a powerful young man capable of hitting a baseball as far as anyone he competed against in the local youth leagues. Guerrero's reputation as a hard-hitting third baseman elicited interest from Cleveland's foremost Latin scout, Reggie Otero, who decided to pay the sixteen-year-old slugger a visit. Describing his first impression of the Dominican prodigy, Otero later noted, "He was five-feet-eleven, 157 pounds. I looked at the width of his shoulders, back and front, and knew that he would get heavier and stronger. He had lived off of rice and beans."

After being signed to a contract by Otero, Guerrero began his professional career in Cleveland's farm system in 1973. However, the Indians traded him to the Dodgers one year later for minor-league left-hander Bruce Ellingsen. Guerrero spent most of the next six seasons in the minors, making brief appearances with the parent club towards the tail end of both the 1978 and 1979 campaigns. During that time, though, he emerged as one of the organization's top prospects, known equally for his hitting prowess and defensive versatility. In fact, only a fractured ankle Guerrero suffered while playing for triple-A Albuquerque in 1977 likely prevented him from being called up to the majors that year. Reflecting back on his temporary setback during a 1982 interview with *Sports Illustrated*, Guerrero recalled, "Before, I wasn't interested in being a good base runner or working on my defense. All I worried about was my hitting. After I got hurt, I had a lot of time to think. There was a lot more money in baseball than when I signed, and I was thinking that, if I played better, I could make good money someday."

After hitting 2 homers, driving in 10 runs, and posting a composite batting average of .286 in 70 total at-bats with the Dodgers in 1978 and 1979, Guerrero arrived in Los Angeles to stay in 1980. Spending most of his time in the outfield and pinch-hitting, the twenty-four-year-old Guerrero, who had grown into a powerfully-built 195-pounder, appeared in a total of 75 games, batting .322, hitting 7 homers, and knocking in 31 runs, in just under 200 plate appearances. Earning a spot in the Dodgers' starting lineup the following year while garnering a significant amount of playing time at both third base and right field, Guerrero earned his first All-Star selection by hitting 12 homers, driving in 48 runs, and batting an even .300 over the course of the strike-shortened campaign. He then helped the Dodgers defeat the Yankees in the World Series by homering twice, driving in 7 runs, and batting .333, en route to earning a share of Series MVP honors, along with teammates Ron Cey and Steve Yeager.

Guerrero followed that up with an outstanding 1982 campaign in which he placed among the NL leaders in six different offensive categories, including home runs (32), RBIs (100), and batting average (.304), earning in the process a third-place finish in the league MVP voting and his lone Silver Slugger. Guerrero continued to perform extremely well after he replaced the departed Ron Cey at third base full time in 1983, earning his second All-Star nomination and a fourth-place finish in the NL MVP balloting by hitting 32 homers, knocking in 103 runs, batting .298, and stealing a career-high 23 bases. However, he also led all NL third sackers with 30 errors, with his struggles in the field leaving him so frustrated that he occasionally let his anger get the better of him.

One particular loss of temper nearly cost Guerrero his life. After leading a charge to the mound against Houston pitcher Frank LaCorte, who Dodger players believed took dead aim at teammate Ken Landreaux's head during a game against the Astros, Guerrero stated during a postgame interview, "He's [LaCorte's] in trouble. I never forget anything like that." Answering Guerrero's challenge, LaCorte's teammate Nolan Ryan "let one slip" in an ensuing meeting between the two clubs, beaning the Dodger third baseman in the head with a fastball that cracked his batting helmet. After saying, "I thought I was dead," following the conclusion of the contest, Guerrero sent his helmet to the Astros clubhouse for Ryan to sign.

Although the Dodgers signed Guerrero to a then-franchise record five-year, $7 million contract prior to the start of the ensuing campaign, the slugger arrived at 1984 spring training feeling somewhat despondent over the free-agent departure of Dusty Baker, his closest friend on the team. Reporting to camp some 12 pounds overweight and appearing disinterested and lethargic at times, Guerrero had to endure rumors about his offseason partying and poor work ethic. However, after getting off to a terrible start during the regular season, Guerrero eventually righted himself following his shift from third base to the outfield in mid-June, concluding the campaign with 16 homers, 72 RBIs, 85 runs scored, and a .303 batting average, even though he spent much of the year battling through shoulder problems.

Returning to top form in 1985, Guerrero earned his third All-Star selection and a third-place finish in the NL MVP voting by hitting 33 homers, driving in 87 runs, scoring 99 times, finishing second in the league with a .320 batting average, and topping the senior circuit with a .422 on-base percentage and a .577 slugging percentage. Unfortunately, though, he ended up missing virtually all of the ensuing campaign after rupturing a tendon in his left knee during spring training. In addition to limiting Guerrero to only 31 games and 61 at-bats in 1986, the injury robbed him of much of his running speed, turning him into a plodder on the base paths and even more of a defensive liability. Nevertheless, Guerrero once again displayed his ability to overcome adversity in 1987, earning NL Comeback Player of the Year honors by hitting 27 homers, knocking in 89 runs, scoring 89 times, and establishing career-high marks in hits (184) and batting average (.338), finishing second in the senior circuit to Tony Gwynn in the last category.

Yet, in spite of the outstanding numbers he posted on offense, the Dodgers grew increasingly impatient with Guerrero, who gradually developed into a destabilizing force in the clubhouse, displaying a lack of prudence with his actions on and off the field, and openly criticizing teammate Mike Marshall for not playing through an injury, leading to a clubhouse altercation between the two men. Furthermore, Guerrero's earlier knee injury transformed him into a completely one-dimensional player, as *Los Angeles Times* columnist Scott Ostler suggested when he wrote during the early stages of the 1988 campaign, "When Guerrero isn't hitting home runs and doubles—which he hasn't been doing much of lately—he hurts you more ways than he helps you. Defense, for instance…The most you can say is that Guerrero sometimes makes the routine plays."

After Guerrero missed nearly two months of the 1988 season while recovering from yet another injury, the Dodgers finally decided to part ways with the enigmatic slugger, trading him to the St. Louis Cardinals for left-handed pitcher John Tudor on August 16. Guerrero left Los Angeles with career totals of 171 home runs, 585 RBIs, 561 runs scored, 1,113 hits, 169 doubles, and 24 triples, a .309 batting average, a .381 on-base percentage, and a .512 slugging percentage.

The outspoken and temperamental Guerrero did not leave Los Angeles quietly, making several disparaging remarks about the Dodger organization and his former teammates to the local media on his way out the door. Continuing to harbor feelings of resentment in the months that followed, Guerrero took offense when the Dodgers graciously offered him a 50% share of their World Series bonuses, later commenting, "What ticked me off is they gave John Tudor more than they gave me. I told them, 'If you want your money back, I'll give it back. I've got more than all you guys put together.'"

Guerrero ended up spending the remainder of his career in St. Louis, having his best year for the Cardinals in 1989, when he earned the last of his five All-Star selections and a third-place finish in the NL MVP voting by hitting 17 homers, driving in 117 runs, batting .311, and leading the league with 42 doubles. Plagued by injuries in subsequent seasons, Guerrero never again reached such heights, seeing his last action as a big leaguer in 1992, when he batted just .219 for St. Louis in a back-up role. Failing to come to terms on a free-agent deal with any other team at season's end, Guerrero ended his fifteen-year major-league career with 215 home runs, 898 RBIs, 730 runs scored, 1,618 hits, 267 doubles, 29 triples, a .300 batting average, a .370 on-base percentage, and a .480 slugging percentage.

Guerrero spent the next two years trying to make it back to the majors, playing for the Sioux Falls Canaries of the Northern League and the Charros de Jalisco of the Mexican League, before retiring from the game for good in 1995.

Following his playing days, Guerrero ran afoul of the law, being implicated as the "money-man" in a 1999 Drug Enforcement Administration investigation on a purchase of 15 kilograms of cocaine. But, while all the evidence pointed towards the guilt of Guerrero, who even confessed to the crime, the shrewdness of his attorney, top-shelf criminal defense lawyer Milton Hirsch, prevented him from going to prison. Arguing that his client's lack of intelligence made him incapable of fully understanding the implications of the alleged drug deal, Hirsch convinced the jury of Guerrero's innocence. Yet, in so doing, Hirsch robbed Guerrero of his pride and dignity, presenting to the jurors a humiliating portrait of the former major-leaguer, referencing his lack of education, low IQ, and inability to perform simple tasks such as writing a check or making a bed.

Almost a decade after the trial, Guerrero experienced a personal rebirth, proclaiming, "I feel like a new man. I know I did a lot of wrong things, and especially when I was playing...I let down a lot of people. Now, I'm a new man. I go to church, I'm reading the Bible, I pray every day. The last three years, I quit drinking. That was my big problem. Now, I'm working with kids in the Dominican. I tell them to stay away from drugs and drinking. I'm one hundred percent different."

After being out of baseball until 2011, Guerrero spent one year serving as a minor league hitting instructor, before being named manager of the Mexican League's Tijuana Tuernos in 2012. More recently, he has managed the Vallejo Admirals of the Pacific Association of Professional Base-

Courtesy of MEARS Online Auctions

Pedro Guerrero established himself as one of the National
League's most feared sluggers during his time in Los Angeles

ball Clubs and the Rieleros de Frontera in the Liga del Norte in the city of
Monclova in the Mexican minor leagues.

In discussing his failure to reach his full potential as a player, Guerrero
says, "I feel I did a good job in the time I played, but not as good as I was
supposed to if I lived the life I'm living now. I would have put up better
numbers and been a better person. I'm not a bad guy. I used to come to the
park with a hangover every day and I could still play like that. Can you
imagine if I had been one hundred percent sober all the time? It's too late
now to think about...."

# Dodger Career Highlights:

**Best Season:** Guerrero performed exceptionally well for the Dodgers in both 1982 and 1983, finishing those two campaigns with nearly identical numbers. After hitting 32 homers, driving in 100 runs, scoring 87 times, batting .304, collecting 175 hits, compiling an OPS of .914, and stealing 22 bases in 1982, en route to becoming the first Dodger player to top 30 home runs and 20 thefts in the same season, Guerrero homered 32 times, knocked in 103 runs, scored 87 times, batted .298, accumulated 174 hits, compiled an OPS of .904, and swiped 23 bags the following season. He had another big year in 1987, concluding the campaign with 27 homers, 89 RBIs, 89 runs scored, a .955 OPS, and career-high marks in batting average (.338) and hits (184). Nevertheless, Guerrero had his finest all-around season in 1985, when, in addition to batting .320 and driving in 87 runs, he established career highs in runs scored (99), home runs (33), on-base percentage (.422), slugging percentage (.577), and OPS (.999), leading the National League in each of the last three categories.

**Memorable Moments/Greatest Performances:** Guerrero had a hand in all 7 runs the Dodgers scored on August 18, 1982, when he led them to a 7-4 win over the Cubs by scoring twice and knocking in 5 runs with a pair of homers and a double.

Guerrero had another big day at the plate against Chicago on July 16, 1983, when he went 4-for-5, with 5 RBIs and one run scored during a 7-4 victory over the Cubs.

Guerrero had the only 5-for-5 day of his career on June 12, 1984, leading the Dodgers to an 8-7 win over the Giants by hitting safely in all five of his trips to the plate, while also knocking in one run and scoring three times. Guerrero topped off his memorable performance by driving in the game's decisive run with a solo homer off Greg Minton in the bottom of the eighth inning.

Guerrero set a Dodgers franchise record by hitting 15 home runs in June 1985, while also knocking in 26 runs and compiling a batting average of .344. He punctuated his fabulous month by giving the Dodgers a 4-3 victory over the Braves on June 30 by hitting a game-winning two-run homer off Atlanta's Bruce Sutter in the bottom of the eighth inning.

Guerrero continued his hot-hitting in the ensuing month, batting .460, compiling a .563 on-base percentage, and posting a .794 slugging percentage in July 1985. Particularly effective from July 23 to July 26, Guerrero led the Dodgers to four straight wins by reaching base safely in 14 consecutive plate appearances, establishing a new National League record in the process. During the streak, Guerrero went a combined 7-for-7, with a pair of homers, three doubles, two singles, six walks, and one hit-by-pitch.

Still, Guerrero will always be remembered most fondly by Dodger fans for his performance against the Yankees in the 1981 World Series. After struggling at the plate against Houston and Montreal in the National League playoffs, Guerrero continued to falter in the first two games of the fall classic, going a combined 0-for-7 against New York pitching. However, he subsequently helped the Dodgers sweep the next four contests by collecting 7 hits in 14 official trips to the plate, hitting 2 homers and driving in 7 runs along the way. After tying Game Five (which the Dodgers eventually won by a score of 2-1) at 1-1 with a home run off Ron Guidry in the bottom of the seventh inning, Guerrero helped lead the Dodgers to a lopsided 9-2 victory in the Series clincher by going 3-for 5, with a homer, triple, and 5 RBIs.

## Notable Achievements:

- Hit more than 30 home runs three times, topping 20 homers one other time.
- Knocked in more than 100 runs twice.
- Batted over .300 six times, topping the .320-mark twice.
- Stole more than 20 bases twice.
- Compiled on-base percentage in excess of .400 twice.
- Posted slugging percentage in excess of .500 five times.
- Led NL in: on-base percentage once, slugging percentage once, and OPS once.
- Finished second in NL in: batting average twice, hits once, total bases once, slugging percentage once, and OPS once.
- Ranks among Dodgers career leaders in: home runs (10th), slugging percentage (seventh), and OPS (seventh).
- June 1985 NL Player of the Month.
- 1981 World Series co-MVP.
- 1982 Silver Slugger winner.
- 1987 NL Comeback Player of the Year.

- Finished in top five in NL MVP voting three times (1982, 1983 & 1985).
- Two-time *Sporting News* All-Star selection (1981 & 1982).
- Four-time NL All-Star (1981, 1983, 1985 & 1987).
- 1981 NL champion.
- 1981 world champion.

# 22

# BURLEIGH GRIMES

The last major-league pitcher permitted to throw the spitball legally, Burleigh Grimes proved to be one of baseball's fiercest competitors over the course of his Hall of Fame career. Earning the nickname "Ol' Stubblebeard" by choosing not to shave the day before he took the mound, Grimes intimidated opposing hitters by routinely throwing at their heads. Described by *The New York Times* as "frightening to the batters he faced," Grimes ended up winning a total of 270 games over 19 big-league seasons, nine of which he spent in Brooklyn. A member of the Dodgers from 1918 to 1926, Grimes posted an overall record for them of 158-121, establishing himself in the process as one of the National League's most consistent winners. Averaging nearly 18 victories per season during his time in Brooklyn, Grimes won more than 20 games four times, topping the senior circuit in wins once and winning percentage once. He also led the league in complete games three times, innings pitched twice, and strikeouts once while pitching for the Dodgers. Grimes' consistently outstanding performance helped him earn a top-10 ranking in franchise history in several pitching categories, as well as eventual induction into the Baseball Hall of Fame by the members of the Veteran's Committee.

Born in Emerald, Wisconsin on August 18, 1893, Burleigh Arland Grimes began his professional career in 1912 with the Eau Claire Commissioners of the Class D Minnesota-Wisconsin League, before spending most of the next four seasons playing for four different minor-league teams, at three different levels. Finally, after compiling a record of 20-11 for the Southern Association's Birmingham Barons in 1916, the twenty-three-year-old right-hander made his major-league debut for Pittsburgh in September of that year, shortly after the Pirates purchased his contract from Birmingham. Appearing in six games for the Pirates during the season's final month, Grimes pitched fairly well, compiling an ERA of 2.36, although he won just two of his five decisions. However, he struggled the following year after being inserted into the starting rotation, going just 3-16, with a 3.53 ERA.

Subsequently included in a five-player trade with Brooklyn that sent Casey Stengel to Pittsburgh, Grimes emerged as one of the senior circuit's best pitchers after joining the Dodgers, concluding the 1918 campaign with a record of 19-9, an ERA of 2.13, 19 complete games, 270 innings pitched, and 7 shutouts. After slipping to 10-11 with a 3.47 ERA the following year, Grimes returned to top form in 1920, ranking among the NL leaders with a record of 23-11, a 2.22 ERA, 131 strikeouts, 5 shutouts, 25 complete games, and 303⅔ innings pitched

After a spitball thrown by Yankees pitcher Carl Mays during an August 1920 contest between New York and Cleveland struck Ray Chapman in the temple, tragically killing the Indians shortstop, the Major Leagues decreed that the spitball be banned from further use, making it an illegal pitch. The only exceptions made were the 17 hurlers active at that time whose pitching repertoires included the newly-outlawed offering, since MLB claimed that those pitchers depended on it to make a living. With Grimes being included in that select group of hurlers, he retained the ability to use the spitball for the remainder of his career.

In discussing his signature pitch, Grimes stated, "The spitter, which has always been an ace in the hole for me, is supposed to be one reason for my success. No doubt it is. But the spitter has its drawbacks. When I'm pitching, I chew slippery elm all the time. I don't like it, but it's the only thing that I can chew that gives me satisfaction."

Grimes further elaborated many years later in *The Man in the Dugout: Fifteen Big League Managers Speak Their Minds*:

> *"I used to chew slippery elm—the bark, right off the tree. Come spring, the bark would get nice and loose and you could slice it free without any trouble. What I checked was the fiber from inside, and that's what I put on the ball. That's what they called the foreign substance. The ball would break like hell, away from right-handed hitters and in on lefties."*

Yet, even though Grimes continued to rely heavily on the spitter in the years that followed, he gradually developed a wide arsenal of pitches that

Courtesy of RMYauctions.com

Burleigh Grimes posted 158 of his 270
major-league victories as a member of the Dodgers

included a slider, a changeup, a live fastball, and a good curve, all of which he threw with an almost straight overhand motion.

Grimes had another big year in 1921, going 22-13, to lead all NL hurlers in wins. He also placed among the league leaders with an ERA of 2.83 and 302⅓ innings pitched, while topping the senior circuit with 136 strikeouts and 30 complete games. After a somewhat subpar performance in 1922 in which he went 17-14 with a 4.76 ERA, Grimes put together back-to-back 20-win seasons, going 21-18 in 1923, before finishing with a mark of 22-13 the following year. He also led the league in complete games and innings pitched both seasons, completing 63 of his starts and tossing a total of 638 innings over the course of those two campaigns.

As Grimes established himself as one of the National League's most formidable pitchers during his time in Brooklyn, he also developed a reputation as one of baseball's toughest and nastiest competitors, antagonizing countless players, fans, and umpires with his aggressive style of play and contentious demeanor. The *New York Times* reported, "When he pitched, he always had a two-day black stubble on his face. He walked with a swagger that infuriated batters, and, when he measured a hitter from the mound, he would peel back his lips to show yellow teeth in a snarl. He often threw at the batters' heads without the slightest hesitation."

Grimes revealed years later that his willingness to brush back opposing hitters stemmed from his pursuit of financial security, explaining, "When I was a teenager, I decided that the best I could make back home was $35 a week driving horses in a lumber camp. Baseball was my answer....There was only one man standing between me and more money, and that was the guy with the bat. I knew I'd always have to fight that man with the bat as if he were trying to rob me in a dark alley."

Still, Grimes often took things too far, beginning a decade-long feud with Frankie Frisch when he got into a fistfight with the Giants second baseman after being spiked by him while covering first on a bunt. Although Grimes later said that the two men eventually ended their personal vendetta against one another after they became teammates in St. Louis, he repeatedly threw at Frisch prior to that, with the latter once revealing, "The only time I was ever scared in my life was one time when Burleigh threw at me on a three-and-oh count."

On another occasion, after future Hall of Fame outfielder Goose Goslin homered against him in his previous at-bat, Grimes paid him back by hitting him with a pitch as he knelt in the on-deck circle awaiting his next trip to the plate. Grimes also berated his teammates for their defensive miscues and quarreled with his managers, later providing insight into his on-field persona when he said, "Why is it there are so many nice guys interested in baseball? Not me, I was a real bastard when I played."

Grimes remained in Brooklyn another two years, being traded to the New York Giants prior to the start of the 1927 campaign after going a combined 24-32 for the Dodgers the previous two seasons. In addition to compiling an overall record of 158-121 during his time in Brooklyn, Grimes posted an ERA of 3.46, struck out 952 batters in 2,426 innings of work, threw 205 complete games and 20 shutouts, and compiled a WHIP of 1.357. He continues to rank among the Dodgers career leaders in wins, complete games, and innings pitched.

Grimes ended up spending just one year with the Giants, winning 19 games for them in 1927, before being reacquired by his original team, the Pittsburgh Pirates, at season's end. He then had two big years for the Pirates, winning a total of 42 games for them in 1928 and 1929, en route to earning a pair of top-five finishes in the NL MVP voting. Grimes subsequently split his final five seasons between the Boston Braves, St. Louis Cardinals, Chicago Cubs, New York Yankees, and Pittsburgh Pirates. During that time, he pitched his best ball for the Cardinals, going a combined 32-17 for them over parts of four seasons, including winning 17 games for their 1931 world championship ball club. Grimes ended his career back in Pittsburgh, announcing his retirement after being released by the Pirates following the conclusion of the 1934 campaign. Over parts of 19 big-league seasons, he posted an overall record of 270-212, giving him a winning percentage of .560. Grimes also compiled an ERA of 3.53, struck out 1,512 batters in 4,180 innings of work, tossed 314 complete games and 35 shutouts, and posted a WHIP of 1.365.

Following his playing days, Grimes began a lengthy managerial career at the minor-league level, although he also spent two seasons (1937-38) piloting the Dodgers. During that time, he continued to display his combative personality, frequently criticizing his young players, while suffering numerous game ejections. Grimes finally began to mellow somewhat after he became a scout, discovering during his time in Baltimore future standouts Jim Palmer and Dave McNally. He retired for good in 1971, seven years after the members of the Veteran's Committee elected him to the

Hall of Fame. Grimes lived another fourteen years, succumbing to cancer on December 6, 1985, at the age of ninety-two.

## Dodger Career Highlights:

**Best Season:** Grimes pitched extremely well for the Dodgers in 1921, leading all NL hurlers with 22 wins, 30 complete games, and 136 strike-outs, while also placing among the leaders with a 2.83 ERA, 302⅓ innings pitched, and a WHIP of 1.287. However, he performed even better the previous season, helping to lead Brooklyn to the 1920 National League pennant by compiling a record of 23-11 that gave him a league-best .676 winning percentage. Grimes also finished among the NL leaders with a 2.22 ERA, 5 shutouts, 131 strikeouts, 25 complete games, 303⅔ innings pitched, and a WHIP of 1.113 that represented the second-lowest mark of his career.

**Memorable Moments/Greatest Performances:** An excellent hitting pitcher over the course of his career, Grimes posted a lifetime batting average of .248, compiling a career-high mark of .306 for the Dodgers in 1920. Grimes had arguably his greatest day at the plate on July 6, 1921, when, during an 11-4 victory over the Giants, he hit one of his two career homers and went 4-for-5, with 3 RBIs and 2 runs scored. He had another big game on August 18, 1924, when he went a perfect 4-for-4 during a 7-4 win over the Pittsburgh Pirates.

Noted far more for his work on the mound, though, Grimes pitched one of his best games for the Dodgers on May 27, 1918, when he won a 1-0 decision over the Cardinals, surrendering just 2 hits and striking out 8 during the contest.

Grimes hurled another gem later in the year, defeating the Cubs by a score of 3-2 in 16 innings on July 18, 1918. Working all 16 frames, Grimes allowed 7 hits and 4 walks to Chicago batsmen, while striking out 4.

Grimes, though, topped that performance exactly one week later, on July 25, 1918, when he tossed a one-hit shutout against the Pittsburgh Pirates, defeating his former team by a score of 10-0.

Turning in another dominant performance the following month, Grimes shut out the Phillies on just 2 hits on August 10, defeating them by a score of 4-0.

Although the Dodgers ended up losing the 1920 World Series to Cleveland in seven games, with Grimes taking the loss in Games 5 and 7, he pitched brilliantly in Game Two, defeating the Indians and 31-game winner Jim Bagby by a score of 3-0.

## Notable Achievements:

- Won more than 20 games four times, surpassing 17 victories on two other occasions.
- Compiled ERA below 3.00 three times, posting mark under 2.50 twice.
- Threw more than 300 innings four times.
- Threw more than 20 complete games four times, topping the 30-mark on three occasions.
- Led NL pitchers in: wins once, winning percentage once, strikeouts once, innings pitched twice, complete games three times, starts twice, putouts twice, and assists three times.
- Ranks among Dodgers career leaders in: wins (sixth), complete games (fourth), innings pitched (fifth), and games started (10th).
- 1920 NL champion.
- Elected to Baseball Hall of Fame by members of Veteran's Committee in 1964.

# 23

# DOLPH CAMILLI

A powerful left-handed hitting first baseman who spent his first few major-league seasons starring for the Philadelphia Phillies, Dolph Camilli helped the Dodgers recover from a long string of dreary seasons after he arrived in Brooklyn in 1938. One of the National League's top sluggers and run-producers for nearly a decade, Camilli finished in the top four in the senior circuit in home runs eight straight times between 1935 and 1942, while also annually ranking among the league leaders in RBIs and runs scored. After hitting more than 25 homers, scoring more than 100 runs, and batting well over .300 in each of his last two seasons in Philadelphia, Camilli continued his outstanding offensive production with the Dodgers, topping 20 homers in each of the next five campaigns, while also driving in more than 100 runs four times. The presence of Camilli's big bat in the middle of their lineup helped establish the Dodgers as perennial pennant contenders, with the slugging first baseman earning NL MVP honors in 1941, when he led Brooklyn to its first league championship in twenty-one years by topping the circuit with 34 home runs and 120 RBIs.

Born in San Francisco, California on April 23, 1907, Adolph Louis Camilli attended local Sacred Heart Cathedral Preparatory High School, before beginning a lengthy eight-year minor league career by splitting the 1926 campaign between the Class C Logan Collegians and the Pacific Coast League's San Francisco Seals. From San Francisco, Camilli moved on to Utah, where he batted .333 as a member of the Salt Lake City Bees in 1928. Camilli then spent the next five seasons playing first base for the Sacramento Solons in the Pacific Coast League, during which time his older brother, who fought under the name Frankie Campbell, died of cerebral hemorrhaging following a match with future heavyweight boxing champion Max Baer.

Courtesy of the Leslie Jones Collection at the Boston Public Library

Dolph Camilli captured NL MVP honors in 1941,
when he led the Dodgers to their first pennant in 21 years

Finally called up to the Major Leagues during the latter stages of the 1933 campaign after having his contract purchased by the Chicago Cubs, Camilli appeared in 16 games over the season's final three weeks, batting .224, driving in 7 runs, and hitting his first two big-league homers. He subsequently spent the first two months of the 1934 season sharing time at first base with Chicago player-manager Charlie Grimm, before being dealt to the Phillies for fellow first sacker Don Hurst on June 11, 1934. Inserted into the everyday starting lineup upon his arrival in Philadelphia, Camilli ended up posting solid numbers as a rookie, finishing his first full season with 16 homers, 87 RBIs, and a .267 batting average, although he also led the league with 94 strikeouts. Camilli had a strong sophomore campaign as well, knocking in 83 runs, scoring 88 times, batting .261, and finishing third in the senior circuit with 25 home runs. However, the free-swinging first baseman also set a new National League record by striking out 113 times.

Camilli emerged as one of the league's foremost sluggers the following year, when, in addition to batting .315, he finished among the NL leaders in most statistical categories, including home runs (28), RBIs (102), runs scored (106), walks (116), and OPS (1.018). Although limited by injuries to 131 games in 1937, Camilli again posted outstanding numbers, finishing the year with 27 homers, 80 RBIs, 101 runs scored, a career-high .339 batting average, and a league-leading .446 on-base percentage.

Yet, in spite of Camilli's standout season, his repeated contract squabbles with team management convinced the Phillies to trade him to the Dodgers for a reported $75,000 in cash and an unknown outfielder named Eddie Morgan prior to the start of the ensuing campaign. Looking back at the difficulties he encountered when trying to negotiate a new contract with team brass, Camilli said, "No matter what kind of year you had, all they wanted to do was give you about a $1,000 raise."

New Brooklyn General Manager Larry MacPhail displayed a great deal of persistence in pursuing Camilli, convincing the Brooklyn Trust Company, which ran the Dodgers' finances at that time, to part with the money necessary to obtain him from the Phillies. Seeking to transform the Dodgers from lovable losers into a contending team, MacPhail viewed the acquisition of Camilli as the first step in that process. The hard-hitting first baseman did not disappoint MacPhail in the least, finishing his first season in Brooklyn with 24 home runs, 100 RBIs, 106 runs scored, and a league-leading 119 bases on balls that gave him a very respectable .393 on-base percentage, even though his batting average slipped to .251. Camilli increased his offensive production in his second season with the Dodgers, earning his first All-Star selection and a 12th-place finish in the 1939 NL MVP voting by batting .290, topping the circuit with 110 walks, and placing among the league leaders with 26 home runs, 104 RBIs, 105 runs scored, 12 triples, a .409 on-base percentage, and a .524 slugging percentage.

Camilli's powerful left-handed stroke proved to be a perfect fit for Brooklyn's cozy Ebbets Field. The muscular 5'10", 185-pound first baseman had a ferocious swing that often drove balls over the ballpark's right field screen onto Bedford Avenue. Dodgers manager Leo Durocher later recalled, "Camilli was a quiet, gentle man, but he was strong as an ox." Durocher added, "Nobody knew how well Dolph could fight because, quite frankly, nobody ever wanted to find out." Camilli also had surprisingly soft hands at first base, annually ranking among the league's top players at his position in putouts, assists, and fielding percentage.

Camilli again posted solid numbers in 1940, batting .287 and finishing among the NL leaders with 23 homers, 96 RBIs, 92 runs scored, 13 triples, a .397 on-base percentage, and a .529 slugging percentage. After being named team captain prior to the start of the ensuing campaign, Camilli reached the apex of his career, earning league MVP honors by leading the Dodgers to their first pennant since 1920. In addition to topping the senior circuit with 34 home runs and 120 RBIs, Camilli batted .285, scored 92 runs, and placed near the top of the league rankings with 104 walks, a .407 on-base percentage, and a .556 slugging percentage. His fine season ended on a sour note, though, when the Dodgers lost the World Series to the Yankees in five games. Camilli knocked in only one run and batted just .167 in his only appearance in the fall classic.

Camilli had another productive year in 1942, finishing second in the NL with 26 homers and 109 runs batted in, en route to breaking Zack Wheat's then club record of 131 career home runs and earning an eighth-place finish in the league MVP voting.

When Camilli got off to a slow start in 1943, hitting just 6 homers and driving in only 43 runs in his first 95 games, new Dodgers General Manager Branch Rickey elected to trade him to the Giants as he began to part ways with several of the team's higher-priced veteran players with more and more major leaguers entering the military to serve in World War II. However, the thirty-six-year-old first baseman refused to report to the Dodgers' bitter rivals, stating years later, "I hated the Giants. This was real serious; this was no put-on stuff. Their fans hated us, and our fans hated them….I said nuts to them, and I quit."

Camilli chose instead to spend the next two years serving as player-manager of the Pacific Coast League's Oakland Oaks, before joining the Boston Red Sox midway through the 1945 campaign. He spent the remainder of the year in Boston, batting just .212, with only 2 homers and 19 RBIs, before announcing his retirement after the Red Sox released him at season's end. Camilli finished his career with 239 home runs, 950 RBIs, 936 runs scored, 1,482 hits, 261 doubles, 86 triples, a .277 batting average, a .388 on-base percentage, and a .492 slugging percentage. Over the course of his six seasons in Brooklyn, he hit 139 homers, knocked in 572 runs, scored 540 times, collected 809 hits, 151 doubles, and 55 triples, batted .270, compiled a .392 on-base percentage, and posted a .497 slugging percentage.

Following his playing days, Camilli returned to the Pacific Coast League, where he spent the next several years managing the Oaks, Sacramento Solons and other minor-league teams, winning a pennant with Spokane in 1948. He later served as a scout for the Yankees and California Angels, before ending his baseball career as a spring training instructor for the Angels in 1971.

Upon being inducted into the Dodgers Hall of Fame in 1984, Camilli fondly recalled the special relationship he and his former teammates shared with the fans of Brooklyn, stating, "All they [the fans] cared about was their family, their job, and the Dodgers. And I don't know which one was the most important." Camilli lived another thirteen years, passing away in San Mateo, California on October 21, 1997, at the age of ninety.

## Dodger Career Highlights:

**Best Season:** Camilli had an outstanding all-around year for the Dodgers in 1939, batting .290, finishing among the NL leaders in eight different offensive categories, including home runs (26), RBIs (104), and runs scored (105), and establishing career-high marks in putouts, assists, and double plays turned at first base. Nevertheless, the 1941 campaign would have to be considered his best in Brooklyn. En route to earning league MVP honors, Camilli topped the senior circuit with a career-best 34 homers and 120 RBIs. He also placed second in the league in slugging percentage (.556), OPS (.962), total bases (294), and walks (104), while providing veteran leadership to a Dodgers team that ended up winning the NL pennant. Particularly effective down the stretch, Camilli hit 15 homers, knocked in 55 runs, and batted .311 during the final two months of the season.

**Memorable Moments/Greatest Performances:** Camilli had the only five-hit game of his career on September 1, 1941, when he led the Dodgers to a 6-5 win over the Braves in 15 innings by going 5-for-7, with a homer, 2 doubles, 3 RBIs, and 2 runs scored. After sending the contest into extra innings by tying the score at 4 runs apiece with a two-out solo homer in the bottom of the eighth inning, Camilli won the game in walk-off fashion with a two-out bases loaded single in the bottom half of the 15th.

Camilli had another big day at the plate just six days later, on September 7, 1941, when he went 3-for-4, with a pair of homers and 5 RBIs, during a 13-1 rout of the New York Giants.

Camilli had a similarly productive afternoon against Cincinnati on April 30, 1942, when he led the Dodgers to an 11-8 win over the Reds by going 3-for-6, with 2 home runs and 6 RBIs, including a game-winning three-run blast in the top of the ninth inning.

Camilli delivered another memorable blow later in the year, on August 23, 1942, when his grand slam homer in the bottom of the 10th inning enabled the Dodgers to defeat the Giants by a score of 6-4. Camilli drove in the first two Dodger runs as well earlier in the contest, giving him a total of 6 RBIs on the day.

Camilli also provided much of the offensive firepower during a 10-3 victory over Pittsburgh on September 16, 1942, going 4-for-5, with a pair of homers, 5 RBIs, and 3 runs scored.

After going 4-for-5, with a double, triple, 2 RBIs, and a career-high 4 runs scored during an extra-inning loss to St. Louis just three days earlier, Camilli paced the Dodgers to an 18-5 win over the Chicago Cubs on June 4, 1943 by going 4-for-4, with a homer, 2 RBIs, 2 runs scored, and 2 walks.

## Notable Achievements:

- Hit more than 20 home runs five times, topping 30 homers once (34 in 1941).
- Knocked in more than 100 runs four times, surpassing 120 RBIs once (120 in 1941).
- Scored more than 100 runs twice.
- Finished in double-digits in triples three times.
- Surpassed 30 doubles once (30 in 1939).
- Drew more than 100 bases on balls three times.
- Compiled on-base percentage in excess of .400 twice.
- Posted slugging percentage in excess of .500 three times.
- Led NL in: home runs once, RBIs once, and walks twice.
- Led NL first basemen in assists once.
- Ranks among Dodgers career-leaders in: bases on balls (ninth), on-base percentage (tied-10th), and OPS (eighth).

- 1941 NL MVP.
- Two-time NL All-Star (1939 & 1941).
- 1941 *Sporting News* All-Star selection.
- 1941 NL champion.

# 24

# WILLIE DAVIS

One of the most enigmatic players ever to wear a Dodgers uniform, Willie Davis tantalized Los Angeles fans with his blazing speed and exceptional all-around athletic ability. Yet, at the same time, he often frustrated them with his inconsistency and inability to live up to his full potential. A world-class sprinter who spent much of his career being viewed as the fastest player in the game, Davis stole as many as 40 bases just once in his fourteen years with the Dodgers. He also batted over .300 in just one of his first nine seasons, before topping the .300-mark three straight times during the latter stages of his tenure in L.A. Still, in spite of his foibles, Davis helped the Dodgers win three pennants and two world championships, earning two All-Star selections and three Gold Gloves along the way. He also ended up scoring more runs and amassing more hits, extra-base hits, triples, total bases, and at-bats than any other player to perform for the Dodgers since they moved to the West Coast in 1958.

Born in Mineral Springs, Arkansas on April 15, 1940, William Henry Davis grew up in Los Angeles, California after moving there with his family as a youngster. Tall and slender, Davis starred in baseball, basketball, and track and field while attending Roosevelt High School, running a 9.5-second 100-yard dash and setting a city record in the long jump by leaping 25 feet, 5 inches. After signing with the Dodgers following his graduation from Roosevelt High in 1958, the left-swinging, lefty-throwing Davis advanced quickly through the Los Angeles farm system, leading his league in runs scored, hits, triples, and batting average in each of the next two seasons, while posting a composite batting average of .352 during that time. Particularly impressive at Class C Reno in 1959, Davis reached near-legendary status by scoring from first base nine times on singles.

Summoned to the big leagues by the Dodgers in September 1960, Davis performed well over the final month of the campaign, hitting 2 homers, driving in 10 runs, scoring 12 times, and batting .318, in 22 games and 88 official at-bats. Replacing Duke Snider as the Dodgers' everyday center-fielder the following year, Davis had a solid rookie season, batting .254, hitting 12 homers, knocking in 45 runs, and scoring 56 times, in fewer than 400 total plate appearances. The twenty-two-year-old outfielder subsequently emerged as one of the Dodgers' top offensive threats in 1962, when, hitting out of the number 3 spot in the batting order, just ahead of NL batting champion Tommy Davis (no relation), he hit 21 homers, drove in 85 runs, scored 103 times, batted .285, finished second in the league with 32 stolen bases, and topped the senior circuit with 10 triples. However, Davis followed that up with a subpar performance in 1963, batting just .245, with only 9 home runs, 60 RBIs, and 60 runs scored.

Davis continued to perform erratically over the course of the next few seasons, compiling batting averages of .294, .238, .284, .257, and .250 from 1964 to 1968, although he managed to steal at least 20 bases each year, including a career-high 42 thefts in 1964. Yet, even that total had to be considered something of a disappointment when Davis' blinding speed is taken into consideration. Built like a greyhound at 6'2" and 180 pounds, the rangy outfielder possessed more natural running speed than any other player of his time, with teammate and close friend Tommy Davis stating, "The first time I saw Willie was at Dodgertown in the spring of 1959. We were put together with several other players to run a sixty-yard dash. I remember that Maury [Wills] was in our group, and I figured Maury would win the race with me right behind him, because I could run in those days. Willie left us in the dust." Davis also recalled, "I once saw him [Willie] score from second base on a sacrifice fly."

In addition to failing to reach his full potential as a base-stealer, Davis never developed into an outstanding run-producer, driving in as many as 90 runs only once, while scoring more than 90 runs just three times. He also lacked patience at the plate, walking as many as 40 times just once his entire career. Longtime Dodger catcher Johnny Roseboro laid most of the blame for Davis' failure to establish himself as a truly elite player squarely on the outfielder's shoulders, saying of his former teammate, "He was egotistical…One time, I asked to help him with his bunting, and he told me he didn't need any help. 'How many … bunts did you beat out

Courtesy of MEARS Online Auctions

Willie Davis (left), seen here with Tommy Davis,
scored more runs and collected more hits
than any other player for the Dodgers
since they moved to Los Angeles in 1958

this year?' he asked me. I never tried to help him after that. Willie wasn't willing to work."

Meanwhile, former Dodgers GM Buzzie Bavasi expressed his feelings about Davis when he told the *Los Angeles Times*, "There was nothing more exciting than to watch Willie run out a triple. He could have been a Hall of Famer, but he had million-dollar legs and a ten-cent head."

Still, after batting just .250, with only 7 homers and 31 RBIs in 1968, Davis began to show signs of maturation the following year, finishing the season with 11 homers, 59 RBIs, and a .311 batting average. He compiled even better numbers in 1970, driving in a career-high 93 runs, scoring 92 times, batting .305, and amassing 181 hits, 38 stolen bases, and a league-leading 16 triples. In addition to winning the first of his three straight Gold Gloves the following year, Davis earned his first All-Star selection by hitting 10 homers, knocking in 74 runs, scoring 84 times, batting .309, and finishing fourth in the league with 198 hits. Davis had another excellent year in 1972, hitting 19 homers, driving in 79 runs, scoring 81 times, and batting .289, before compiling extremely similar numbers in 1973, when he earned his second All-Star nomination by hitting 16 homers, knocking in 77 runs, scoring 82 times, and batting .285.

Yet, with the Dodgers desperately needing bullpen help, they elected to trade the thirty-four-year-old Davis to Montreal for reliever Mike Marshall prior to the start of the 1974 campaign. Davis left Los Angeles with career totals of 154 home runs, 849 RBIs, 1,004 runs scored, 2,091 hits, 321 doubles, 110 triples, and 335 stolen bases, a batting average of .279, a .312 on-base percentage, and a .413 slugging percentage.

When asked by *Sports Illustrated* to describe how he felt about being traded to Montreal, Davis said, "Now I can just be me. When I first started, I never wanted to be great, to be another Mays. I just wanted to play. But the pressure got to me. One day I would try to be Musial, to hit like him; the next day, Mays; the next, somebody else. I kept trying to be somebody else, and I got the short end. Now, with Buddhism, I've found the real Willie Davis. In Montreal, I will have a new life, a new challenge. Now I'm dredging up all my potential, getting the true value out of myself. Everything is beautiful."

Davis ended up spending just one year in Montreal, hitting 12 homers, driving in 89 runs, scoring 86 times, and batting .295 for the Expos in 1974, before being dealt to the Texas Rangers at season's end. He subsequently split the next two seasons between Texas, St. Louis, and San Diego, before signing with the Japanese Chunichi Dragons. After two years in Japan, Davis returned to the States, where he spent his final season as an active player serving the California Angels primarily as a pinch-hitter. Announcing his retirement following the conclusion of the 1979 campaign, Davis ended his career with 182 home runs, 1,053 RBIs, 1,217 runs scored, 2,561 hits, 395 doubles, 138 triples, 398 stolen bases, a .279 batting average, a .311 on-base percentage, and a .412 slugging percentage. In addition to his offensive accomplishments, Davis ranks third all-time among major-league center-fielders in games played and fifth in putouts.

Following his playing career, Davis experienced a number of personal problems that included drug and alcohol abuse. He also was arrested in 1996 for allegedly threatening to kill his parents and burn down their home unless they gave him money. Helped by his brother and former Laker Tommy Hawkins, then part of the Dodgers' front office, Davis overcame his addiction and joined the Dodgers' speakers' bureau, where he spent the next several years counseling youngsters on the evils of drug use. Davis lived until March 9, 2010, when a neighbor found him dead in his home in Burbank, California, apparently of natural causes. He was sixty-nine years old at the time of his passing. Dodgers' owner Frank McCourt subsequently issued a statement that read:

> *"Willie Davis was beloved by generations of Dodger fans and remains one of the most talented players ever to wear the Dodger uniform. Having spent time with him over the past six years, I know how proud he was to have been a Dodger. He will surely be missed and our sincere thoughts are with his children during this difficult time."*

Maury Wills also paid tribute to his former teammate when he told *The Los Angeles Times*, "He [Davis] was so talented. God really blessed him with some great tools—for any sport, really—speed, strength, agility—everything an athlete needs in order to make the big time."

## Dodger Career Highlights:

**Best Season:** Davis had one of his finest all-around seasons for the Dodgers in just his second full year in the big leagues, concluding the 1962 campaign with career-high marks in home runs (21) and runs scored (103), a league-leading 10 triples, a batting average of .285, 85 RBIs, and 32 stolen bases, which placed him second in the league to teammate Maury Wills. He also performed extremely well in 1964, when he hit 12 homers, drove in 77 runs, scored 91 times, batted .294, and stole a career-high 42 bases. Nevertheless, the feeling here is that Davis played his best ball for the Dodgers in 1970, when, in addition to establishing career-high marks with 93 RBIs and a league-leading 16 triples, he hit 8 homers, scored 92 runs, stole 38 bases, batted .305, and led all NL center-fielders with a .991 fielding percentage.

**Memorable Moments/Greatest Performances:** Davis established a franchise record by hitting safely in 31 consecutive games from August 1 to September 3, 1969, batting .435, with a homer, 23 RBIs, and 20 runs scored during that time. He also hit in 25 straight games two years later.

Although the Dodgers lost their May 27, 1961 match-up with the Braves by a score of 10-8, Davis had a big day at the plate, going 3-for-5, with a pair of homers, a triple, and 5 RBIs.

Davis helped lead the Dodgers to a lopsided 14-3 victory over Cincinnati on June 23, 1962 by going 4-for-4, with a career-high 4 runs scored.

Davis broke out of a slump on May 8, 1963 by hitting a pair of homers, tripling, knocking in 3 runs, and scoring 3 times during an 11-5 pounding of the St. Louis Cardinals.

Davis had the first 5-for-5 day of his career on April 21, 1971, helping the Dodgers defeat the San Diego Padres by a score of 10-2 in the process. He duplicated his earlier feat some four months later, on August 24, 1971, when he hit safely in all 5 of his trips to the plate and drove in 3 runs during a 6-4 victory over the Montreal Expos.

Davis led the Dodgers to a 12-11 win over the Giants on August 2, 1972 by going 3-for-5, with a homer and a career-high 5 RBIs.

Davis turned in a number of outstanding performances in his final year with the Dodgers, with one of those coming on May 2, 1973, when he went 4-for-4, with 2 homers, a double, and 3 RBIs during a 4-1 victory over the Chicago Cubs.

Less than two weeks later, on May 13, Davis helped lead the Dodgers to a lopsided 15-3 win over the Giants by going 4-for-5, with a pair of doubles and a career-high 4 runs scored.

Although the Dodgers lost a 19-inning marathon to the Mets by a score of 7-3 on May 24, 1973, Davis collected a career-high 6 hits during the contest, going 6-for-9, with 1 RBI and 1 run scored.

Davis also set a pair of World Series records during his time in Los Angeles, stealing 3 bases against Minnesota in Game Five of the 1965 fall classic, and committing 3 errors in the fifth inning of Game Two of the 1966 Series, one when he lost a fly ball in the sun, and the other two when he dropped a fly ball and then overthrew third base.

## Notable Achievements:

- Batted over .300 four times.
- Hit more than 20 home runs once (21 in 1962).
- Scored more than 100 runs once (103 in 1962).
- Finished in double-digits in triples four times.
- Surpassed 30 doubles twice.
- Stole more than 30 bases four times, topping 40 thefts once (42 in 1964).
- Led NL in triples twice.
- Led NL outfielders in putouts twice.
- Led NL center-fielders in: putouts twice, assists twice, fielding percentage once, and double plays turned twice.
- Ranks among Dodgers career leaders in: RBIs (ninth), runs scored (sixth), hits (third), extra-base hits (fourth), doubles (sixth), triples (second), total bases (fourth), stolen bases (third), games played (sixth), plate appearances (fourth), and at-bats (third).
- Holds Dodger record for longest consecutive games hitting streak (31 in 1969).
- Holds World Series record with 3 stolen bases in one game (Game Five of 1965 Series).
- Ranks among MLB all-time leaders in games played (third) and putouts (fifth) by a center-fielder.
- Three-time Gold Glove winner (1971, 1972 & 1973).
- August 1969 NL Player of the Month.
- 1971 *Sporting News* All-Star selection.
- Two-time NL All-Star (1971 & 1973).
- Three-time NL champion (1963, 1965 & 1966).
- Two-time world champion (1963 & 1965).

# 25

# JIM GILLIAM

An extremely versatile player who manned every position on the diamond except for pitcher, catcher, and shortstop at some point during his career, Jim Gilliam contributed to the Dodgers in many different ways in his fourteen years with the club, helping them capture seven National League pennants and four world championships in the process. Doing all the little things to help his team win, Gilliam used his intelligence and relentless focus to establish himself as one of the Dodgers' most important players, even though he lacked exceptional natural ability. Displaying tremendous patience at the plate, Gilliam annually ranked among the NL leaders in bases on balls, topping the senior circuit in that category once, and finishing second on three other occasions. An excellent base-runner, Gilliam also scored more than 100 runs and stole more than 20 bases four times each, placing second in the league in the last category three times as well. Meanwhile, whether playing second base, third base, or the outfield, Gilliam did a solid job wherever the Dodgers put him, finishing among the league's top players at his position in assists eight times, putouts six times, and fielding percentage seven times. And, following the conclusion of his playing career, Gilliam continued to contribute to the Dodgers for another twelve years as a member of their coaching staff.

Born in Nashville, Tennessee on October 17, 1928, James William Gilliam attended Pearl High School, during which time he also began playing on a local semi-pro team. Dropping out of high school in his senior year to pursue a career in baseball, Gilliam signed with the Nashville Black Vols, an affiliate of the Negro National League's Baltimore Elite Giants. After one season at Nashville, the right-handed hitting Gilliam joined the Giants, with whom he spent the next five seasons, earning All-Star honors as a second baseman three straight times. During his time in

Jim Gilliam, seen here in his minor league days,
earned All-Star honors as both a second baseman
and third baseman in his years with the Dodgers

Baltimore, Gilliam acquired the nickname "Junior," being assigned that moniker by Giants manager George "Tubby" Scales, who also taught him how to switch-hit.

Gilliam's success in the Negro Leagues prompted the Dodgers to sign him prior to the start of the 1951 campaign. Gilliam spent the next two years playing for Brooklyn's top farm team in Montreal, earning International League MVP honors in 1952 by batting .303, knocking in 109 runs, and topping the circuit with 133 runs scored and 41 doubles. Royals' skipper Walter Alston, who later managed Gilliam with the Dodgers, recalled the young infielder's days at Montreal, stating, "He didn't hit with power, he had no arm, and he couldn't run. But he did the little things to win ball games. He never griped or complained. He was one of the most unselfish ballplayers I know."

Promoted to the Dodgers in 1953, the twenty-four-year-old Gilliam took over at second base for Jackie Robinson, who spent his remaining years with the team playing third base and left field. Assuming the leadoff spot in Brooklyn's batting order in his first big-league season, Gilliam ended up being named NL Rookie of the Year after helping the Dodgers capture their second straight pennant by driving in 63 runs, batting .278, leading the league with 17 triples, and placing near the top of the league rankings with 125 runs scored, 21 stolen bases, and 100 bases on balls.

Although the Dodgers failed to repeat as NL champions in 1954, Gilliam had another outstanding season, hitting a career-high 13 homers, knocking in 52 runs, scoring 107 times, and batting .282. However, he experienced something of a drop-off the following year, driving in only 40 runs and batting just .249, although he still managed to finish fifth in the league with 110 runs scored. Gilliam then had one of his finest offensive seasons in 1956, earning the first of his two All-Star selections and a fifth-place finish in the NL MVP voting by scoring 102 runs, stealing 21 bases, walking 95 times, and establishing career-high marks in hits (178), batting average (.300), and on-base percentage (.399).

Even though Gilliam proved to be one of the league's better leadoff hitters his first few seasons with the Dodgers, team management always seemed to be looking to replace him with some young phenom. Yet, Gilliam's versatility, reliability, and strong relationship with Dodger manager Walter Alston enabled him to retain his starting job, although he often found himself moving around the diamond. In addition to his seven seasons as the Dodgers' primary second baseman, Gilliam spent five years playing mostly third base and another two seasons splitting his time between second, third, and the outfield. Perhaps most effective as a second baseman, Gilliam used his knowledge of hitters and cerebral approach to his craft to get the most out of his somewhat limited natural ability, with former teammate Ron Farily stating, "He had a tremendous feel for playing the hitters. Knowing the pitcher, knowing what the pitcher might throw, and then positioning himself defensively accordingly."

Meanwhile, in discussing Alston's comfort level with Gilliam, Fairly said, "He never missed a sign; all the years he played for Alston, Walt would say the one player who never missed a sign was Jim Gilliam."

Alston, himself, said of his favorite player, "He gets on base. He can punch the ball on the hit and run. He steals and never throws to the wrong base. He knows how to get a walk. He has all the little things that go to make up a good ball club….I don't think he's ever been late a day in his life."

After a pair of subpar seasons in 1957 and 1958, in which he posted batting averages of .250 and .261 and totaled only 80 RBIs and 170 runs scored, Gilliam earned his second All-Star nomination in 1959 by batting .282, scoring 91 runs, stealing 23 bases, and leading the National League with 96 bases on balls. He also did a solid job in his first full season at third base, finishing fifth among NL third sackers in assists, putouts, double plays, and fielding percentage.

With Maury Wills establishing himself as the team's starting shortstop and leadoff hitter the following year, Gilliam assumed the number two spot in the Dodgers batting order. Slumping somewhat at the plate while continuing to man the hot corner, Gilliam batted just .248 and drove in only 40 runs, although he also scored 96 times and finished third in the league with 96 bases on balls. Gilliam posted even less impressive numbers in 1961, concluding the campaign with only 32 RBIs, 74 runs scored, and a .244 batting average. However, he experienced something of an offensive resurgence in 1962, raising his batting average nearly 30 points, to .270, while driving in 43 runs and scoring 83 times. More importantly, Gilliam served as the perfect complement to Wills, helping the latter to amass a record-setting 104 steals by displaying tremendous intelligence and patience at the plate. In discussing the approach he used each time he stepped into the batter's box with Wills at first base, Gilliam explained, "I try to help him …Lots of times, there are pitches I could swing at, but I see Maury out of the corner of my eye and take the pitch if I think he's going to get the base. Or else I'll take a strike, even two strikes, to give him a chance to steal it. If it looks like he could be caught, I'll hit at the pitch. Maybe I'll punch it through and Maury will be able to make it to third. Or else I'll foul it off and he's not out."

Commenting on Gilliam's ability to handle the bat, Leo Durocher, who returned to the Dodgers as a coach in 1961, stated, "Not a man in baseball can do it better because Jim's a real mechanic with that bat. He's the best two-strike hitter in baseball."

Former teammate Jeff Torborg later described Gilliam as the ideal number two hitter, saying, "What a great team player he was. He'd hit behind Maury, take pitch after pitch after pitch. And, when Maury got to second, he'd give himself up by hitting the ball to the right side, even with two strikes, which most hitters won't do."

Ron Fairly also praised Gilliam for his selfless attitude, suggesting, "Junior played to win ballgames. He didn't care which player won the game, as long as the Dodgers won the game. Jim didn't worry about personal things like that."

Gilliam again contributed significantly to the Dodger cause in 1963, helping them capture the NL flag by scoring 77 runs, stealing 19 bases, and batting .282, en route to earning a sixth-place finish in the league MVP voting. Assuming a part-time role the following year, Gilliam batted just .228 and scored only 44 runs, before being named a player-coach at season's end. Yet, even though the thirty-six-year-old veteran expected to see very little playing time in 1965, injuries and substandard performances by his replacements forced the Dodgers to depend on him much more than they originally anticipated. Appearing in a total of 111 games at four different positions, Gilliam ended up batting .280, with 39 RBIs and 54 runs scored, in helping the Dodgers win their second pennant in three years. Spending the vast majority of his time at third base, Gilliam also served as part of the Major Leagues' first all-switch-hitting infield, sharing that distinction with first baseman Wes Parker, second baseman Lim Lefebvre, and shortstop Maury Wills.

Although the Dodgers repeated as NL champions in 1966, Gilliam proved to be much less effective in his dual role, batting just .217 in 88 games, before announcing his retirement as a player following the conclusion of the campaign. He ended his career with 65 home runs, 558 RBIs, 1,163 runs scored, 1,889 hits, 304 doubles, 71 triples, 203 stolen bases, a .265 batting average, a .360 on-base percentage, and a .355 slugging percentage. Extremely difficult to strike out over the course of his career, Gilliam fanned only 416 times, in more than 8,300 total plate appearances, while drawing 1,036 bases on balls—the second-highest total in franchise history.

Gilliam subsequently spent the next 12 years serving the Dodgers as their first-base coach, never expressing any anger over the fact that, in spite of his vast knowledge of the sport, he never received an offer to manage any major-league team. When asked about the possibility of other African American candidates receiving managerial job offers before him, Gilliam told *Los Angeles Times* reporter Ross Newhan, "No, it doesn't bother me, although I think I may be better prepared than any of the others. I've been in baseball for twenty-five years and, during that time, I haven't just gone through the motions. I've studied and applied myself. I know I'll get the chance and I'll be ready."

Unfortunately, Gilliam's dream of managing in the Major Leagues never became a reality. On September 15, 1978, Gilliam suffered a massive brain hemorrhage and went into a coma from which he never awoke. He died a little over three weeks later, on October 8, 1978, just nine days shy of his fiftieth birthday, the day after the Dodgers won their 10th National League pennant with him as a member of the organization. The Dodgers retired Gilliam's uniform number 19 prior to Game One of the 1978 World Series, which they won by a score of 11-5 behind a pair of home runs by second baseman Davey Lopes, who earlier called his mentor a "father, friend, and locker room inspiration." Gilliam's number is the only one retired by the Dodgers of a player not in the Hall of Fame.

Following Gilliam's passing, Dodgers manager Tommy Lasorda said of his longtime friend, "He was a unique man in the sense that, in twenty-eight years, no one heard one person say a bad word about Jim Gilliam. He loved country, God, family, and the organization. He didn't have a bitter bone in his body. Although always struggling, he never had any resentment."

## Career Highlights:

**Best Season:** Gilliam earned his lone top-five finish in the NL MVP balloting in 1956 by hitting 6 homers, driving in 43 runs, scoring 102 times, stealing 21 bases, walking 95 times, and establishing career-high marks in hits (178), batting average (.300), and on-base percentage (.399). However, he posted slightly better overall numbers as a rookie in 1953, concluding the campaign with 6 homers, 168 hits, 21 stolen bases, a .278 batting average, a .383 on-base percentage, a .415 slugging percentage, and a career-best 63 RBIs, 125 runs scored, 31 doubles, and league-leading 17 triples. In addition to topping the senior circuit in three-baggers, Gilliam finished second in walks, third in stolen bases, and fourth in runs scored.

**Memorable Moments/Greatest Performances:** Although the Dodgers ended up losing the 1953 World Series to the Yankees in six games, Gilliam performed extremely well in his first fall classic, hitting 2 homers, driving in 4 runs, scoring 4 times, batting .296, and compiling an OPS of .951.

Gilliam homered twice in the same game for the only time in his career on April 29, 1954, when he led the Dodgers to a 7-5 win over Cincinnati by going 3-for-5, with 3 RBIs and 3 runs scored.

Gilliam had another big day against Cincinnati some six weeks later, on June 13, 1954, helping the Dodgers defeat the Reds by a score of 14-2 by going 4-for-5, with a homer, 2 RBIs, and 3 runs scored.

Gilliam led the Dodgers to a 5-0 win over Pittsburgh on April 20, 1956 by homering, stealing a base, scoring twice, and driving in a career-high 4 runs.

Gilliam again victimized Pittsburgh's pitching staff nearly four months later, on August 9, 1956, going 4-for-4, with a pair of doubles, 1 RBI, and 3 runs scored, during a 7-3 Dodger victory over the Pirates.

Gilliam helped pace the Dodgers to a lopsided 20-4 victory over the Braves on July 15, 1957 by going 4-for-6, with a career-high 4 runs scored.

Gilliam matched that total six years later, on September 6, 1963, when he went 3-for-4, with a homer and 4 runs scored, during a 5-2 win over the Giants

Still, Gilliam experienced arguably the most memorable moment of his career in Game Seven of the 1965 World Series, when he helped preserve Sandy Koufax's 2-0 lead over the Minnesota Twins in the bottom of the fifth inning by saving at least one run with a spectacular backhanded grab of a sharp grounder hit down the third base line by AL MVP Zoilo Versalles with two runners on base. After Gilliam forced the runner at third, Koufax settled down, allowing the Twins just one more hit over the final four frames, en route to posting a 2-0 win that gave the Dodgers their second world championship in three years.

## Notable Achievements:

- Batted over .300 once (.300 in 1956).
- Scored more than 100 runs four times, topping the 120-mark once (125 in 1953).
- Finished in double-digits in triples once (17 in 1953).
- Surpassed 30 doubles once (31 in 1953).
- Stole more than 20 bases four times.
- Walked more than 100 times once (100 in 1953).
- Led NL in: triples once; bases on balls once; and sacrifice hits once.
- Led NL second basemen with .986 fielding percentage in 1957.
- Ranks among Dodgers career leaders in: runs scored (fourth), hits (eighth), doubles (eighth), total bases (ninth), bases on balls (second), games played (fifth), plate appearances (third), and at-bats (fifth).
- 1953 NL Rookie of the Year.
- Finished in top 10 of NL MVP voting twice, placing fifth once (1956).
- 1963 *Sporting News* All-Star selection.
- Two-time NL All-Star (1956 & 1959).
- Seven-time NL champion (1953, 1955, 1956, 1959, 1963, 1965 & 1966).
- Four-time world champion (1955, 1959, 1963 & 1965).26

# 26

# BABE HERMAN

His legacy tarnished by the media's unfair portrayal of him as something of a clown, Babe Herman has never received the credit he deserves for being one of the elite hitters of his era. Focusing far more on his occasional fielding lapses, base-running blunders, and off-the-field malapropisms than on his outstanding batting feats, the members of the press corps that covered the Dodgers during Herman's time in Brooklyn failed to acknowledge the fact that the right-fielder ranked among the finest hitters of his time. The holder of several single-season Dodger batting records, including highest batting average, highest slugging percentage, and most hits, Herman compiled a lifetime batting average of .324, posting an overall mark of .339 over the course of his seven seasons in Brooklyn that ranks as the second-highest in franchise history. In addition to batting well in excess of .300 five times for the Dodgers, the left-handed swinging Herman surpassed 20 homers, 100 RBIs, 100 runs scored, and 200 hits two times each, earning in the process one top-10 finish in the NL MVP voting and the respect of pitchers throughout the league. Yet, Herman, unfortunately, continues to be remembered more than anything for the occasional miscues he committed on the playing field.

Born in Buffalo, New York on June 26, 1903, Floyd Caves Herman grew up in Los Angeles, California, where he attended Glendale Union High School. After establishing himself as a multi-sport star at Glendale, earning varsity letters in baseball, football, basketball, and track, Herman signed with the Edmonton Eskimos of the Western Canada League at the age of eighteen. Excelling at the bat in his first professional season, Herman topped the circuit in hits and triples, prompting *The Sporting News* to observe, "There is yet a youthful prodigy who tops the others as a prospect

Courtesy of MEARS Online Auctions

Babe Herman's 241 hits, 416 total bases, .393 batting average, .678 slugging percentage, and 1.132 OPS in 1930 all represent single-season franchise records

of future greatness. This is the eighteen-year-old high school giant. Herman is a left-handed colossus."

While playing north of the border, Herman also acquired the nickname he retained for the rest of his life. Referred to as "Babe" by an admiring female fan who frequently exhorted him to get a hit during games, Herman carried his new moniker with him to the training camp of the Detroit Tigers, who purchased his contract prior to the start of the 1922 campaign. After being returned to the minor leagues by Detroit before the regular season got underway, Herman batted .416 for the Omaha Buffaloes of the Western League in 1922, before spending the next two seasons in the farm system of the Boston Red Sox. Sold to the Pacific Coast League's Seattle Indians at the end of 1924, Herman ended his five-year minor-league sojourn in Seattle, where he spent the entire 1925 campaign before having his contract purchased by the Brooklyn Robins, whose scout said of his latest acquisition, "He's kind of funny in the field, but, when I see a guy go six-for-six, I've got to go for him."

Manning first base for the Robins in 1926, Herman had a solid rookie season, hitting 11 homers, driving in 81 runs, and batting .319, although he struggled somewhat in the field, committing a total of 14 errors. Herman proved to be somewhat less productive the following year, concluding the 1927 campaign with 14 homers, 73 RBIs, and a .272 batting average, while leading all NL first sackers with 21 fielding miscues.

After being shifted to right field by the Robins prior to the start of the 1928 season, Herman compiled the best numbers of his young career, hitting 12 homers, driving in 91 runs, and finishing among the NL leaders with 37 doubles and a .340 batting average. Nevertheless, he continued to perform erratically in the field, leading all players at his position in errors for the second of four times.

With the National League employing a livelier ball in 1929, offensive numbers throughout the senior circuit rose dramatically, with Herman's statistics proving to be no exception. En route to earning an eighth-place finish in the NL MVP voting, the Brooklyn right-fielder established new career highs with 21 homers, 113 RBIs, 105 runs scored, 217 hits, 13 triples, 42 doubles, a .381 batting average, a .436 on-base percentage, and a .612 slugging percentage, placing him among the league leaders in all but two of those categories (RBIs and runs scored). Herman also finished near the top of the league rankings with 21 stolen bases. He followed that up with an even stronger 1930 campaign in which he hit 35 homers, knocked in 130 runs, scored 143 times, amassed 241 hits, 48 doubles, and 416 total bases, stole 18 bases, batted .393, compiled a .455 on-base percentage, and posted a .678 slugging percentage, finishing in the league's top five in each category.

Long and lean, the 6'4", 195-pound Herman possessed a slashing style of hitting he developed early in his career under the tutelage of Ty Cobb, who taught him to concentrate on hitting the ball back up the middle. Admired by Rogers Hornsby, who claimed that he hit the ball harder than anyone, Herman also drew praise from former Brooklyn teammate and longtime major-league manager Al Lopez, who once stated, "Babe swung a bat with more ease and grace than any man I ever saw."

Yet, even though he earned their begrudging respect, Herman angered opposing pitchers at times with his pre-at-bat ritual, which sportswriter Ned Cronin described thusly: "He takes his time, swinging his bats and loosening up his long, powerful arms. With what must be maddening unconcern for the opposing pitcher, Babe slowly selects a war club and then kneels down and carefully scoops a hole so he can get a toehold in the batter's box." As a result, Herman often found himself ducking away from inside pitches, noting specifically on one occasion that Chicago Cubs hurler Charlie Root frequently knocked him down with his high, hard one.

As Herman evolved into one of the National League's most potent batsmen, he also became a source of amusement to the New York media, which frequently made light of his defensive shortcomings and baserunning mishaps in the local newspapers. Particularly critical of Herman's ability to judge fly balls, the local scribes claimed that the right-fielder typically circled an area of the field where he thought the ball might drop and blindly stuck out his glove hoping it might land there. They also suggested that he had once been hit on the head while trying to catch a fly ball. Former Brooklyn teammate Fresco Thompson joined in the fun, once stating, "He [Herman] wore a glove for one reason: it was a league custom. The glove would last him a minimum of six years because it rarely made contact with the ball." Herman's style of play, along with that of the entire team, led to Brooklyn being dubbed "The Daffiness Boys," with sportswriter Frank Graham noting, "They were not normally of a clownish nature, and some of them were very good ballplayers, indeed, but they were overcome by the atmosphere in which they found themselves as soon as they had put on Brooklyn uniforms."

In truth, the writers grossly exaggerated Herman's deficiencies in the field and on the base paths. In fact, he eventually turned himself into a competent outfielder, leading all NL right-fielders in putouts once, while finishing second in assists and fielding percentage twice each. But, with the local newspapers the primary source of information at the time, Herman had no way of refuting the claims made by the members of the press corps. As a result, he had to endure their barbs, developing over time a self-deprecating attitude he once revealed when a local bank informed him that someone had been impersonating him and cashing bad checks. In response, Herman said, "Hit him a few fly balls. If he catches any, it ain't me." On another occasion, Herman quipped, "Never once did I get hit on the head by a fly ball; once or twice on the shoulder maybe, but never on the head."

Never showing any animosity towards the sportswriters, Herman stated matter of factly, "They had to make a living, too."

Still, the image the writers created of Herman tended to make people think that he had more deficiencies than strengths—a notion that former Dodgers manager Charlie Dressen contradicted when he said, "People think Herman was a stupid clown when he was at the height of his career. I know different because I played with him and also managed him. Let me tell you, Herman was a good outfielder. He could hit and throw. He was nobody's fool."

After the National League began using a more conventional ball again in 1931, Herman compiled less impressive offensive numbers than he had the previous two seasons. Nevertheless, he still managed to finish among the league leaders in several statistical categories, concluding the campaign with 18 homers, 97 RBIs, 93 runs scored, 191 hits, 43 doubles, 16 triples, and a .313 batting average, before being dealt to the Cincinnati Reds at season's end following a salary dispute with team ownership. Herman left Brooklyn with career totals of 112 home runs, 594 RBIs, 540 runs scored, 1,093 hits, 232 doubles, 66 triples, and 69 stolen bases, a .339 batting average, a .396 on-base percentage, and a .557 slugging percentage that ranks as the third best in franchise history.

Herman had an excellent year for the Reds in 1932, earning a 12th-place finish in the NL MVP balloting by placing among the league leaders with 16 homers, 87 RBIs, and a .326 batting average, while topping the senior circuit with a career-high 19 triples. Yet, in spite of his outstanding performance, Cincinnati traded him to the Chicago Cubs for four players shortly after the regular season ended. Herman subsequently spent two productive years in Chicago, having the biggest day of his career for the Cubs on July 20, 1933, when he hit 3 home runs and knocked in 8 runs against the Phillies. He then split the 1935 campaign between the Pirates and Reds, remaining in Cincinnati through the end of 1936, when he joined the Detroit Tigers as a backup. After being released by the Tigers early in 1937, Herman returned to the minor leagues, where he spent the next six seasons playing for the Hollywood Stars in the Pacific Coast League. Ironically, Herman rejoined the Dodgers at forty-two years of age in 1945, appearing in 37 games for them, almost exclusively as a pinch-hitter, before announcing his retirement at season's end. He concluded his major-league career with 181 home runs, 997 RBIs, 882 runs scored, 1,818 hits, 399 doubles, 110 triples, 94 stolen bases, a .324 batting average, a .383 on-base percentage, and a .532 slugging percentage.

Following his playing days, Herman spent brief periods of time serving as a coach for the Pittsburgh Pirates and a minor-league manager, before beginning a lengthy career in scouting. He lived until the age of eighty-four, passing away at his home in Glendale, California on November 27, 1987, following a bout with pneumonia and a series of strokes. In discussing her husband's final days, Herman's widow said, "His legs gave out. He fell a lot. He used a walker, then a wheelchair. Now he's free."

Part of Herman's obituary that subsequently appeared in the *New York Times* read: "Though he was an outstanding hitter, he was perhaps best remembered for what were viewed as his misadventures in the field and on the base paths." Meanwhile, another obituary headline read, "Daffiest of the Dodgers." Once again, Herman had no way of refuting the claims made by the members of the media.

## Dodger (Robins) Career Highlights:

**Best Season:** Although Herman also compiled exceptional numbers for Brooklyn the previous year, he unquestionably had the greatest season of his career in 1930. Placing in the league's top three in eight different offensive categories, Herman finished runner-up in the batting race to New York's Bill Terry (.401) with a mark of .393. He also ranked among the NL leaders with 35 home runs, 130 RBIs, 143 runs scored, 241 hits, 48 doubles, 416 total bases, 18 stolen bases, a .455 on-base percentage, and a .678 slugging percentage, establishing in the process single-season franchise records for highest batting average, highest slugging percentage, highest OPS (1.132), most hits, and most total bases.

**Memorable Moments/Greatest Performances:** Herman nearly tied a National League record when he hit safely in 9 consecutive trips to the plate against Pittsburgh, from August 9 to August 11, 1926.

Herman had a big day at the plate for the Robins on July 3, 1926, when, after going 2-for-5 during a 4-3 loss to the Giants in the first game of a doubleheader, he led his team to a 9-2 win in the nightcap by going 3-for-5, with a homer, double, and 5 RBIs.

Performing extremely well throughout May of 1927, Herman had one of his best games on the second of the month, when he led the Robins to a 10-7 victory over the Giants by going 3-for-4, with a pair of homers, 5 RBIs, and 3 runs scored. Although the Robins lost their May 20 matchup with the Cubs by a score of 7-5, Herman had another huge game, going 3-for-5, with 2 homers and 3 RBIs. He followed that up two days later with a 5-for-5 effort against Philadelphia, in leading his team to a 20-4 pasting of the Phillies. Herman also knocked in 2 runs and scored 4 times during the contest.

Herman again tormented Philadelphia's pitching staff on May 18, 1929, when he led the Robins to a 20-16 victory over the Phillies by going 5-for-6, with 5 RBIs and 2 runs scored.

Herman turned in a number of exceptional performances over the course of his brilliant 1930 campaign, with the first of those coming on April 29, when he collected 3 hits, including a homer and a triple, drove in 7 runs, and scored 3 times during a 19-15 win over the Giants.

Some three weeks later, on May 20, 1930, Herman led Brooklyn to a 16-9 victory over Philadelphia by going 5-for-6, with a homer, 6 RBIs, 2 runs scored, and 2 stolen bases.

Herman put together outstanding back-to-back efforts against Pittsburgh on June 22 and June 23, 1930, leading the Robins to 9-6 and 19-6 wins over the Pirates by hitting a pair of homers in each contest. Over the course of those two games, he went a combined 5-for-8, with 8 RBIs and 6 runs scored.

Although the Robins lost their July 31, 1930 matchup with Philadelphia by a score of 12-7, Herman had another big day at the plate, going 5-for-5, with a homer, 2 doubles, and 4 RBIs.

Just 8 days later, on August 8, 1930, Herman led Brooklyn to an 11-5 win over St. Louis by going 4-for-4, with 2 homers, a double, 4 RBIs, and 4 runs scored.

Herman also hit for the cycle twice during his time in Brooklyn, doing so both times in 1931. He accomplished the feat for the first time on May 18, when he led Brooklyn to a lopsided 14-4 victory over Cincinnati by going 4-for-5, with 5 RBIs and 4 runs scored. Herman duplicated his earlier effort a little over two months later, on July 24, when he went 4-for-5 with 3 runs scored during an 8-7 loss to Pittsburgh.

Yet, Herman is perhaps remembered most for his fielding miscues and base-running blunders, being called out twice on the base paths in 1930 after stopping to watch a home run and being passed by the hitter, who subsequently found himself being credited with just a single.

In an even more uncommon occurrence, Herman doubled into a double play during an August 15, 1926 contest when he drove a ball into the outfield gap with the bases loaded. As Herman rounded second base and headed towards third, the third base coach yelled at him to go back since the runner advancing from first, Chick Fewster, had not yet rounded third. Misinterpreting the coach's instructions, the runner from second, pitcher Dazzy Vance, headed back to third, even though he could have scored easily. With Herman ignoring his coach, he continued on to third, leaving all three base-runners there. The opposing third baseman subsequently tagged all three runners, retiring Fewster and Herman, but not Vance, who the rules of the game dictated was entitled to the bag.

## Notable Achievements:

- Batted over .300 five times, topping the .380-mark twice.
- Hit more than 20 home runs twice, surpassing 30 homers once (35 in 1930).
- Knocked in more than 100 runs twice, topping 120 RBIs once (130 in 1930).
- Scored more than 100 runs twice, topping 120 runs scored once (143 in 1930).
- Surpassed 200 hits twice, accumulating 241 safeties in 1930.
- Finished in double-digits in triples four times.
- Surpassed 30 doubles five times, topping 40 two-baggers on three occasions.

- Surpassed 400 total bases once (416 in 1930).
- Stole more than 20 bases once (21 in 1929).
- Compiled on-base percentage in excess of .400 twice.
- Posted slugging percentage in excess of .500 five times, topping the .600-mark twice.
- Posted OPS in excess of 1.000 twice.
- Finished second in NL in: batting average twice, on-base percentage once, OPS once, triples once, and stolen bases twice.
- Holds Dodgers single-season records for: highest batting average (.393), highest slugging percentage (.678), highest OPS (1.132), most hits (241), and most total bases (416) – all in 1930.
- Ranks among Dodgers career leaders in: batting average (second), on-base percentage (seventh), slugging percentage (third), and OPS (fourth).

# 27

# WILLIE KEELER

Nicknamed "Wee Willie" for his diminutive 5'4 ½", 140-pound frame, Willie Keeler spent parts of 19 seasons in the Major Leagues, establishing himself during that time as arguably the greatest slap hitter of his era. En route to compiling a lifetime batting average of .341, Keeler accumulated a total of 2,932 hits, with 85 percent of those being singles. In addition to batting more than .350 on seven separate occasions, Keeler surpassed 200 hits and 100 runs scored eight straight times while starring in right field for the National League's Baltimore Orioles and Brooklyn Superbas from 1894 to 1902. In his four seasons in Brooklyn alone, Keeler batted over .350 twice, never compiling a mark any lower than .333. He also collected more than 200 hits, scored more than 100 runs, and finished in double-digits in triples three times each as a member of the Superbas, in helping them capture two National League pennants.

Born to Irish immigrant parents in Brooklyn, New York on March 3, 1872, William Henry O'Kelleher got his start in organized baseball at the age of fourteen, when he joined a local amateur team. After quitting school one year later to play semi-pro ball, young William continued to compete at the semi-pro level until 1892, when, after starting the season with the Crescents of Plainfield, New Jersey, he began his professional career with Binghamton in the Eastern League. The left-handed hitting infielder, who changed his last name to "Keeler" at some point, spent the remainder of 1892 compiling a .373 batting average but struggling in the field for the Bingos, before being converted into an outfielder shortly after he joined the New York Giants in late September. Keeler spent most of the ensuing campaign in the minors as well, before being dealt to the Baltimore Orioles in January 1894.

Immediately inserted into the leadoff spot in the Baltimore batting order by manager Ned Hanlon, Keeler began an extraordinary five-year run for the Orioles during which he batted in excess of .370 each season, including a league-leading mark of .424 in 1897 that ranks as the highest single-season mark by a left-handed hitter in baseball history. Keeler also scored 145 runs, stole 64 bases, amassed 19 triples, and topped the senior circuit with a career-high 239 hits in 1897, while setting a National League record that still stands by hitting safely in 45 consecutive games. He followed that up by again leading the league in batting average (.385) and hits (216) in 1898, while scoring another 126 runs. In addition to batting over .370 in each of his five seasons with the Orioles, Keeler amassed well in excess of 200 hits and 120 runs scored each year, crossing the plate as many as 165 times in 1894.

Keeler, who had virtually no power at the plate (he hit just 33 home runs over the course of his career, with only three of those traveling over the outfield fence), learned to take full advantage of his outstanding running speed and exceptional bat control during his time in Baltimore. With the help of legendary groundskeeper Tom Murphy, the diminutive outfielder perfected what became known as the "Baltimore Chop," driving the ball into the infield dirt in front of home plate and beating out the resulting high hop for an infield single. Usually hitting immediately in front of John McGraw in the Orioles' batting order, Keeler collaborated with the future Giants manager to turn the hit-and-run into an art form. Keeler also possessed superior bunting skills and excelled at fouling off pitches with his tiny 30-inch bat, which weighed only 29 ounces. In discussing Keeler's hitting style, McGraw said:

"Keeler had the best batting eye I have ever seen. He held his bat away up in the middle with only about a foot of it extending beyond his hands, and he could slap the ball to either field. It was impossible to play for him. I have seen the outfield come in behind the infield or the infielders close up till you'd think you couldn't have dropped the ball into an open spot if you had it in your hand—but Keeler would invariably punch a base hit in there somewhere."

Legendary Pittsburgh Pirates shortstop Honus Wagner further elaborated on Keeler's extraordinary ability to place the ball wherever he wanted in the *50th Anniversary Hall of Fame Yearbook*, being quoted in that publication as saying, "Keeler could bunt any time he chose. If the third baseman came in for a tap, he invariably pushed the ball past the fielder.

If he stayed back, he bunted. Also, he had a trick of hitting a high hopper to an infielder. The ball would bounce so high that he was across the bag before he could be stopped."

In describing his approach at the plate, Keeler suggested, "Learn what pitch you can hit good, then wait for that pitch." He became much better known, though, for the description he gave to *Brooklyn Eagle* writer Abe Yager, who he told, "Keep your eye clear and hit 'em where they ain't; that's all."

Keeler also developed into an excellent defensive right-fielder, with Baltimore teammate Steve Brodie recalling, "He knew his territory like a child its ABC's."

With Hanlon and Orioles owner Henry Von der Horst acquiring majority ownership of the National League's Brooklyn franchise prior to the start of the 1899 campaign, they transferred the contracts of Keeler and fellow future Hall of Famers Joe Kelley and Hughie Jennings from Baltimore to Brooklyn, where they joined Hanlon, who assumed the managerial reins of the newly-named "Superbas." Elated to be returning to his hometown, Keeler told the *Brooklyn Eagle*, "I can say frankly that I would rather play in Brooklyn, my home, than anywhere else."

Keeler continued his exceptional play in Brooklyn, where he lived in his parents' house on Pulaski Street. Combining with Kelley, Jennings, and star shortstop Bill Dahlen, "Wee Willie" helped lead the Superbas to the NL pennant in 1899 by batting .379, collecting 216 hits, stealing 45 bases, and topping the senior circuit with 140 runs scored. Brooklyn repeated as league champions the following year, with Keeler batting .362, scoring 106 runs, driving in 68 others, stealing 41 bases, topping the circuit with 204 hits, and hitting 4 homers, which represented the second-highest total of his career (he hit 5 for Baltimore in 1894). Keeler had another solid year in 1901, batting .339, scoring 123 runs, and continuing his string of eight straight seasons with more than 200 hits by amassing 202 safeties. After seriously considering joining the newly-formed American League at season's end, Keeler ultimately decided to return to Brooklyn, telling the *New York Times*, "I expect to play ball for six or seven years longer, and, while it is not absolutely necessary for me to continue on the diamond as I have been unusually lucky in my investments, still the question was whether I should take a chance on a couple of years elsewhere, or a longer period here, where I am known and where my future is the brightest. If I ever get out of baseball, it is here that I shall be, and it is here that I expect to make friends. Consequently, I decided to stick to Brooklyn."

However, after batting .333, scoring 86 runs, and accumulating 186 hits for the Superbas in the final year of his contract with the club, Keeler elected to jump to the rival league in 1903 when AL President Ban Johnson offered him $11,000 to play for the New York Highlanders. Baseball's first $10,000-a-year-player, Keeler told the *New York Clipper*, "We can count on our fingers the number of years we will be able to play. That makes it plain that we must make all the money we can during the short period we may be said to be star players." Keeler left Brooklyn having batted .352, hit 8 homers, knocked in 219 runs, scored 469 times, collected 833 hits, 64 doubles, 43 triples, and 130 stolen bases, compiled a .389 on-base percentage, and posted a .425 slugging percentage as a member of the Superbas. His .352 batting average is the highest in franchise history.

Keeler spent the next seven seasons playing for the Highlanders, batting over .300 four more times, before becoming a part-time player in 1907. Released by the Highlanders early in 2010, he signed with the New York Giants, appearing in only 19 games with them over the course of the campaign, before announcing his retirement at season's end. One of a select few to play for all three New York teams that represented the city during the first half of the twentieth century, Keeler ended his career with 33 home runs, 810 RBIs, 1,719 runs scored, 2,932 hits, 241 doubles, 145 triples, 495 stolen bases, a .341 batting average, a .388 on-base percentage, and a .415 slugging percentage. Nearly impossible to strike out, he fanned only 136 times in more than 9,600 total plate appearances. Keeler's .341 batting average places him 14th all-time among major-league players. Meanwhile, his 366 sacrifice hits represent the fourth-highest total in the history of the game.

Following his retirement, Keeler returned to Brooklyn in 1912 to serve as a coach and scout under former teammate Bill Dahlen. He later joined the coaching staff of the Federal League's Brooklyn Tip-Tops, before leaving the game for good after spending one year scouting for the Boston Braves. Extremely wealthy upon his retirement due to a number of wise investments he made during his playing career, Keeler eventually lost most of his holdings when the real-estate market experienced a sharp decline after World War I. He also spent much of his retirement suffering

Courtesy of MEARS Online Auctions

En route to compiling a franchise-record .352
career batting average, Willie Keeler never batted
any lower than .333 as a member of the Superbas

from chest pains and rapid breathing, before passing away at only fifty
years of age early on New Year's Day 1923. Keeler's cause of death was
diagnosed as chronic endocarditis, an inflammation of the lining of the
heart. Some sixteen years later, in June 1939, the Baseball Hall of Fame
in Cooperstown, New York opened its doors to Willie Keeler and 25 other
baseball immortals at the formal opening of that institution.

Later ranked 75th on *The Sporting News* list of Baseball's 100 Greatest
Players, Keeler received the additional honor of being named as a finalist
for the Major League Baseball All-Century Team in 1999, even though he
had most of his finest seasons in the nineteenth century. Once called "the
most wonderful hitter that ever lived" by Hall of Fame radio broadcaster
Bill Stern, Keeler also received the following praise in *The Biographical
Encyclopedia of Baseball* (2000):

*"Wee Willie Keeler was one of the smallest men ever to play major-league baseball, but he was often the most important man on the field."*

## Dodger (Superbas) Career Highlights:

**Best Season:** Keeler's first season in Brooklyn proved to be his best as a member of the team. In addition to finishing fourth in the National League with a .379 batting average in 1899, Keeler topped the circuit with 140 runs scored and placed among the leaders with 216 hits, 45 stolen bases, a .425 on-base percentage, and an OPS of .876. He also struck out only two times in 633 total plate appearances.

**Memorable Moments/Greatest Performances:** Keeler, whose 45-game hitting streak as a member of the Orioles remains the longest in National League history, also put together a lengthy streak for the Superbas in 1902, hitting safely in 26 consecutive games from August 8 to September 3.

Although Keeler hit just one home run in 1899, it provided him with one of the most memorable moments of his career. With Brooklyn facing Philadelphia at Washington Park on May 15, Keeler stepped to the plate with the bases loaded and two men out in the bottom of the eighth inning. Noticing Philadelphia's Ed Delahanty playing him extremely shallow in left field, Keeler laced a line drive past him and raced around the bases for a grand slam home run that ended up giving Brooklyn an 8-5 victory. The grand slam homer was the only one of Keeler's career.

## Notable Achievements:

- Batted over .330 four times, topping the .360-mark twice.
- Scored more than 100 runs three times, surpassing 120 runs scored twice.
- Surpassed 200 hits three times.
- Finished in double-digits in triples three times.
- Stole more than 40 bases twice.
- Compiled on-base percentage in excess of .400 twice.
- Led NL in runs scored once and hits once.
- Finished second in NL in runs scored once and hits twice.
- Led NL outfielders in fielding percentage twice.

- Holds Dodgers franchise record for highest career batting average (.352).
- Number 75 on *The Sporting News'* 1999 list of Baseball's 100 Greatest Players.
- Two-time NL champion (1899 & 1900).
- 1900 world champion.
- Elected to Baseball Hall of Fame by members of BBWAA in 1939.

# 28

# DIXIE WALKER

Although Dixie Walker has been remembered through the years primarily for his unwillingness to accept Jackie Robinson as a teammate in Brooklyn, the Southern-born outfielder contributed significantly to any success the Dodgers experienced during his nine years in New York. Nicknamed "The People's Choice" due to his tremendous popularity with the local fans, Walker batted over .300 seven times for the Dodgers, winning the National League batting title in 1944, when he compiled a career-high mark of .357. Walker also surpassed 100 RBIs twice and 100 runs scored once during his time in Brooklyn, earning in the process four All-Star selections and five top 10 finishes in the league MVP voting. Still, even though Walker's outstanding all-around play helped the Dodgers win two National League pennants, the lack of tolerance he displayed in his final days with the team has created a negative image of him in the minds of most modern fans of the game.

Born in a log cabin in the small railroad and factory town of Villa Rica, Georgia on September 24, 1910, Fred "Dixie" Walker acquired his nickname from his father, who pitched for the Washington Senators from 1909 to 1912. Young Fred left school at the age of fifteen to take a job with the Tennessee Coal and Iron Company, a Birmingham steel mill, where he worked at the open hearth. But, with baseball in his blood, he decided to pursue a career in pro ball, leaving the mills in 1928 to play for Greensboro of the Piedmont League. After splitting the next two seasons between four different minor league teams, Walker began to draw attention to himself by posting a batting average of .401 for Class B Greenville of the South Atlantic Association over the first half of the 1930 campaign. Subsequently purchased by the New York Yankees, the nineteen-year-old outfielder spent the remainder of 1930 playing for Jersey City of the International League, where he batted .335 in 83 games.

The success Walker experienced at the minor-league level made him one of the top prospects in the Yankee organization, with the team believing that his combination of power, speed, and outfield defense made him a leading candidate to eventually succeed Babe Ruth in right field. However, shortly after being called up to New York for the first time early in 1931, Walker experienced a setback when he crashed into an outfield fence and suffered a shoulder injury that impaired his throwing. Forced to undergo surgery, Walker missed the remainder of 1931 and all of the ensuing campaign, before resurfacing in 1933, when, serving as the Yankees' fourth outfielder, he hit 15 homers, knocked in 51 runs, scored 68 times, and batted .274, in 98 games and 328 official at-bats, en route to earning a spot on *The Sporting News'* unofficial American League All-Rookie Team.

Unfortunately, Walker suffered a series of injuries over the course of the next few seasons that stunted his development, forcing him to spend most of his time back in the minor leagues. As a result, after appearing in a total of only 25 games in 1934 and 1935, the twenty-five-year-old Walker found himself headed to Chicago in May of 1936 when the Yankees sold him to the White Sox to clear a roster spot for Joe DiMaggio.

Walker's earlier shoulder woes returned after he joined the White Sox, limiting him to just 26 games in 1936 and forcing him to undergo a second surgery at season's end that involved the refastening of tendons. After resting the arm all winter, Walker made a full recovery, leaving him injury-free for the first time in years. Establishing himself as Chicago's starting right-fielder after he re-joined the team in 1937, Walker appeared in all 154 games for the White Sox, concluding his first full major-league season with 9 home runs, 95 RBIs, 105 runs scored, a .302 batting average, and a league-leading 16 triples.

In spite of the excellent numbers Walker compiled for them in 1937, the White Sox elected to include him in a six-player trade they completed with the Tigers at season's end that netted them, among others, popular Detroit outfielder "Gee" Walker (no relation). The Georgia native subsequently spent one and a half tumultuous years in Detroit, frequently being booed by Tiger fans, who resented him for replacing his popular namesake in left field. Yet, Walker continued to perform well at the plate, batting .308 in 1938, before being placed on waivers by the Tigers midway through the ensuing campaign after tearing ligaments in his knee. After being claimed by Brooklyn on July 24, 1939, Walker spent the rest of the year manning centerfield for the Dodgers, hitting 2 homers, driving in 38 runs, and batting .280 over the season's final 61 games.

Impressing manager Leo Durocher with his solid line-drive stroke and excellent outfield defense, the left-handed hitting Walker remained the Dodgers' starting centerfielder in 1940, earning a sixth-place finish in the NL MVP voting by batting .308, with 6 home runs, 66 RBIs, 75 runs scored, 171 hits, 8 triples, and 37 doubles. Furthermore, Walker's hustle in the field and on the base paths, as well as the .435 batting average he compiled against the hated New York Giants in his first full season with the Dodgers, quickly turned him into a fan favorite, eventually earning him the title of "The People's Choice" (or, as Brooklyn fans pronounced it with their local accent, "The People's Cherce"). Shifted to right field the following season to make room in center for brilliant rookie Pete Reiser, Walker continued to perform well, helping the Dodgers capture their first league championship in twenty-one years by batting .311, with 9 home runs, 71 RBIs, 88 runs scored, and a .391 on-base percentage. Limited to just 118 games by ankle and leg injuries in 1942, Walker posted his least-impressive numbers as a member of the Dodgers, concluding the campaign with a .290 batting average, 6 home runs, and only 54 RBIs.

With Walker's numerous baseball injuries making him exempt from military service, he remained active in the Major Leagues during World War II, compiling some of the best numbers of his career against lesser competition. After earning his first All-Star selection in 1943 by batting .302, with 71 RBIs and 83 runs scored, Walker topped the senior circuit with a .357 batting average the following year. He also hit 13 homers, knocked in 91 runs, scored 77 times, amassed 191 hits, and finished second in the league with a .434 on-base percentage, en route to earning his second straight All-Star nomination and a third-place finish in the NL MVP balloting. Walker followed that up by batting .300, scoring 102 times, and driving in a league-leading 124 runs in 1945, before earning a runner-up finish in the 1946 MVP voting by placing in the league's top five in nine different offensive categories, including RBIs (116), batting average (.319), and hits (184).

Widely considered to be one of the most popular players in Dodgers history by the conclusion of the 1946 campaign, Walker subsequently experienced a precipitous fall from grace shortly after Jackie Robinson

Dixie Walker (left), seen here with Joe Medwick, batted over .300
in seven of his nine seasons with the Dodgers

joined the team the following spring. Upon learning of Robinson's impending arrival, Walker joined a number of his teammates in signing a petition imploring the Dodgers not to add the rookie infielder to the roster. When that failed, he wrote a letter to Branch Rickey, asking the club president to trade him to another team. Although Walker remained somewhat evasive in his letter as to the reason behind his request, he admitted years later that concerns over the profitability of his Alabama business served as his primary motive. Fearful that playing with a black man might deter his Southern neighbors from frequenting his hardware store, Walker chose not to challenge the Jim Crow laws that prevailed at the time, stating on one occasion, "I didn't know if people would spit on me or not [for playing with a black man]."

After reluctantly trying to trade one of his team's best players prior to the start of the regular season, Rickey found himself unable to work out a suitable deal, forcing Walker to remain in Brooklyn for one more year. During that time, he shared a somewhat awkward relationship with Robinson, with the two men rarely acknowledging one another on the field. However, Walker never went out of his way to be unpleasant to Robinson, who later described his teammate as a man of innate fairness. In fact, Walker eventually came to respect Robinson for the manner in which he conducted himself both on and off the field, calling him "as outstanding an athlete as I ever saw." And, after the Dodgers captured the 1947 National League pennant, Walker praised Robinson, suggesting, "He is everything Branch Rickey said he was when he came up from Montreal."

Walker ended up being a key contributor to Brooklyn's 1947 NL championship ball club, finishing the year with 9 homers, 94 RBIs, 77 runs scored, and a .306 batting average, en route to earning All-Star honors for the fourth and final time in his career. But, after declining an offer to remain in the organization as manager of the American Association's St. Paul Saints, Walker headed to Pittsburgh when Branch Rickey granted his earlier request by including him in a six-player trade he completed with the Pirates on December 8, 1947. Walker left the Dodgers having hit 67 homers, driven in 725 runs, scored 666 times, collected 1,395 hits, 274 doubles, and 56 triples, batted .311, compiled a .386 on-base percentage, and posted a .441 slugging percentage as a member of the team.

Walker spent the final two seasons of his playing career in Pittsburgh, batting .316 as the team's starting right-fielder in 1948, before batting .282 in a part-time role the following year. He announced his retirement after the Pirates released him following the conclusion of the 1949 campaign, ending his big-league career with 105 home runs, 1,023 RBIs, 1,038 runs scored, 2,064 hits, 376 doubles, 96 triples, a .306 batting average, a .383 on-base percentage, and a .437 slugging percentage. Always a very difficult man to strike out, Walker fanned a total of only 325 times in nearly 7,700 plate appearances.

Following his playing days, Walker spent most of the 1950s managing in the minor leagues, before serving as batting coach for the Cardinals, Braves, and Dodgers at the major-league level. During that time, as he continued to interact more and more with black and Latino players, his position on integration softened considerably. In fact, Roger Kahn's 1993 memoir of baseball in New York during the 1950s entitled *The Era: 1947-1957, When the Yankees, the Giants, and the Dodgers Ruled the World* included a quote from Walker in which the latter expressed regret over attempting to block Jackie Robinson's arrival in Brooklyn due to his concerns over his off-season business in Alabama. Speaking of his involvement in the conspiracy, Walker told Kahn, "That's why I started that thing. It was the dumbest thing I ever did in my life. Would you tell everybody that I'm deeply sorry?"

Walker continued to coach Dodger batsmen until 1976, when he retired to his home in Alabama. He lived another six years, losing his battle with colon cancer on May 17, 1982, at seventy-one years of age.

## Dodger Career Highlights:

**Best Season:** Walker played his best ball for the Dodgers from 1944 to 1946, compiling the most impressive offensive numbers of his career over the course of those three seasons. In addition to leading the NL with 124 RBIs in 1945, Walker batted .300, scored 102 runs, and finished second in the league with a career-high 42 doubles. He followed that up by finishing among the NL leaders in 10 different offensive categories in 1946, including placing in the league's top three in RBIs (116), batting average (.319), and hits (184), en route to earning a runner-up finish in the MVP voting. Nevertheless, the 1944 campaign would have to be considered the finest of Walker's career, even though he compiled the numbers he did against lesser competition. In addition to topping the senior circuit with a career-high .357 batting average, Walker knocked in 91 runs and established career-high marks in hits (191), total bases (283), on-base percentage (.434), and slugging percentage (.529). Walker's outstanding performance earned him his lone *Sporting News* All-Star selection and a close third-place finish in the league MVP balloting, in spite of the fact that the Dodgers finished in seventh place, 42 games behind the pennant-winning Cardinals.

**Memorable Moments/Greatest Performances:** Walker keyed an 8-4 win over the New York Giants on August 7, 1940 by going 4-for-5, with a homer, triple, 4 RBIs, and 3 runs scored.

Walker again torched New York's pitching staff later in the year, on September 1, 1940, when he went 5-for-5 during a 7-3 victory over the Giants.

Although the Dodgers lost their matchup with the Giants eight days later by a score of 7-4, Walker continued his assault against Giant hurlers, turning in another 5-for-5 effort.

Walker hit 2 home runs in one game for the first time in his career on May 6, 1941, when he led the Dodgers to a 7-3 victory over Pittsburgh with a pair of long balls and 5 RBIs. He again homered twice in the same contest on September 5, 1942, when he knocked in 4 runs and scored 3 times during a 7-6 loss to the Giants. Walker went deep twice in the same game for the third and final time on June 19, 1943, when he led the Dodgers to a 7-5 win over the Phillies by going 4-for-4, with a pair of homers, 3 RBIs, and 4 runs scored.

After entering the game as a pinch-hitter during the early stages of the contest, Walker had a huge day at the plate on July 2, 1941, leading the Dodgers to a 9-3 win over Philadelphia by going 3-for-4, with a pair of triples and 5 RBIs.

Continuing his practice of excelling against the hated Giants, Walker led the Dodgers to an 8-4 win over their crosstown rivals on September 2, 1944 by hitting for the cycle, knocking in 4 runs, and scoring twice.

Walker continued to be a thorn in the side of Giant pitchers on August 25, 1945, when he homered, singled, and drove in a career-high 6 runs during a 13-3 Dodgers victory.

## Notable Achievements:

- Batted over .300 seven times, topping the .350-mark once (.357 in 1944).
- Knocked in more than 100 runs twice, topping 120 RBIs once (124 in 1945).

- Scored more than 100 runs once (102 in 1945).
- Surpassed 30 doubles six times, topping 40 two-baggers once (42 in 1945).
- Compiled on-base percentage in excess of .400 twice.
- Posted slugging percentage in excess of .500 once (.529 in 1944).
- Led NL in batting average once and RBIs once.
- Led NL outfielders in assists once and double plays turned once.
- Led NL right-fielders in: putouts once, assists once, double plays turned once, and fielding percentage once.
- Finished in top five of NL MVP voting twice, placing second in 1946 and third in 1944.
- Four-time NL All-Star (1943, 1944, 1946 & 1947).
- 1944 *Sporting News* All-Star selection.
- Two-time NL champion (1941 & 1947).

# 29

# JAKE DAUBERT

An outstanding all-around first baseman who excelled both at the bat and in the field, Jake Daubert spent nine of his 15 major-league seasons in Brooklyn, during which time he proved to be the National League's finest player at his position. An excellent contact hitter with occasional power, the left-handed swinging Daubert batted over .300 seven times for the Dodgers, en route to winning a pair of batting titles. Superb with the glove as well, Daubert drew comparisons to Hal Chase, who gained widespread acclaim during the first two decades of the twentieth century as the greatest defensive first baseman of the Deadball Era, by annually ranking among the top players at his position in assists, putouts, double plays, and fielding percentage. Daubert's stellar all-around play earned him seven selections to *Baseball Magazine's* All-American team and the 1913 Chalmers Award, presented at that time to the league's Most Valuable Player. He also finished in the top-10 in the MVP voting two other times, while helping the Dodgers capture their first league championship since the turn of the century.

Born in Shamokin, Pennsylvania on April 17, 1884, Jacob Ellsworth Daubert quit school at the age of eleven to join his father and two older brothers in the local coal mines, where he became a breaker boy who separated slate and other impurities from the coal. Not wishing to experience the same fate as his brother Calvin, who lost his life while working in the mines, Daubert left his job in 1906 to play for a semi-pro baseball team in Lykens, Pennsylvania. He continued to play semi-pro ball until late in 1907, when he signed with a minor-league team situated in Marion, Ohio.

After subsequently signing with the Cleveland Indians in 1908, Daubert spent most of the year with Nashville of the Southern Association following his release by Cleveland. He then split the 1909 campaign between Toledo of the American Association and Memphis of the Southern Association, before having his contract purchased by the Dodgers after being discovered by Brooklyn scout Larry Sutton while playing for Memphis.

Finally making his major-league debut on April 14, 1910, three days before he celebrated his twenty-sixth birthday, Daubert had a solid first year in Brooklyn, batting .264, driving in 50 runs, scoring 67 others, stealing 23 bases, and finishing among the NL leaders with 8 home runs and 15 triples. He followed that up with an excellent all-around 1911 campaign in which he scored 89 runs, stole a career-high 32 bases, placed near the top of the league rankings with a .307 batting average and 176 hits, led all NL first basemen in double plays, and ranked among the league's top players at his position in both putouts and assists, en route to earning the first of his seven selections to *Baseball Magazine's* All-American team and a ninth-place finish in the Chalmers Award balloting. Daubert again placed in the top-10 in the voting in 1912 after batting .308, driving in a career-high 66 runs, scoring 81 times, collecting 172 hits, stealing 29 bases, finishing fourth in the league with 16 triples, and leading all NL first basemen with a .993 fielding percentage.

Just as they had done in Daubert's first three years with the club, the Dodgers (or Robins, as they were known at the time) continued to struggle in 1913, finishing sixth in the eight-team National League with a record of only 65-84. Nevertheless, the Brooklyn first baseman ended up being named the winner of the Chalmers Award after topping the senior circuit with a .350 batting average, finishing second in the league with 178 hits, and placing third with a .405 on-base percentage.

Possessing a solid line-drive swing, Daubert batted over .300 a total of 10 times over the course of his career, placing in the league's top five in that category on five separate occasions. He also finished in double-digits in triples eight times, with his excellent running speed also enabling him to steal more than 20 bases six times. Meanwhile, Daubert's extraordinary bat control allowed him to amass a total of 392 sacrifice bunts—the second-highest total in major-league history.

Yet, in spite of his offensive skills, Daubert became equally well known for his defensive prowess, with *Baseball Magazine* stating in 1913, "Jake Daubert is easily one of the greatest infielders baseball has ever seen. Flashing and sensational like [Hal] Chase, he is, unlike Chase, never erratic, never prone to sudden error, never sulky or indifferent in his play." The magazine went on to say that Daubert "is universally popular; he is the most valuable first sacker playing the game."

Daubert was indeed one of the most liked and respected players of his era, being elected to the Baseball Players Fraternity by his peers, who eventually named him Vice President of that organization. Extremely intelligent, Daubert also became quite popular with the sportswriters, who enjoyed conversing with him on a wide variety of subjects beyond the game.

Daubert continued his strong all-around play in 1914, winning his second straight batting title with a mark of .329, while also finishing third in the league with 89 runs scored and placing sixth in the circuit with a .432 slugging percentage. After another solid performance the following year, Daubert helped the Dodgers win the NL pennant in 1916 by placing second in the league with a .316 batting average, scoring 75 runs, and leading all players at his position with a .993 fielding percentage. Unfortunately, he failed to perform well in the World Series, batting just .176, as Brooklyn lost to Boston in five games.

After a subpar 1917 season in which he batted a career-low .261, Daubert rebounded in the war-shortened 1918 campaign to hit .308, with a league-leading 15 triples. However, he subsequently entered into a contentious disagreement with Brooklyn owner Charles Ebbets that ultimately led to his being traded to Cincinnati. With the season cut short to 126 games by the United States' involvement in World War I and the influenza epidemic, team owners chose to prorate player salaries. But Daubert, who had been among the founding members of the Players' Fraternity, maintained that Ebbets owed him the remainder of his salary since he had signed a multi-year contract with the Dodgers. After suing Ebbets for the balance of his pay, Daubert ended up recovering most of his losses in an out-of-court settlement. But Ebbets had the final say, exacting a measure of revenge against Daubert by trading him to the Reds for outfielder Tommy Griffith. Daubert left Brooklyn with career totals of 33 home runs, 415 RBIs, 648 runs scored, 1,387 hits, 138 doubles, 87 triples, and 187 stolen bases, a lifetime .305 batting average, a .365 on-base percentage, and a .395 slugging percentage.

Upon Daubert's arrival in Cincinnati, the Reds immediately named him team captain, a title he continued to hold throughout his six-year tenure with the club. Serving in that capacity, Daubert helped lead the Reds to

Jake Daubert won a pair of batting titles
while playing for Brooklyn during the second decade
of the 20th century

the world championship in 1919, when they defeated the heavily-favored
Chicago White Sox in the World Series that has since become known as
the infamous *Black Sox Scandal of 1919*. With the advent of the "Live-
Ball Era" the following year, Daubert ended up posting some of the best
offensive numbers of his career the next few seasons, compiling his most
impressive stat-line in 1922, when he batted .336 and established career-
high marks with 12 homers, 205 hits, 114 runs scored, and a league-leading 22 triples.

Daubert continued to play well for Cincinnati until the tail end of the
1924 campaign, when he left the team after falling ill during a road trip
to New York. Subsequently diagnosed with appendicitis and gallstones,

Daubert also suffered from frequent headaches and a lack of sleep after being hit in the head by a pitch earlier in the season. After having an appendectomy performed by Cincinnati's team doctor on October 2, Daubert failed to make a full recovery, passing away one week later, on October 9, 1924, at only forty years of age. Although doctors initially cited "exhaustion, resulting in indigestion" as the immediate cause of death, it later surfaced that Daubert suffered from a hereditary blood disorder called hemolytic spherocytosis that contributed to his death, and to that of his son years later as well.

The life and playing career of Jake Daubert ended with him having hit 56 home runs, driven in 722 runs, scored 1,117 times, collected 2,326 hits, 250 doubles, 165 triples, and 251 stolen bases, batted .303, compiled a .360 on-base percentage, and posted a .401 slugging percentage. He subsequently never came close to gaining induction into the Baseball Hall of Fame, failing to garner more than 1.3% of the votes in any election his name appeared on the ballot.

## Dodger Career Highlights:

**Best Season:** It could be argued that Daubert had his finest all-around season for the Dodgers in 1912, when he knocked in a career-high 66 runs, scored 81 times, accumulated 172 hits, 16 triples, and 29 stolen bases, batted .308, and led all NL first basemen with a .993 fielding percentage. Nevertheless, the 1913 campaign is generally considered to be Daubert's best season in Brooklyn. En route to earning league MVP honors, Daubert topped the senior circuit with a career-high .350 batting average, drove in 52 runs, scored 76 others, stole 25 bases, and finished among the NL leaders with 178 hits, a career-best .405 on-base percentage, and an OPS of .829.

**Memorable Moments/Greatest Performances:** An exceptional fielder throughout his career, Daubert recorded 21 putouts at first base during an 8-5 loss to the Boston Braves on May 6, 1910, falling just one putout shy of tying the major-league record.

Daubert had one of his best days at the plate for the Dodgers on May 11, 1911, when he keyed a 10-1 victory over the St. Louis Cardinals by going 4-for-4, with a homer, triple, 3 runs scored, and a career-high 4 runs batted in.

Later that same season, on September 12, 1911, Daubert went 4-for-6, with a career-best 4 runs scored during an 11-6 win over the Philadelphia Phillies.

Daubert had another big game on June 17, 1918, when he led the Dodgers to a come-from-behind 4-3 victory over the Chicago Cubs by going 4-for-5, with 3 RBIs, including a game-winning run-scoring single with one man out in the bottom of the ninth inning.

Daubert had a similarly productive afternoon a little over two months later, on August 28, 1918, when he went 4-for-5, with 2 RBIs and 2 runs scored, during an 8-7 win over the rival New York Giants.

Daubert exhibited his exceptional bat control on August 15, 1914, when he set a major-league record by laying down 6 successful sacrifice bunts during a doubleheader sweep of the Phillies.

## Notable Achievements:

- Batted over .300 seven times, reaching the .350-mark once (.350 in 1913).
- Finished in double-digits in triples three times, topping 15 three-baggers all three times.
- Stole more than 20 bases six times, surpassing 30 thefts once (32 in 1911).
- Compiled on-base percentage in excess of .400 once (.405 in 1913).
- Led NL in batting average twice and triples once.
- Led NL first basemen in: assists once, fielding percentage twice, and double plays turned twice.
- Ranks fourth in Dodgers history in triples (87).
- Hold National League career record for most sacrifice hits (392).
- 1913 NL MVP.
- Seven-time *Baseball Magazine* All-Star selection (1911, 1913, 1914, 1915, 1916, 1917 & 1918).
- 1916 NL champion.

# 30

# CLAUDE OSTEEN

A durable left-hander who often pitched in hard luck during his time in Los Angeles, Claude Osteen won at least 15 games and threw more than 250 innings seven times each in his nine seasons with the Dodgers, eventually establishing himself as the ace of their pitching staff, after spending his first two years in L.A. pitching in the shadow of Sandy Koufax and Don Drysdale. Compiling an ERA under 3.00 four times as a member of the team, Osteen managed to win 20 games twice for the Dodgers, even though he frequently received poor run support from his teammates. A three-time NL All-Star, Osteen made significant contributions to the Dodgers' pennant-winning ball clubs of 1965 and 1966, posting a total of 32 victories for them over the course of those two seasons, with his clutch performance in Game Three of the 1965 World Series completely changed the momentum of the fall classic and enabling the Dodgers to overcome an early 2-0 deficit to the Minnesota Twins. By the time Osteen left Los Angeles following the conclusion of the 1973 campaign, he had compiled a total of 147 wins for the Dodgers, placing him seventh in team annals in that category. He also continues to rank among the franchise's all-time leaders in shutouts (fifth), innings pitched (sixth), and starts (third).

Born in the rural community of Caney Springs, Tennessee on August 9, 1939, Claude Wilson Osteen moved with his family to Cincinnati, Ohio during his freshman year of high school in 1954. After enrolling in Reading High School, Osteen went on to establish himself as the greatest pitcher in that institution's history, compiling a record of 23-1 during his career, which included a magnificent senior year in which he went 16-0, with an ERA of 0.13 and 221 strikeouts in 103⅔ innings pitched.

Pursued by several major-league teams following his graduation from Reading High, the seventeen-year-old Osteen elected to sign with the local Cincinnati Reds, who guaranteed him a spot on their big-league roster. Upon inking his deal with the Reds, Osteen commented, "I have the confidence that I can win in the majors right now, and I want the chance to prove it."

However, it ended up being quite some time before Osteen had an opportunity to prove himself at the major-league level. After appearing in only 3 games and working a total of just 4 innings in 1957, he spent virtually all of the next two seasons in the minors, before finally earning a return trip to Cincinnati. After rejoining the Reds, Osteen experienced more of the same, languishing in their bullpen for most of 1960 and spending much of the ensuing campaign back in the minors. He finally received his reprieve on September 16, 1961, when the Reds traded him to the expansion Washington Senators for pitcher Dave Sisler. Years later, Osteen called the deal that sent him to Washington "probably one of the biggest breaks in my career because I got to go there as a starting pitcher with little pressure."

Pitching for one of baseball's worst teams, Osteen compiled an overall record of 33-41 over the course of the next three seasons. Nevertheless, he established himself during that time as Washington's most reliable and consistent starter, throwing well over 200 innings in both 1963 and 1964, while posting earned run averages of 3.35 and 3.33, respectively. Particularly effective in the second of those campaigns, Osteen won 15 games and tossed 257 innings for a Senators team that finished ninth in the 10-team American League with a record of just 62-100.

Taking note of the twenty-five-year-old southpaw's strong performance, the Dodgers worked out a seven-player trade with the Senators on December 4, 1964 that sent slugging outfielder Frank Howard, third baseman Ken McMullen, first baseman Dick Nen, and pitchers Phil Ortega and Pete Richert to Washington for Osteen and infielder John Kennedy. Recalling his feelings upon learning that he had been dealt from the lowly Senators to a team that had won the World Series just one year earlier, Osteen said, "It was such a joyous thing to go to a team that I knew wanted me all along, and one with a great pitching staff led by Sandy Koufax and Don Drysdale. In one year, I went from a last-place team in Washington with the Senators to one that won the World Series in Los Angeles. It's hard to top that."

Yet, while Osteen basked in the glow of joining a contending team, the Los Angeles media criticized the trade since its members felt that Howard represented the Dodgers' lone power threat. But, even though the massive Howard eventually went on to establish himself as one of the game's premier sluggers, the Dodgers never regretted making the deal since they got everything they wanted, and more, out of Osteen. Although the 5'11", 175-pound left-hander finished just 15-15 for the pennant-winning Dodgers in 1965, he pitched much better than his record would seem to indicate, placing in the league's top 10 with a 2.79 ERA and 287 innings pitched, while striking out 162 batters, posting a WHIP of 1.153, and finishing third in the league with 40 starts. Osteen subsequently came up big for the Dodgers in the World Series, compiling an ERA of 0.64 in his two starts, which included a five-hit shutout of the Twins in Game Three, after Minnesota victories over Drysdale and Koufax in the first two contests put Los Angeles in an early 2-0 hole. Osteen followed that up with an outstanding 1966 campaign in which he went 17-14 with a 2.85 ERA, while allowing only 6 home runs in 240 innings of work, making him the most difficult pitcher in the National League to take deep.

With the Dodgers compiling a losing record in each of the next two seasons, Osteen posted a composite mark of just 29-35. Nevertheless, he continued to pitch well, especially in 1967, when he earned his first All-Star selection by placing among the league leaders with 17 wins, 5 shutouts, 39 starts, 14 complete games, and 288⅓ innings pitched. Osteen then had arguably the finest season of his career in 1969, when he finished 20-15, with a 2.66 ERA, 183 strikeouts, 16 complete games, 7 shutouts, and 321 innings pitched, placing second in the league in each of the last two categories.

Osteen gradually emerged as one of the National League's top hurlers even though he lacked dominating stuff. Blessed with exceptional control of all his pitches, which included a slider, sinking fastball, curve, and changeup, Osteen relied primarily on the location and movement on his pitches to thwart opposing hitters, as he revealed years later when he explained, "Learning how to pitch, and then knowing how to throw to hitters' tendencies, made the difference in my career. I had a ninety-plus mph fastball when I got to the majors, but I was wild. So, I worked on my mechanics and sacrificed some of that velocity to gain greater control and movement on my pitches. From then on, I never tried to overthrow, but, instead, pitched to contact. I think that saved my arm."

Courtesy of MEARS Online Auctions

Claude Osteen's pivotal win in Game Three of the
1965 World Series helped the Dodgers overcome
an early 2-0 deficit to Minnesota

Osteen's durability also proved to be a key to his success, with him noting, "Except for a bout of tendonitis in the beginning of my career, I never had arm trouble. I think it's because I had wiry strength from growing up on a farm, hauling hay bales and riding a combine. My hands and arms were strong. There wasn't a nut or bolt that I couldn't loosen." Osteen added, "I had a delivery that didn't put pressure on any key points of my shoulder, elbow, or arm."

Osteen's delivery and physical make-up enabled him to remain the focal point of the Dodgers' starting rotation through 1973, when he threw more than 230 innings for the 10th straight time. He also earned his third

All-Star nomination that year by winning 16 games, after pitching some of the best ball of his career the previous season, when he went 20-11, with a 2.64 ERA and 14 complete games.

Still, with the Dodgers seeking to add power to their lineup, they completed a trade with the Astros on December 6, 1973 that sent the thirty-four-year-old Osteen to Houston for hard-hitting outfielder Jim Wynn. Osteen left the Dodgers having compiled an overall record of 147-126 as a member of the team, along with an ERA of 3.09, a WHIP of 1.217, 34 shutouts, 1,162 strikeouts in 2,397 innings of work, and 100 complete games.

Osteen spent most of 1974 with the Astros, before being dealt to St. Louis during the latter stages of the campaign. After being released by the Cardinals at season's end, Osteen signed as a free agent with the Chicago White Sox, with whom he finished his career in 1975. He retired with an overall record of 196-195, an ERA of 3.30, a WHIP of 1.275, 40 shutouts, 140 complete games, and 1,612 strikeouts in 3,460⅔ innings pitched. Osteen's teams suffered 47 shutouts with him on the mound, prompting him to later comment, "These games sure make you a better pitcher. I know it is up to me to pitch a shutout."

After retiring as an active player, Osteen transitioned seamlessly into a role he had spent years preparing for, both mentally and physically, as he noted when he said, "Toward the end of my career, I paid particular attention to my delivery and keeping my body in shape. I learned more about myself over the last five years of my career than at any other time. I was training myself to be a pitching coach, and to relay the knowledge I gained from coaches like the Dodgers' Red Adams and the Redlegs' Tom Ferrick."

Osteen began his coaching career in the farm system of the Philadelphia Phillies in 1976, before spending the next twenty-four years splitting his time between the Cardinals, Phillies, Rangers, and Dodgers at the major-league level. In discussing the philosophy he employed while working with younger pitchers, Osteen stated, "I thought of myself as a psychologist and tried to get the most out of each pitcher. From a delivery standpoint, I looked for flaws. ...I tried to make the delivery as perfect as I could mechanically so he [the pitcher] has a chance to not hurt his arm, and to take the pressure points off the key parts of the delivery." After leaving the Dodger organization at the end of 2000, Osteen remained close to the game the next several years as a scout and consultant for the Arizona Diamondbacks, before finally retiring to his home in Tennessee in 2009.

## Dodger Career Highlights:

**Best Season:** Osteen had a big year for the Dodgers in 1972, going 20-11, with a 2.64 ERA, 4 shutouts, 14 complete games, 252 innings pitched, and a WHIP of 1.194. However, he had his finest all-around season three years earlier, concluding the 1969 campaign with a record of 20-15, an ERA of 2.66, and career-best marks in strikeouts (183), shutouts (7), complete games (16), innings pitched (321), starts (41), and WHIP (1.143). In addition to finishing fifth in the league in wins, Osteen placed among the NL leaders in shutouts (second), innings pitched (second), starts (second), complete games (ninth), and WHIP (10th).

**Memorable Moments/Greatest Performances:** A pretty fair hitting pitcher, Osteen hit 8 homers and knocked in 76 runs over the course of his career, with his greatest day at the plate coming on May 26, 1970, when he went 4-for-5, with a homer, double, 4 RBIs, and 3 runs scored during a lopsided 19-3 victory over the Giants.

Osteen performed brilliantly in his very first start for the Dodgers, surrendering just 2 hits and 2 walks, while striking out 8, during a complete-game 3-1 win over the Pirates on April 14, 1965.

Osteen tossed the only one-hitter of his career a little over two months later, when he allowed just a second-inning single to San Francisco catcher Jack Hiatt during a 3-0 win over the Giants on June 17, 1965.

Although Osteen lost his next start four days later to the Mets by a score of 1-0, he again pitched exceptionally well, allowing just 2 hits and 3 walks to Mets batters.

Osteen turned in his most dominant performance of the 1966 campaign on September 9, when he surrendered just 3 hits and struck out 5 during a 7-0 whitewashing of the Houston Astros.

Osteen posted almost identical numbers on August 23, 1967, when he allowed only 3 hits and recorded 6 strikeouts during an 8-0 shutout of the Cincinnati Reds.

Despite winning only one of his three World Series starts, Osteen proved to be an outstanding postseason pitcher during his time in Los Angeles, compiling an ERA of 0.86, a WHIP of 0.857, and surrendering only

12 hits in 21 total innings of work. He pitched easily the most memorable game of his career against Minnesota in the 1965 fall classic, when, after Don Drysdale and Sandy Koufax suffered defeats in the first two contests, the Dodgers placed their hopes squarely on Osteen's shoulders as they headed back to Los Angeles for Game Three. Recalling the tension that existed on the team's charter flight back to L.A., Osteen commented, "My teammates had confidence in me. I was sitting with my wife on the airplane. Players went up and down the aisle and tapped me on the shoulder and said, 'You'll get 'em.' By the time I got off the plane I was a nervous wreck." After giving up a leadoff double to Zoilo Versalles in the top of the first inning, Osteen settled down, surrendering only 4 more hits the rest of the way, in leading the Dodgers to a 4-0 win that gave them momentum in a Series they eventually won in seven games.

## Notable Achievements:

- Won 20 games twice, topping 15 victories five other times.
- Compiled ERA under 3.00 four times.
- Threw more than 300 innings once, topping 250 innings pitched six other times.
- Led NL pitchers in assists three times.
- Finished second among NL pitchers in shutouts three times and innings pitched once.
- Ranks among Dodgers career leaders in: wins (seventh), shutouts (fifth), innings pitched (sixth), and starts (third).
- Three-time NL All-Star (1967, 1970 & 1973).
- Two-time NL champion (1965 & 1966).
- 1965 world champion.

# 31

# DAVEY LOPES

The offensive catalyst of Dodger teams that won four pennants and one world championship, Davey Lopes proved to be one of the National League's most prolific base stealers and top second basemen of the 1970s. The Dodgers' starter at second from 1973 to 1981, Lopes swiped more than 30 bags seven straight times, surpassing 50 thefts on three occasions. In addition to topping the senior circuit in steals twice, the speedy Lopes placed in the league's top three in that category three other times, en route to amassing a total of 418 stolen bases for the Dodgers that places him second only to Maury Wills in franchise history. Meanwhile, Lopes' career total of 557 steals in only 671 attempts gives him a success rate of 83.01% that ranks third all-time among players with at least 400 stolen bases (behind only Tim Raines and Willie Wilson). In addition to his base-stealing prowess, Lopes possessed unusual power for a middle infielder of his day, once hitting as many as 28 home runs in a season. Lopes also scored more than 100 runs twice and led all NL second sackers in assists once, with his varied skill-set earning him four All-Star nominations and two *Sporting News* All-Star selections.

Born in East Providence, Rhode Island on May 3, 1945, David Earl Lopes played high school baseball at local LaSalle Academy, before splitting his college years between Iowa Wesleyan College and Washburn University in Topeka, Kansas. Initially drafted by San Francisco in the eighth round of the 1967 amateur draft, Lopes chose not to sign with the Giants, instead waiting until his stock rose to the point that the Dodgers picked him in the second round of the January phase of the following year's draft.

After signing with the Dodgers, Lopes spent the next five years advancing through their vast farm system, before finally making his major-league debut with the club during the latter stages of the 1972 campaign.

Appearing in a total of 11 games over the season's final two weeks, the twenty-seven-year-old Lopes batted .214, scored 6 runs, and stole 4 bases. Named the starter at second early the following year, Lopes went on to have a solid rookie season, hitting 6 homers, driving in 37 runs, scoring 77 times, batting .275, and finishing fifth in the league with 36 stolen bases, while hitting mostly out of the leadoff spot in the batting order. Lopes subsequently emerged as an offensive force in 1974, when he helped the Dodgers capture the NL pennant by hitting 10 homers, scoring 95 runs, batting .266, and finishing second in the league with 59 steals. He followed that up with another strong performance in 1975, when, despite batting just .262, he managed to compile a very respectable .358 on-base percentage by drawing 91 bases on balls. Lopes also finished third in the league with 108 runs scored and topped the senior circuit with 77 stolen bases.

Limited by injuries to only 117 games in 1976, Lopes struggled somewhat at the plate, batting just .241, hitting only 4 homers, and driving in just 20 runs. Nevertheless, he recorded 63 stolen bases, edging out Cincinnati's Joe Morgan (60) for the league lead in that category. Although forced to miss nearly a month of the ensuing campaign with various injures, Lopes returned to top form, hitting 11 homers, knocking in 53 runs, scoring 85 times, stealing 47 bases, and batting .283 for a Dodgers team that won the pennant. A healthier Lopes helped lead the Dodgers to their second straight NL flag in 1978 by establishing new career highs with 17 home runs and 58 RBIs, while also scoring 93 runs, batting .278, and stealing 45 bases in 49 attempts. His contributions to the success of the team earned him All-Star honors for the first of four straight times and MVP consideration (he finished 16th in the voting). Lopes also won the only Gold Glove of his career. Although the Dodgers ended up losing the World Series to the Yankees in six games, Lopes had a memorable postseason, hitting a pair of homers, driving in 5 runs, and batting .389 against Philadelphia in the NLCS, before homering 3 times, knocking in 7 runs, and batting .308 against New York in the fall classic.

Lopes' power surge during the 1978 playoffs and World Series proved to be a portent of things to come, since the 5'9", 170-pound second baseman hit a career-high 28 home runs the following year, while also batting .265, stealing 44 bases in 48 attempts, and establishing new career highs with 73 RBIs, 109 runs scored, and 97 bases on balls.

Lopes' combination of power and speed made him one of the more unique middle infielders of his time. In fact, his 28 homers in 1979 enabled him to join Rogers Hornsby and Davey Johnson as the only second basemen in major-league history to reach the seats that many times in one season, to that point. However, it was with his legs that Lopes made his greatest impact, proving to be one of his era's top base-stealers and most disruptive forces on the base paths. Praised by Dusty Baker, who said of his former teammate, "He was the best base-runner I played with," Lopes challenged opposing pitchers and catchers, served as a distraction to opposing infielders, and often got his teammates better pitches to hit. He also possessed a keen batting eye, twice finishing in the league's top five in bases on balls. Those are the qualities that made Lopes one of the most effective leadoff hitters in baseball for much of his career.

Following his offensive outburst in 1979, Lopes remained in Los Angeles only two more years. After hitting 10 homers, driving in 49 runs, scoring 79 times, stealing 23 bases, and batting .251 in 1980, Lopes found himself splitting time at second with veteran Derrell Thomas and rookie Steve Sax during the strike-shortened 1981 campaign. With Sax waiting in the wings and Lopes having batted just .206 in 58 games in 1981, the Dodgers elected to part ways with the thirty-six-year-old second baseman at season's end, trading him to the Oakland Athletics for minor league infielder Lance Hudson. Lopes left Los Angeles with career totals of 99 home runs, 384 RBIs, 759 runs scored, 1,204 hits, 165 doubles, 39 triples, and 418 stolen bases in only 503 attempts, a .262 batting average, a .349 on-base percentage, and a .380 slugging percentage.

Lopes spent most of the next three seasons in Oakland, having his best year for the A's in 1983, when he hit 17 homers, knocked in 67 runs, scored 64 times, stole 22 bases, and batted .277. After being traded to the Cubs during the latter stages of the 1984 campaign, Lopes split his final three seasons between Chicago and Houston, ending his career as a backup with the Astros in 1987. While with the Cubs, the forty-year-old Lopes amazingly stole 47 bases in 51 attempts in 1985, doing so in only 99 games. Choosing to announce his retirement after Houston released him on November 12, 1987, Lopes finished his career with 155 home runs, 614 RBIs, 1,023 runs scored, 1,671 hits, 232 doubles, 50 triples, 557 stolen bases, a .263 batting average, a .349 on-base percentage, and a .388 slugging percentage.

Following his playing days, Lopes served as first base coach for the Baltimore Orioles from 1992 to 1994, before assuming the same role for the San Diego Padres from 1995 to 1999. Subsequently hired to manage the Milwaukee Brewers in 2000, Lopes remained in that post until 15 games into the 2002 season, when team management replaced him with former Dodger teammate Jerry Royster. After being relieved of his duties in Milwaukee, Lopes rejoined the Padres as first base coach from 2003 to 2005. He then held the same position with the Washington Nationals in 2006 and the Philadelphia Phillies from 2007 to 2010, before returning home to coach first base for the Dodgers from 2011 to 2015. Leaving the Dodgers following the conclusion of the 2015 campaign, Lopes currently serves as first base coach for the Washington Nationals.

## Dodger Career Highlights:

**Best Season:** Lopes played extremely well for the Dodgers in 1975, scoring 108 runs, walking 91 times, compiling a .358 on-base percentage, and leading the National League with a career-high 77 stolen bases. He also served as an offensive spark for their 1978 NL championship ball club, hitting 17 homers, driving in 58 runs, scoring 93 times, stealing 45 bases, and batting .278, en route to earning his first All-Star selection. Nevertheless, Lopes undoubtedly had his finest season in 1979, when, in addition to stealing 44 bases, compiling a .372 on-base percentage, and posting a .464 slugging percentage, he established career-high marks in home runs (28), RBIs (73), runs scored (109), and bases on balls (97), placing third in the league in each of the last two categories. He also had arguably his best year defensively, leading all NL second basemen with 384 assists, while also finishing second among players at his position with a career-high 341 putouts.

**Memorable Moments/Greatest Performances:** En route to stealing a league-leading 77 bases in 1975, Lopes swiped 38 consecutive bags without getting caught, breaking in the process a fifty-three-year-old record previously set by Pittsburgh's Max Carey in 1922. Vince Coleman eventually surpassed Lopes' mark 14 years later.

Lopes had the greatest day of his career on August 20, 1974, when he homered three times during an 18-8 pasting of the Chicago Cubs at Wrigley Field. He finished the game 5-for-6, with 3 round-trippers, a double, 4 RBIs, and 3 runs scored.

Davey Lopes (right) served as the offensive catalyst
for four pennant-winning Dodger teams

Lopes delivered one of the most memorable hits of his career on September 2, 1979, when his walk-off grand slam off Hall of Fame reliever Bruce Sutter with two men out in the bottom of the ninth inning gave the Dodgers a 6-2 victory over the Cubs.

Lopes excelled on the base paths in the 1981 NLCS, helping the Dodgers defeat Montreal in five games by stealing five bases.

However, Lopes had his finest postseason in 1978, when he also experienced the most emotional moment of his career. After leading the Dodgers to a four-game victory over Philadelphia in the NLCS by hitting 2 homers, driving in 5 runs, and batting .389, Lopes dedicated his World Series to fallen Dodger coach, Jim Gilliam, who passed away just prior to the start of the fall classic. Lopes then went out and led his team to an 11-5 win over the Yankees in Game One by hitting a pair of homers and driving in 5 runs. Paying tribute to his close friend and mentor, Lopes pointed to the sky with one hand as he rounded first base on his first home run trot.

After hitting his second homer, he pointed with both arms extended, each forefinger pointing straight up.

## Notable Achievements:

- Hit more than 20 home runs once (28 in 1979).
- Scored more than 100 runs twice.
- Stole more than 30 bases seven times, topping 50 thefts on three occasions, including 77 steals in 1975.
- Led NL in stolen bases twice.
- Led NL second basemen in assists once.
- Ranks among Dodgers career leaders in stolen bases (second) and bases on balls (eighth).
- Set new Major League record in 1975 (since broken) by recording 38 consecutive successful stolen base attempts.
- Hit three home runs in one game vs. Chicago on August 20, 1974.
- 1978 Gold Glove winner.
- Two-time *Sporting News* All-Star selection (1978 & 1979).
- Four-time NL All-Star (1978, 1979, 1980 & 1981).
- Four-time NL champion (1974, 1977, 1978 & 1981).
- 1981 world champion.

# 32

# JOHNNY PODRES

Earning a permanent place in Dodger lore with his brilliant perfor-mance in arguably the single most important game in franchise history, Johnny Podres ended years of frustration for Brooklyn fans with his 2-0 shutout of the Yankees in Game Seven of the 1955 World Series. Podres' win over the Yankees gave the Dodgers their only world championship in Brooklyn, helping to ease the pain of five previous losses to their longtime nemesis in the fall classic. Yet, even though the twenty-three-year-old left-hander's victory over New York proved to be easily the highlight of his career, Podres should be remembered for more than just that one game. In addition to handcuffing New York's potent lineup that early October afternoon, Podres won at least 14 games for the Dodgers five times, post-ing as many as 18 victories in 1961, when he led all NL hurlers with a winning percentage of .783. Podres also finished first among NL pitchers in ERA, WHIP, and shutouts once each, en route to earning three All-Star selections. An exceptional postseason performer during his career, Podres helped the Dodgers capture four world championships by compiling a re-cord of 4-1 and an ERA of 2.11 in World Series play.

Born in Witherbee, New York on September 30, 1932, John Joseph Podres grew up rooting for the Dodgers, listening to Red Barber broad-cast their games on the radio. Excelling on the mound while attending local Mineville High School, Podres signed with the Dodgers following his graduation and spent the next two years advancing through their farm system, before making his major-league debut in Brooklyn early in 1953.

The twenty-year-old southpaw experienced a moderate amount of success in his first big-league season, compiling a record of 9-4 and an ERA of 4.23, while starting 18 games and making another 15 appearances coming out of the bullpen. Assuming a similar role the following year,

Podres went 11-7 with a 4.27 ERA, before suffering through an injury-marred 1955 campaign during which he injured his shoulder and later sustained bruised ribs after being struck by the Ebbets Field batting cage while groundskeepers busied themselves preparing the field for a pregame workout. However, after finishing just 9-10 with a 3.95 ERA during the regular season, Podres ended up being the hero of the 1955 World Series, helping the Dodgers defeat the Yankees in seven games by winning both his starts, including tossing a five-hit shutout in Game Seven that earned him Series MVP honors.

After subsequently missing the entire 1956 season while serving in the military, Podres returned to the Dodgers in 1957 to compile a record of 12-9 and a league-leading 2.66 ERA, 6 shutouts, and 1.082 WHIP for a Brooklyn team that finished third in the National League. Despite winning just 13 of his 28 decisions after the Dodgers moved to Los Angeles the following year, Podres pitched relatively well, finishing third in the league with 143 strikeouts and tossing more than 200 innings for the first time in his career, en route to earning his first All-Star selection. He followed that up with a pair of 14-win campaigns, before having the most successful season of his career in 1961, when he posted a mark of 18-5 that gave him a league-best .783 winning percentage.

Podres, who possessed an exceptional fastball when he first entered the Major Leagues, actually became more of a complete pitcher after the Dodgers moved to Los Angeles. Having lost some of his velocity, Podres perfected the circle-change, which eventually became his "out" pitch. Years later, Tim McCarver discussed the southpaw's favorite offering in *Baseball for Brain Surgeons and Other Fans*, noting, "Brooklyn Dodgers left-hander Johnny Podres threw the most effective circle-change, and it still serves as the prototype. He gripped the ball with only his last three fingers while his thumb and index finger formed a circle halfway up on the ball. It was a changeup that he could throw on any count."

Meanwhile, fellow Dodger hurler Carl Erskine commented on the success that Podres experienced after the team moved to the West Coast, stating, "Most people don't realize that Johnny had a lot of good pitching left in Los Angeles. Most people remember him for that big game in the 1955 World Series. But he was a strong pitcher for the early teams in Los Angeles."

Courtesy of RMYauctions.com

Johnny Podres gave the Dodgers their first
World Series victory with his 2-0 shutout
of the Yankees in Game 7 of the 1955 fall classic

Erskine added, "Johnny always had good command; he was always around the plate."

Podres had two more solid years for the Dodgers, going a combined 29-25 from 1962 to 1963, and tossing a career-high 255 innings in the first of those campaigns, before his skills began to diminish. After missing most of 1964 with an injury, Podres went just 7-6 the following year, prompting the Dodgers to trade him to Detroit during the early stages of the 1966 season. Podres left Los Angeles with a career record of 136-104, an ERA of 3.66, 1,331 strikeouts in 2,029⅓ innings of work, 74 complete games, 23 shutouts, and a WHIP of 1.320. He continues to rank among the franchise's all-time leaders in wins, strikeouts, and shutouts.

Podres spent most of the next two seasons in Detroit, compiling an overall record of 7-6 for the Tigers while working mostly in relief. After being released by the Tigers following the conclusion of the 1967 campaign, Podres sat out all of 1968, before signing with the San Diego Padres, with whom he spent his final season. He announced his retirement at the end of 1969, finishing his career with a record of 148-116, an ERA of 3.68, 1,435 strikeouts in 2,265 innings of work, 77 complete games, 24 shutouts, and a WHIP of 1.317.

Following his playing days, Podres began a twenty-three-year career in coaching, serving at different times as pitching coach of the Padres, Boston Red Sox, Minnesota Twins, and Philadelphia Phillies. He eventually settled in Queensbury, New York, where he lived until January 13, 2008, when he passed away at the age of seventy-five after being hospitalized for heart and kidney problems and a leg infection.

In mourning Podres' passing, longtime Dodgers General Manager Buzzie Bavasi said of his former pitcher, "He was one in a million. I have said this many times:

> *I've had many good pitchers on my teams during my career, including the best in the business in Sandy Koufax, and I am sure that all these pitchers will agree that, if a club had to win one game, it would be Podres that would get the call."*

## Dodger Career Highlights:

**Best Season:** It could certainly be argued that Podres had his finest season in 1961, when he posted easily the best won-lost record of his career. However, aside from finishing 18-5, Podres did not compile overly impressive numbers in any other statistical category, concluding the campaign with an ERA of 3.74, a WHIP of 1.330, just 6 complete games and 1 shutout, and surrendering more hits (192) than innings pitched (182⅔). That being the case, the feeling here is that Podres actually pitched his best ball for the Dodgers in 1957, when, in addition to going 12-9, he led all NL pitchers with an ERA of 2.66, 6 shutouts, and a WHIP of 1.082, establishing career-best marks in all three categories.

**Memorable Moments/Greatest Performances:** Podres turned in his first dominant performance for the Dodgers on September 14, 1954, when he shut out the Reds by a score of 4-0, allowing just 3 hits and 1 walk during the contest.

Podres put forth an extremely similar effort on May 29, 1957, winning a 1-0 pitcher's duel with Pittsburgh's Ron Kline, while surrendering only 3 hits and 1 walk to Pirates batsmen.

Podres tossed another three-hit shutout on September 6, 1957, defeating the Giants by a score of 3-0 in the process.

Podres also threw three two-hitters during his career, doing so during an 8-0 blanking of the Giants on May 25, 1959, an 11-0 win over the Phillies on June 11, 1959, and a 1-0 victory over the Reds on July 5, 1963.

Podres hurled another gem on July 10, 1963, following up his two-hit shutout of Cincinnati with a 1-0 win over the Mets during which he surrendered just 3 hits and struck out 11.

Still, it is for his performance in the 1955 World Series that Podres will always be remembered most. After the Yankees won the first two games of the fall classic, Podres got the Dodgers back in the Series with a complete-game, 8-3, win in Game Three. Returning to the mound for the Series finale, Podres defeated the Yankees by a score of 2-0, with the game's pivotal play taking place in the bottom of the sixth inning, when Sandy Amoros' superb running catch of a fly ball hit by Yogi Berra into the left-field corner with two men on base and no one out resulted in a rally-killing double play. Reflecting back on his exceptional performance, Podres said, "There was no pressure on me. Who expected a guy 9-10, a young kid pitching against the Yankees, to beat them in the third game, and then, pitching again on the fourth day, to beat them again in the seventh game? If I get beat, I go home and they say, 'Dem Bums, wait till next year' But we changed all that."

Podres also proved to be a thorn in the side of the Yankees in the 1963 World Series, winning Game Two by a score of 4-1, while surrendering just 1 run and 6 hits over 8⅓ innings.

## Notable Achievements:

- Topped 15 victories twice, winning 18 games in 1961.
- Posted winning percentage in excess of .700 once (.783 in 1961).
- Compiled ERA under 3.00 once (2.66 in 1957).
- Threw more than 250 innings once (255 in 1962).
- Led NL pitchers in: winning percentage once, ERA once, shutouts once, and WHIP once.

- Ranks among Dodgers career leaders in: wins (ninth), strikeouts (eighth), shutouts (tied-10th), and starts (eighth).
- Won two games in 1955 World Series, including Game Seven shutout of Yankees.
- 1955 World Series MVP.
- Three-time NL All-Star (1958, 1960 & 1962).
- Five-time NL champion (1953, 1955, 1959, 1963 & 1965).
- Four-time world champion (1955, 1959, 1963 & 1965).

# 33

# ERIC KARROS

A powerful right-handed batter who topped the 30-homer mark in five of his 11 seasons in Los Angeles, Eric Karros hit more home runs for the Dodgers than any other player since the team relocated to the West Coast nearly 60 years ago. An outstanding run-producer as well, the former National League Rookie of the Year knocked in more than 100 runs for the Dodgers on five separate occasions, en route to also establishing himself as one of the franchise's all-time leaders in RBIs. In addition to his slugging feats, Karros proved to be an outstanding leader and solid defensive first baseman during his time in Los Angeles, leading all players at his position in assists twice and fielding percentage once, while annually placing near the top of the league rankings in putouts and double plays. Although Karros never had the good fortune to play for a pennant-winning team, his strong all-around play helped the Dodgers capture three NL West titles, earning him one Silver Slugger and one top-five finish in the league MVP voting.

Born in Hackensack, New Jersey on November 4, 1967, Eric Peter Karros moved with his family to California as a young boy. Excelling more in the classroom than on the ball field while attending Patrick Henry High School in San Diego, Karros garnered little interest from college recruiters as he approached graduation. However, displaying the same determination he carried with him to the playing field, Karros eventually convinced UCLA head baseball coach Gary Adams to offer him a conditional scholarship—one in which Adams agreed not to cut him from the squad before the end of fall tryouts if he enrolled at that institution.

After making the Bruins' roster as a freshman, Karros ended up spending most of his first year at UCLA serving the team as a glorified bullpen catcher. But he began to emerge as one of the school's foremost hitters and top RBI-men the following year, before improving even more as a junior, prompting the Dodgers to select him in the sixth round of the 1988 amateur draft

Karros spent the next four years advancing through the Los Angeles farm system, before finally joining the Dodgers during the latter stages of the 1991 campaign. Accumulating only 14 at-bats over the final month of the season, Karros failed to make much of an impression, striking out six times and collecting just one hit, giving him a batting average of .071.

Replacing the departed Eddie Murray as the Dodgers' starting first baseman the following year, Karros went on to have a solid first season, earning NL Rookie of the Year honors by hitting 20 homers, driving in 88 runs, and batting .257. The 6'4", 210-pound first baseman posted similar numbers in 1993, finishing the year with 23 homers, 80 RBIs, and a .247 batting average, before hitting 14 homers, knocking in 46 runs, and batting .266 during the strike-shortened 1994 campaign.

Developing into the one of the senior circuit's top sluggers in 1995, Karros finished among the league leaders with 32 home runs and 105 RBIs, while also scoring 83 times and batting .298. With his strong performance helping the Dodgers capture the NL West title, Karros earned a fifth-place finish in the league MVP voting. Although his batting average slipped to .260 the following year, Karros compiled similar power numbers, concluding the campaign with 34 homers and 111 RBIs.

In addition to adding a significant amount of power to the Dodgers' lineup, Karros' emergence as a top offensive threat enabled him to evolve into one of the team's foremost leaders, with teammate Brett Butler telling Lawrence Rocca in the December 1995 edition of *Baseball Digest*, "He [Karros] understands the game. He knows what it takes to win, which is hard work. He's talented and works hard, which is very rare among many young major leaguers today. He wasn't gifted with tremendous speed, unbelievable power, a tremendous arm. His whole life, he's had to prove himself. He believes in himself. A leader is not someone who walks around and says he's a leader. A leader leads by example. That's what he does."

Karros again put up excellent numbers for the Dodgers in 1997, finishing in the league's top 10 with 31 homers, while also driving in 104 runs, scoring a career-high 86 times, and batting .266. Despite missing nearly a month of the ensuing campaign with various injuries, Karros had another solid year, hitting 23 homers, knocking in 87 runs, and batting .296. He

Eric Karros (right), seen here with Mike Piazza, hit more than 30 home runs five times for the Dodgers

followed that up with perhaps his finest offensive season, tying his career high in home runs (34), while establishing new career-bests in RBIs (112), batting average (.304), hits (176), doubles (40), and OPS (.912).

However, after hitting 31 homers, driving in 106 runs, and batting .250 in 2000, Karros experienced a precipitous decline in offensive production the next two seasons, totaling only 28 home runs and 136 RBIs in 2001 and 2002. With the thirty-five-year-old first baseman apparently on the downside of his career, the Dodgers elected to include him in a four-player trade they completed with the Cubs on December 4, 2002 that also sent Mark Grudzielanek to Chicago for outfielder Chad Hermansen and catcher Todd Hundley. Karros left Los Angeles with career totals of 270 home runs, 976 RBIs, 752 runs scored, 1,608 hits, 302 doubles, and 10 triples, a .268 batting average, a .325 on-base percentage, and a .457 slugging percentage. He currently ranks third in franchise history in home runs and sixth in RBIs. Meanwhile, only Brooklyn sluggers Duke Snider and Gil Hodges can match the five 30-homer, 100-RBI seasons that Karros turned in as a member of the team.

Karros ended up spending just one year in Chicago, hitting 12 homers, knocking in 40 runs, and batting .286 for the Cubs in a part-time role in 2003, before signing with the Oakland A's when he became a free agent at season's end. Released by the A's four months into the 2004 campaign after hitting just 2 homers, driving in only 11 runs, and batting just .194 in his 40 games with them, Karros subsequently announced his retirement, ending his career with 284 home runs, 1,027 RBIs, 797 runs scored, 1,724 hits, 324 doubles, 11 triples, a .268 batting average, a .325 on-base percentage, and a .454 slugging percentage.

Shortly after retiring as an active player, Karros entered into a career in broadcasting, accepting a position with Fox Sports. After initially doing the pregame shows for the MLB playoffs, Karros moved to ESPN, where he continued to share with viewers his insights, both as a studio and in-game analyst. Hired to call regional games for Fox Saturday Baseball in 2007, Karros eventually earned a spot on the No. 2 broadcast team—a post he currently holds.

## Dodger Career Highlights:

**Best Season:** Karros had his finest statistical season in 1999, when he established career-high marks in home runs (34), RBIs (112), batting average (.304), hits (176), doubles (40), total bases (318), slugging percentage (.550), and OPS (.912). However, he finished in the league's top 10 in only one offensive category ($10^{th}$ in doubles) and failed to receive any support in the NL MVP voting. On the other hand, Karros placed near the top of the league rankings in six different offensive categories, earned his lone Silver Slugger, and finished fifth in the NL MVP balloting in 1995, when he compiled offensive numbers that rivaled the figures he posted four years later. In addition to finishing fifth in the league with 32 homers and placing fourth with 105 RBIs, Karros batted .298 and ranked in the league's top 10 in hits (164), total bases (295), slugging percentage (.535), and OPS (.905). All things considered, Karros played his best ball for the Dodgers in 1995.

**Memorable Moments/Greatest Performances:** Although Karros collected just one hit in 14 at-bats after being called up by the Dodgers in September 1991, he made it a big one. Pinch-hitting for reliever John Wetteland in the bottom of the $12^{th}$ inning of a September 16 contest the Dodgers trailed by a score of 5-4, Karros drove home the tying run with a line-drive double to deep left-center field. Jeff Hamilton followed Karros' two-bagger with an RBI single to centerfield, giving the Dodgers a come-from-behind 6-5 victory over Cincinnati.

Karros got off to an excellent start in the ensuing campaign, hitting his first career home run in his initial at-bat of the 1992 season, in helping the Dodgers defeat San Diego by a score of 6-3 on April 9.

Karros had a big day at the plate on August 24, 1993, leading the Dodgers to a lopsided 13-4 victory over the Pittsburgh Pirates by going 3-for-5, with a pair of homers, 2 runs scored, and a career-high 6 runs batted in.

Less than two weeks later, on September 4, 1993, Karros helped the Dodgers record a decisive 9-4 win over the Marlins by going 4-for-5, with a homer, 4 RBIs, and 2 runs scored.

Karros turned in another 4-for-5 performance on July 25, 1994, collecting a single, double, and a pair of homers, knocking in 4 runs, and scoring 3 times during a 10-5 win over the Giants.

Karros defeated St. Louis almost single-handedly on June 3, 1998, going 4-for-5, with a homer and 5 RBIs, during a 7-4 victory over the Cardinals.

Karros equaled his single-game career-high in RBIs on August 11, 1999, leading the Dodgers to a 9-7 win over Montreal by driving in 6 runs with a homer and a pair of singles.

Karros came up big for the Dodgers on April 8, 2000, helping them overcome a 5-1 deficit to the New York Mets heading into the ninth inning by hitting a pair of homers. After contributing to a four-run, game-tying rally in the top of the ninth by hitting a leadoff homer off John Franco, Karros delivered the game's winning run with another blast in the ensuing frame, this one off Armando Benitez.

Later that year, on August 22, 2000, Karros became the only Dodger player ever to hit two home runs in the same inning when he homered twice against Montreal in the sixth inning of a contest the Dodgers went on to win by a score of 14-6. Karros' round-trippers knocked in 4 of the 9 runs the Dodgers scored that inning.

## Notable Achievements:

- Hit more than 30 home runs five times, topping 20 homers on three other occasions.
- Knocked in more than 100 runs five times.
- Batted over .300 once (.304 in 1999).
- Topped 30 doubles twice, surpassing 40 two-baggers once (40 in 1999).
- Posted slugging percentage in excess of .500 twice.
- Led NL in games played once.
- Led NL first basemen in assists twice and fielding percentage once.
- Ranks among Dodgers career leaders in: home runs (third), RBIs (sixth), extra-base hits (fifth), doubles (ninth), total bases (eighth), and games played (10th).
- Holds Los Angeles Dodgers career records for most home runs (270) and most sacrifice flies (74).
- Hit two home runs in same inning vs. Montreal on August 22, 2000.
- 1992 NL Rookie of the Year.
- 1995 Silver Slugger winner.
- Finished fifth in 1995 NL MVP voting.
- 1995 *Sporting News* All-Star selection.

# 34

# SHAWN GREEN

Considered to be an emerging star when the Dodgers acquired him prior to the start of the 2000 campaign, Shawn Green continued his ascension into baseball's elite after arriving in Los Angeles, topping 40 homers, 100 RBIs, and 100 runs scored in two of the next three seasons, en route to earning a pair of top-10 finishes in the NL MVP voting. Noted for his smooth left-handed swing, Green set the Dodgers' single-season home run record in his second year in L.A. by reaching the seats 49 times, breaking in the process the previous mark of 43 held jointly by Duke Snider (1956) and Gary Sheffield (2000). Green also had one of the greatest days of any batter in the history of the game the following season, when he tied a major-league record by hitting four home runs in one game, while also setting a new mark by collecting 19 total bases. In all, Green hit 162 home runs in his five seasons with the Dodgers, surpassing 20 homers four times. Although the Dodgers failed to advance to the World Series in any of those five seasons, Green's potent bat helped them finish first in the NL West once and second on two other occasions.

Born in Des Plaines, Illinois on November 10, 1972, Shawn David Green grew up in Orange County, California, where he attended Tustin High School. After earning a first-team selection to the 1991 *USA Today* All-USA High School Team, Green accepted a scholarship offer from Stanford University. Selected at the same time by the Toronto Blue Jays with the 16th overall pick of the 1991 MLB amateur draft, Green reached an agreement with the Blue Jays that allowed him to play in the minor leagues during the summer, but that also enabled him to attend classes at Stanford during the offseason. Green spent most of the next three seasons in the minors, earning multiple All-Star selections, while also being named the International League's Best Batting Prospect, Best Outfield

Arm, and Most Exciting Player in *Baseball America's* 1994 "Tools of the Trade" poll.

After making brief appearances with the Blue Jays in each of the previous two seasons, Green arrived in Toronto to stay in 1995. Manning right field mostly against right-handed pitching, the 6'4", 200-pound Green performed well in a platoon situation, hitting 15 homers, driving in 54 runs, scoring 52 times, and batting .288, in 121 games and 379 official at-bats. He also did a good job in the outfield, using his deceptive speed to finish third among AL right-fielders in putouts, while leading all players at his position with 9 assists. Used primarily against right-handed pitching again in 1996 and 1997, Green continued to post solid numbers, totaling 27 homers and 98 RBIs over the course of those two campaigns, while compiling batting averages of .280 and .287, respectively.

Green truly began to excel after the Blue Jays inserted him into their everyday starting lineup in 1998. Facing all types of pitching, the twenty-five-year-old outfielder hit 35 homers, knocked in 100 runs, scored 106 times, stole 35 bases, and batted .278, becoming in the process the first player in franchise history to top 30 homers and 30 steals in the same season. Green followed that up by earning his first All-Star selection and a ninth-place finish in the AL MVP voting in 1999 by batting .309, placing among the league leaders with 42 home runs, 123 RBIs, 134 runs scored, and 190 hits, and topping the circuit with 45 doubles and 361 total bases. He also won the only Gold Glove of his career by finishing second among AL right-fielders in putouts, while leading all players at his position with a .997 fielding percentage.

Yet, in spite of the notoriety he received as a result of his excellent all-around play, Green remained unhappy in Toronto, expressing a desire to return to his California roots when he eventually became a free agent following the conclusion of the 2000 campaign. Accommodating the disgruntled outfielder, Toronto worked out a deal with the Dodgers on November 8, 1999 in which they sent Green and minor league second baseman Jorge Nuñez to Los Angeles for reliever Pedro Borbón, Jr. and the equally unhappy Raúl Mondesí. Upon learning of the trade, an elated Green said, "I'm excited to get a chance to play at home in Los Angeles. It's a dream come true for me."

In explaining why he traded away his team's best all-around player, Blue Jays General Manager Gord Ash stated, "Shawn made it clear that

Shawn Green's 49 home runs in 2001 established
a new single-season franchise record

his intention was not to sign a long-term contract in Toronto, and his preference was to play in a U.S. market, specifically Los Angeles. Shawn advised the club that his decision was based on his desire to settle down and return home."

Meanwhile, Dodgers General Manager Kevin Malone praised his latest acquisition, saying, "We know what he's capable of doing. He sets the tone with his work ethic. He's a baseball player with a work ethic. His most important assets are his integrity and character."

Dodgers chairman Bob Daly added, "It was important that there's somebody here who wants to be a Dodger. I was unbelievably impressed, not only with his statistics, but also with what a fine young man he is."

Green, who earlier rejected a five-year, $48 million contract extension from the Blue Jays, quickly signed a six-year, $84 million deal with the Dodgers.

Although Green subsequently performed erratically at times during his first year in Los Angeles, he ended up posting good overall numbers, concluding the 2000 campaign with 24 homers, 99 RBIs, 98 runs scored, 24 stolen bases, 44 doubles, and a .269 batting average, while appearing in all 162 games for the Dodgers. He also compiled one of the longest consecutive games on-base streaks in major-league history, at one point reaching base safely in 53 straight contests. Green followed that up with a career year in 2001, batting .297 and placing among the NL leaders with 49 home runs, 125 RBIs, 121 runs scored, 370 total bases, a .598 slugging percentage, and a .970 OPS.

In addition to drawing attention to himself with his fabulous offensive performance, Green made headlines in 2001 by missing a game for the first time in more than two years. Choosing to sit out the Dodgers' September 26 meeting with the Giants since it coincided with Yom Kippur, the holiest of all Jewish holidays, Green failed to take the field for the first time in 415 contests. In explaining his decision, Green said, "I felt like it was the right thing to do...I didn't do this to gain approval. I thought it was the right example to set for Jewish kids, a lot of whom don't like to go to synagogue." Green subsequently donated his day's pay of $75,000 to a charity for survivors of the New York 9/11 terrorist attacks.

Although the 2001 season proved to be the highlight of Green's career, he followed that up with another big year, concluding the 2002 campaign with 42 home runs, 114 RBIs, 110 runs scored, and a .285 batting average, earning in the process his second All-Star selection and a fifth-place finish in the NL MVP balloting. Bothered by tendinitis in his left shoulder in 2003, Green hit only 19 homers and knocked in just 85 runs, although he managed to bat .280 and amass a career-high 49 doubles, which placed him second in the league rankings. Green's power numbers improved somewhat in 2004, as he helped the Dodgers advance to the playoffs by hitting 28 homers, driving in 86 runs, and scoring 92 times, even though his batting average slipped to .266.

With the Dodgers believing that the thirty-two-year-old Green's best days lay in the past, they elected to trade him to the Arizona Diamondbacks for four prospects on January 11, 2005, ending his five-year association with them. Green left Los Angeles having hit 162 homers, driven in 509 runs, scored 505 times, collected 842 hits, 183 doubles, 12 triples, and 63 stolen bases, batted .280, compiled an on-base percentage of .366, and posted a slugging percentage of .510.

Green ended up spending almost two full seasons in Arizona, hitting 33 homers, knocking in 124 runs, scoring 146 others, and batting .285 during that time, before being dealt to the New York Mets during the latter stages of the 2006 campaign. He subsequently ended his career in New York, retiring at the end of the following season with career totals of 328 home runs, 1,070 RBIs, 1,129 runs, scored, 2,003 hits, 445 doubles, 35 triples, and 162 stolen bases, a lifetime batting average of .283, an on-base percentage of .355, and a slugging percentage of .494. Green's home run and RBI totals leave him trailing only Hank Greenberg all-time among Jewish major league players.

## Dodger Career Highlights:

**Best Season:** Green clearly had his finest season for the Dodgers in 2001, when, in addition to scoring 121 runs, stealing 20 bases, and batting .297, he established career-high marks in home runs (49), RBIs (125), total bases (370), and slugging percentage (.598). Although Green's 49 homers only tied him for the fourth–highest total in the league, behind Barry Bonds, Sammy Sosa, and Luis Gonzalez, they established a new single-season Dodger record.

**Memorable Moments/Greatest Performances:** Green paced the Dodgers to a 5-4 win over Arizona on April 12, 2001 by hitting a pair of homers and knocking in 4 runs.

Green had a similarly productive afternoon on May 19, 2001, when he led the Dodgers to a lopsided 10-2 victory over the Mets by going 3-for-4, with 2 homers, 4 RBIs, and 3 runs scored.

Green turned in arguably his finest all-around effort of the 2001 campaign on September 7, when he went 4-for-5, with a pair of homers, 3 RBIs, 3 runs scored, and a stolen base, during a 7-1 win over the Cardinals

Green came up big in the clutch for the Dodgers on August 3, 2002, when, after hitting a solo home run earlier in the game, he delivered a game-tying two-run homer with 2 men out in the top of the ninth inning, to even up the score with the Phillies at 6-6. The Dodgers went on to win the game by a score of 8-6 in 12 innings, with Green finishing the contest 4-for-6, with a pair of homers, a double, 3 RBIs, and 3 runs scored.

Green had a memorable day at the plate on August 15, 2001, leading the Dodgers to a 13-1 mauling of the Montreal Expos by hitting 3 home runs and driving in a career-high 7 runs.

However, Green topped that effort on May 23, 2002, when he turned in arguably the finest single-game performance in Major League history, leading the Dodgers to a 16-3 victory over the Brewers in Milwaukee by going 6-for-6, with 4 homers, a double, 7 RBIs, and 6 runs scored. Green's 4 home runs and 5 extra-base hits both tied major-league records, while his 19 total bases established a new mark, surpassing by one Joe Adcock's previous record of 18 set in 1954. In addressing Green's extraordinary performance, Mike Cameron, who homered 4 times in one game for the Seattle Mariners just three weeks earlier, said, "He's kind of been in that zone. He has the kind of swing that can get it up in the air. I wish the best for him. He's now part of the young men who did some damage in one particular day." Green subsequently homered in each of the next two games as well, making him the only Major League player ever to hit 7 home runs in a three-game span.

## Notable Achievements:
- Hit more than 20 home runs four times, topping 40 homers twice.
- Knocked in more than 100 runs twice, topping 120 RBIs once (125 in 2001).
- Scored more than 100 runs twice, surpassing 120 runs scored once (121 in 2001).
- Topped 30 doubles four times, surpassing 40 two-baggers twice.
- Surpassed 20 stolen bases twice.
- Posted slugging percentage in excess of .500 twice.
- Led NL in games played once.
- Led NL right-fielders in putouts once.
- Holds Dodgers single-season home-run record (49 in 2001).
- Ranks among Dodgers career leaders in slugging percentage (eighth) and OPS (10th).
- Hit four home runs in one game vs. Milwaukee on May 23, 2002.
- Hit three home runs in one game vs. Montreal on August 15, 2001.
- Holds Major League record for most total bases in one game (19, on May 23, 2002).
- Holds Major League record for most home runs over a three-game span (7, from May 23-25, 2002).
- Finished fifth in 2002 NL MVP voting.
- 2002 NL All-Star.

# 35

# DUSTY BAKER

With more than twenty years of managerial experience at the major-league level, Dusty Baker is known mostly to younger fans of the game as someone who has led his teams to six division titles and one National League pennant. However, the three-time NL Manager of the Year previously carved out quite a successful career for himself as a hard-hitting outfielder for four different teams over the course of 19 big-league seasons. Remembered best for his years in Atlanta and Los Angeles, Baker surpassed 20 home runs six times, 90 RBIs twice, and 100 runs scored once, while also batting over .300 three times. Part of the first quartet of teammates in baseball history to reach the 30-homer mark in the same season, Baker joined fellow sluggers Steve Garvey, Ron Cey, and Reggie Smith in accomplishing the feat for the pennant-winning Dodgers in 1977. Baker also helped the Dodgers capture two other pennants and one world championship in his eight years with the club, earning in the process a pair of All-Star selections and two top-10 finishes in the NL MVP voting.

Born in Riverside, California on June 15, 1949, Johnnie B. Baker had the nickname "Dusty" given to him by his mother after he repeatedly came home covered with dirt from playing baseball. After starring in baseball and basketball at Del Campo High School, near Sacramento, California, Baker turned down a basketball scholarship to the University of Santa Clara when the Atlanta Braves selected him in the 26th round of the 1967 amateur draft. Baker spent most of the next five years advancing through Atlanta's farm system, making brief appearances with the Braves each season from 1968 to 1971, before joining them for good in 1972.

Assigned the task of patrolling centerfield for the Braves in his first full season in Atlanta, Baker performed extremely well, hitting 17 homers, driving in 76 runs, finishing third in the National League with a .321

batting average, and ranking third among all players at his position in put-outs. He followed that up with another outstanding year in 1973, hitting 21 homers, knocking in 99 runs, scoring 101 times, batting .288, stealing 24 bases, and leading all NL centerfielders with 394 putouts. Although Baker proved to be somewhat less productive after the Braves moved him to right field in 1974, he still posted decent numbers in each of the next two campaigns, totaling 39 home runs and 141 RBIs, while compiling batting averages of .256 and .261.

In spite of the solid offensive production Baker gave them the previous four seasons, the Braves elected to include him in a six-player trade they completed with the Dodgers on November 17, 1975 that sent the twenty-six-year-old outfielder and journeyman infielder Ed Goodson to Los Angeles for promising young infielder Jerry Royster and veterans Lee Lacy, Jim Wynn, and Tom Paciorek. Baker, who grew up rooting for the Dodgers, later expressed the delight he felt upon learning of the deal by saying, "This was where I always wanted to play because, as a kid, I was a Dodger fan and I always had my radio, listening to Vin Scully and sort of imagining myself one day playing in Dodger Stadium."

Nevertheless, Baker's first season in L.A. ended up being an extremely difficult one, with the Dodgers' new center-fielder struggling through the worst year of his career. Although Los Angeles finished second in the NL West with a record of 92-70 in 1976, Baker contributed little to the cause, hitting just 4 homers, driving in only 39 runs, and batting just .242. Commenting on Baker's poor performance years later, Tommy Lasorda said, "I knew one thing—he wasn't that kind of a hitter. He had just a great kind of talent."

With Lasorda replacing Walter Alston as manager of the Dodgers the following season, Baker shifted from centerfield to left, where he remained the rest of his time in Los Angeles. Responding well to the change in positions and his new skipper's upbeat personality, Baker helped the Dodgers capture the NL pennant by hitting 30 homers, knocking in 86 runs, scoring 86 times, and batting .291. He followed that up with an exceptional post-season performance, hitting a pair of homers, driving in 8 runs, and batting .357 against Philadelphia, en route to earning NLCS MVP honors, before homering once, knocking in 5 runs, and batting .292 against the Yankees in the World Series.

The right-handed hitting Baker failed to perform as well for the pennant-winning Dodgers in 1978, hitting just 11 homers, driving in only 66 runs, and batting just .262. However, he had another big NLCS against Philadelphia, leading both teams with a .467 batting average. Baker then put together back-to-back outstanding seasons, hitting 23 homers, knocking in 88 runs, scoring 86 times, and batting .274 in 1979, before earning a fourth-place finish in the NL MVP voting the following year by hitting 29 homers, driving in 97 runs, scoring 80 times, and batting .294.

Baker continued his excellent play in each of the next two seasons, compiling a .320 batting average during the strike-shortened 1981 campaign, before hitting 23 homers, knocking in 88 runs, scoring 80 times, and batting an even .300 the following year. But, after the thirty-four-year-old outfielder slumped to 15 homers, 73 RBIs, and a .260 batting average in 1983, the Dodgers decided not to actively pursue him when he became a free agent at season's end, leaving him to sign a three-year deal with the arch-rival Giants. Baker left Los Angeles having compiled 144 home runs, 586 RBIs, 549 runs scored, 1,144 hits, 179 doubles, 12 triples, 73 stolen bases, a .281 batting average, a .343 on-base percentage, and a .437 slugging percentage in his eight years with the Dodgers.

Baker ended up spending just one year in San Francisco, batting .292, with only 3 homers and 32 RBIs in 100 games in 1984, before being dealt to the Oakland Athletics for a pair of minor leaguers prior to the start of the ensuing campaign. After spending the next two seasons in Oakland serving as a part-time player, Baker announced his retirement when his contract expired at the end of 1986. He retired with career totals of 242 home runs, 1,013 RBIs, 964 runs scored, 1,981 hits, 320 doubles, 23 triples, and 137 stolen bases, a .278 batting average, a .347 on-base percentage, and a .432 slugging percentage. In addition to earning two All-Star selections and a pair of top-10 finishes in the NL MVP balloting, Baker won a Gold Glove and a Silver Slugger.

Following his playing days, Baker became a coach for the Giants, manning the coaching box at first base for them in 1988, before spending the next four years serving as their batting instructor. He then became manager of the Giants in 1993, beginning in the process a lengthy managerial career that has seen him earn NL Manager of the Year honors on three separate occasions. After earning that distinction in his very first season as skipper of the Giants by leading them to a record of 103-59 in 1993, Baker won the award again in 1997 and 2000 by piloting them to a pair of division titles. He also directed the Chicago Cubs to a first-place finish in the NL Central in 2003, before leading the Cincinnati Reds to that same division title in both 2010 and 2012. After being relieved of his duties in Cincinnati following the conclusion of the 2013 campaign, Baker resurfaced some two years later as manager of the Washington Nationals, who he led to the NL East title in 2016.

## Dodger Career Highlights:

**Best Season:** Although Baker also performed extremely well for the Dodgers in 1977, 1981, and 1982, he had his finest all-around season for them in 1980, when, en route to earning a fourth-place finish in the NL MVP voting and his lone *Sporting News* All-Star selection, he batted .294, scored 80 runs, and placed near the top of the league rankings with 29 home runs, 97 RBIs, 291 total bases, a .503 slugging percentage, and an OPS of .842.

**Memorable Moments/Greatest Performances:** Baker had the only 5-for-5 day of his career on April 26, 1978, when he collected 3 doubles and 2 singles, knocked in a pair of runs, and scored twice during a lopsided 14-4 victory over the Cincinnati Reds.

Baker nearly matched that effort later in the year, when he helped lead the Dodgers to a 7-4 win over Houston on July 7, 1978 by going 4-for-4, with a homer, double, 4 RBIs, and 2 runs scored.

Baker turned in a pair of outstanding back-to-back-efforts during the final week of July 1979, collecting 3 hits, including a homer, driving in 4 runs, and scoring 3 times during a 15-3 rout of the Phillies on the 24th of the month, before leading the Dodgers to a 16-8 win over the Phillies the very next day by going 4-for-5, with a pair of doubles, 4 RBIs, and 3 runs scored.

Baker continued his hot-hitting the following month, pacing the Dodgers to an 11-3 win over the Giants on August 3, 1979 by going 4-for-4, with a homer, 2 runs scored, and a career-high 6 runs batted in.

Baker had another big day at the plate on May 4, 1980, when he homered twice and knocked in 5 runs during a 12-10 win over the Phillies.

Baker had a similarly productive afternoon against Montreal on May 8, 1982, when he led the Dodgers to a 10-8 win over the Expos by going 5-for-6, with a pair of homers and 5 RBIs.

Courtesy of MEARS Online Auctions

Dusty Baker earned NLCS MVP honors in 1977 by homering twice, knocking in 8 runs, and batting .357 against the Phillies

Baker proved to be a thorn in the side of his former team on August 1, 1982, helping the Dodgers record a 9-4 victory over Atlanta by hitting 2 homers, driving in 3 runs, and scoring 3 times.

Baker hit arguably his most dramatic home run as a member of the Dodgers on July 11, 1983, when he gave them a 7-6 win over the Cardinals by hitting a walk-off two-run homer off relief ace Bruce Sutter with one man out in the bottom of the ninth inning. The blast concluded a 4-for-5 day for Baker, who hit another homer and knocked in 4 runs during the contest.

Yet, Baker may have experienced the most memorable moment of his career on October 2, 1977, when he took part in what is generally considered to be the first ever "high five." The incident, which ESPN featured in a documentary entitled "The High Five," took place on the final day of the regular season, after Baker homered off Houston right-hander J.R. Richard to join Steve Garvey, Ron Cey, and Reggie Smith in the 30-home run club, making them the first quartet of teammates ever to reach that plateau in the same season. As Baker approached home plate after circling the bases, on-deck hitter Glenn Burke thrust his hand enthusiastically over his head to greet him. Not knowing what else to do, Baker smacked it, recalling years later, "His hand was up in the air, and he was arching way back. So I reached up and hit his hand. It seemed like the thing to do."

## Notable Achievements:

- Hit more than 20 home runs four times, reaching 30-homer mark once (30 in 1977).
- Batted over .300 twice, reaching .320-mark once (.320 in 1981).
- Posted slugging percentage in excess of .500 twice.
- Finished third in NL with .320 batting average in 1981.
- Led NL left-fielders in double plays twice and fielding percentage once.
- Two-time NL Player of the Month (June, 1980 & July, 1983).
- 1981 Gold Glove winner.
- Two-time Silver Slugger winner (1980 & 1981).
- Finished fourth in 1980 NL MVP voting.
- 1977 NLCS MVP.
- 1980 *Sporting News* All-Star selection.
- Two-time NL All-Star (1981 & 1982).
- Three-time NL champion (1977, 1978 & 1981).
- 1981 world champion.

# 36

# ADRIAN BELTRE

One of the finest all-around third basemen of his generation, Adrian Beltre has been an excellent hitter and a superb fielder over the course of his career, which began in Los Angeles nearly two decades ago. Originally signed by the Dodgers as an underage amateur free agent in 1994, the Dominican-born Beltre performed somewhat erratically at the plate and in the field his first few years in the majors. However, since putting together the greatest offensive season of any third baseman in franchise history in 2004, Beltre has been a consistently productive hitter and arguably the finest glove man at his position in all of baseball. Unfortunately for the Dodgers, Beltre has experienced much of his success while playing for other teams, earning all four of his All-Star selections, all five of his Gold Gloves, and three of his four Silver Sluggers since leaving Los Angeles. Nevertheless, Beltre accomplished enough in his seven years with the Dodgers to be included in these rankings, with the aforementioned 2004 campaign solidifying his place on this list.

Born in Santo Domingo, Distrito Nacional, Dominican Republic on April 7, 1979, Adrian Perez Beltre honed his baseball skills on the sandlots of his hometown competing against older boys and men. After starting out as a middle infielder, the thin but muscular Beltre moved to third base at the age of twelve and fell in love with the position.

Beltre attended Liceo Maximo Gomez High School, where he developed into one of the school's top players. Discovered by Dodger scouts Ralph Avila and Pablo Peguero while working out at the team's Dominican-based training facility at Campo Las Palmas in 1994, the fifteen-year-old infielder impressed the organization's top two Latin American scouts with his quick bat and powerful throwing arm, prompting the Dodgers to sign him to a contract that included a $23,000 bonus. A few years later, when Beltre's agent Scott Boras discovered that the Dodgers had violated the rules set forth by MLB for signing foreign amateurs by inking his client to a deal prior to his sixteenth birthday, Boras attempted to have Beltre declared a free agent. However, instead of rewarding the young third baseman by allowing him to sign with the highest bidder, Baseball Commissioner Bud Selig punished the Dodgers by suspending their scouting operations in the Dominican Republic for one year.

After competing in the Dominican Summer League in 1995, Beltre began his minor-league career with the Savannah Sand Gnats of the South Atlantic League the following spring. Despite being one of the circuit's youngest players at only seventeen years of age, Beltre held his own against more experienced competition, hitting 16 homers, driving in 59 runs, and batting .307, earning himself a midseason promotion to High Class-A San Bernardino, where he hit another 10 homers, knocked in 40 more runs, and batted .261. Beltre subsequently established himself as the top prospect in the entire Los Angeles farm system in 1997 by batting .317 and leading the Florida State League with 26 home runs and 104 RBIs while playing for Vero Beach, earning in the process FSL MVP and *Baseball America* Class A Player of the Year honors.

After being promoted to the Dodgers midway through the 1998 campaign, the right-handed hitting Beltre struggled at third base while platooning with the switch-hitting Bobby Bonilla, committing 13 errors in only 74 games at the hot corner, while hitting 7 homers, knocking in 22 runs, and batting just .215. However, while Beltre continued to perform somewhat erratically in the field over the course of the next two seasons, committing a total of 52 errors, he acquitted himself far better at the plate, hitting 15 homers, driving in 67 runs, scoring 84 times, and batting .275 in 1999, before homering 20 times, knocking in 85 runs, scoring 71 others, and batting .290 the following year.

Beltre, though, regressed significantly as a hitter in each of the next three seasons, showing very little patience at the plate, while increasing his strikeout total each year. After drawing close to 60 bases on balls in each of his first two full seasons, Beltre became a free-swinger with very little sense of the strike zone, walking a total of only 102 times between 2001 and 2003. He also saw his batting average decline each season, until it finally reached a low of .240 in 2003.

Courtesy of Will Liu

Adrian Beltre (left) put together the greatest offensive season of any Dodger third baseman in 2004, when he hit 48 homers, drove in 121 runs, and batted .334

Certainly, at least part of the blame for Beltre's failure to mature as a hitter during that period of time can be placed on an appendectomy he underwent in the spring of 2001. Thin and weak upon his return to the team, Beltre ended up hitting only 13 homers, knocking in just 60 runs, and batting .265, in 126 games over the course of the regular season. But, even though Beltre increased his power numbers in each of the next two seasons after putting on some much-needed weight during the 2001 offseason (he totaled 44 home runs and 155 RBIs in 2002 and 2003), he degenerated into someone with very little plate awareness, walking a total of only 74 times, while simultaneously accumulating 199 strikeouts. Fortunately, Beltre did not allow his hitting woes to affect him in the field, since he gradually emerged as one of the National League's better defensive third basemen during that time.

Having agreed to a one-year deal with the Dodgers worth $3.7 million following the conclusion of the 2003 campaign, Beltre knew that he needed to improve his overall performance if he wished to receive a lucrative long-term contract offer when he became a free agent at the end of the year. Perhaps more focused and motivated than ever before, the twenty-five-year-old third baseman became a veritable hitting machine, excelling more at the plate than anyone could have reasonably expected. In easily his finest offensive season to that point, Beltre led the NL with 48 homers, scored 104 runs, and placed near the top of the league rankings with 121 RBIs, 200 hits, 376 total bases, a .334 batting average, a .388 on-base percentage, and a .629 slugging percentage, earning in the process a runner-up finish to Barry Bonds in the league MVP voting.

Much of the success Beltre experienced over the course of his fabulous season could be attributed to his improved pitch recognition and patience at the plate (he drew 53 bases on balls and struck out only 87 times). He also learned to trust his swing and use the whole field with two strikes, developing into a much better situational hitter in the process. Furthermore, Beltre committed only 10 errors in the field, with his quickness and powerful throwing arm enabling him to finish second among NL third basemen in both putouts and assists.

In addressing his improved defensive play, Beltre commented, "I work hard on my defense. It's something I take pride in, but it's nothing that I want to brag about. It's part of my game."

And, for anyone who wished to suggest that Beltre put forth more of an effort in 2004 due to his impending free agency, he stated, "I don't like to play slow or softly. I like to play hard; always."

Although the Dodgers attempted to re-sign Beltre when he became a free agent, he ended up accepting a five-year, $65 million contract offer from the Seattle Mariners. Beltre left Los Angeles with career totals of 147 home runs, 510 RBIs, 456 runs scored, 949 hits, 176 doubles, 18 triples, and 62 stolen bases, a .274 batting average, a .332 on-base percentage, and a .463 slugging percentage.

Beltre performed relatively well over the course of the next five seasons, having his best year for the Mariners in 2007, when he hit 26 homers, knocked in 99 runs, scored 87 times, batted .276, and won his first Gold Glove. However, he didn't begin to approach the level of excellence he reached in his final season with the Dodgers until after he left Seattle.

A free agent again following the conclusion of the 2009 campaign, Beltre inked a one-year deal with the Boston Red Sox, for whom he posted outstanding numbers in 2010. En route to earning All-Star honors for the first of three straight times and a ninth-place finish in the A.L MVP voting, Beltre hit 28 homers, drove in 102 runs, batted .321, and led the league with 49 doubles.

Following his one year in Boston, Beltre signed as a free agent with the Texas Rangers, with whom he spent the last six seasons. Since joining the Rangers, Beltre has established himself as arguably the junior circuit's finest all-around third baseman, earning three All-Star selections, three Gold Gloves, two Silver Sluggers, and four top-10 finishes in the league MVP balloting. He performed particularly well his first three seasons with the Rangers, concluding the 2011 campaign with 32 home runs, 105 RBIs, and a .296 batting average, before hitting 36 homers, driving in 102 runs, and finishing third in the league with a .321 batting average the following year, en route to earning a third-place finish in the MVP voting. Beltre then hit 30 homers, knocked in 92 runs, batted .315, and led the league with 199 hits in 2013. Despite being thirty-seven years old as of this writing, Beltre shows no signs of slowing down, finishing this past season with 32 home runs, 104 RBIs, and a .300 batting average. He will enter the 2017 campaign with career totals of 445 home runs, 1,571 RBIs, 1,428 runs scored, 2,942 hits, 591 doubles, 36 triples, and 119 stolen bases, a .286 lifetime batting average, a .338 on-base percentage, and a .480 slugging percentage.

## Dodger Career Highlights:

**Best Season:** There can be no doubting that Beltre had his finest season for the Dodgers in 2004, when he established career-high marks in nine different offensive categories. In addition to topping the senior circuit with 48 home runs, Beltre finished second in the league in total bases (376), fifth in OPS (1.017), and fourth in RBIs (121), batting average (.334), slugging percentage (.629), and hits (200).

**Memorable Moments/Greatest Performances:** Beltre helped lead the Dodgers to a 16-11 win over the Rockies in Colorado on July 27, 2000 by going 4-for-6, with a homer, 2 runs scored, and a career-high 6 runs batted in.

Beltre proved to be the difference in a 5-3 victory over the Chicago Cubs on August 25, 2000, going a perfect 4-for-4, with a homer, double, 4 RBIs, and 2 runs scored. Beltre's two-out, three-run homer off Chicago reliever Todd Van Poppel in the top of the eighth inning broke a 2-2 tie, giving the Dodgers a lead they protected the final two frames.

Beltre helped the Dodgers defeat Cincinnati by a score of 11-5 on July 31, 2002 by hitting a pair of late-inning homers, driving in 3 runs, scoring 3 times, and stealing a base.

After the Dodgers spotted Colorado an early 5-run lead on September 5, 2003, Beltre helped lead his team to a come-from-behind 8-7 victory by going 4-for-5, with a pair of homers, 3 RBIs, and 3 runs scored.

Beltre paced the Dodgers to a 10-5 win over the Angels on June 27, 2004 by going 3-for-5, with 2 home runs and 5 RBIs.

Some two months later, on August 28, 2004, Beltre had his only 5-for-5 day as a member of the Dodgers, hitting safely in all 5 of his trips to the plate, homering once, driving in 2 runs, and scoring twice during a 4-2 victory over the Mets.

## Notable Achievements:

- Surpassed 20 home runs four times, topping 40 homers once (48 in 2004).
- Knocked in more than 100 runs once (121 in 2004).
- Scored more than 100 runs once (104 in 2004).
- Batted over .300 once (.334 in 2004).
- Topped 200 hits once (200 in 2004).
- Surpassed 30 doubles three times.
- Posted slugging percentage in excess of .600 once (.629 in 2004).
- Compiled OPS in excess of 1.000 once (1.017 in 2004).
- Led NL with 48 home runs in 2004.
- Finished second in NL with 376 total bases in 2004.
- Led NL third basemen in putouts once and double plays once.
- September 2004 NL Player of the Month.
- 2004 Silver Slugger winner.
- Finished second in 2004 NL MVP voting.

# 37

# TOMMY JOHN

Although he is perhaps remembered most for the revolutionary surgery that came to bear his name, Tommy John had quite a successful major-league career that saw him pitch for six different teams over a twenty-seven-year period. Having most of his finest seasons in Los Angeles and New York, John ended up winning a total of 288 games, with 87 of his victories coming as a member of the Dodgers, who he helped lead to back-to-back pennants in 1977 and 1978 after making a remarkable recovery from a serious arm injury that earlier threatened to end his career at only thirty-one years of age. Going a combined 37-17 for the Dodgers over the course of those two seasons, the crafty southpaw earned one All-Star nomination and one runner-up finish in the NL Cy Young voting, before moving on to New York, where he helped the Yankees capture two division titles and one American League pennant, surpassing 20 victories two straight times in the process. Subsequently pitching well into his forties, John remained in the big leagues until 1989, when he finally succumbed to Father Time after making the eighth-most starts in baseball history. Since that time, though, John's name has remained prominent in baseball circles, with the groundbreaking medical procedure he underwent some forty years ago helping to save the careers of countless pitchers.

Born in Terre Haute, Indiana on May 22, 1943, Thomas Edward John attended local Gerstmeyer High School, where he starred in baseball and basketball, before signing with the Cleveland Indians as an amateur free agent in 1961. Considered to be a finesse pitcher with a major-league-ready curve but only a mediocre fastball, John advanced rapidly through Cleveland's farm system, making his big-league debut with the Indians during the latter stages of the 1963 campaign, at only twenty years of age. After John went a combined 2-11 over parts of the next two seasons, the

Indians decided to include him in a three-team trade they completed with the Chicago White Sox and Kansas City Athletics early in 1965 that also saw such notable players as Rocky Colavito and Tommie Agee switch teams. John ended up spending the next seven seasons in Chicago, serving the White Sox primarily as a middle-of-the-rotation type starter during that time, while compiling an overall record of 82-80 and a very respectable 2.95 ERA. Although John twice won 14 games for the White Sox, he actually pitched his best ball for them in 1968, when he earned his first All-Star selection by going 10-5 with a 1.98 ERA over his first 25 starts, before seeing his season come to an abrupt end in early August when he injured his shoulder in a fight with Detroit's Dick McAuliffe, who charged the mound after being driven off the plate by a high-and-tight fastball thrown by the left-hander. After John returned to the team the following year, he failed to perform as well over the course of the next three seasons, prompting Chicago to work out a deal with the Dodgers in early December 1971 that sent him to Los Angeles for enigmatic slugger Dick Allen.

Arriving in L.A. with a career record of just 84-91, John soon found his fortunes about to change, with the help of Dodger pitching coach Red Adams, who suggested to him that he rely more on his fastball. Crediting Adams with much of the success he experienced in Los Angeles, John revealed that his new pitching coach told him that he had a good fastball with a lot of movement, stating years later, "When I joined the club, I was still convinced that I had only a mediocre fastball and that I was going to have to depend chiefly on my breaking pitches to win ball games. But Red disagreed with me, emphatically."

After going 11-5 with a 2.89 ERA in 1972, John performed even better his second season with the Dodgers, concluding the 1973 campaign with a record of 16-7 that gave him a league-leading .696 winning percentage, while also compiling an ERA of 3.10. However, after getting off to the finest start of his career the following year, John suffered an injury that nearly brought his playing days to an end.

The incident occurred on July 17, 1974, during a twilight game at home against the Montreal Expos. John, who entered the contest with a record of 13-3 and an ERA of 2.59, took the mound in the top of the fourth inning trying to protect a 4-0 Dodger lead. Facing the right-handed hitting Hal Breeden with two men on base, John attempted to induce a rally-killing double play grounder from the Montreal first baseman by throwing him a sharp sinker on the outside half of the plate. Suggesting that his body may have been "too far ahead of his arm at the critical moment when the ball is released," and noting that he felt the "strangest sensation I had ever known," John later described the events that subsequently transpired:

> *"Right at the point where I put force on the pitch, the point where my arm is back and bent, something happened. It felt as if I had left my arm someplace else. It was as if my body continued to go forward and my left arm had just flown out to right field, independent of the rest of me."*

After testing his arm out on the mound by moving it in a circular motion, John attempted to throw another pitch. But the same thing happened, with the ball heading softly towards home plate in "bloop" fashion, well out of the strike zone. Meanwhile, John revealed that he heard a "thumping" sound in his forearm, typically made by two hard objects bumping into each other. Although he felt no pain, he knew that he could no longer pitch, telling manager Walter Alston at the time, "You'd better get somebody in there. I've hurt my arm."

As it turned out, John permanently damaged the ulnar collateral ligament in his pitching arm, forcing him to undergo radical surgery in which he had the ligament in his elbow replaced with a tendon from his right forearm. The procedure, which has since become known as "Tommy John Surgery," ended up adding fourteen years to his pitching career, enabling him to post another 164 victories—40 more than he had recorded prior to the injury. Making light of his situation a few years later, John quipped, "When they operated on my arm, I asked them to put in a Koufax fastball. They did, but it turned out to be Mrs. Koufax."

Working extensively with teammate Mike Marshall while sitting out the entire 1975 campaign, John learned from the 1974 NL Cy Young Award winner how to alter his delivery so that he no longer turned his leg and faced home plate directly, greatly reducing the chance of him hurting his knee and arm. Miraculously returning to the Dodgers in 1976, John compiled a record of 10-10 and an ERA of 3.09, before beginning the finest stretch of his career the following year, when he helped the Dodgers capture the NL pennant by going 20-7, with a 2.78 ERA and 11 complete games. John again pitched extremely well for the pennant-winning Dodgers in 1978, finishing 17-10 with a 3.30 ERA, before going a perfect 2-0 in the postseason.

With John becoming a free agent following the conclusion of the 1978 campaign, he elected to sign with the Yankees, bringing to an end his association with the Dodgers. John's six-year stay in Los Angeles resulted in an overall record of 87-42 that gave him an excellent winning percentage of .674—the fifth best in franchise history. He also compiled an ERA of 2.97, recorded 649 strikeouts in 1,198 total innings of work, threw 37 complete games and 11 shutouts, and posted a WHIP of 1.223 while pitching for the Dodgers.

John continued to experience success in New York, earning AL All-Star honors in each of his first two seasons with the Yankees. After compiling a record of 21-9 and an ERA of 2.96 in 1979, the thirty-seven-year-old southpaw went 22-9, with a 3.43 ERA and a league-leading 6 shutouts the following year. Making an extremely favorable impression on American League hitters with his ability to navigate his way through opposing lineups despite his relative lack of velocity, John drew praise from seven-time AL batting champion Rod Carew, who later said, "Tommy John never made it easy for you to hit."

Former catcher and big-league manager Buck Martinez further elaborated on the difficulties opposing batters faced when they stepped up to the plate to hit against John, stating, "Tommy John was a guy you'd go up there and say, 'Man, I saw the ball pretty good,' and it felt like a shot put when it left your bat....He was never really a guy you felt uncomfortable against—but you just knew you were gonna have to battle your ass off all day long. Screwball down and away and that big, slow breaking ball inside. He had such a smooth delivery that the ball got on you and then disappeared. You never had a ball out over the plate to hit."

Although the 1980 campaign turned out to be John's last big season, he remained in the majors another nine years, winning another 74 games during that time. In addition to spending parts of six more seasons with the Yankees, John spent three years with the California Angels and briefly pitched for the Oakland A's. Finally announcing his retirement after being released by the Yankees during his second tour of duty with them in May 1989, John left the game with a career record of 288-231, an ERA of 3.34, 2,245 strikeouts in 4,710⅓ total innings of work, 162 complete games, 46 shutouts, and a WHIP of 1.283. His 288 victories rank as the seventh highest total among left-handed pitchers in major league history. A four-time All-Star, John also earned three top-five finishes in his league's Cy Young voting, placing second in the balloting on two separate occasions.

Tommy John, seen here as a member of the Cleveland Indians, won a total of 37 games for the Dodgers' pennant-winning teams of 1977 & 1978.

Following his playing days, John occasionally served as a color commentator on televised baseball broadcasts, before spending nearly three years managing the Bridgeport Bluefish in the Atlantic League, an independent minor league in the Northeast. Since resigning as skipper of the Bluefish on July 8, 2009 to pursue a "non-baseball position" with Sportable Scoreboards, John has remained away from the game in any official capacity.

## Dodger Career Highlights:

**Best Season:** John had easily his best year for the Dodgers in 1977, when he earned a runner-up finish to Steve Carlton in the NL Cy Young voting by going 20-7, with a 2.78 ERA, 11 complete games, and a WHIP of 1.248. In addition to finishing fourth in the league with a .741 winning percentage, he ranked among the league leaders in wins (third), ERA (fifth), and complete games (sixth). John, himself, identified 1977 as the highlight of his career, saying, "I loved playing for Tommy Lasorda because he made it fun. That was the first time I won twenty games, and then I beat Steve Carlton four-to-one in a rainstorm in Veterans Stadium, and that got us to the World Series. It was probably the best game I ever pitched. I won more games in my years with the Yankees, but the first time winning twenty and being in the World Series with the Dodgers, that was special."

**Memorable Moments/Greatest Performances:** John tossed his first shutout as a member of the Dodgers on August 3, 1972, blanking the Giants by a score of 3-0 on just 3 hits, while striking out 7 and allowing 3 bases on balls.

Although John failed to earn a decision in his next start, a 2-1, 19-inning loss to Cincinnati on August 8, 1972, he pitched magnificently, surrendering just 3 hits and 1 run in 9 innings of work, while recording a career-high 13 strikeouts.

John turned in another outstanding effort against the hard-hitting Reds on June 23, 1973, going the distance and allowing only 3 hits and 1 run during a 5-1 Dodgers win.

However, John topped that performance some two months later, surrendering just 3 hits and 2 walks, while striking out 7, during a 3-0 shutout of the Phillies.

John pitched perhaps his finest game as a member of the Dodgers on August 8, 1977, when he tossed a two-hit shutout against the Reds, defeating the two-time defending National League champions by a score of 4-0. He finished the game with 5 strikeouts and just one walk.

Nevertheless, as noted earlier, John considers his performance against Steve Carlton and the Phillies in Game Four of the 1977 NLCS to be the best of his career. Pitching on a rain-soaked evening in Philadelphia, John clinched the pennant for the Dodgers by defeating Carlton and the Phillies by a score of 4-1, allowing 7 hits and recording 8 strikeouts during the contest.

John hurled another gem against Philadelphia in the 1978 NLCS, surrendering just 4 hits and 2 walks during a complete-game 4-0 win that gave the Dodgers a 2-0 lead in the series.

## Notable Achievements:

- Won 20 games in 1977.
- Surpassed 16 victories two other times.
- Posted winning percentage in excess of .700 twice.
- Compiled ERA under 3.00 three times.
- Threw more than 200 innings four times.
- Led NL pitchers in winning percentage twice.
- Ranks sixth in Dodgers history with career winning percentage of .674.
- April, 1974 NL Player of the Month.
- 1976 Hutch Award winner.
- 1976 *Sporting News* NL Comeback Player of the Year.
- Finished second in 1977 NL Cy Young voting.
- 1978 NL All-Star.
- Three-time NL champion (1974, 1977 & 1978).

# 38

# TOMMY DAVIS

One of the National League's best all-around players early in his career, Tommy Davis appeared headed to Cooperstown after his first few seasons with the Dodgers. An outstanding line-drive hitter capable of delivering the long ball as well, Davis won back-to-back batting titles in 1962 and 1963, putting together one of the finest offensive seasons in franchise history in the first of those campaigns, when, in addition to topping the senior circuit with a batting average of .346, he hit 27 homers, scored 120 runs, and led the league with 153 RBIs and 230 hits. Davis followed that up by hitting a league-leading .326 in 1963, earning in the process his second straight All-Star selection and second consecutive top-10 finish in the NL MVP voting. However, a moment of hesitation on the base paths a little over one year later caused Davis to break his ankle, greatly diminishing his once-considerable running speed, forcing him to change his approach at the plate, and altering the course of history.

Born in the Bedford-Stuyvesant section of Brooklyn, New York on March 21, 1939, Herman Thomas Davis grew up rooting for the hometown Dodgers and his favorite player, Jackie Robinson. A multi-sport star at local Boys High School, Davis earned All-City honors on the basketball court, competed in the long-jump in track and field, and starred at catcher on the baseball squad. Scouted by several major-league teams while still in high school, Davis received a great deal of attention from the Yankees, who allowed him to work out at the Stadium whenever he pleased. Davis later recalled, "I would hit with the pitchers and shag when the regulars hit. I probably did that three or four times."

New York's kindness towards Davis prompted the seventeen-year-old youngster to seriously consider signing with the Yankees when he graduated from high school in 1956. However, the Dodgers also sought his services, with scout Al Campanis using as bargaining tools Davis' Brooklyn roots and the pleasant environment that the team offered its black players. Finally, a phone call from Jackie Robinson placed only days before Davis planned to sign with the Yankees convinced the teenager to join the Dodger organization instead.

Ironically, the Dodgers left Brooklyn one year later, with Davis later revealing, "That was really a blow at first. But the Dodgers' move turned out to be a blessing. I escaped the distraction of my childhood friends. I was able to concentrate on baseball when I got to the majors. It also gave me a chance to explore new horizons and grow up a little bit."

After winning batting titles in the Midwest League and Pacific Coast League during his four-year minor-league sojourn, Davis made the Dodgers out of spring training in 1960. Seeing action at all three outfield positions, he ended up having a solid rookie year, batting .276, hitting 11 homers, and driving in 44 runs, in 110 games and 352 official at-bats. Although Davis moved all over the outfield again in 1961, he spent the greatest amount of time at third base, starting 57 games at the hot corner, before manager Walter Alston abandoned the idea of converting him into an infielder after watching him struggle with his throws to first base, as Davis later noted when he said, "They never really explained to me how you had to short-arm the ball at third. I was throwing it like an outfielder and the ball was sailing over Hodges's head." Yet, despite the lack of success he experienced in the field, Davis continued to hit, batting .278, with 15 homers, 58 RBIs, and 60 runs scored, in 132 games and 460 official at-bats.

Moved to left field and inserted into the cleanup spot in the Dodgers' batting order during the early stages of the ensuing campaign, Davis emerged as an offensive force, establishing himself as one of the game's elite hitters. Displaying remarkable consistency over the course of the season, the right-handed swinging Davis rarely went more than a day or two without collecting at least one hit. He also did an exceptional job of driving in runs, with Sandy Koufax recalling, "Every time Tommy came up with a man on second, he would drive him in with a single. When he came up with a man on first, he drove him in with a double." After amassing 100 RBIs before the end of July, Davis finished the year with a league-leading and franchise-record 153 runs batted in. He also hit 27 homers, scored 120 runs, collected 9 triples and 27 doubles, stole 18 bases, and topped the senior circuit with 230 hits and a .346 batting average, earning in the process a third-place finish in the league MVP voting and a spot on the *Sporting News* All-Star Team. Looking back at his brilliant performance, Davis said, "Starting and playing every day was the key. Maury [Wills], [Jim] Gilliam, and Willie [Davis] all had good years in front of me, and Frank Howard behind me hit thirty-one bombs, so I saw a lot of fastballs."

Although Davis compiled far less prolific numbers in 1963, concluding the campaign with 16 home runs, 88 RBIs, 69 runs scored, and 181 hits, he earned his second straight *Sporting News* All-Star selection and an eighth-place finish in the NL MVP balloting by leading the league with a .326 batting average. He subsequently displayed his ability to perform well under pressure by batting .400 during the Dodgers' four-game sweep of the Yankees in the World Series, prompting Sandy Koufax to later say, "For two years, Tommy was the best hitter in baseball. He just didn't get the recognition. He was part of a team that had a lot of good parts to it."

The Dodgers and Davis both slumped somewhat in 1964, with Los Angeles finishing sixth in the National League, with a record of only 80-82. Meanwhile, Davis batted just .275, with 14 home runs and 86 RBIs. Nevertheless, he displayed his speed and range in the outfield by leading all NL left-fielders with a career-high 267 putouts, while also finishing first among players at his position with a .982 fielding percentage.

Unfortunately, the 1964 campaign ended up being Davis' last year as a full-time starter in Los Angeles. After appearing in only 17 games the following year, Davis saw his career take a sudden turn for the worse on May 1, 1965, when he broke and dislocated his right ankle sliding into second base while trying to break up a double play against the Giants. The incident took place in the bottom of the fourth inning, with Davis occupying first base following a leadoff single. Ron Fairly hit a ground ball to San Francisco first baseman Orlando Cepeda, who flipped to Giants pitcher Gaylord Perry for the out at first. Davis, who took off for second on the play, described the events that subsequently transpired:

> "I was running on the inside of the baseline expecting Cepeda to throw to [Jose] Pagan. As I approached the bag, I did a crossover step with my left leg and the back spike of my right leg caught in the clay and turned my footcompletely around. Perry dove to tag me and I never felt it. I was in shock. [Dodger trainer] Wayne Anderson came on the field and snapped my foot back in place right on the base path."

Tommy Davis won consecutive batting titles
for the Dodgers during the early 1960's

Davis said that he felt much better after having his leg placed in a balloon cast in the clubhouse. However, he added, "Then Dr. Kerlan came to see me, popped off the cast, and said it felt like a bag of walnuts in my ankle. I said, 'Oh man, don't tell me that.'"

Davis ended up missing the remainder of the season, failing to return to the Dodgers in time to take part in their World Series victory over the Minnesota Twins. And, even after he rejoined the club the following year, Davis found himself unable to perform at the same lofty level to which he had become accustomed. Although never considered to be a true home run hitter, Davis previously tended to drive the ball with authority to all fields. However, no longer able to generate the same amount of power by pushing off on his right (back) foot, Davis had to adjust his batting style so that he became much more of a singles hitter. Appearing in 100 games with the Dodgers in 1966, Davis still managed to lead the team with a .313 batting average. But he hit only 3 homers, knocked in just 27 runs, and collected a total of only 15 extra-base hits. Furthermore, he displayed little of the speed that made him one of the league's better defensive outfielders earlier in his career.

The Dodgers subsequently elected to trade Davis to the New York Mets for second baseman Ron Hunt and outfielder Jim Hickman at season's end, returning the Brooklyn native to his hometown. Davis ended his time with the Dodgers with career totals of 86 home runs, 465 RBIs, 392 runs scored, 912 hits, 109 doubles, 22 triples, and 65 stolen bases, a .304 batting average, a .338 on-base percentage, and a .441 slugging percentage.

After arriving in New York, Davis regained some of his power, concluding the 1967 campaign with 16 homers, 73 RBIs, 72 runs scored, 32 doubles, and a .302 batting average. In spite of the earlier success he experienced with the Dodgers, Davis identified 1967 as his greatest triumph, stating years later, "I had to prove myself again. By having a decent year, I was able to play until 1976. I was certified good enough to play, thanks to 1967 with the Mets."

The 1967 season actually began the second stage of Davis' career— one in which he led an extremely nomadic existence. The former two-time National League batting champion spent the next 10 seasons playing for nine different teams, with his lengthiest stay proving to be a three-year stint in Baltimore, where he spent virtually all his time serving the Orioles as a designated hitter. Other teams for which Davis played included the Chicago White Sox, Seattle Pilots, Houston Astros, Oakland A's, Chicago Cubs, California Angels, and Kansas City Royals. Davis experienced his greatest success during that period with the Orioles, helping them capture the AL East title in 1973 and earning a 10th-place finish in the league MVP voting by batting .306 and knocking in 89 runs. After being released by Kansas City following the conclusion of the 1976 campaign, Davis elected to call it quits, ending his career with 153 home runs, 1,052 RBIs, 811 runs scored, 2,121 hits, 272 doubles, 35 triples, 136 stolen bases, a .294 batting average, a .329 on-base percentage, and a .405 slugging percentage.

Following his retirement, Davis returned to the Dodgers, serving them as a minor-league batting instructor and, also, as part of their community relations department. He also spent one season coaching the Mariners hitters in Seattle.

Looking back at his former teammate's career, Maury Wills noted, "That injury changed Tommy's career and changed his whole life. I have no doubt that, with two good legs, he would have had three thousand hits and hit three hundred fifty to four hundred home runs."

Wills added, "Tommy was one of the best hitters I've ever seen, especially in the clutch. And he had speed. In the minors, Tommy, Earl Robinson, Willie Davis, and I could run about the same. And Tommy was bigger than the rest of us. Were it not for that injury, he'd be remembered with all the greats."

## Dodger Career Highlights:

**Best Season:** Davis unquestionably had his finest season in 1962, when he established career-high marks in virtually every offensive category, including home runs (27), RBIs (153), runs scored (120), hits (230), triples (9), batting average (.346), on-base percentage (.374), and slugging percentage (.535). In addition to leading the NL in RBIs, hits, and batting average, he placed in the league's top five in runs scored, triples, total bases (356), slugging percentage, and OPS, earning in the process a third-place finish in the MVP voting and the first of two consecutive selections to *The Sporting News* All-Star Team.

**Memorable Moments/Greatest Performances:** Although the Dodgers lost their July 30, 1960 match-up with the Braves by a score of 8-7,

Davis had a big day at the plate, homering twice and collecting a career-high 5 RBIs.

Davis turned in a number of exceptional performances over the course of the 1962 campaign, with one of those coming on May 5, when he led the Dodgers to a 10-1 victory over the Pirates by going 4-for-5, with a homer, double, 2 RBIs, and 3 runs scored.

Later that month, on May 25, Davis went 4-for-6, with 3 RBIs and 3 runs scored, during a 17-8 pounding of the New York Mets.

Davis delivered arguably his most dramatic hit of the year on June 18, 1962, when he gave Sandy Koufax a 1-0 victory over Bob Gibson and the St. Louis Cardinals by homering in the bottom of the ninth inning off the Hall of Fame right-hander.

Just five days later, on June 23, Davis helped lead the Dodgers to a lopsided 14-3 win over Cincinnati by going 4-for-5, with a double, triple, 2 runs scored, and career-high 5 RBIs.

Although the Dodgers ended up losing their three-game playoff with the Giants in 1962, dropping the series finale by a score of 6-4, Davis demonstrated his ability to hit in the clutch, reaching Giants ace Juan Marichal for a two-run homer in the bottom of the sixth inning that gave the Dodgers a 3-2 lead.

Davis again came up big in the clutch in the 1963 World Series, batting .400 during the Dodgers' four-game sweep of the Yankees, tying a Series record by tripling twice in Game Two, and driving in the only run of Game Three with a first-inning single off Jim Bouton.

## Notable Achievements:

- Batted over .300 three times, topping the .340-mark once (.346 in 1962).
- Hit more than 20 home runs once (27 in 1962).
- Knocked in more than 100 runs once (153 in 1962).
- Scored more than 100 runs once (120 in 1962).
- Surpassed 200 hits once (230 in 1962).
- Posted slugging percentage in excess of .500 once (.535 in 1962).
- Led NL in: batting average twice, RBIs once, and hits once.

- Led NL left-fielders in: putouts once, fielding percentage twice, and double plays turned twice.
- Holds Dodgers single-season record for most runs batted in (153 in 1962).
- Finished third in 1962 NL MVP voting.
- Two-time *Sporting News* All-Star selection (1962 & 1963).
- Two-time NL All-Star (1962 & 1963).
- Three-time NL champion (1963, 1965 & 1966).
- Two-time world champion (1963 & 1965).

# 39

# RAUL MONDESI

Considered to be a potential superstar when he first arrived in Los Angeles in 1993, Raul Mondesi had all the requisite physical tools to become a truly great player. Blessed with good speed, excellent power, and one of the strongest throwing arms in the game, Mondesi appeared headed for greatness after he earned NL Rookie of the Year honors in 1994. However, after compiling solid numbers for the Dodgers in each of the next five seasons, the hard-hitting outfielder experienced a precipitous fall from grace, never again experiencing the same level of success, while splitting his final six years in the majors between six different teams. Yet, even though Mondesi failed to attain the level of excellence originally predicted for him, he managed to compile a fairly impressive stat-line over the course of his career, performing especially well for the Dodgers from 1993 to 1999. Serving as the team's starting right-fielder in six of those seasons, Mondesi hit more than 20 home runs five times, surpassing 30 homers on three separate occasions. He also batted over .300 and topped 90 RBIs two times each, scored more than 90 runs four times, and swiped more than 30 bases twice, becoming in 1997 the first Dodger player ever to surpass 30 homers and 30 stolen bases in the same season—a feat he accomplished again two years later.

Born in San Cristobal, in the Dominican Republic, on March 12, 1971, Raúl Ramón Mondesí Avelino attended high school locally at Liceo Manual Maria Valencia, before signing with the Dodgers as a seventeen-year-old amateur free agent in 1988. After beginning his pro career in the Los Angeles farm system later that year, Mondesi began to flourish at Great Falls in 1990, where he earned a spot on the Pioneer League All-Star team by batting .303 and stealing 30 bases. Mondesi subsequently split the 1991 campaign between three different teams, before spending most of 1992

Although he never lived up to his full potential,
Raul Mondesi topped 30 homers three times
while playing for the Dodgers

Courtesy of Bradley Park

at Albuquerque, where he posted a batting average of .296. Returning to Albuquerque in 1993, Mondesi again compiled solid numbers, prompting the Dodgers to call him up at midseason. Appearing in 42 games over the final two and a half months of the regular season, Mondesi made a favorable impression by batting .291, hitting 4 homers, driving in 10 runs, and scoring 13 times, in only 86 official at-bats.

After making the Dodgers' opening day roster the following year, Mondesi ended up starting all but two of the 114 games the team played over the course of the strike-shortened campaign, earning NL Rookie of the Year honors by hitting 16 homers, knocking in 56 runs, scoring 63 times, batting .306, and leading all NL outfielders with 16 assists from his post in right field. The twenty-four-year-old outfielder followed that up by hitting 26 homers, driving in 88 runs, scoring 91 times, batting .285, stealing 27 bases, and once again topping the senior circuit with 16 outfield assists in 1995, en route to earning his lone All-Star selection and first Gold Glove. The right-handed hitting Mondesi subsequently posted comparable numbers in 1996, concluding the campaign with 24 homers, 88 RBIs, 98 runs scored, and a .297 batting average, while also leading all NL right-fielders in putouts for the first of two straight times.

In addition to possessing outstanding power at the plate, Mondesi, who stood 5'11" and weighed just over 200 pounds, displayed an ability to hit for a fairly high batting average his first few years with the Dodgers, with his only real flaw as a hitter being his lack of selectivity. Showing little patience at the plate, Mondesi rarely walked, drawing a total of only 65 bases on balls over the course of his first two full seasons, while striking out as many as 122 times in 1996. Meanwhile, despite being somewhat erratic in the outfield (he led all NL outfielders with 12 errors in 1996), Mondesi possessed good range and a powerful throwing arm that earned him the respect of National League base-runners. In fact, after amassing a league-leading 16 outfield assists in both 1994 and 1995, Mondesi threw out as many as 10 base-runners only two more times as a member of the Dodgers since opposing players simply refused to challenge him on the base paths.

Mondesi continued his strong play for the Dodgers in 1997, hitting 30 homers, driving in 87 runs, scoring 95 times, stealing 32 bases, and placing among the league leaders with 191 hits, 42 doubles, and a .310 batting average. In addition to winning his second Gold Glove, Mondesi finished 15th in the NL MVP voting, receiving consideration for the award for the only time in his career. He followed that up with another very solid year in 1998, concluding the campaign with 30 home runs, 90 RBIs, 85 runs scored, and a batting average of .279. Although Mondesi's batting average slipped to .253 in 1999, he established career-high marks in homers (33), RBIs (99), runs scored (98), and stolen bases (36), topping 30 homers and 30 steals for the second time in three seasons.

Yet, in spite of his outstanding offensive production, Mondesi gradually wore out his welcome in Los Angeles with his somewhat indifferent attitude, occasional mental lapses, and failure to hustle at times. As a result, the Dodgers completed a trade with the Blue Jays on November 8, 1999 that sent Mondesi and left-handed relief pitcher Pedro Borbón,

Jr. to Toronto, for star outfielder Shawn Green and minor league second baseman Jorge Nunez. In announcing the deal, Blue Jays general manager Gord Ash stated, "In making this trade, Toronto gets two players who can contribute to our club immediately. Raul Mondesi is an exciting and multi-talented player whose contract status is not an issue. He will be an impact player in the American League."

Meanwhile, in explaining the trade from the Dodger perspective, Los Angeles general manager Kevin Malone said, "We want players who want to be here. Raul expressed a desire to be elsewhere. Shawn Green wanted to be a Los Angeles Dodger."

Mondesi played well for the Blue Jays in 2000 until he suffered a ligament injury to his right elbow in early August that ended his season prematurely. Appearing in only 96 games, the twenty-nine-year-old out-fielder concluded his first season north of the border with 24 home runs, 67 RBIs, 78 runs scored, and a .271 batting average. Healthy again in 2001, Mondesi put up good numbers for Toronto, finishing the year with 27 homers, 84 RBIs, 88 runs scored, 30 stolen bases, and a batting average of .252, while leading all AL outfielders with 18 assists.

However, as had been the case in Los Angeles, the Blue Jays soon began to grow weary of Mondesi's somewhat apathetic attitude and in-ability to reach his full potential, prompting them to deal him to the Yan-kees midway through the 2002 campaign. The trade to New York ushered in the final phase of Mondesi's career—one in which he rarely stayed in one place for very long. After remaining with the Yankees for a little over one season, hitting 27 homers, driving in 92 runs, and batting .250, during that time, Mondesi found himself headed to Arizona, where he spent the remainder of the 2003 campaign. He subsequently signed with Pittsburgh as a free agent at the end of the year, after which he spent two injury-marred seasons splitting his time between the Pirates, Angels, and Braves. Released by Atlanta on May 31, 2005, Mondesi chose to announce his re-tirement, ending his career at only thirty-four years of age with 271 home runs, 860 RBIs, 909 runs scored, 1,589 hits, 319 doubles, 49 triples, 229 stolen bases, a .273 batting average, a .331 on-base percentage, and a .485 slugging percentage. Over parts of seven seasons in Los Angeles, Mondesi hit 163 homers, knocked in 518 runs, scored 543 times, accumulated 1,004 hits, 190 doubles, 37 triples, and 140 stolen bases, batted .288, compiled an on-base percentage of .334, and posted a slugging percentage of .504.

Following his playing days, Mondesi entered into a career in politics, gaining election to the Dominican Republic's Chamber of Deputies in 2006. Four years later, he began a six-year term as mayor of his home province of San Cristóbal.

## Dodger Career Highlights:

**Best Season:** Mondesi performed extremely well for the Dodgers in 1996, when he hit 24 homers, knocked in 88 runs, batted .297, and amassed 188 hits, 40 doubles, and a career-high 98 runs scored. However, he had his finest all-around season one year later, concluding the 1997 campaign with 30 home runs, 87 RBIs, 95 runs scored, 32 stolen bases, and career-high marks in hits (191), doubles (42), total bases (333), batting average (.310), on-base percentage (.360), and slugging percentage (.541). Mondesi finished in the league's top 10 in six different offensive categories, placing fourth in hits and fifth in doubles. Furthermore, Mondesi's 30 homers and 32 steals made him the first player in franchise history to top the 30-mark in both categories in the same season.

**Memorable Moments/Greatest Performances:** Mondesi hit the first home run of his career on July 31, 1993, capping a 5-run Dodger rally in the top of the 13th inning with a two-run shot off Chicago Cubs reliever Bob Scanlan in a game the Dodgers won by a score of 7-2.

Mondesi had a big day at the plate on April 17, 1994, going 4-for-6, with a homer, triple, 2 singles, 3 RBIs, and a career-high 4 runs scored, during a 19-2 pasting of the Pirates.

Mondesi helped the Dodgers begin the 1995 season on a positive note by homering twice and driving in 4 runs on opening day, in leading them to an 8-7 win over the Florida Marlins.

Finding Colorado's Coors Field very much to his liking, Mondesi homered twice and knocked in a career-high 6 runs during a 9-6 victory over the Rockies on August 1, 1995.

Although the Dodgers lost their June 30, 1996 matchup with Colorado by a score of 16-15, Mondesi again displayed his fondness for the Rockies' home ballpark by going 4-for-6, with a pair of homers, a triple, 6 RBIs, and 3 runs scored.

Mondesi recorded the only five-hit game of his career on April 27, 1998, hitting safely in 5 of his 6 trips to the plate during a 3-2 loss to the

Milwaukee Brewers in 13 innings. Mondesi's 5 hits, which amounted to half of the Dodgers' total, included a homer and a double.

Mondesi helped the Dodgers begin the 1999 season in dramatic fashion by hitting a two-out, two-run homer in the bottom of the 11$^{th}$ inning, giving them an 8-6 extra-inning win over Arizona in the regular-season opener. Mondesi's blast concluded a 4-for-5 afternoon in which he homered twice and tied his career high by knocking in 6 runs.

## Notable Achievements:

- Hit more than 20 home runs five times, topping 30 homers on three occasions.
- Batted over .300 twice.
- Topped 40 doubles twice.
- Stole more than 20 bases three times, swiping more than 30 bags twice.
- Posted slugging percentage in excess of .500 twice.
- Led NL outfielders in assists twice.
- Led NL right-fielders in putouts twice and double plays once.
- Ranks ninth in Dodgers history with career slugging percentage of .504.
- 1994 NL Rookie of the Year.
- Two-time Gold Glove winner (1995 & 1997).
- 1995 NL All-Star.

# 40

# PETE REISER

A supremely gifted athlete and tremendous all-around ballplayer, Pete Reiser suffered a series of debilitating injuries over the course of his career that prevented him from ever attaining the level of greatness for which he appeared destined when he first arrived in Brooklyn. In just his first full season in 1941, Reiser earned a second-place finish in the NL MVP voting by topping the senior circuit in seven different offensive categories, with his fabulous performance helping the Dodgers capture their first pennant since 1920. Blessed with a rare combination of power and speed, Reiser possessed more natural ability than anyone else in the game at that time. However, the Dodger center-fielder also played the game with a reckless abandon that ended up being his undoing. Exhibiting virtually no fear of the consequences involved, Reiser repeatedly ran into outfield walls, causing him to be carried off the field on a stretcher 11 times during his career—completely unconscious on six of those occasions. Reiser's fool-hardiness robbed him of his once blinding speed and exceptional ability to hit a baseball, leaving us all to wonder what might have been had he remained healthy.

Born in St. Louis, Missouri on March 17, 1919, Harold Patrick Reiser came to be known as "Pete" to his family members, who named him after the cowboy movie hero *Two-Gun Pete* due to his fondness for westerns. Excelling in several different sports while attending William Beaumont High School, Reiser proved to be especially proficient at baseball, prompting the St. Louis Cardinals to sign him to a contract following his graduation. However, after spending the 1937 campaign playing in the St. Louis farm system, Reiser became a free agent when Baseball Commissioner Kenesaw Mountain Landis forced Cardinals GM Branch Rickey to surrender many of the minor-league players he had stockpiled within the

Injuries likely prevented Pete Reiser
from going down as one of the all-time greats

Courtesy of RMYauctions.com

organization. Not wishing to lose Reiser, the extremely shrewd Rickey subsequently reached a gentlemen's agreement with close personal friend Larry MacPhail in which he prevailed upon the Dodgers General Manager to hide the nineteen-year-old prospect within the Brooklyn farm system for a year or two, before returning him to St. Louis. While MacPhail initially intended to live up to his part of the arrangement, Reiser's extraordinary play eventually forced him to change his mind.

After being converted from a right-handed hitter to a left-handed batter in the minor leagues to take better advantage of his exceptional running speed, the ambidextrous Reiser arrived at Dodgers spring training in 1939. Making an immediate impression on Brooklyn player-manager Leo Durocher, Reiser proceeded to reach base safely in his first 11 trips to the plate against major-league pitchers, walking three times, collecting four singles, and hitting four home runs. Nevertheless, MacPhail instructed Durocher to return Reiser to the minor leagues shortly thereafter, causing a heated discussion to ensue between the two men that resulted in Durocher punching his superior in the face. MacPhail eventually won out, though, convincing his manager to remove Reiser from the major-league roster, although he later reneged on the earlier agreement he had reached with Rickey, choosing not to part with the young phenom.

Despite being signed originally as a shortstop, Reiser played the outfield at Class A Elmira in 1939, appearing in only 38 games before undergoing surgery to remove bone chips from his right elbow. Promoted to Brooklyn's top farm team in Montreal early the following year, Reiser compiled a batting average of close to .400, prompting the Dodgers to call him up to the big leagues in late July. Acquitting himself well while splitting his time between third base and the outfield the rest of the season, the twenty-one-year-old Reiser batted .293 in 58 games, with 3 homers, 20 RBIs, and 34 runs scored.

Moved to the outfield full-time in 1941, Reiser did an outstanding job of patrolling centerfield for the Dodgers, leading all players at his position with 14 assists, while also finishing second among NL centerfielders with 355 putouts. He made an even greater impact on offense, though, hitting 14 homers, driving in 76 runs, placing among the league leaders with 184 hits and a .406 on-base percentage, and topping the senior circuit with 117 runs scored, 39 doubles, 17 triples, 299 total bases, a .343 batting average, a .558 slugging percentage, and a .964 OPS. Reiser's brilliant performance for the pennant-winning Dodgers earned him the first of his three All-Star selections and a runner-up finish to teammate Dolph Camilli in the NL MVP voting.

Possessing tremendous power at the plate in spite of his relatively modest 5'11", 185-pound frame, Reiser impressed others even more with his exceptional running speed and powerful throwing arm, with Arthur Patterson writing in the *New York Herald Tribune*, "Any manager in the National League would give up his best man to obtain Pete Reiser. On every bench, they're talking about him. Rival players watch him take his cuts during batting practice, announce when he's going to make a throw to the plate or third base during outfield drill. They just whistle their amazement when he scoots down the first base line on an infield dribbler or a well-placed bunt."

Reiser remained the talk of the baseball world throughout the first half of 1942, entering play on July 19 leading the National League in batting average (.356), slugging percentage (.531), and OPS (.947). However, his career took a sudden turn for the worse during a doubleheader loss to the Cardinals in St. Louis that afternoon. After the Cardinals won the opener by a score of 8-5, the two teams entered the 11th inning of the nightcap tied at 6-6. Batting in the bottom of the frame, Enos Slaughter hit a ball well over Reiser's head to deep centerfield. After narrowly avoiding the flagpole that rose from the playing field, Reiser made a superb running catch of Slaughter's drive, before having the ball jarred loose from his glove a moment later when he crashed into the unpadded concrete wall. Although dazed, Reiser returned the ball to the infield, albeit too late to prevent Slaughter from circling the bases with a game-winning inside-the-park home run. He then collapsed in the outfield, where he lay motionless for several minutes, blood trickling from his ears. Carried off the field on a stretcher, Reiser awoke the next morning in the hospital with a fractured skull and a brain injury.

Failing to heed the advice of his doctors, Reiser amazingly returned to the playing field less than a week later. However, he suffered from dizziness and headaches the rest of the season, preventing him from performing at the same lofty level he had reached prior to his mishap. Batting just .244 and displaying little power at the plate over the final two months of the campaign, Reiser finished the year with 10 home runs, 64 RBIs, 89 runs scored, and a .310 batting average, although he still managed to lead the NL with 20 stolen bases and earn a sixth-place finish in the league MVP voting. Meanwhile, the Dodgers, who led second-place St. Louis by

8 games in the standings before Reiser suffered his injury, ended up finishing 2 games behind the pennant-winning Cardinals, even though they compiled an exceptional record of 104-50.

Although Reiser never fully recovered from the after-effects of his collision with the outfield wall at Sportsman's Park, continuing to experience problems with dizziness and headaches the remainder of his career, he managed to pass his Army physical and enlist in the military following the conclusion of the 1942 campaign. He spent the next three years in the service, during which time he suffered what he considered to be the injury that did the most to bring his career to a premature end.

"I plowed through a fence playing with Fort Riley [Kansas], rolled down a twenty-five-foot embankment, and came up with a shoulder separation," Reiser later said. "It wasn't as serious as the head injuries, but it did more to end my career. The shoulder kept popping out of place, more bone chips developed, and there was constant pain in the arm and shoulder."

Reiser remained an effective player after he returned to the Dodgers in 1946, when, despite appearing in only 122 games, he earned his third All-Star selection and a ninth-place finish in the NL MVP voting by batting .277, driving in 73 runs, scoring 75 times, and leading the league with 34 stolen bases, including a record 7 steals of home. However, with his shoulder proving to be a constant source of discomfort, Reiser altered his swing somewhat, causing him to lose much of his power at the plate. His performance declined even more after he fractured his fibula by running into another outfield wall.

Refusing to alter his aggressive style of play, Reiser suffered another serious injury in early June 1947, when he ran into the centerfield wall at Ebbets Field while chasing down a fly ball against the Pirates, once again being knocked unconscious. Yet, despite missing the next six weeks of the campaign, he helped the Dodgers capture the National League pennant by batting .309, scoring 68 runs, and stealing 14 bases.

Unfortunately, the 1947 season ended up being Reiser's last as a full-time player. Slowed by his many injuries, he never again appeared in more than 84 games. After batting just .236, hitting only one home run, and knocking in just 19 runs in 64 games with the Dodgers in 1948, Reiser asked to be traded at season's end. Team management granted his request on December 15, 1948, dealing him to the Boston Braves for a pair of nondescript players. Reiser left Brooklyn with career totals of 44 home runs, 298 RBIs, 400 runs scored, 666 hits, 135 doubles, 35 triples, and 78 stolen bases, a batting average of .306, an on-base percentage of .384, and a slugging percentage of .460.

Reiser remained in the Major Leagues another four years, spending two seasons in Boston, one in Pittsburgh, and one in Cleveland. During that time, he never batted any higher than .271 or accumulated more than 221 official at-bats in any single season. Reiser announced his retirement following the conclusion of the 1952 campaign, ending his career with 58 homers, 368 RBIs, 473 runs scored, 786 hits, 155 doubles, 41 triples, 87 stolen bases, a .295 batting average, a .380 on-base percentage, and a .450 slugging percentage.

Following his playing days, Reiser remained in the game another twenty-nine years, spending the first twelve of those serving as a coach with the Dodgers. He later worked for the Cubs, Angels, and Phillies as well, finally announcing his retirement from baseball in October 1981. Reiser died of emphysema just two days later, on October 25, 1981, losing his lengthy battle with the respiratory illness at only sixty-two years of age.

Over the course of his playing career, Pete Reiser had to be carried off the field a total of 11 times, regaining consciousness either in the clubhouse or in the hospital in nine of those instances. He broke a bone in his right elbow while throwing and tore the muscles in his left leg while sliding. He broke both ankles and tore cartilage in his left knee. Seven times he crashed into outfield walls, dislocating his left shoulder, breaking his right collarbone, and, five times, ending up in an unconscious heap on the ground. He also was beaned twice.

Former Dodgers' Vice President and General Manager Buzzie Bavasi paid homage to Reiser on one occasion by suggesting that he might have been the greatest player he ever saw. Quoted in *Out By a Step: The 100 Best Players Not in the Baseball Hall of Fame*, Bavasi stated,

> *"Pete might have been the best of all of them, including DiMag. He could do it all, a true five-tool player. Joe couldn't run with him. Reiser had more power, and he hit from both sides of the plate and could throw equally well with both hands. He was the fastest and the strongest guy in the game. The only trouble is, he didn't do it long enough. He was more than aggressive. He was reckless."*

Leo Durocher also paid tribute to Reiser in his 1976 autobiography entitled *Nice Guys Finish Last*, writing, "There will never be a ballplayer as good as Willie Mays, but Reiser was every bit as good, and he might have been better. Pete Reiser might have been the best ballplayer I ever saw. He had more power than Willie. He could throw as good as Willie. Mays was fast, but Reiser was faster. Name whoever you want to, and Pete Reiser was faster. Willie Mays had everything. Pete Reiser had everything but luck."

## Dodger Career Highlights:

**Best Season**: Was there ever any doubt? Fully healthy for an entire season for the only time as a major-leaguer, Reiser established career-high marks in virtually every statistical category in 1941, leading the National League in batting average (.343), slugging percentage (.558), OPS (.964), runs scored (117), doubles (39), triples (17), and total bases (299). Although he finished second to teammate Dolph Camilli in the league MVP balloting, it could certainly be argued that Reiser had the better all-around year and made more of an overall impact on the pennant race.

**Memorable Moments/Greatest Performances:** A daring base-runner throughout his career, Reiser established a new major-league record by stealing home seven times in 1946.

Reiser turned in his finest performance as a rookie on September 8, 1940, when he led the Dodgers to a 4-2 extra-inning victory over the Giants by going 4-for-5, with a double.

Reiser's exceptional 1941 campaign included a number of outstanding efforts, with the first of those coming on April 18, when he homered, singled, drove in 3 runs, and scored 3 times during an 11-6 win over the Boston Braves.

Just two days later, on April 20, Reiser helped lead the Dodgers to a 10-9 victory over the Giants by going 4-for-5, with a pair of doubles and 2 runs scored.

Reiser provided the winning margin in an 8-4 win over Philadelphia on May 25, 1941, when his sixth-inning grand slam put the Dodgers ahead to stay. He finished the game with a career-high 5 runs batted in.

The following year, on May 31, 1942, Reiser sparked a 10-2 victory over the Boston Braves by going 3-for-4, with a homer, double, 3 RBIs, and a career-high 4 runs scored.

Reiser had another huge game just two days later, on June 2, 1942, when he led the Dodgers to a 17-2 pasting of Pittsburgh by going 5-for-5, with a homer, 3 doubles, 3 RBIs, and 3 runs scored.

Reiser celebrated his return to the Dodgers early in 1946 by going 4-for-5, with a pair of doubles, a stolen base, 2 RBIs, and 1 run scored during a 5-4, 10-inning win over the Braves on April 22.

Later in the year, on June 20, 1946, Reiser led the Dodgers to a 7-3 victory over the Pirates by going 3-for-4, with a pair of doubles and 4 RBIs.

Reiser tied his single-game career-high for RBIs on April 29, 1948, when he led the Dodgers to a 17-7 pounding of the Giants by homering, tripling, knocking in 5 runs, and scoring twice.

## Notable Achievements:

- Batted over .300 three times, topping the .340-mark once (.343 in 1941).
- Scored more than 100 runs once (117 in 1941).
- Finished in double-digits in triples once (17 in 1941).
- Surpassed 30 doubles twice.
- Surpassed 20 stolen bases twice, topping 30 steals once (34 in 1946).
- Compiled on-base percentage in excess of .400 twice.
- Posted slugging percentage in excess of .500 once (.558 in 1941).
- Led NL in: batting average once, run scored once, triples once, stolen bases twice, slugging percentage once, OPS once, and total bases once.
- Led NL center-fielders in assists once.
- Set major-league record by stealing home seven times in 1946.
- Finished second in 1941 NL MVP voting.
- 1941 *Sporting News* All-Star selection.
- Three-time NL All-Star (1941, 1942 & 1946).
- Two-time NL champion (1941 & 1947).

# 41

# STEVE SAX

An aggressive, high-energy player who served as an offensive catalyst during his time in Los Angeles, Steve Sax spent seven full seasons starting at second base for the Dodgers, excelling at the bat and on the base paths while hitting out of the leadoff spot in the batting order. After winning NL Rookie of the Year honors in 1982, Sax went on to earn three All-Star nominations as a member of the Dodgers, helping them capture three division titles, one pennant, and one world championship in the process. Along the way, Sax consistently ranked among the league leaders in hits and stolen bases, amassing more than 200 safeties once and 40 thefts on four separate occasions. Meanwhile, after inexplicably developing a mental block when throwing the ball to first base early in his career, Sax gradually evolved into one of the senior circuit's more reliable defenders at second, annually finishing among the top few players at his position in both putouts and assists.

Born in Sacramento, California on January 29, 1960, Stephen Louis Sax attended James Marshall High School (now known as River City High School) in West Sacramento, where he starred on the diamond before being drafted by the Dodgers in the ninth round of the 1978 amateur draft. After spending most of the next four years advancing through the Los Angeles farm system, Sax made his major-league debut with the Dodgers on August 18, 1981. Starting 28 games at second base over the final six weeks of the campaign, the right-handed hitting Sax made a favorable impression on team brass by batting .277, scoring 15 runs, and stealing 5 bases.

Convinced that Sax had all the tools needed to succeed at the major-league level, the Dodgers elected to trade Davey Lopes to Oakland during the subsequent offseason, leaving the starting second base job to the twenty-two-year-old infielder. Rewarding team management for the faith

Courtesy of George A. Kitrinos

Steve Sax stole more than 40 bases four times
as a member of the Dodgers

it placed in him, Sax went on to earn All-Star and NL Rookie of the Year honors by batting .282, scoring 88 runs, and finishing fifth in the league with 49 stolen bases. Sax followed that up with another solid offensive performance in 1983, batting .281 and establishing career-high marks in runs scored (94) and stolen bases (56). However, while Sax made significant contributions to the division-winning Dodgers out of his leadoff spot in the batting order, he proved to be very much a liability in the field, committing a league-leading 30 errors at second base, mostly on throws to first.

Sax's throwing woes began innocently enough in the first week of the campaign, when he made a poor throw home as the relay man on a ball hit to the outfield. After his errant toss to the plate allowed the runner at third to score, Sax found himself being overwhelmed by self-doubt, later revealing in *This Great Game*, "I made that error, and then I made another one, and pretty soon I let doubt and fear creep into my psyche. And, when that happens, you're a goner."

Things only got worse for Sax when he subsequently lapsed into an inexplicable funk that prevented him from accurately throwing the ball to first base. The young infielder's inability to deliver the ball accurately, which later came to be known in baseball circles as "Steve Sax Syndrome," served as a source of amusement to opposing fans seated behind first base, who openly mocked him by wearing batting helmets and covering themselves with bed sheets adorned with bulls-eye targets. The beleaguered Sax later admitted, "I went to bed with it. I woke up with it. I was the laughingstock of the league."

Even some of Sax's teammates found a certain amount of humor in his predicament, with Dodger third baseman Pedro Guerrero once poking fun at his fellow infielder during a private meeting with manager Tommy Lasorda. With Guerrero also committing his fair share of miscues in the field, Lasorda decided to probe the mind of his struggling slugger, posing to him an imaginary scenario in which he asked him to envision himself at third base with the game on the line in the ninth inning. Asked by his manager what would likely be going through his mind in such a situation, Guerrero responded, "God, please don't let him hit the ball to me." When Lasorda asked him what else he would be thinking, Guerrero answered, "God, please don't let him hit the ball to Sax."

After committing 24 errors by the All-Star break, Sax finally overcame his phobia during the latter stages of the campaign following an emotional conversation with his dying father. Chronicled by Sax in *Shift: Change Your Mindset and You Change Your World*, the exchange took place in the hospital, where the confused infielder went to visit his father after the latter suffered his fifth heart attack. Told by his father that he had experienced the exact same problem in high school, Sax became encouraged when his dad suggested to him, "One day, you are going to wake up and this problem is going to be gone." Although John Sax died six hours later, his words lived on in his son's mind, bringing him comfort and relief. His spirits buoyed, Sax slowly regained his confidence, going the final 36 games of the season without making a single error. Following his retirement, though, Sax's mother, who had known his dad since the fifth grade, revealed the truth to her son, telling him that his father never had a throwing problem. In addressing the psychology employed by his dad, Sax later told *The Arizona Republic*, "He lied. He didn't want to see me fail, so he lied. He bailed me out on his death bed. And it changed my life."

His mind finally free of worry, Sax began to enjoy baseball again. Displaying tremendous hustle and enthusiasm in everything he did on the playing field, Sax served as an inspiration to his teammates, with fellow Dodger Alfredo Griffin stating in *Miracle Men: Hershiser, Gibson, and the Improbable 1988 Dodgers,*

*"He was a machine, Saxy, in and out every day. I don't
know how he did it. He gave one hundred percent one day.
The next day, he comes back and gives one hundred and
ten percent. I thought, 'Where does this guy get all this
energy?' It was unbelievable. He'd hit a grounder, and he's
flying to first base; Doesn't matter if we're down one run or
up ten runs. This guy was the best."*

Although Sax suffered through a subpar 1984 campaign in which he
batted just .243 and scored only 70 runs, he performed extremely well for
the Dodgers in each of the next four seasons, with his finest year coming in
1986, when he earned his third All-Star selection and lone Silver Slugger
by hitting 6 homers, driving in 56 runs, scoring 91 times, stealing 40 bases,
and finishing second in the league with 210 hits, 43 doubles, and a .332
batting average. Sax also batted .280, scored 84 runs, and stole 37 bases
in 1987, before batting .277 and stealing 42 bases for the Dodgers' 1988
world championship ball club. Meanwhile, although Sax never developed
into a Gold Glove caliber second baseman, he eventually established himself as one of the more dependable fielders at his position, reducing his
error total to just 14 in both 1987 and 1988, while leading all NL second
sackers in putouts in 1986.

The 1988 season ended up being Sax's last in Los Angeles since he
elected to sign with the Yankees as a free agent following the conclusion
of the campaign. Upon announcing his decision to leave the Dodgers, Sax
explained, "There was a great difference in the tone of negotiations between [Yankees GM] Bob Quinn and [Dodgers GM] Fred Claire. The attitude was completely different. The Yankees treated me as someone they
greatly respected. I felt it wasn't the same with the Dodgers. I felt Claire
was really aloof. The tone of voice he spoke to me in and the way he
looked at me really turned me off." Sax left the Dodgers with career totals
of 30 home runs, 333 RBIs, 574 runs scored, 1,218 hits, 159 doubles, 35
triples, and 290 stolen bases, a .282 batting average, a .339 on-base percentage, and a .356 slugging percentage.

Sax spent the next three seasons in New York, sandwiching two excellent years around a rather mediocre one. En route to earning the fourth of
his five All-Star nominations in 1989, Sax batted .315, collected 205 hits,
knocked in a career-high 63 runs, scored 88 times, stole 43 bases, and led
all AL second sackers in double plays and fielding percentage. He had
another fine season in 1991, batting .304, with 198 hits, 85 runs scored,

31 steals, and a career-high 10 homers, before being dealt to the Chicago White Sox for three young players during the subsequent offseason. Sax remained in Chicago through the end of 1993, gradually seeing his performance deteriorate until the club released him just prior to the start of the 1994 campaign. After being picked up by Oakland, Sax appeared in only seven games with the A's, before announcing his retirement. He ended his career with 54 home runs, 550 RBIs, 913 runs scored, 1,949 hits, 278 doubles, 47 triples, 444 stolen bases, a .281 batting average, a .335 on-base percentage, and a .358 slugging percentage.

Following his playing days, Sax became involved in a number of ventures, including working as a baseball analyst on television, owning a nightclub and restaurant in Folsom, California, working as a financial consultant for RBC Dain Rauscher, LLC, and piloting a sports networking site called allsportsconnection.com. He also spent one season coaching first base for the Arizona Diamondbacks, before returning to the Dodger organization in 2015 as an Alumni member of the team's Community Relations Department.

## Dodger Career Highlights:

**Best Season:** Sax unquestionably had his best season for the Dodgers in 1986, when, in addition to scoring 91 runs and stealing 40 bases, he established career-high marks in on-base percentage (.390), slugging percentage (.441), batting average (.332), hits (210), and doubles (43), finishing second in the league in each of the last three categories. Sax also did a solid job defensively, leading all NL second basemen with a career-best 367 putouts.

**Memorable Moments/Greatest Performances:** Sax put together an impressive 25-game hitting streak in 1986 that lasted from September 1 to September 27, going 43-for-106 (.406), with 10 doubles, 13 RBIs, 15 runs scored, and 11 stolen bases during that time.

Sax turned in an outstanding all-around effort for the Dodgers on April 16, 1983, helping them record an 8-5 victory over the San Diego Padres by going 4-for-5, with a double, triple, 2 stolen bases, 2 RBIs, and 2 runs scored.

Sax led the Dodgers to an 8-4 win over the Cubs at Wrigley Field on May 7, 1986 by driving in a career-high 5 runs with a single and a grand slam homer.

Later that same season, on September 3, 1986, Sax sparked the Dodgers to a 5-3 win over Montreal by going 4-for-5, with a pair of doubles, 2 stolen bases, and 2 runs scored.

Sax again served as the Dodgers' offensive catalyst exactly one week later, going a perfect 4-for-4, with a double, a stolen base, an RBI, and 2 runs scored, during a 5-1 win over the Astros on September 10, 1986.

Sax homered twice in one game for the only time in his career on May 26, 1988, when he collected a pair of homers, a double, 4 RBIs, and 3 runs scored during a 10-8 victory over Philadelphia.

Sax had another big day at the plate the following week, going 5-for-6 and scoring a pair of runs, in leading the Dodgers to a 13-5 win over Cincinnati on June 3, 1988.

Sax helped lead the Dodgers to a stunning seven-game victory over the heavily-favored New York Mets in the 1988 NLCS by batting .267, stealing 5 bases, and tying a franchise record by scoring 7 runs in a single postseason series. Coming up big in the Dodgers' 6-0 pennant-clinching win in Game Seven, Sax went 3-for-5, with 2 RBIs and 2 runs scored. He also performed well against Oakland in the World Series, posting a batting average of .300, scoring three times, and stealing a base.

## Notable Achievements:

- Batted over .300 once (.332 in 1986).
- Topped 200 hits once (210 in 1986).
- Surpassed 40 doubles once (43 in 1986).
- Stole more than 30 bases six times, topping 40 thefts on three occasions.
- Led NL in plate appearances once and at-bats once.
- Finished second in NL in: batting average once, hits once, and doubles once.
- Led NL second basemen in putouts once.
- Ranks fifth in Dodgers history with 290 career steals.
- 1982 NL Rookie of the Year.
- September, 1986 NL Player of the Month.
- 1986 Silver Slugger winner.
- 1986 *Sporting News* All-Star selection.

- Three-time NL All-Star (1982, 1983 & 1986).
- Two-time NL champion (1981 & 1988).
- Two-time world champion (1981 & 1988).

# 42

# RON PERRANOSKI

One of baseball's premier relief pitchers for nearly a decade, Ron Perranoski spent his first seven big-league seasons in Los Angeles, before moving on to Minnesota, where he continued to excel in late-game situations. The Major Leagues' all-time saves leader among left-handed pitchers at the time of his retirement in 1973, Perranoski annually placed near the top of the NL rankings in saves and games finished during his time with the Dodgers, helping them capture three pennants and two world championships in the process. Meanwhile, his 16 victories in 1963 remain one of the highest single-season win totals ever compiled by a reliever.

Born in Paterson, New Jersey on April 1, 1936, Ronald Peter Perzanowski changed his last name to Perranoski sometime after he moved with his family to nearby Fair Lawn as a youngster. Attracting scouts from several colleges while pitching for Fair Lawn High School, Perranoski eventually accepted a scholarship offer to attend Michigan State University, where he ended up earning First-Team All-Big Ten honors as a senior in 1958. Following his graduation from MSU, Perranoski signed with the Chicago Cubs, who sent him to the minors for two years, before trading him to the Dodgers for infielder Don Zimmer prior to the start of the 1960 campaign. Subsequently converted into a relief pitcher during his one year in the Los Angeles farm system, Perranoski arrived in the Major Leagues to stay in the spring of 1961.

The twenty-five-year-old Perranoski had a solid rookie year for the Dodgers, compiling 6 saves, a record of 7-5, and a 2.65 ERA, over 91⅔ innings and 53 mound appearances. Assuming the role of closer the following year, Perranoski emerged as one of the senior circuit's top relievers, going 6-6 with a 2.85 ERA, finishing second in the league with 19 saves, throwing more than 100 innings (107⅓) for the first of four straight times, and leading all NL pitchers with 70 appearances. Perranoski then had the finest season of his career in 1963, helping the Dodgers capture the NL flag by going 16-3, with 21 saves and an ERA of 1.67, while tossing 129 innings and appearing in a league-leading 69 games, en route to earning a fourth-place finish in the MVP voting.

Perranoski owed much of the success he experienced his first few seasons in Los Angeles to his wide assortment of pitches that included a live fastball he used primarily to set up his sinker and curve. A master at inducing double plays, Perranoski established himself as one of the game's dominant closers, even though he typically allowed nearly as many hits as innings pitched.

Perranoski continued to anchor the Dodgers' bullpen through 1967, contributing significantly to two more pennants and one more world championship over the course of the next four seasons. Particularly effective in the championship campaign of 1965, Perranoski finished 6-6, with a 2.24 ERA, 18 saves, and a WHIP of 1.194, which represented his best mark as a member of the team. Yet, even though Perranoski performed extremely well in 1967, saving 16 games and compiling an ERA of 2.45, the Dodgers elected to include him in a five-player trade they completed with the Minnesota Twins at season's end that netted them pitcher Jim "Mudcat" Grant and former AL MVP shortstop Zoilo Versalles in return.

Perranoski found the American League very much to his liking, being named AL Fireman of the Year in back-to-back years by *The Sporting News*, after spending his first season in Minnesota serving as the setup man for Al Worthington. Helping the Twins capture the AL West title in both 1969 and 1970, Perranoski amassed a total of 65 saves those two seasons, topping the junior circuit in that category both years. However, after the thirty-five-year-old reliever began to show signs of aging in 1971, going just 1-4 with a 6.75 ERA over the course of the first four months of the campaign, Minnesota placed him on waivers. Subsequently claimed by Detroit, Perranoski spent exactly one year in Motown, before returning to Los Angeles when the Dodgers signed him in August 1972 following his release by the Tigers. Perranoski finished out the year in Los Angeles, going 2-0 with a 2.70 ERA in 9 appearances, before ending his career with the California Angels the following season. He retired with a lifetime record of 79-74, 178 saves, an ERA of 2.79, a WHIP of 1.332, and 687 strikeouts in 1,174⅔ innings pitched, while allowing the opposition a total of 1,097 hits. Over parts of eight seasons with the Dodgers, Perranoski

Courtesy of MEARS Online Auctions

Ron Perranoski (left), seen here with Johnny Podres
after beating the Yankees in the 1963 World Series, posted 16
victories for the pennant-winning Dodgers in 1963 as a reliever

went 54-41, with a 2.56ERA, 100 saves, a WHIP of 1.302, and 461 strike-outs in 766⅔ innings of work.

Following his playing days, Perranoski spent eight years serving as a minor league pitching coordinator for the Dodgers, during which time he helped develop the pitching skills of talented young hurlers such as Rick Sutcliffe, Bob Welch, Steve Howe, Orel Hershiser, and Fernando Valenzuela. Named Dodgers' pitching coach in 1981, Perranoski spent the next 14 seasons mentoring a staff that led the National League in team ERA five times. After leaving the Dodgers, Perranoski continued his coaching career with the San Francisco Giants, serving as their minor league pitching coordinator for two years, before being promoted to bench coach in 1997, and then to pitching coach the following year. Since 2000, he has been a special assistant to general manager Brian Sabean.

## Dodger Career Highlights:

**Best Season:** Perranoski unquestionably had his greatest season for the Dodgers in 1963, when he helped them capture the NL pennant by compiling a record of 16-3 that gave him a league-best .842 winning percentage. By posting 16 victories in relief, he tied Philadelphia's Jim Konstanty (1950) for the second highest win total in a season, trailing only Roy Face, who won 18 games working out of the Pittsburgh bullpen in 1959. Perranoski also compiled an ERA of 1.67, finished second in the league with 21 saves, posted a WHIP of 1.202, struck out 75 batters and surrendered 112 hits in a career-high 129 innings of work, and led all NL hurlers with 69 mound appearances, en route to earning his only top-10 finish in the league MVP voting.

**Memorable Moments/Greatest Performances:** Replacing Dodger starter Stan Williams after just one inning, Perranoski turned in the longest outing of his career on May 13, 1961, when he worked the final eight frames of a 7-3 victory over the Chicago Cubs, allowing 7 hits and 2 runs along the way.

Perranoski again excelled in relief of Williams on August 25, 1962, surrendering just 1 hit and 1 walk over the final 4⅔ innings of an 8-2 win over the New York Mets.

Perranoski turned in another exceptional effort against the Mets on May 19, 1963, when he worked the final seven frames of a 13-inning contest the Dodgers finally won by a score of 4-2 on a walk-off two-run homer by Frank Howard. Perranoski allowed no runs, 4 hits, 4 walks, and struck out 4 batters after entering the game in the seventh inning.

Perranoski again performed heroically on September 18, 1963, when he helped the Dodgers defeat St. Louis by a score of 6-5 in 13 innings by shutting out the Cardinals over the final six frames, allowing just 3 hits and 2 bases on balls to the Redbirds.

Working in relief of Los Angeles starter Phil Ortega on September 5, 1964, Perranoski earned a 6-2 victory over the Mets by pitching six scoreless innings, surrendering just 1 hit and 1 walk to the New Yorkers.

Perranoski again dominated Mets batters on September 12, 1966, allowing just 3 hits and striking out 7 during a four-inning stint that resulted in a 3-2 Dodgers win.

Yet, the highlight of Perranoski's career would have to be considered the save he earned in Game Two of the 1963 World Series, when he preserved Johnny Podres' 4-1 victory over the Yankees by stifling a rally by the New Yorkers in the bottom of the ninth inning.

## Notable Achievements:

- Saved more than 20 games once (21 in 1963).
- Won 16 games in 1963.
- Compiled ERA below 3.00 five times, posting mark under 2.00 once (1.67 in 1963).
- Compiled winning percentage in excess of .800 once (.842 in 1963).
- Threw more than 100 innings five times.
- Led NL pitchers in winning percentage once and appearances three times.
- Ranks among Dodgers career leaders in: saves (sixth), ERA (sixth), pitching appearances (fourth), and games finished (second).
- Finished fourth in 1963 NL MVP voting.
- Three-time NL champion (1963, 1965 & 1966).
- Two-time world champion (1963 & 1965).

# 43

# ANDRE ETHIER

A solid all-around player with a flair for the dramatic, Andre Ethier has spent most of the last 11 seasons in Los Angeles serving as one of the central figures on Dodger teams that have won six division titles and advanced to the NLCS on three separate occasions. En route to earning two All-Star selections and one top-10 finish in the league MVP voting, the left-handed hitting Ethier has hit more than 20 homers four times, driven in more than 100 runs once, and batted over .300 twice. A strong defender as well, Ethier has led all NL outfielders in fielding percentage and double plays once each, going an entire season at one point without committing a single error in the field. Meanwhile, despite being overshadowed much of the time by the more spectacular Matt Kemp, Ethier boasts career totals that rival those of the former Dodger standout, ranking among the franchise's all-time leaders in both doubles (seventh) and extra-base hits (ninth).

Born in Phoenix, Arizona on April 10, 1982, Andre Everett Ethier grew up in a multicultural household. Born to a father with a mixed French Canadian and Cherokee background and a Mexican American mother, Ethier attended local St. Mary's High School, where he starred in baseball while also playing for a travel team called the Firebirds during the summer. After earning First-Team All-Region and Second-Team All-State honors as a senior at St. Mary's in 2000, Ethier accepted a scholarship offer from Arizona State University. However, he decided to transfer to Chandler-Gilbert Community College after playing with ASU in the fall of 2000 when the latter institution's coaching staff told him that they thought he lacked Division I talent, and that he would do better to play junior college ball. Ethier, though, re-enrolled at ASU in 2002 after he earned All-Conference honors and an honorable mention as a Junior College All-American by batting .468 at CGCC the previous year.

Courtesy of Keith Allison

Andre Ethier has helped the Dodgers
win six division titles

After spending the remainder of his collegiate career starring in the outfield for the Sun Devils, Ethier signed with the Oakland Athletics when they made him the 62$^{nd}$ overall pick of the 2003 amateur draft. He subsequently spent the next three years advancing through Oakland's farm system, earning Texas League Most Valuable Player and Oakland Athletics Minor League Player of the Year honors in 2005 by hitting 18 homers, driving in 88 runs, scoring 104 times, and batting .319 for the Class AA Texas League champion Midland RockHounds.

With the Dodgers seeking to part ways with troubled outfielder Milton Bradley, who had earlier experienced problems with several of his teammates, they worked out a deal with the A's on December 13, 2005 that sent Bradley and utility infielder Antonio Perez to Oakland for Ethier. After spending the first month of the 2006 campaign at triple-A Las Vegas, Ethier arrived in Los Angeles to stay in early May. He then gradually worked his way into the Dodger starting lineup as the team's everyday left-fielder by hitting 11 homers, knocking in 55 runs, scoring 50 times, and batting .308 over the season's final five months, en route to earning a fifth-place finish in the NL Rookie of the Year voting. Splitting each of the next two seasons between both corner outfield positions, Ethier continued to post solid numbers for the Dodgers, concluding the 2007 campaign with 13 home runs, 64 RBIs, 50 runs scored, and a .284 batting average, before increasing his offensive output to 20 homers, 77 RBIs, 90 runs scored, and a .305 batting average the following year.

Ethier, who the Dodgers played almost exclusively in right field the next few seasons, subsequently emerged as a full-fledged star in 2009, earning a sixth-place finish in the NL MVP balloting by hitting 31 homers, scoring 92 runs, batting .272, and placing among the league leaders with 106 RBIs and 42 doubles. The twenty-seven-year-old outfielder also developed into one of the senior circuit's finest clutch performers, tying a National League record by hitting four walk-off homers. As Ethier evolved into one of the league's better players, he drew further attention to himself with the tremendous level of intensity he displayed on the playing field, prompting Dodgers skipper Joe Torre to liken him to a young Paul O'Neill, who Torre earlier managed in New York. But, while Torre suggested that Ethier's ability to eventually tame his inner anger allowed him to improve as a player, former Dodger Randy Wolf disagreed, claiming that the outfielder's explosive temper added to his on-field performance.

Despite missing nearly a month of action with various injuries in 2010, Ethier had another solid season, earning All-Star honors for the first of two straight times by hitting 23 homers, driving in 82 runs, scoring 71 others, and batting .292. He then experienced an up-and-down year in 2011, hitting just 11 homers, knocking in only 62 runs, and scoring just 67 times, although he also batted .292 and compiled a perfect 1.000 fielding percentage in right field. Ethier also became embroiled in controversy for the first time in his career that season, when *Los Angeles Times* columnist T.J. Simers wrote an article that quoted Ethier as saying that his offensive production had fallen off because of a bothersome knee injury. With Ethier implying that he had been forced to take the field against his wishes, Dodger Manager Don Mattingly called himself "blindsided" by the story and responded that he would never make anyone play hurt. After meeting with Mattingly and GM Ned Colletti, Ethier retracted his earlier comments and said that it had been his decision to play hurt.

Ethier rebounded somewhat in 2012 after signing a five-year, $85 million contract extension with the Dodgers, concluding the campaign with 20 home runs, 89 RBIs, 79 runs scored, and a .284 batting average. However, after injuries to Matt Kemp forced the Dodgers to move Ethier to centerfield for the first time in his career the following year, Ethier himself suffered an injury to his foot that severely limited his playing time and effectiveness the final few weeks of the season. Appearing in 142 games in 2013, Ethier finished the season with only 12 home runs, 52 RBIs, 54 runs scored, and a .272 batting average.

The arrival of top prospect Yasiel Puig and the return of Kemp in 2014 forced Ethier to the bench for much of the season's second half, limiting him to just 4 homers, 42 RBIs, 29 runs scored, and a career-low .249 batting average. Yet, even though Ethier remained unhappy with his new role, he accepted it, drawing praise from his teammates for the level of professionalism he displayed. The *Los Angeles Times* also applauded Ethier for not complaining about his lack of playing time, and for continuing to attend pre-game photo and autograph-signing sessions. Although the departure of Kemp created additional room in the Dodger outfield in 2015, Ethier essentially remained a part-time player, finishing the year with 14 home runs, 53 RBIs, 54 runs scored, and a .294 batting average, in 142 games and fewer than 400 official at-bats. Ethier subsequently suffered a fractured right tibia after fouling a ball off his shin during a 2016 spring training game, forcing him to miss virtually the entire season. After finally returning to action on September 10, he hit one homer, knocked in two runs, and batted .208 over the final three weeks of the campaign. Ethier will enter the 2017 season with career totals of 160 home runs, 684 RBIs, 638 runs scored, 1,359 hits, 302 doubles, 34 triples, and 29 stolen bases, a .285 batting average, a .359 on-base percentage, and a .463 slugging percentage.

## Career Highlights:

**Best Season:** Although Ethier also performed well for the Dodgers in 2008, hitting 20 homers, driving in 77 runs, scoring 90 times, batting .305, and establishing career-high marks in on-base percentage (.375) and slugging percentage (.510), he had his finest all-around season one year later. In addition to batting .272, compiling a .361 on-base percentage, and posting a .508 slugging percentage in 2009, Ethier reached career-bests in home runs (31), RBIs (106), runs scored (92), hits (162), doubles (42), walks (72), and total bases (303), earning in the process his lone Silver Slugger and only top-10 finish in the league MVP voting. Doing much of his damage at home, Ethier hit 22 homers at Dodger Stadium, the most ever in a season by any member of the team.

**Memorable Moments/Greatest Performances:** Ethier had his break-out game for the Dodgers on May 19, 2006, going 5-for-5, with a homer, 3 RBIs, and 4 runs scored, during a 16-3 rout of the Anaheim Angels.

Although the Dodgers lost their July 24, 2006 meeting with the San Diego Padres by a score of 7-6 in 11 innings, Ethier turned in the first 2-homer performance of his career, going deep twice, collecting 4 hits, knocking in 3 runs, and scoring 3 times during the contest.

Ethier came off the bench on September 6, 2007 to hit a pinch-hit three-run homer in the top of the ninth inning that gave the Dodgers a 6-4 lead over the Chicago Cubs. The Dodgers pushed across another run later in the frame, going on to win the game by a score of 7-4.

Ethier delivered the first game-winning walk-off home run of his career on August 17, 2008, when he gave the Dodgers a 7-5 victory over Milwaukee with a two-run blast off Brewers reliever Carlos Villanueva in the bottom of the ninth inning. Ethier's homer, his second of the game, concluded a 3-for-5 afternoon during which he also doubled, drove in 3 runs, and scored 3 times.

Ethier had the second 5-for-for-5 day of his career on September 5, 2008, homering once, doubling twice, collecting a pair of singles, and knocking in 5 runs, in leading the Dodgers to a 7-0 win over the Arizona Diamondbacks.

Earning in the process the nickname "Captain Clutch," Ethier tied a single-season Major League record by hitting four walk-off home runs in 2009. He delivered his first such blow on June 6, when, just one day after beating Philadelphia with a run-scoring double in the bottom of the ninth inning, he launched his second homer of the game in the bottom of the 12th inning, to give the Dodgers a 3-2 victory over the Phillies. Ethier provided further heroics on June 29, when his two-run blast off Colorado reliever Joel Peralta in the bottom of the 13th gave the Dodgers a 4-2 win over the Rockies. Ethier continued to play the role of Superman on August 6, when his three-run homer in the bottom of the ninth inning off Atlanta reliever Rafael Soriano turned an apparent 4-2 loss to the Braves into a 5-4 Dodger victory. Ethier subsequently tied the Major League record for most walk-off homers in a season on September 15, giving the Dodgers a 5-4 win over Pittsburgh by reaching Pirates reliever Phil Dumatrait for a two-run homer in the bottom of the 13th.

Ethier has also put together a pair of extremely impressive hitting streaks during his time in Los Angeles, with the first of those being a string of 30 consecutive games in which he collected at least one hit. Ethier's 30-game hitting streak, which represents the second-longest in franchise history, lasted from April 2 to May 6, 2011, a period during which he went 46-for-116 (.397), with 3 home runs, 10 doubles, 17 RBIs, and 15 runs scored.

Ethier compiled another impressive streak the following year, hitting safely in 10 straight trips to the plate from August 23 to August 25, 2012. Ethier's string of successful at-bats, which tied the Dodger franchise record previously set by Ed Konetchy in 1919, included a particularly strong performance on August 24 in which he went 4-for-4, with a homer, 4 RBIs, and 3 runs scored.

Ethier had a big day at the plate on May 12, 2015, when he helped lead the Dodgers to a resounding 11-1 victory over the Florida Marlins by going 5-for-5, with a home run and 3 RBIs.

Ethier continued to display his penchant for coming up big in the clutch on August 2, 2015, when he hit a pair of go-ahead home runs during a 10-inning, 5-3 victory over the Anaheim Angels. Ethier delivered his second homer of the contest in walk-off fashion, going deep against Anaheim reliever Drew Rucinski with one man aboard in the bottom of the 10th.

Still, Ethier turned in his most memorable performance on June 26, 2009, when he led the Dodgers to an 8-2 win over the Seattle Mariners by hitting 3 homers and driving in a career-high 6 runs.

## Notable Achievements:

- Has hit more than 20 home runs four times, surpassing 30 homers once (31 in 2009).
- Has knocked in more than 100 runs once (106 in 2009).
- Has batted over .300 twice.
- Has topped 30 doubles seven times, surpassing 40 two-baggers once (42 in 2009).

- Has posted slugging percentage in excess of .500 twice.
- Has led NL outfielders in fielding percentage once and double plays once.
- Has led NL right-fielders in fielding percentage three times.
- Ranks among Dodgers career leaders in doubles (seventh) and extra-base hits (ninth).
- 2009 Silver Slugger winner.
- 2011 Gold Glove winner.
- Finished sixth in 2009 NL MVP voting.
- Two-time NL All-Star (2010 & 2011).

# 44

# JIM BREWER

Although he is perhaps remembered most for his on-field altercation with Billy Martin as a rookie with the Chicago Cubs in 1960, Jim Brewer went on to establish himself as one of the finest relief pitchers in Dodgers history, ranking among the team's all-time leaders in both saves and pitching appearances. An extremely reliable member of the Los Angeles bullpen for more than a decade, Brewer compiled a record of 61-51 and an ERA of 2.62 in his 12 seasons with the Dodgers, while also amassing 126 saves. Depending heavily on a screwball he learned from Warren Spahn, the lefty-throwing Brewer proved to be one of the most difficult pitchers for opposing hitters to solve during his time in Los Angeles, posting an ERA under 2.00 and a WHIP under 1.000 three times each, while saving at least 20 games on four separate occasions. In addition to earning him one All-Star selection, Brewer's stellar work helped the Dodgers capture three National League pennants and one world championship.

Born in Merced, California on November 14, 1937, James Thomas Brewer grew up in Oklahoma, where he attended Broken Arrow High School. Signed by the Chicago Cubs as an amateur free agent following his graduation from Broken Arrow in 1956, Brewer spent most of the next four seasons in the minor leagues, before being summoned to the majors for the first time midway through the 1960 campaign. However, after appearing in only five games with the Cubs, Brewer saw his rookie season come to an abrupt end on August 4, when, after driving Cincinnati Reds second baseman Billy Martin off the plate with an inside pitch, the southpaw fell victim to the streetwise Martin's brawling tactics. An incensed Martin swung and intentionally missed the next pitch, purposefully throwing his bat in Brewer's direction in the process. When no one offered to return it to him, Martin headed towards the mound to retrieve it himself.

But, as Martin approached Brewer, he sucker-punched him in the right eye, knocking him to the ground with a broken cheekbone that required two surgeries to repair. Although the Cubs eventually dropped their $1 million lawsuit against Martin, a judge later ordered him to pay $10,000 in damages to Brewer.

Returning to the Cubs the following year, Brewer experienced little success over the course of the next three seasons, compiling an overall record of just 4-10 and earned run averages of 5.82, 9.53, and 4.89, respectively, while seeing limited action as both a starter and a reliever. He received his big break, though, on December 13, 1963, when Chicago traded him to the Dodgers for journeyman right-hander Dick Scott.

After arriving in Los Angeles, Brewer quickly developed into one of the most dependable members of the Dodgers' bullpen, concluding his first season in L.A. with a record of 4-3, an ERA of 3.00, a WHIP of 1.118, and 63 strikeouts in 93 innings of work. Having learned from Warren Spahn the intricacies of throwing the screwball, which is a change-up pitch that, when thrown properly by a left-handed pitcher, tends to break away from right-handed hitters, Brewer subsequently emerged as one of the National League's top relievers. After serving primarily as a situational reliever and spot starter from 1964 to 1967, Brewer assumed the role of closer following the trade of Ron Perranoski to Minnesota prior to the start of the 1968 campaign. Over the course of the next six seasons, the 6'1", 190-pound Brewer compiled a total of 118 saves for the Dodgers, placing in the league's top five in that category each year. He also won 42 games and twice finished with more strikeouts than innings pitched during that time. After recording a career-high 24 saves in 1970, while also posting a record of 7-6 and a WHIP of 1.112, surrendering only 66 hits in 89 innings of work, and striking out 91 batters, Brewer pitched even better the following year, concluding the 1971 campaign with a record of 6-5, 22 saves, an ERA of 1.88, a WHIP of 0.971, 66 strikeouts in 81⅓ innings pitched, and just 55 hits allowed. He had another great year in 1972, going 8-7, with 17 saves, a 1.26 ERA, a WHIP of 0.843, 69 strikeouts in 78⅓ innings pitched, and only 41 hits allowed.

After earning his lone All-Star selection in 1973, Brewer continued to pitch well for the Dodgers in 1974, helping them win the pennant by posting 4 victories, an ERA of 2.52, and a WHIP of 0.992. However, with the addition of NL Cy Young Award winner Mike Marshall, who assumed the role of team closer, Brewer failed to save a single game. And, after the

Jim Brewer (far left), with other Dodger southpaws
(left to right) Claude Osteen, Sandy Koufax,
Ron Perranoski, Johnny Podres & Mike Kekich

thirty-seven-year-old left-hander compiled an ERA of 5.18 through the first three and a half months of the ensuing campaign, the Dodgers elected to trade him to the California Angels, ending his nearly twelve-year association with the ball club. Brewer left Los Angeles having compiled an overall record of 61-51, an ERA of 2.62, a WHIP of 1.129, and a total of 126 saves as a member of the team. He also struck out 672 batters in 822 innings of work, while surrendering just 630 hits to the opposition. Brewer's total of 474 pitching appearances for the Dodgers places him third in team annals, behind only Don Sutton and Don Drysdale.

Brewer subsequently pitched for the Angels through the end of 1976, announcing his retirement after compiling a record of 4-1 and 7 saves for them over the previous year-and-a-half. He ended his career with a record of 69-65, an ERA of 3.07, 133 saves, a WHIP of 1.209, and 810 strikeouts in 1,040⅓ innings pitched.

Following his playing days, Brewer joined the coaching staff of the Montreal Expos for three years, before becoming a college pitching coach, first at Oral Roberts University in Tulsa, Oklahoma, and, then, at Northwestern University. Brewer returned to the Dodger organization in 1987 to serve as a coach at the minor-league level. However, he tragically passed away later that year, on November 17, 1987, after sustaining fatal injuries in an automobile accident that took place in a small Texas town near the Louisiana border. Brewer had celebrated his fiftieth birthday just two days earlier.

## Dodger Career Highlights:

**Best Season:** Brewer had a tremendous year for the Dodgers in 1971, going 6-5, with a 1.88 ERA and a WHIP of 0.971, and finishing third in the league with 22 saves. However, he proved to be even more dominant the following season, concluding the 1972 campaign with a record of 8-7, 17 saves, an ERA of 1.26, and a WHIP of 0.843, posting career-best marks in each of the last two categories. Brewer also surrendered just 41 hits in 78⅓ innings of work, while striking out 69 batters.

**Memorable Moments/Greatest Performances:** Brewer, who started a total of only 18 games in his 12 seasons with the Dodgers, turned in one of his finest performances on the next-to-last day of the 1964 regular season, tossing a complete-game five-hit shutout against the Houston Colt 45s, defeating them by a score of 7-0. He also recorded 6 strikeouts during the contest.

Relieving ineffective Dodger starter John Purdin after only 3 innings on August 28, 1965, Brewer worked 5 scoreless frames, surrendering just 1 hit and striking out 7, in gaining an 8-4 victory over the Philadelphia Phillies. Ironically, Sandy Koufax came out of the bullpen to retire the final three batters in the bottom of the ninth, earning one of his 9 career saves in the process.

Making one of the 11 starts he made for the Dodgers in 1967, Brewer allowed only 4 hits and 1 walk over 7 scoreless innings, in defeating the Cincinnati Reds by a score of 5-0.

Brewer turned in one of his most dominant performances as a reliever on April 22, 1968, when he struck out 5 of the 6 batters he faced during a 5-3 victory over the Pittsburgh Pirates.

Brewer similarly dominated Philadelphia's lineup on August 19, 1969, saving a 2-0 Dodger win over the Phillies by surrendering just 1 hit and striking out 5 batters over 2⅔ innings.

Working in relief of Los Angeles starter Claude Osteen, who pitched into the eighth inning, Brewer helped the Dodgers defeat the Atlanta Braves by a score of 2-1 in 13 innings on July 24, 1971 by allowing just 2 hits and recording 9 strikeouts during a lengthy 5⅔-inning stint.

## Notable Achievements:

- Topped 20 saves four times.
- Compiled ERA below 3.00 seven times, posting mark under 2.00 on three occasions.
- Compiled winning percentage in excess of .700 once (.727 in 1968).
- Posted WHIP under 1.000 three times.
- Threw more than 100 innings once (100⅔ in 1967).
- Holds Dodgers career record for games finished (302).
- Ranks among Dodgers career leaders in: saves (fifth), ERA (tied-eighth), WHIP (ninth), and pitching appearances (third).
- 1973 NL All-Star.
- Three-time NL champion (1965, 1966 & 1974).
- 1965 world champion.

# 45

# BILL RUSSELL

The fourth and final member of a Dodger infield that remained together longer than any other in baseball history, Bill Russell spent his entire eighteen-year career in Los Angeles, serving as the Dodgers' starting shortstop from 1972 to 1983. During that time, Russell proved to be a key contributor to four pennant-winning teams and one world championship ball club, earning three NL All-Star selections and one *Sporting News* All-Star nomination. An extremely consistent player who batted somewhere between .264 and .286 in nine of his 12 seasons as a starter, Russell provided steady hitting from his number two spot in the batting order, while also teaming up with second baseman Davey Lopes to give the Dodgers one of the National League's top middle-infield tandems. Meanwhile, as one of the team's longest tenured players, Russell ranks among the franchise's all-time leaders in several categories, including most games played (second), most hits (sixth), and most total bases (10th).

Born in Pittsburg, Kansas on October 21, 1948, William Ellis Russell found his home state very much to his liking, attending Pittsburgh High School, before enrolling at Pittsburg State University. Russell's horizons began to expand after Los Angeles selected him in the ninth round of the 1966 amateur draft. Spending most of the next three seasons advancing through the Dodger farm system as a right-handed hitting outfielder, Russell emerged as one of the organization's top prospects. Finally arriving in Los Angeles in 1969, Russell served the Dodgers primarily as a utility outfielder in each of the next two seasons, appearing in a total of 179 games, accumulating 490 total at-bats, and hitting 5 homers, driving in 43 runs, and posting a composite batting average of .245.

Although Russell continued to assume the role of a utility player in 1971, he saw his first extensive action as an infielder, starting 52 games,

34 of those at second base. With Maury Wills turning thirty-nine years of age during the subsequent offseason, the Dodgers moved Russell to short-stop – a position he ended up manning for the next twelve years. Starting 118 games at short in 1972, Russell batted .272, with 4 homers, 34 RBIs, 47 runs scored, and 14 stolen bases. Yet, while the twenty-three-year-old infielder posted decent offensive numbers, he struggled somewhat defensively, committing a league-leading 34 errors in the field.

Russell raised his level of play the following season, earning All-Star honors for the first time by driving in 56 runs, scoring 55 times, batting .265, and topping the senior circuit with 560 assists and 162 games played. He followed that up with a similarly productive 1974 campaign, helping the Dodgers capture their first pennant in eight years by batting .269, knocking in 65 runs, scoring 61 times, and finishing second among NL shortstops with 491 assists, although he also led all players at his position with a career-high 39 errors.

After suffering through an injury-plagued 1975 season in which he batted just .206 in 84 games, Russell rebounded the following year to earn his second All-Star selection by batting .274 and driving in 65 runs. Four more solid seasons followed, with Russell earning one more All-Star nomination, while twice ranking among the leading players at his position in both putouts and assists. Performing particularly well for the Dodgers' 1977 and 1978 NL championship teams, Russell batted .278 and scored 84 runs in the first of those campaigns, before posting a career-high .286 batting average in the second.

Perhaps the biggest criticism that could be made of Russell during his peak seasons with the Dodgers is that he lacked patience at the plate, recording as many as 50 bases on balls in a season just twice in his career, en route to compiling a very mediocre .310 on-base percentage. Russell also never developed into anything more than a marginal defensive shortstop, although he eventually improved himself to the point that he no longer represented a liability in the field.

After having his right forefinger broken by a pitch thrown by Cincinnati's Mike Lacoss in September 1980, Russell suffered through a horrendous 1981 campaign in which he scored only 20 runs and batted just .233 for the world champion Dodgers. However, he bounced back the following year to score 64 runs and compile a .274 batting average. Russell remained the Dodgers' starting shortstop one more year, before assuming more of a utility role his last three seasons in Los Angeles. After batting .250 while appearing in 105 games at several different positions in 1986, Russell announced his retirement, ending his career with 46 home runs, 627 RBIs, 796 runs scored, 1,926 hits, 293 doubles, 57 triples, 167 stolen bases, a .263 batting average, a .310 on-base percentage, and a .338 slugging percentage. Only Hall of Famer Zack Wheat played in more games as a Dodger than the 2,181 contests Russell appeared in as a member of the team.

After retiring as a player, Russell became a coach for the Dodgers, serving as a member of Tommy Lasorda's staff from 1987 to 1991, before assuming the managerial reins of the Dodger's top farm club, the Albuquerque Dukes, in 1992. Following a brief two-year stint at Albuquerque, Russell returned to the Dodgers in 1994, resuming his coaching career until he replaced Lasorda at the helm midway through the 1996 campaign after the sixty-eight-year-old skipper suffered a mild heart attack. Russell remained manager of the Dodgers for nearly two years, being relieved of his duties on June 21, 1998 after the team got off to a 36-38 start. His thirty-year association with the organization ended with him having led the Dodgers to an overall record of 173-149 as manager. Russell subsequently went on to coach for the Tampa Bay Rays and manage in the minors for both Tampa Bay and San Francisco, before taking a position with Major League Baseball's umpiring division, where he currently works.

## Career Highlights:

**Best Season:** Russell played his best ball for the Dodgers in the pennant-winning campaigns of 1977 and 1978, batting .278 and scoring a career-high 84 runs in the first of those years, before reaching career-high marks in batting average (.286), hits (179), and doubles (32) in the second. But 1978 steps to the forefront as his finest season when it is considered that he batted over .400 in both the NLCS and World Series that year.

**Memorable Moments/Greatest Performances:** Russell hit arguably the most memorable home run of his career on August 2, 1972, when he hit a two-out walk-off homer in the bottom of the ninth inning off San Francisco reliever Jim Barr, to give the Dodgers a 12-11 win over the Giants. He finished the day 4-for-4, with a homer, triple, 1 RBI, and 3 runs scored.

Courtesy of Griffin Lauerman

Bill Russell served as the starting shortstop
on four pennant-winning Dodger teams

Russell had another big day at the plate on May 30, 1973, when he led the Dodgers to a 9-4 victory over the Phillies by going 4-for-5, with 4 RBIs.

Russell turned in another 4-for-5 performance less than three weeks later, on June 18, 1973, scoring twice and driving in a career-high 5 runs during a lopsided 13-3 win over the Braves.

Russell equaled his career-high mark in RBIs on May 10, 1979, when he homered, singled twice, scored 3 times, knocked in 5 runs, and stole a base during a 14-1 rout of the New York Mets.

Russell performed exceptionally well against Pittsburgh in the 1974 NLCS, collecting 7 hits, driving in 3 runs, and batting .389 during the Dodgers' four-game victory over the Pirates.

However, Russell turned in his finest postseason performance in 1978, batting .412 against the Phillies in the NLCS, before leading the Dodgers with 11 hits and a .423 batting average during their six-game loss to the Yankees in the World Series. Russell experienced the most memorable moment of his career in Game Four of the NLCS, when he delivered an RBI single off Phillies' reliever Tug McGraw in the bottom of the 10th inning that drove home Ron Cey with the winning run of a 4-3 victory that clinched the pennant for the Dodgers.

## Notable Achievements:

- Surpassed 30 doubles once (32 in 1978).
- Led NL in games played once (162 in 1973).
- Led NL shortstops in assists once and double plays turned once.
- Ranks among Dodgers career leaders in: hits (sixth), total bases (10th), games played (second), plate appearances (fifth), and at-bats (fourth).
- 1973 Sporting News All-Star selection.
- Three-time NL All-Star (1973, 1976 & 1980).
- Four-time NL champion (1974, 1977, 1978 & 1981).
- 1981 world champion.

# 46

# ERIC GAGNE

Although the legitimacy of the numbers Eric Gagne compiled during his time in Los Angeles can certainly be questioned due to his use of performance-enhancing drugs, the fact remains that the hard-throwing right-hander pitched as well as any other reliever in the game for three straight seasons. En route to earning a second-place ranking on the Dodgers' all-time saves list, Gagne set a major-league record by successfully converting 84 consecutive save opportunities, going almost two whole years without failing in such situations. The franchise's single-season record-holder in that category, Gagne earned numerous accolades while serving as the Dodgers' closer, including becoming the first reliever in eleven years to be named the NL Cy Young Award winner. Gagne also earned one *Sporting News* All-Star selection, three NL All-Star nominations, and two NL Reliever of the Year awards, cementing himself as one of the finest closers of his time.

Born in Montreal, Canada on January 7, 1976, Eric Serge Gagne grew up in nearby Mascouche, a suburb less than 10 miles north of the French-speaking city. A huge fan of the Montreal Canadiens and Montreal Expos, Gagne played both hockey and baseball as a youngster, excelling in both sports while attending Montreal's highly regarded Polyvalente Edouard Montpetit High School. Spending much of his time in high school trying to decide which sport he should pursue as a career, Gagne finally settled on baseball after he spent two years serving as the ace of Team Canada's Junior World Championship pitching staff.

Selected by the Chicago White Sox in the 30th round of the 1994 MLB amateur draft, Gagne instead chose to enroll at Seminole State Junior College in Oklahoma, where he spent his freshman year pitching for head coach Lloyd Simmons and learning the English language. Gagne, who only spoke French when he first arrived at Seminole State, taught himself English by taping classroom lectures and then listening to them repeatedly. He also met with a tutor twice a day and picked up some of the language's more commonly used phrases by watching a lot of television. Meanwhile, Gagne ingratiated himself to Simmons by displaying a mean streak on the mound and a wide assortment of pitches that included an overpowering fastball, a slider, a splitter, and an outstanding curveball.

Scouted by Claude Pelletier, a Canadian native working for the Dodgers, Gagne signed as an amateur free agent with Los Angeles after just one year at Seminole State. However, after excelling at Class A Savannah in the South Atlantic League in 1996, Gagne sat out the entire 1997 campaign after undergoing Tommy John surgery on his right elbow.

Returning to the playing field in 1998, Gagne gradually worked his way back into top form, even improving himself to some extent by developing an excellent changeup. He continued to evolve into more of a complete pitcher after being promoted to San Antonio in the Texas League the following year, mastering a four-seam changeup that became his out pitch. Subsequently named the Dodgers Minor League Pitcher of the Year for compiling a record of 12-4 and leading the Texas League with 185 strikeouts in 1999, Gagne earned a brief call-up to the majors, where he started 5 games, posted a record of 1-1 and an ERA of 2.10, and recorded 30 strikeouts in 30 innings of work over the season's final three weeks.

Expected to join the Dodgers' starting rotation in 2000, Gagne ended up spending most of the year at triple-A Albuquerque after failing to impress during spring training. Summoned to Los Angeles on three separate occasions over the course of the campaign, Gagne struggled mightily with his control, issuing 60 walks in 101⅓ innings of work, while striking out 79 batters and compiling a record of 4-6 and an ERA of 5.15 in his 19 starts. More of the same followed in 2001, when, appearing in a total of 33 games and making 24 starts for the Dodgers, Gagne went 6-7 with a 4.75 ERA, while recording 130 strikeouts and issuing 46 bases on balls in 151⅔ innings pitched.

Gagne finally received his big break in 2002, when the Dodgers converted him from a starting pitcher into a reliever following the retirement of closer Jeff Shaw. Inserted into the role of closer shortly thereafter, Gagne took to his new post immediately, commenting at the time, "This

Courtesy of John Verive

Eric Gagne ranks second on the Dodgers'
all-time saves list

role is perfect for me. I love the adrenaline rush that I get as I jog out to the mound with the fans cheering me on. There is nothing like it."

Excelling on the mound as never before, Gagne ended up finishing second in the league with 52 saves, while also compiling a record of 4-1 and an ERA of 1.97, striking out 114 batters in 82⅓ innings of work, issuing only 16 bases on balls, and posting a WHIP of 0.862. Gagne's exceptional performance earned him the first of his three straight All-Star selections and a fourth-place finish in the NL Cy Young voting. Gagne amazingly improved upon his performance slightly in 2003, converting all 55 of his save opportunities en route to becoming the first pitcher to record as many as 50 saves in more than one season. In addition to leading the league in that category, Gagne compiled an ERA of 1.20, posted a WHIP of 0.692, and struck out 137 batters and issued only 20 walks in 82⅓ innings of work, earning in the process NL Cy Young honors, a sixth-place finish in the league MVP voting, and a spot on the *Sporting News* NL All-Star team.

The success Gagne experienced as a closer made him a tremendous fan favorite, with those in attendance at Dodger Stadium cheering him wildly as he entered contests to the tune of Guns N' Roses' "*Welcome to the Jungle*," with the words "Game Over" flashing across the scoreboard. Practically unhittable, Gagne featured a wide array of pitches, with his four-seam fastball and sharp-breaking changeup proving to be his most commonly-used offerings. In describing Gagne's pitching arsenal, sports-writer Dan Habib wrote:

"Most closers depend on one pitch that becomes synonymous with their success: Trevor Hoffman's changeup, Mariano Rivera's cut fastball. Gagné thrives on the dizzying oscillation between his changeup and his fastball. They have the same release point and the same arm speed. The fastball is straight gas ... but the changeup is a devious thing, a bowling ball rolled off a picnic table. It travels some ten mph slower than his fast-ball, anywhere from eighty-three to eighty-eight mph, and, like a splitter, it breaks late and sharp."

Gagne's aggressive approach to pitching and unrestrained enthusiasm added to his popularity with the local fans, with the 6'2", 215-pound right-hander stating, "I like to show my emotion, be real aggressive, and give everything I've got for one-half inning."

Gagne had another great year in 2004, continuing his record-setting string of 84 consecutive successfully converted save opportunities through July 5, when he faltered for the first time since August 26, 2002. In addi-tion to finishing third in the league with 45 saves, Gagne went 7-3, with a 2.19 ERA, 114 strikeouts in 82⅓ innings pitched, and a WHIP of 0.911.

The 2004 season ended up being Gagne's last year as a dominant closer. After battling through numerous injuries during the early stages of the ensuing campaign, Gagne pitched effectively through mid-June, suc-cessfully converting all 8 of his save opportunities while compiling an ERA of 2.70. However, his season came to an abrupt end on June 21, when it was announced that he needed to undergo Tommy John surgery to repair a sprained ligament in his right elbow. Although surgeons even-tually performed a less-invasive procedure after amending their initial diagnosis, Gagne never regained his earlier form after undergoing two more operations—one to remove the nerve in his elbow that doctors had previously attempted to stabilize, and the other to repair two herniated discs in his back.

With Gagne having missed virtually all of the previous two campaigns, the Dodgers chose not to extend his $12 million contract at the end of 2006, making him a free agent. After signing with the Texas Rangers on December 19, 2006, Gagne ended up splitting two injury-marred years between the Rangers, Red Sox, and Milwaukee Brewers, serving as a setup man for all three teams. He then spent most of 2009 with the Quebec Capitales of the independent Can-AM League, before mounting an attempted comeback with the Dodgers in the spring of 2010. Having failed in his brief trial with the Dodgers, Gagne elected to announce his retirement on April 18, 2010, ending his career with 187 saves, a record of 33-26, an ERA of 3.47, 718 strikeouts in 643⅔ innings of work, and a WHIP of 1.156. In his years with the Dodgers, Gagne accumulated 161 saves, compiled a record of 25-21, pitched to an ERA of 3.27, struck out 629 batters over 545⅓ innings, and posted a WHIP of 1.111.

With the release of the Mitchell Report on December 13, 2007, Gagne became known as a user of HGH, an issue he addressed during a 2009 interview with the *Los Angeles Times*. Expressing remorse for his actions, while simultaneously apologizing for his inability to go into much detail about his involvement with steroids, Gagne told the newspaper, "I'm not denying it. I'm not saying I did it. I just can't talk about it. It's a touchy subject. It doesn't just involve me. I've been straightforward about everything. It stinks that I can't be more open about this. I'm not looking for sympathy anyway. I have to live with this the rest of my life. I'm going to have to explain this to my kids. It's going to be on my resume the rest of my life."

Gagne went on to say that, while others had looked up to him as a role model, he considered himself to be an example of what one should not do. However, when asked whether he had given an honest performance to Dodgers fans, he maintained that he had always worked hard to do so.

## Dodger Career Highlights:

**Best Season:** While Gagne performed brilliantly for the Dodgers from 2002 to 2004, he unquestionably pitched his best ball for them in 2003, when, in addition to successfully converting all 55 of his save opportunities, he compiled a career-best ERA of 1.20, struck out 137 batters and issued only 20 walks in 82⅓ innings pitched, surrendered just 37 hits to the opposition, and posted a WHIP of 0.692. Gagne's 137 strikeouts and 37 hits allowed produced a strikeout-to-hit ratio of 3.7 that represents a single-season record for relievers with at least 50 innings pitched.

**Memorable Moments/Greatest Performances:** Gagne pitched exceptionally well in his major-league debut on September 7, 1999, allowing no runs, just 2 hits, and striking out 8 over the first six innings of a game the Dodgers eventually lost to Florida by a score of 2-1.

Gagne turned in one more strong performance as a starter before being converted into a reliever in 2002, surrendering just 1 run and 1 hit in seven innings of work during a May 6, 2001 game against Chicago that the Dodgers ended up losing by a score of 3-2.

Gagne, though, did most of his best work out of the bullpen, performing brilliantly in April 2002, at one point retiring 19 consecutive batters en route to compiling an ERA of 0.69 and accumulating 9 saves for the month. Gagne also earned NL Pitcher of the Month honors for June 2002 by successfully converting 19 save opportunities.

Gagne made history on August 24, 2002, when he tied Todd Worrell's single-season franchise record by recording his 44th save. He broke the record four days later against Arizona.

Gagne put his name in the record books again in August 2003, when he successfully converted his 40th consecutive save opportunity, breaking in the process Jose Mesa's mark for perfection to start a season. He saved his 44th straight on the 28th of the month, giving him a new single-season record previously held by Tom Gordon.

Gagne took over first place on the Dodgers' all-time saves list on July 15, 2004, when he recorded his 130th save as a member of the team, surpassing in the process Jeff Shaw, the previous record-holder. Kenley Jansen has since replaced Gagne in the top spot.

## Notable Achievements:

- Topped 50 saves twice, surpassing 40 saves on another occasion.
- Compiled ERA below 2.50 four times, posting mark under 2.00 twice.
- Compiled winning percentage in excess of .700 three times.
- Posted WHIP under 1.000 four times.
- Posted more strikeouts than innings pitched four times.
- Led NL pitchers in saves once and games finished once.
- Finished second in NL in saves once.
- Holds Dodgers single-season record for most saves (55 in 2003).
- Holds Dodgers career record for most strikeouts per 9 innings pitched (10.381).
- Ranks among Dodgers career leaders in: saves (second), WHIP (sixth), fewest hits allowed per 9 innings pitched (fourth), strikeouts-to-walks ratio (fourth), and games finished (seventh).
- Holds major-league record for most consecutive save opportunities converted (84).
- June 2002 NL Pitcher of the Month.
- Finished sixth in 2003 NL MVP voting.
- 2003 NL Cy Young Award winner.
- 2003 *Sporting News* NL Pitcher of the Year.
- Two-time *Rolaids* NL Reliever of the Year (2003 & 2004).
- 2003 *Sporting News* All-Star selection.
- Three-time NL All-Star (2002, 2003 & 2004).

# 47

# GARY SHEFFIELD

One of baseball's most feared sluggers for much of his career, Gary Sheffield played for eight different teams over the course of 22 big-league seasons, amassing 509 home runs and 1,676 RBIs during that time, while also compiling a lifetime batting average of .292. Spending less than four full seasons in Los Angeles, Sheffield posted the vast majority of those numbers while playing for other teams. Nevertheless, the contentious out-fielder ended up earning a place in these rankings with his prolific slugging and clutch hitting. Hitting more than 30 home runs, driving in more than 100 runs, and batting over .300 in each of his three full seasons in L.A., Sheffield gave the Dodgers a potent bat in the middle of their lineup, earn-ing two All-Star selections and one top-10 finish in the NL MVP voting as a member of the team. Unfortunately, just as he did everywhere else, Shef-field eventually wore out his welcome in Los Angeles with his combative nature and surly disposition, forcing the Dodgers to part ways with him earlier than they would have liked.

Born in Tampa, Florida on November 18, 1968, Gary Antonian Shef-field grew up in Belmont Heights, near the notoriously dangerous Ponce de Leon projects, where shootings and stabbings occurred frequently. Living in the same household as his uncle Dwight Gooden until 1976, Sheffield learned how to hit a fastball from the future New York Mets star pitcher, who was four years his elder. Putting those lessons to good use, Sheffield excelled in Little League ball, eventually earning a spot on the Belmont Heights All-Stars, who ended up making it to the Little League World Series. However, Sheffield displayed his bad temper even as a youngster, once chasing his coach all over the field with a bat after being benched for having been late for practice, causing him to be kicked off the team for a year. Sheffield continued to display violent tendencies as a young

Courtesy of George A. Kitrinos

Gary Sheffield hit more than 30 homers,
knocked in more than 100 runs, and batted over
.300 in each of his three full seasons with the Dodgers

teenager, running with a local gang known as the Alleycats, to the top of whose hierarchy he rose by beating and bludgeoning anyone who stood in his path. Fortunately, Sheffield's love of baseball proved to be strong enough to eventually lure him away from a life of crime.

Shortly after Sheffield enrolled at Hillsborough High School, he made the varsity baseball team, starring at third base and pitcher as a junior, before earning Gatorade National Player of the Year honors as a senior by batting .500 and hitting 15 home runs, in just 62 official at-bats. Subsequently selected by the Milwaukee Brewers with the sixth overall pick of the 1986 MLB draft, Sheffield began his professional career as an infielder with Helena of the Pioneer League, where he batted .365 and knocked in 71 runs, in only 57 games. Sheffield spent two more years in Milwaukee's farm system, before being called up to the big leagues for the first time in September 1988. Appearing in 24 games at shortstop over the season's final month, Sheffield hit 4 homers, drove in 12 runs, and batted .238. After assuming the role of a utility infielder the following year, Sheffield became Milwaukee's starting third baseman in 1990, a season in which he hit 10 homers, knocked in 67 runs, and batted .294. Plagued by injuries and inconsistency in 1991, Sheffield performed horribly, prompting the

Brewers to trade him to the San Diego Padres for three players prior to the start of the ensuing campaign.

Sheffield emerged as a star in San Diego, earning the first of his nine All-Star selections and a third-place finish in the 1992 NL MVP voting by placing among the league leaders with 33 home runs and 100 RBIs, while topping the circuit with a .330 batting average and 323 total bases. Although Sheffield followed that up with another strong performance in 1993, the Padres elected to include him in a five-player trade they completed with the Florida Marlins at midseason that brought Trevor Hoffman to San Diego.

Shifted to the outfield upon his arrival in Florida, Sheffield ended up spending parts of five seasons with the Marlins, having easily his best year for them in 1996, when he hit 42 homers, knocked in 120 runs, scored 118 times, batted .314, drew 142 bases on balls, and led the league with a .465 on-base percentage and an OPS of 1.090. Making an extremely favorable impression on teammate Jeff Conine during his time in Florida, Sheffield drew praise from the slugging first baseman, who said, "He [Sheffield] likes to win. His commitment to the team is above everything else." Yet, with the Marlins conducting a huge fire-sale after winning the World Series in 1997, Sheffield found himself switching cities once again, this time being included in a seven-player trade Florida completed with the Dodgers on May 14, 1998 that sent Sheffield, Bobby Bonilla, Charles Johnson, Jim Eisenreich, and Manuel Barrios to Los Angeles for Mike Piazza and Todd Zeile.

After performing somewhat erratically over the course of his first 10 big-league seasons, the twenty-nine-year-old Sheffield developed into a consistent run-producer and elite hitter during his time in Los Angeles. Finishing the 1998 campaign strong by hitting 16 homers, driving in 57 runs, and batting .316 in his 90 games with the Dodgers, Sheffield followed that up with an exceptional three-year run during which he established himself as one of the most feared sluggers in the game. The hard-hitting outfielder earned the fifth All-Star selection of his career in his first full season in Los Angeles, concluding the 1999 campaign with 34 home runs, 101 RBIs, 103 runs scored, a .301 batting average, a .407 on-base percentage, and a .523 slugging percentage. Sheffield then hit 43 homers, knocked in 109 runs, scored 105 times, batted .325, compiled a .438 on-base percentage, and posted a .643 slugging percentage in 2000, en route to earning another All-Star nomination and a ninth-place finish in the NL

MVP voting. Although Sheffield failed to make the All-Star team again in 2001, he had another big year, finishing the season with 36 home runs, 100 RBIs, 98 runs scored, a .311 batting average, a .417 on-base percentage, and a .583 slugging percentage.

The success Sheffield experienced as a member of the Dodgers earned him the admiration of GM Kevin Malone, who suggested, "I believe Gary can do pretty much whatever he puts his mind to—if he's healthy." Teammate Charles Johnson added, "He's a guy who can change a game with one swing."

Sheffield did indeed have the ability to alter a game with one swing of the bat. Possessing arguably the hardest swing in all of baseball, the right-handed hitting Sheffield whipped his bat through the hitting zone with amazing speed and precision, using his entire 5'11", 200-pound frame to launch fierce line drives to all parts of the ballpark. Though primarily a pull-hitter, Sheffield drove the ball with power to the opposite field as well upon occasion. And, when he made solid contact with the sphere, no one in the game hit the ball any harder. Meanwhile, in spite of his ferocious swing, Sheffield did not strike out a great deal, never fanning more than 83 times in any single season.

Still, in spite of Sheffield's tremendous offensive production, Dodger management eventually came to view him as a clubhouse cancer and a liability to team morale. Finding fault with many of the moves the team made during his time in Los Angeles, Sheffield began lobbying for a trade following the conclusion of the 2000 campaign. Prior to the start of spring training, he used the press to insult his teammates, criticize club management, and call Chairman Bob Daly a liar. Sheffield even screamed racism when the team refused to double the value of his contract. However, after a proposed trade with the New York Mets failed to come to fruition, a disingenuous Sheffield fired his agent of fifteen years and called a press conference, during which he apologized to Dodger fans for his behavior through a prepared statement

Although Sheffield remained in Los Angeles one more year, team management acted quickly to rid itself of the confrontational outfielder when the Braves offered the Dodgers Brian Jordan and Odalis Perez for his services during the 2001 offseason. Packing his bags for Atlanta, Sheffield left L.A. with totals of 129 home runs, 367 RBIs, 358 runs scored, 583 hits, 88 doubles, and 6 triples as a member of the Dodgers, along with a batting average of .312 and franchise-record marks in on-base percentage (.424), slugging percentage (.573), and OPS (.998).

Sheffield continued to produce on the playing field over the course of the next two seasons, performing particularly well for the Braves in 2003, when he earned a third-place finish in the NL MVP voting by finishing among the league leaders in nine different offensive categories, including home runs (39), RBIs (132), runs scored (126), and batting average (.330). Meanwhile, Braves manager Bobby Cox sang the praises of his team's right-fielder, stating, "The guy generates the most awesome bat speed I've ever seen—he doesn't just hit balls, he kills them." Atlanta GM John Schuerholz chimed in, "He's one of the most dynamic and consistent hitters in baseball."

Nevertheless, Sheffield again found himself on the move when he signed as a free agent with the Yankees following the conclusion of the 2003 campaign. He then had two huge years in New York, totaling 70 home runs, 244 RBIs, and 221 runs scored in 2004 and 2005, while compiling batting averages of .290 and .291. Sheffield's outstanding play for the Bronx Bombers earned him a pair of All-Star selections and two top-10 finishes in the AL MVP balloting, including a runner-up finish in 2004. But, after missing most of the 2006 season with a wrist injury, Sheffield once again displayed his abrasive personality when he insulted beloved Yankees manager Joe Torre by claiming that he mistreated him during his time in New York. Sheffield, who often attempted to use the "race card" to his advantage, insisted that Torre treated black players differently than white players. When reminded of Derek Jeter's bi-racial background, Sheffield made further headlines by stating that the Yankee captain wasn't "all the way black."

Eager to rid themselves of the cantankerous Sheffield, the Yankees dealt him to the Detroit Tigers shortly thereafter. Sheffield subsequently spent the next two seasons serving the Tigers almost exclusively as a DH, before ending his career back in New York as a part-time outfielder with the Mets. He retired following the conclusion of the 2009 campaign with career totals of 509 home runs, 1,676 RBIs, 1,636 runs scored, 2,689 hits, 467 doubles, 27 triples, and 253 stolen bases, a batting average of .292, an on-base percentage of .393, and a slugging percentage of .514. In addition to his nine All-Star selections, Sheffield earned three *Sporting News* All-Star nominations, five Silver Sluggers, and six top-10 finishes in the league MVP voting over the course of his career.

Still, in spite of his outstanding on-field accomplishments, Sheffield likely will have a difficult time gaining admittance to Cooperstown in the coming years. Identified in the 2007 Mitchell Report as a user of performance-enhancing drugs, Sheffield accepted culpability for his actions, after earlier denying on numerous occasions that he ever used steroids. Unfortunately, the lack of integrity Sheffield displayed on this issue closely parallels the behavior he exhibited over the course of his playing career.

## Dodger Career Highlights:

**Best Season:** Although Sheffield performed extremely well in each of his three full seasons with the Dodgers, he had his best year for them in 2000, when he earned a ninth-place finish in the NL MVP voting by driving in 109 runs, scoring 105 times, and finishing among the league leaders with 43 home runs, 101 walks, a .325 batting average, a .438 on-base percentage, and a .643 slugging percentage.

**Memorable Moments/Greatest Performances:** Sheffield led the Dodgers to a 9-7 win over the Phillies on August 22, 1999 by driving in 6 runs with a double and a grand slam home run.

Sheffield had another productive day at the plate on April 29, 2000, when he helped the Dodgers win a 13-12 slugfest with the Florida Marlins by going 3-for 4, with a pair of homers, a double, 2 walks, and 5 RBIs.

Sheffield had a hand in 7 of the 8 runs the Dodgers scored during an 8-3 win over the Angels on June 3, 2000, going 3-for-4, with a pair of homers, 4 RBIs, and 3 runs scored.

Sheffield delivered the game's decisive blow in leading the Dodgers to a 7-6 win over Houston on June 21 2000, hitting a two-out solo homer in the top of the eighth inning that provided the margin of victory. He finished the game 4-for-5, with 2 home runs, 2 RBIs, and 4 runs scored.

Sheffield had another big day a little over one week later, hitting a pair of homers, knocking in 4 runs, and scoring 3 times during a 9-2 rout of the Giants on June 30, 2000.

Sheffield made significant contributions to a lopsided 22-7 victory over the Rockies in Colorado on July 21, 2001 by going 3-for-4, with a pair of homers, a double, 4 RBIs, and 4 runs scored.

## Notable Achievements:

- Hit more than 30 home runs three times, topping 40 homers once (43 in 2000).
- Knocked in more than 100 runs three times.
- Scored more than 100 runs twice.
- Batted over .300 four times, topping the .320-mark once (.325 in 2000).
- Walked more than 100 times twice.
- Compiled on-base percentage in excess of .400 four times.
- Posted slugging percentage in excess of .500 four times, topping the .600-mark once (.643 in 2000).
- Compiled OPS in excess of 1.000 twice.
- Holds Dodgers career records for highest: on-base percentage (.424); slugging percentage (.573); and OPS (.998).
- Two-time NL All-Star (1999 & 2000).

# 48

# RAMON MARTINEZ

Idolized by his younger brother Pedro, Ramon Martinez preceded the Hall of Fame pitcher into the Los Angeles farm system by four years, joining the Dodger organization at the tender age of sixteen in 1984. Eventually establishing himself as the ace of the Dodgers' pitching staff, the elder Martinez brother spent the next 11 seasons in Los Angeles, compiling a total of 123 victories during that time. Winning 20 games once and posting 17 victories on two other occasions, Martinez earned one All-Star selection and two top-five finishes in the Cy Young voting, placing as high as second in the balloting in 1990, when he reached the 20-win plateau for the only time in his career. One of the senior circuit's better pitchers for nearly a decade, Martinez also compiled an ERA under 3.00 twice and led all NL hurlers in complete games once, with his solid pitching helping the Dodgers capture three division titles, one National League pennant, and one world championship.

Born in Santo Domingo, Distrito Nacional, Dominican Republic on March 22, 1968, Ramon Jaime Martinez came from humble beginnings. After moving with his family to the town of Manoguayabo while still just a toddler, young Ramon grew up with his parents and five siblings in a home that had dirt floors, a tin roof, and three bedrooms formed by sheets hung from wires.

Seeking to escape his impoverished upbringing, Martinez chose to pursue a career in baseball, first gaining the attention of major-league scouts at the 1984 Olympic Games, when he pitched for a Dominican team chosen to replace the boycotting Cuban squad. Although the Dominican club did not fare particularly well, Martinez made an extremely favorable impression on those scouts in attendance with his blazing fastball and composure on the mound. Having observed Martinez in action, Dodgers scout Ralph Avila signed the sixteen-year-old right-hander as an amateur free agent shortly thereafter, telling the *Los Angeles Times* early in 1988, "When I first saw him work out, I had my doubts. He was six-foot-two and a hundred and thirty-two pounds. But he showed good mechanics and a good breaking ball and good control. We figured if we put more weight on him, it would improve his breaking ball. He was just a baby then—barely sixteen years old. You give him the ball now, and he thinks he can pitch in the big leagues. He's a good kid, a mature kid. He's got a good head on his shoulders."

After spending his first two years in the Dodger organization advancing slowly through the Los Angeles farm system, Martinez made a statement by going 16-5 with a 2.17 ERA for Class A Vero Beach in the Florida State League in 1987. He followed that up by compiling a record of 13-6 and an ERA of 2.58, while splitting his time between double-A San Antonio and triple-A Albuquerque in 1988, prompting the Dodgers to summon him to the big leagues on August 12 to replace the recently-released forty-three-year-old Don Sutton in the starting rotation. With Martinez having established himself as the organization's most prized pitching prospect since Fernando Valenzuela, Dodgers general manager Fred Claire weighed in on any comparisons being made between the two men, telling the *Los Angeles Times* upon Martinez's promotion, "It's not fair to compare anyone to Fernando, especially the way he started. But, with Fernando and Ramon, you have two players who have an inner confidence that helps in a situation like this."

Making his major-league debut at only twenty years of age, Martinez appeared in a total of nine games for the eventual world champions over the final seven weeks of the campaign, winning just one of his four decisions, while compiling an ERA of 3.79, striking out 23 batters, and surrendering 22 walks in 35⅔ innings of work. After beginning the 1989 campaign back in the minors, Martinez arrived in Los Angeles to stay later in the year, going 6-4 with a 3.19 ERA in his 15 starts with the Dodgers after becoming a regular member of the starting rotation at midseason. Martinez emerged as the ace of the Dodgers pitching staff the following year, finishing the 1990 season with a record of 20-6, an ERA of 2.92, 223 strikeouts in 234⅓ innings pitched, and a league-leading 12 complete games, en route to earning his lone All-Star selection and a runner-up finish to Pittsburgh's Doug Drabek in the NL Cy Young voting.

Martinez again pitched well for the Dodgers in 1991, going 17-13 with a 3.27 ERA, and finishing second in the league with 4 shutouts. However, he slumped somewhat in each of the next two seasons, posting an overall record of just 18-23, while compiling earned run averages of 4.00 and 3.44, respectively. Rebounding somewhat in 1994, Martinez compiled a record of 12-7 before the season ended prematurely due to a players' strike. Returning to top form the following year, Martinez went 17-7 with a 3.66 ERA, earning in the process a fifth-place finish in the Cy Young balloting. He followed that up with another solid performance in 1996, concluding the campaign with a record of 15-6 and an ERA of 3.42, before going 10-5 with a 3.64 ERA in 1997.

Although Martinez continued to pitch effectively for the Dodgers throughout much of the 1990s, he gradually evolved into more of a finesse pitcher, after beginning his career as a flamethrower. Learning how to change speeds and work the corners of the plate, Martinez depended far more on his breaking pitches than he did earlier in his career. In fact, after recording 223 strikeouts in his first full season, Martinez never again fanned more than 150 batters in any single campaign.

Unfortunately, 1997 proved to be Martinez's last full season in Los Angeles. After suffering a torn rotator cuff and torn cartilage during the first half of the ensuing campaign, Martinez had his shoulder surgically repaired on June 30, bringing his season to an early end. With the Dodgers subsequently choosing not to pick up his $5.6 million option at the end of the year, Martinez signed as a free agent with the Boston Red Sox, where he joined his younger brother Pedro. Martinez left Los Angeles with a career record of 123-77, an ERA of 3.45, 1,314 strikeouts in 1,731⅔ innings pitched, 37 complete games, 20 shutouts, and a WHIP of 1.283.

After spending much of 1999 rehabilitating his shoulder in the minor leagues, Martinez joined the Red Sox, with who he remained through the end of 2000, compiling an overall record of 12-9 during his time in Boston. He then finished out his career with the Pittsburgh Pirates, announcing his retirement early in 2001 after going 0-2 with an 8.62 ERA in his four appearances with them during the season's first month. Martinez ended his career with an overall record of 135-88, an ERA of 3.67, 1,427 strikeouts in 1,895⅔ total innings of work, 37 complete games, 20 shutouts, and a WHIP of 1.311.

Following his playing days, Martinez returned to Los Angeles in 2010, where he spent the next few years working in the Dodger front office as a senior advisor in Latin America. He currently holds the same position for the Baltimore Orioles.

## Dodger Career Highlights:

**Best Season:** Although Martinez also pitched well for the Dodgers in 1991 and 1995, he clearly had his finest season for them in 1990, when he established career-best marks in wins (20), ERA (2.92), strikeouts (223), complete games (12), innings pitched (234⅓), and WHIP (1.101), placing among the NL leaders in all six categories.

**Memorable Moments/Greatest Performances:** Far more comfortable on the mound than in the batter's box, Martinez hit just one home run during his career, experiencing one of his greatest thrills on September 22, 1991, when he took Tom Glavine deep during a 3-0 victory over the Braves. Martinez also worked seven scoreless innings during the contest, allowing just 2 hits, while walking 6 and recording 8 strikeouts.

Martinez made a strong impression in his major-league debut, surrendering just 1 run and 4 hits in 7⅔ innings of work during an August 13, 1988 game against San Francisco that the Dodgers eventually won by a score of 2-1 in 11 innings.

Martinez turned in the first truly dominant performance of his career on April 22, 1990, when he shut out Houston by a score of 2-0, allowing just 3 hits and 1 walk, while striking out 9 during the contest.

Martinez, though, topped that effort later in the year, surrendering just 3 hits and 1 walk, while striking out a career-high 18 batters, in defeating the Braves by a score of 6-0 on June 4, 1990.

Martinez tossed the first of his three career two-hitters on July 24, 1990, when he allowed just a pair of singles and a walk during a 9-2 win over the Giants.

Martinez pitched his best game of the 1992 campaign on May 29, when he surrendered just 3 hits and 1 walk, in winning a 1-0 pitcher's duel with Chicago's Frank Castillo.

Martinez threw his second two-hitter on June 21, 1993, allowing just a first-inning single to Craig Biggio and a second-inning double to Luis Gonzalez, in shutting out Houston by a score of 7-0.

Courtesy of Bardley Park

Ramon Martinez's strong pitching helped the Dodgers
win three division titles, one NL pennant,
and one world championship

Nearly one year later, on June 7, 1994, Martinez hurled another gem, scattering 3 harmless singles and recording 7 strikeouts during a 2-0 win over the Florida Marlins.

Although Atlanta swept the Dodgers in three straight games in the 1996 NLDS, Martinez pitched brilliantly in the series opener, allowing just 3 hits and 1 run over the first 8 innings of a game the Dodgers eventually lost by a score of 2-1 in 10 innings.

Martinez tossed his final two-hitter on May 23, 1998, when he allowed just a single to Andy Fox and a homer to Brent Brede during a 7-1 victory over the Arizona Diamondbacks.

However, Martinez experienced his finest moment on July 14, 1995, when he no-hit the Florida Marlins, defeating them by a score of 7-0. Martinez's only blemish on the day proved to be a walk to Tommy Gregg with two men out in the eighth inning.

## Notable Achievements:

- Won 20 games in 1990.
- Posted 17 victories on two other occasions.
- Posted winning percentage in excess of .700 four times.
- Compiled ERA under 3.00 twice.
- Struck out more than 200 batters once (223 in 1990).
- Threw more than 200 innings four times.
- Finished in double-digits in complete games once (12 in 1990).
- Led NL pitchers in shutouts once and complete games once.
- Finished second in NL in: wins once, winning percentage twice, strikeouts once, and shutouts three times.
- Ranks ninth in Dodgers history with 1,314 career strikeouts.
- Threw no-hitter vs. Florida on July 14, 1995.
- June 1990 NL Pitcher of the Month.
- Finished second in 1990 NL Cy Young voting.
- 1990 NL All-Star.
- 1988 NL champion.
- 1988 world champion.

# 49

# PREACHER ROE

An outstanding left-handed pitcher who depended on guile, superb control, and an occasional spitball to navigate his way through opposing lineups, Preacher Roe compiled a winning percentage of .715 as a member of the Dodgers that remains the second-highest mark in franchise history. Posting an overall record of 93-37 during his seven seasons in Brooklyn, Roe won 22 games once and 19 games another time, en route to helping the Dodgers capture three NL pennants. Along the way, the lanky southpaw earned four All-Star selections, one top five finish in the league MVP voting, and one *Sporting News* NL Pitcher of the Year nomination. The success Roe experienced during his relatively brief stay in Brooklyn prompted Roy Campanella to identify him as the best pitcher he ever caught, with the Hall of Fame receiver noting long after his career ended, "He [Roe] was a guy who knew what he was doing every second of every minute."

Born in Ash Flat, Arkansas on February 26, 1916, Elwin Charles Roe grew up some 28 miles northwest, in the town of Viola, where he acquired the nickname "Preacher" as a young boy, telling the *West Plains Gazette* years later, "I had an uncle that came back from the first World War who hadn't ever seen me. He said, 'What's your name, young man?' And, for some reason, I said, 'Preacher.'...My mother said maybe it was because I liked the preacher we had at our church so well."

After starring on the mound while attending Viola High School, Roe enrolled at Harding University, a religious school in Searcy, Arkansas, where he gained national attention in 1937 by striking out 26 batters in a 13-inning game. Signed by a St. Louis Cardinals scout the following year, Roe left college one semester shy of completing his degree to pursue a career in pro ball. He appeared in one game for the Cardinals prior to the conclusion of the 1938 campaign, before spending the next five years toiling in the minor leagues. While playing for Burt Shotton during his time in the St. Louis farm system, the spindly 6'2", 170-pound Roe made a lasting impression on the future Dodgers manager, who said years later, "He was fast as hell and wilder than any human I ever saw."

After being traded to Pittsburgh and declared unfit for military service because of a back injury he suffered when a tree fell on him the previous winter, Roe finally returned to the Major Leagues with the Pirates in 1944. Pitching well as a rookie, the twenty-eight-year-old Roe finished 13-11, with a 3.11 ERA. He followed that up by going 14-13, with a 2.87 ERA and a league-leading 148 strikeouts in 1945, before experiencing a major setback during the subsequent offseason.

While coaching a high-school basketball game back in Arkansas in February 1946, Roe got into an argument with a referee, who struck him, knocking him to the floor and fracturing his skull. Suffering from headaches and dizzy spells after he returned to the Pirates, Roe ended up winning just 3 of his 11 decisions and compiling an ERA of 5.14 in 1946, before returning home in August. Having lost much of the velocity on his fastball, Roe continued to struggle in 1947, going just 4-15 with a 5.25 ERA, before Brooklyn General Manager Branch Rickey acquired him in a six-player trade he completed with the Pirates on December 8, 1947.

No longer a hard thrower by the time he arrived in Brooklyn, the thirty-two-year-old Roe set about remaking himself as a control pitcher who depended primarily on changing speeds and occasionally resorting to the spitball to retire opposing batters. In describing his newfound pitching style, Roe said, "I try to keep the hitters off balance, never giving them a decent pitch. I'm always aiming for the corners, never throwing the same pitch twice or what the hitter is expecting." Roe added that his pitching repertoire included a fastball, a changeup off his fastball, a curveball, and a slider, failing to mention at the time that he also threw the spitball, which his teammates called a "Beech-Nut curve," after the pitcher's favorite brand of chewing gum.

Although Roe lacked the ability to consistently throw the ball by opposing hitters after he joined the Dodgers, he developed into much more of a complete pitcher, compiling a record of 12-8 and placing among the league leaders with an ERA of 2.63 and a WHIP of 1.064 in 1948. In comparing the new Roe to the out-of-control hurler he had managed

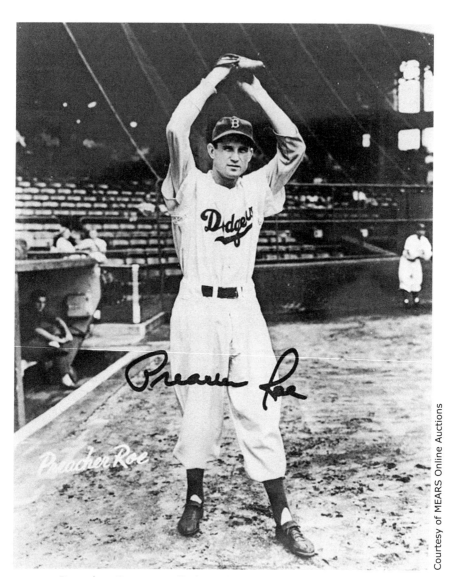

Preacher Roe compiled a winning percentage of .715
as a member of the Dodgers that represents
the second-highest mark in franchise history

years earlier in the minor leagues, Dodgers manager Burt Shotten said, "He'd become a pitcher because he knew where to throw the ball, and he had a change of speed...though not his old speed. Didn't seem like the same pitcher."

Roe emerged as one of the senior circuit's best pitchers in 1949, earning the first of his four straight All-Star selections by posting a record of 15-6 that gave him the league's second-best winning percentage (.714). He also ranked among the NL leaders with an ERA of 2.79 and a WHIP of 1.152. Roe had another outstanding year in 1950, placing near the top of the league rankings in wins (19), winning percentage (.633), ERA (3.30), complete games (16), innings pitched (250⅔), and WHIP (1.241). He improved upon those numbers the following year, though, concluding the 1951 season with a league-best record of 22-3, an ERA of 3.04, and a WHIP of 1.207, while tossing a career-high 19 complete games and 257⅔ innings. Roe's fabulous performance earned him *Sporting News* NL Pitcher of the Year honors.

Having turned thirty-six years of age prior to the start of the 1952 campaign, Roe ended up starting only 25 games for the Dodgers. Nevertheless, he remained an effective pitcher, going 11-2 with a 3.12 ERA during the regular season, before posting another victory against the Yankees in the World Series. Following Roe's 5-3 complete-game win over New York in Game Three of the fall classic, Yankees manager Casey Stengel said of the crafty left-hander, "He's a smart operator—about the smartest pitcher there is in the game today."

Although Roe's ERA climbed to 4.36 in 1953, he compiled another outstanding record for the pennant-winning Dodgers, finishing the year with a mark of 11-3. However, after he won just 3 of his 7 decisions and compiled an ERA of 5.00 the following year, the Dodgers traded him to the Baltimore Orioles at season's end. Instead of going to Baltimore, though, the thirty-nine-year-old Roe decided to announce his retirement, ending his career with a record of 127-84, an ERA of 3.43, 956 strikeouts in 1,914⅓ innings of work, 101 complete games, 17 shutouts, and a WHIP of 1.259. In addition to compiling an overall record of 93-37 as a member of the Dodgers, Roe posted an ERA of 3.26, struck out 632 batters in 1,277⅓ innings of work, threw 74 complete games and 12 shutouts, and compiled a WHIP of 1.222 in his seven years with the club.

Following his playing days, Roe opened a supermarket with his wife in West Plains, Missouri. One year after he retired from the game, he also admitted to throwing the spitball, describing the technique he used in a *Sports Illustrated* article entitled "The Outlawed Spitball Was My Money Pitch." Roe told of wiping his left hand across his brow and spitting on his thumb with juice from his bubblegum, using the base of his hand as a shield. Tugging at his belt, he subsequently transferred the moisture to his fingertips. Roe then gripped the baseball on a smooth spot and delivered it to home plate with a fastball motion, getting a sharp downward break on his offering. When a hitter complained, prompting the umpire to ask for the ball, Roe rolled it towards home plate. Or, if the ball happened to already be in Campanella's possession, the Dodger catcher dropped it to the ground and stepped on it to erase the evidence.

Revealing that his illicit actions did not leave him feeling the least bit guilty, Roe said, "It never bothered me none throwing a spitter. If no one is going to help the pitcher in this game, he's got to help himself."

Roe expressed his lone regret years later, stating during an October 2000 telephone interview, "I had a wonderful career. My only regret is I never got a World Series ring. The Yankees just beat us. Believe it or not, they're still my favorite team…in the American League."

Roe lived another eight years, passing away from colon cancer at the age of ninety-two, on November 9, 2008. Upon learning of his former teammate's passing, Ralph Branca recalled, "He enjoyed playing the role of a country bumpkin, but he wasn't one. He was real smart and real crafty on the mound."

Carl Erskine, another former member of Brooklyn's starting rotation, told *The New York Times*, "The Preach was a master of his craft. He was a smart control pitcher with a phenomenal sense of timing."

Dodgers' owner Frank McCourt and team president Jamie McCourt also paid tribute to Roe, saying in a prepared statement, "Preacher Roe left an indelible mark in Dodger history. He was one of the original 'Boys of Summer' and his success in the World Series against the Yankees in 1949, 1952 and 1953 helped pave the way for the 1955 world champions."

## Dodger Career Highlights:

**Best Season:** Although Roe compiled the lowest ERA (2.63) and WHIP (1.064) of his career in 1948, he unquestionably had his greatest season in 1951, when he finished 22-3 with a league-leading .880 winning percentage, compiled an ERA of 3.04 and a WHIP of 1.207, and posted career-high marks in complete games (19) and innings pitched (257⅔). Over the course of the campaign, Roe put together two 10-game winning streaks, earning in the process a fifth-place finish in the league MVP voting and recognition as *The Sporting News* NL Pitcher of the Year.

**Memorable Moments/Greatest Performances:** A notoriously bad-hitting pitcher (he had a lifetime batting average of .110), Roe hit the only home run of his career on July 7, 1953, when, during a 9-5 victory over the Pirates, he homered off Pittsburgh's Bob Hall, prompting his teammates to lay down a congratulatory carpet of towels between home plate and the Dodger dugout as he rounded the bases. Following the contest, Roe said in his Southern drawl, "I reckon it means that I've finally come out of my slump."

Roe turned in one of his most dominant performances for the Dodgers on August 28, 1948, when he tossed a three-hit shutout against Cincinnati, defeating the Reds by a score of 2-0.

Roe performed heroically for the Dodgers two starts later, working all 12 innings and recording a career-high 11 strikeouts during a 4-3 extra-inning win over the Giants on September 5, 1948.

Roe ironically matched his career-high in strikeouts exactly one year later, fanning 11 batters during a lopsided 13-2 victory over the Boston Braves on September 5, 1949.

Roe proved to be even more dominant a little over two weeks later, helping the Dodgers move to within ½ game of first-place St. Louis on September 21, 1949 by surrendering just two singles and striking out five during a 5-0 shutout of the Cardinals.

Yet, Roe turned in arguably the most memorable performance of his career in Game Two of the 1949 World Series, when he tossed a six-hit shutout against the Yankees, defeating the Bronx Bombers by a score of 1-0 despite being struck in the right forefinger by Johnny Lindell's line drive back to the box during the early stages of the contest. Pitching in intense pain for most of the game, Roe later revealed, "Between innings they had to drill holes in my fingernail to relieve the swelling. It was after the game when I felt the most pain. I had to sleep on a pillow in the bathroom with my hand in a tub of water all night." Roe called the shutout the highlight of his career.

## Notable Achievements:

- Won more than 20 games once, posting 19 victories on another occasion.
- Posted winning percentage in excess of .700 four times, topping the .800-mark twice.
- Compiled ERA under 3.00 twice.
- Threw more than 250 innings twice.
- Led NL pitchers with .880 winning percentage in 1951.
- Ranks second in Dodgers history with career winning percentage of .715.
- Finished fifth in 1951 NL MVP voting.
- 1951 National League *Sporting News* Pitcher of the Year.
- 1951 *Sporting News* All-Star selection.
- Four-time NL All-Star (1949, 1950, 1951 & 1952).
- Three-time NL champion (1949, 1952 & 1953).

# 50

# WHIT WYATT

Plagued by arm problems for much of his career, Whit Wyatt accomplished very little over the course of his first nine big-league seasons, compiling an overall record of just 26-43 for three American League teams. However, after joining the Dodgers in 1939, the hard-throwing right-hander flourished as never before, having easily the best years of his career while pitching at Ebbets Field. Already thirty-one years of age by the time he arrived in Brooklyn, Wyatt nevertheless posted a composite mark of 78-39 for the Dodgers between 1939 and 1943, helping them capture the 1941 National League pennant in the process. Wyatt's stellar pitching earned him four consecutive All-Star selections and a third-place finish in the NL MVP voting in 1941, when he topped the senior circuit with 22 victories.

Born in Kensington, Georgia on September 27, 1907, John Whitlow Wyatt attended Cedartown High School, where he starred as a fullback in football and a pitcher in baseball, once striking out 23 college batters in a single game. Signed by the Detroit Tigers following his graduation from Cedartown High, Wyatt initially chose to enroll at the Georgia Institute of Technology, which he attended briefly, before putting his education on hold to begin a career in pro baseball. Joining the Evansville Hubs of the Class B Three-I League in 1928, Wyatt spent the next two seasons excelling in the minor leagues, compiling an overall record of 36-18 for Evansville in 1928 and 1929. Called up to Detroit during the latter stages of the 1929 campaign, Wyatt pitched ineffectively for the Tigers, going 0-1 with a 6.75 ERA in his four starts. Although he remained in Detroit throughout all of 1930, the Tigers used him sparingly, with the twenty-two-year-old right-hander compiling a record of 4-5 and an ERA of 3.57 in his 21 appearances and 7 starts.

Whit Wyatt earned four straight All-Star selections
while pitching for the Dodgers

Wyatt developed arm problems for the first time in his career the following spring, with *The Sporting News* reporting in April 1931, "The Georgia boy is having trouble with his arm. He thought it was fine when he reported, but, as soon as he was called upon to pitch, he found he was wrong. His arm was not sore, but weak. The Detroit coaches are seriously concerned."

Wyatt ended up spending most of 1931 in the minor leagues, strengthening his arm with the Beaumont Exporters of the Class A Texas League, before returning to Detroit the following year. Yet, in spite of his improved physical condition, Wyatt continued to struggle on the mound, going just 9-13 with a 5.03 ERA for the fifth-place Tigers.

Traded to the Chicago White Sox midway through the 1933 campaign, Wyatt worked primarily out of the bullpen the next three seasons, compiling an overall record of 11-18 for the Sox and undergoing arm surgery in 1934, before being sent back down to the minor leagues in 1936. Subsequently acquired by the Cleveland Indians in the Rule 5 draft prior to the start of the ensuing campaign, Wyatt spent one year in Cleveland, posting a record of 2-3 and an ERA of 4.44 in 1937 while pitching mostly in relief.

Released by the Indians at season's end, Wyatt strongly considered leaving the game and retiring to his farm in Buchanan, Georgia, stating years later, "I wasn't going anyplace. I wasn't making progress. I thought, 'Well, I'll just give it up; I'll just stay home and farm.'"

However, after receiving an offer to play for the American Association's Milwaukee Brewers, Wyatt resurrected his career back in the minors under the tutelage of manager Al Sothoron. Working harder than ever on perfecting his curveball, Wyatt later recalled, "Suddenly it came to me. From that time on I could throw the hook at three-and-two with as much confidence as I could my fastball. No longer were the hitters able to dig in up there and guess on me." Wyatt ended up leading the American Association with 23 victories, earning in the process league MVP honors, and prompting the Dodgers to purchase his contract.

Wyatt began his time in Brooklyn in fine fashion, winning his first four starts in 1939, before tearing cartilage in his knee in a collision at first base while running out a bunt during a midseason contest against the Cincinnati Reds. Forced to undergo season-ending surgery, Wyatt concluded the campaign with a record of 8-3 and a 2.31 ERA, earning in the process the first of his four straight All-Star selections.

Returning to the Dodgers fully healthy in 1940, Wyatt compiled a record of 15-14 and an ERA of 3.46, while establishing new career highs with 16 complete games, 239⅓ innings pitched, 124 strikeouts, and a league-leading 5 shutouts. Having developed a slider to go with his fastball and curve prior to the start of the ensuing campaign, Wyatt emerged as the senior circuit's best pitcher, finishing the season with a record of 22-10, an ERA of 2.34, 176 strikeouts, 23 complete games, 288⅓ innings pitched, and a league-leading 7 shutouts and 1.058 WHIP. Wyatt's superb pitching helped lead the Dodgers to the NL pennant, earning him a third-place finish in the league MVP voting. It also earned him the admiration and respect of his teammates, with Brooklyn center-fielder Pete Reiser commenting, "If I could sculpt a statue of what a pitcher should look like, for form and grace and style, it would look like Whitlow Wyatt."

As Wyatt established himself as one of baseball's top hurlers, he furthered his reputation as one of the game's nastiest pitchers. A notorious headhunter throughout his career, Wyatt displayed little restraint in knocking down opposing hitters, with Joe DiMaggio once calling him "the meanest guy I ever saw." In fact, Wyatt, who came up and in to DiMaggio after Yankees teammate Tommy Henrich homered against him in Game Five of the 1941 World Series, said earlier that same season, "If DiMaggio was playing in the National League, he'd have to swing while he's flat on his ass." Wyatt's combative attitude greatly pleased pugnacious Dodgers manager Leo Durocher, who regularly rewarded the right-hander for his intimidation tactics by leaving $100 bills on top of his locker. Durocher also identified Wyatt as the pitcher he would start if he had to win one game.

Wyatt had another big year for the Dodgers in 1942, compiling a record of 19-7, an ERA of 2.73, and a WHIP of 1.141, while also tossing 16 complete games and 217⅓ innings. He followed that up by going 14-5 with a 2.49 ERA and a league-leading 1.007 WHIP in 1943, before arm problems began to plague him again during the latter stages of the campaign. Limited to only 9 starts in 1944, Wyatt went just 2-6 with a 7.17 ERA, prompting the Dodgers to sell him to the Philadelphia Phillies at season's end. Wyatt left Brooklyn having compiled a record of 80-45 as a member of the Dodgers, giving him an excellent winning percentage of .640. He also posted an ERA of 2.86, struck out 540 batters in 1,072⅓ innings of work, threw 75 complete games and 17 shutouts, and compiled a WHIP of 1.141 in his six seasons with the Dodgers.

Wyatt ended up spending just one season in Philadelphia, losing all 7 of his decisions in 1945, before announcing his retirement after the Phillies released him following the conclusion of the campaign. He ended his career with a record of 106-95, an ERA of 3.79, 872 strikeouts in 1,761 innings of work, 97 complete games, 17 shutouts, and a WHIP of 1.321.

Following his playing days, Wyatt spent the next few years back on his farm in Buchanan, before returning to the game in 1950 as a minor-league pitching coach. He later served on the coaching staffs of the Phillies and Braves as well, continuing to espouse to his pupils his philosophy of pitching inside to hitters that he explained when he said, "Never be afraid to pitch inside. If you have to flip someone, do it." Wyatt added, "I think you ought to play it mean like Durocher did. They ought to hate you on the field."

After leaving the game for good during the 1970s, Wyatt retired to his native Georgia, where he died of pneumonia on July 16, 1999, at ninety-one years of age.

## Dodger Career Highlights:

**Best Season:** Wyatt pitched the best ball of his career for the Dodgers in 1941, helping them capture the NL pennant by posting a record of 22-10 that tied him with teammate Kirby Higbe for the league lead in victories. He also topped the senior circuit with 7 shutouts and a WHIP of 1.058, while ranking third in innings pitched (288⅓) and placing second in ERA (2.34), strikeouts (176), and complete games (23). Wyatt's magnificent performance earned him a third-place finish in the league MVP voting, putting him behind only teammates Dolph Camilli and Pete Reiser in the balloting.

**Memorable Moments/Greatest Performances:** Wyatt proved to be a pretty fair hitting pitcher over the course of his career, compiling a lifetime batting average of .219, with 7 home runs, including a particularly effective 1941 campaign in which he batted .239, hit 3 homers, and knocked in 22 runs, in only 109 official at-bats. However, he had his biggest day at the plate the previous year, going 3-or-4, with a homer, double, 2 RBIs, and 2 runs scored, during a lopsided 10-1 victory over the Pittsburgh Pirates on July 15, 1940.

Despite allowing 15 hits during the contest, Wyatt performed hero-ically for the Dodgers on June 27, 1939, working the first 16 innings of a game that ended in a 23-inning, 2-2 tie with the Braves.

Wyatt nearly attained perfection on August 17, 1941, when he allowed just a one-out single to Boston catcher Phil Masi in the bottom of the ninth inning, in defeating the Braves by a score of 3-0. Wyatt struck out 9 batters during the contest.

Wyatt threw another gem against Boston later in the year, clinching the pennant for the Dodgers on September 25 by allowing just 5 hits dur-ing a 6-0 victory over the Braves.

In between those two efforts, Wyatt engaged in a memorable pitching duel with Mort Cooper of the St. Louis Cardinals on September 13, allow-ing just 3 hits and striking out 9 batters during a 1-0 Dodgers win. The Car-dinals ace also surrendered only 3 hits and struck out 6 during the contest.

In addition to his near-perfect game, Wyatt tossed two other one-hit-ters during his time in Brooklyn, with one of those coming on August 20, 1942, when he surrendered only a second-inning home run to Johnny Mize and recorded 7 strikeouts, in defeating the Giants by a score of 2-1. Wyatt accomplished the feat again on September 8, 1943, when he allowed just a single and a walk during a 3-0 whitewashing of the Braves.

Yet, Wyatt experienced what he later called the highlight of his career in Game Two of the 1941 World Series, when he recorded a complete-game 3-2 victory over the Yankees that put an end to New York's 10-game winning streak in the fall classic that dated back to 1937. Wyatt, who al-lowed 9 hits and struck out 5 batters during the contest, recalled years later, "I was proud of that game. They had all those hitters and had won all those consecutive games in the World Series, and I beat them."

## Notable Achievements:

- Won more than 20 games once, posting 19 victories on another occasion.
- Posted winning percentage in excess of .700 three times.
- Compiled ERA under 3.00 four times.
- Threw more than 20 complete games once (23 in 1941).
- Threw more than 250 innings once (288⅓ in 1941).

- Led NL pitchers in: wins once, winning percentage once, shutouts twice, and WHIP twice.
- Finished third in 1941 NL MVP voting.
- 1941 *Sporting News* All-Star selection.
- Four-time NL All-Star (1939, 1940, 1941 & 1942).
- 1941 NL champion.

# SUMMARY AND HONORABLE MENTIONS

## (The Next 25)

Having identified the 50 greatest players in Brooklyn/Los Angeles Dodgers history, the time has come to select the best of the best. Based on the rankings contained in this book, the members of the Dodgers all-time team for each city are listed below. Our squads include the top player at each position, along with a pitching staff that features a five-man starting rotation, a set-up man, and a closer. The closer for the Brooklyn team was taken from the list of honorable mentions that will soon follow. Following the two separate squads, I have listed the members of the Dodgers all-time team for both cities combined.

## Brooklyn Dodgers Starting Lineup:

| Player: | Position: |
|---|---|
| Jackie Robinson | 2B |
| Pee Wee Reese | SS |
| Duke Snider | CF |
| Roy Campanella | C |
| Zack Wheat | LF |
| Gil Hodges | 1B |
| Carl Furillo | RF |
| Jim Gilliam | 3B |

## Brooklyn Dodgers Pitching Staff:

| | |
|---|---|
| Dazzy Vance | SP |
| Don Newcombe | SP |
| Burleigh Grimes | SP |
| Johnny Podres | SP |
| Preacher Roe | SP |
| Whit Wyatt | SU |
| Hugh Casey | CL |

## Los Angeles Dodgers Starting Lineup:

| Player: | Position: |
|---|---|
| Davey Lopes | 2B |
| Maury Wills | SS |
| Mike Piazza | C |
| Pedro Guerrero | LF |
| Steve Garvey | 1B |
| Matt Kemp | RF |
| Willie Davis | CF |
| Ron Cey | 3B |

## Los Angeles Dodgers Pitching Staff:

| | |
|---|---|
| Sandy Koufax | SP |
| Clayton Kershaw | SP |
| Don Drysdale | SP |
| Don Sutton | SP |
| Fernando Valenzuela | SP |
| Jim Brewer | SU |
| Ron Perranoski | CL |

## Brooklyn/Los Angeles Dodgers:

| Player: | Position: |
|---|---|
| Jackie Robinson | 2B |
| Pee Wee Reese | SS |
| Duke Snider | CF |
| Roy Campanella | C |
| Zack Wheat | LF |
| Gil Hodges | 1B |
| Carl Furillo | RF |
| Ron Cey | 3B |

## Brooklyn/Los Angeles Dodgers Pitching Staff:

| | |
|---|---|
| Sandy Koufax | SP |
| Clayton Kershaw | SP |
| Dazzy Vance | SP |
| Don Drysdale | SP |
| Don Sutton | SP |
| Jim Brewer | SU |
| Ron Perranoski | CL |

Although I limited my earlier rankings to the top 50 players in Dodgers history, many other fine players have performed for the fans of Brooklyn and Los Angeles over the years, some of whom narrowly missed making the final cut. Following is a list of those players deserving of an honorable mention. These are the men I deemed worthy of being slotted into positions 51 to 75 in the overall rankings. The statistics they compiled during their time with the Dodgers, and their most notable achievements as a member of the team are also included.

## 51 – Zack Greinke (P, 2013-15)

**Dodger Numbers:** 51-15; .773 Win Pct.; 2.30 ERA; 2 CG; 1 Shutout; 602⅔ IP; 555 Strikeouts; 1.027 WHIP

**Notable Achievements:**

- Surpassed 15 victories three times, winning 19 games once.
- Posted winning percentage in excess of .700 twice, topping the .800-mark once (.864 in 2015).
- Compiled ERA under 3.00 three times, posting mark under 2.00 once (1.66 in 2015).
- Struck out more than 200 batters twice.
- Threw more than 200 innings twice.
- Compiled WHIP under 1.000 once (0.844 in 2015).
- Led NL pitchers in: winning percentage twice, ERA once, WHIP once, and putouts once.
- Holds Dodgers career records for: lowest ERA (2.30), highest winning percentage (.773), and best strikeouts-to-walks ratio (4.302).
- Ranks second all-time on Dodgers with WHIP of 1.027.
- Threw 46 consecutive scoreless innings from 6/13/15 to 7/26/15.
- August 2013 NL Pitcher of the Month.
- Finished second in 2015 NL Cy Young voting.
- Finished seventh in 2015 NL MVP voting.
- 2015 Silver Slugger winner.
- Two-time Gold Glove winner (2014 & 2015).
- 2015 *Sporting News* NL Pitcher of the Year.
- Two-time NL All-Star (2014 & 2015).

## 52 – Jeff Pfeffer (P, 1913-21)

**Dodger Numbers:** 113-80; .585 Win Pct.; 2.31 ERA; 157 CG; 25 Shutouts; 1,748⅓ IP; 656 Strikeouts; 1.134 WHIP

### Notable Achievements:

- Surpassed 20 victories twice, topping 17 wins two other times.
- Compiled ERA below 2.50 four times, finishing with mark under 2.00 twice.
- Threw more than 250 innings five times, topping 300 innings pitched twice.
- Threw more than 20 complete games six times, completing 30 of his starts in 1916.
- Finished second in NL in: wins once, shutouts once, innings pitched once, and complete games twice.
- Ranks among Dodgers career leaders in: ERA (second), WHIP (10th), shutouts (eighth), and complete games (seventh).
- Two-time NL champion (1916 & 1920).

## 53 – Burt Hooton (P, 1975-84)

**Dodger Numbers:** 112-84; .571 Win Pct.; 3.14 ERA; 61CG; 22 Shutouts; 1,861⅓ IP; 1,042 Strikeouts; 1.181 WHIP

### Notable Achievements:

- Surpassed 18 victories twice.
- Posted winning percentage in excess of .700 once (.720 in 1975).
- Compiled ERA under 3.00 five times, posting mark under 2.50 once (2.28 in 1981).
- Threw more than 200 innings six times.
- Three-time NL Pitcher of the Month.
- Finished second in 1978 NL Cy Young voting.
- 1981 NLCS MVP.
- 1981 NL All-Star.
- Three-time NL champion (1977, 1978 & 1981).
- 1981 world champion.

## 54 – Bob Welch (P, 1978-87)

**Dodger Numbers:** 115-86; .572 Win Pct.; 3.14 ERA; 47 CG; 23 Shutouts; 8 Saves; 1,820⅔ IP; 1,292 Strikeouts; 1.206 WHIP

### Notable Achievements:

- Surpassed 15 victories three times.
- Posted winning percentage in excess of .700 once (.778 in 1985).
- Compiled ERA under 3.00 three times, posting mark under 2.50 twice.
- Threw more than 200 innings five times.
- Led NL pitchers with 4 shutouts in 1987.
- Finished second in NL with 251⅔ innings pitched in 1987.
- Ranks among Dodgers career leaders in strikeouts (10th) and shutouts (tied-10th).
- 1980 NL All-Star.
- Two-time NL champion (1978 & 1981).
- 1981 world champion.

## 55 – Jack Fournier (1B, 1923-26)

**Dodger Numbers:** 82 HR; 396 RBIs; 322 Runs Scored; 629 Hits; 85 Doubles; 35 Triples; 22 SB; .337 AVG; .421 OBP; .552 SLG PCT; .973 OPS

### Notable Achievements:

- Hit more than 20 home runs three times.
- Knocked in more than 100 runs three times, topping 130 RBIs once (130 in 1925).
- Batted over .300 three times, topping the .350-mark twice.
- Finished in double-digits in triples twice.
- Topped 30 doubles once (30 in 1923).
- Compiled on-base percentage in excess of .400 three times.
- Posted slugging percentage in excess of .500 three times.
- Compiled OPS in excess of 1.000 once (1.015 in 1925).
- Led NL in home runs once and bases on balls once.
- Finished second in NL in: home runs once, RBIs twice, triples once, on-base percentage once, slugging percentage once, and OPS once.

- Led NL first basemen in assists once.
- Ranks among Dodgers career leaders in: batting average (third), slugging percentage (fifth), and OPS (second).
- Had six hits in one game vs. Philadelphia on June 29, 1923.
- Hit three home runs in one game vs. St. Louis on July 13, 1926.

## 56 – Jerry Reuss (P, 1979-87)

**Dodger Numbers:** 86-69; .555 Win Pct.; 3.11 ERA; 44 CG; 16 Shutouts; 8 Saves; 1,407⅔ IP; 685 Strikeouts; 1.220 WHIP

### Notable Achievements:

- Won 18 games twice.
- Posted winning percentage in excess of .700 twice.
- Compiled ERA under 3.00 four times, posting mark under 2.50 once (2.30 in 1981).
- Threw more than 200 innings four times.
- Led NL pitchers with 6 shutouts in 1980.
- Finished second in NL in winning pct. once and WHIP once.
- Threw no-hitter vs. San Francisco on June 27, 1980.
- June 1980 NL Pitcher of the Month.
- Finished second in 1980 NL Cy Young voting.
- 1980 NL Comeback Player of the Year.
- 1980 NL All-Star.
- 1981 NL champion.
- 1981 world champion.

## 57 – Hugh Casey (P, 1939-42, 1946-48)

**Dodger Numbers:** 70-41; .631 Win Pct.; 3.34 ERA; 24 CG; 3 Shutouts; 49 Saves; 867⅔ IP; 325 Strikeouts; 1.302 WHIP

### Notable Achievements:

- Won 15 games in 1939.
- Finished in double digits in saves twice.
- Posted winning percentage in excess of .700 twice.
- Compiled ERA under 3.00 three times, posting mark under 2.00 once (1.99 in 1946).
- Threw more than 200 innings once (227⅓ in 1939).
- Led NL pitchers in saves twice and games finished once.
- Two-time NL champion (1941 & 1947).

## 58 – Hideo Nomo (P, 1995-98, 2002-2004)

**Dodger Numbers:** 81-66; .551 Win Pct.; 3.74 ERA; 12 CG; 7 Shutouts; 1,217⅓ IP; 1,200 Strikeouts; 1.279 WHIP

### Notable Achievements:

- Won 16 games three times.
- Posted winning percentage in excess of .700 once (.727 in 2002).
- Compiled ERA under 3.00 once (2.54 in 1995).
- Struck out more than 200 batters three times.
- Threw more than 200 innings four times.
- Led NL pitchers in: strikeouts once, shutouts once, and fewest hits allowed per 9 innings once.
- Finished second in NL in: ERA once, strikeouts once, shutouts once, and WHIP once.
- Threw no-hitter vs. Colorado on September 17, 1996.
- Two-time NL Pitcher of the Month.
- 1995 NL Rookie of the Year.
- Finished fourth in NL Cy Young voting twice.
- 1995 NL All-Star.

## 59 – Reggie Smith (OF, 1976-81)

**Dodger Numbers:** 97 HR; 301 RBIs; 314 Runs Scored; 516 Hits; 89 Doubles; 11 Triples; 32 SB; .297 AVG; .387 OBP; .528 SLG PCT; .915 OPS

### Notable Achievements:

- Hit more than 20 home runs twice, topping 30 homers once (32 in 1977).
- Scored more than 100 runs once (104 in 1977).
- Batted over .300 twice.
- Drew more than 100 bases on balls once (104 in 1977).
- Compiled on-base pct. in excess of .400 once (.427 in 1977).
- Posted slugging percentage in excess of .500 three times.
- Led NL in on-base percentage once and sacrifice flies once.
- Finished second in NL in slugging percentage once and OPS once.
- Ranks among Dodgers career leaders in slugging percentage (sixth) and OPS (sixth).
- Finished fourth in NL MVP voting twice (1977 & 1978).

- Three-time NL All-Star (1977, 1978 & 1980).
- Three-time NL champion (1977, 1978 & 1981).
- 1981 world champion.

## 60 – Wes Parker (1B, OF, 1964-72)

**Dodger Numbers:** 64 HR; 470 RBIs; 548 Runs Scored; 1,110 Hits; 194 Doubles; 32 Triples; 60 SB; .267 AVG; .351 OBP; .375 SLG PCT; .726 OPS

**Notable Achievements:**

- Knocked in more than 100 runs once (111 in 1970).
- Batted over .300 once (.319 in 1970).
- Surpassed 40 doubles once (47 in 1970).
- Led NL in doubles once and sacrifice hits once.
- Led NL first basemen in putouts once and fielding percent six times.
- Hit for cycle vs. New York Mets on May 7, 1970.
- Finished fifth in 1970 NL MVP voting.
- Six-time Gold Glove winner (1967, 1968, 1969, 1970, 1971 & 1972).
- Two-time NL champion (1965 & 1966).
- 1965 world champion.

## 61 – Carl Erskine (P, 1948-59)

**Dodger Numbers:** 122-78; .610 Win Pct.; 4.00 ERA; 71 CG; 14 Shutouts; 13 Saves; 1,718⅔ IP; 981 Strikeouts; 1.328 WHIP

**Notable Achievements:**

- Won 20 games once, surpassing 16 victories two other times.
- Posted winning percentage in excess of .700 three times.
- Compiled ERA under 3.00 once (2.70 in 1952).
- Threw more than 200 innings three times.
- Tossed 16 complete games in 1953.
- Led NL pitchers with .769 winning percentage in 1953.
- Finished second in NL with 187 strikeouts in 1953
- Threw two no-hitters (vs. Chicago Cubs on June 19, 1952 & vs. New York Giants on May 12, 1956).
- Finished ninth in 1953 NL MVP voting.
- 1954 NL All-Star.

- Six-time NL champion (1949, 1952, 1953, 1955, 1956 & 1959).
- Two-time world champion (1955 & 1959).

## 62 – Adrian Gonzalez (1B, 2012-16)

**Dodger Numbers:** 98 HR; 418 RBIs; 309 Runs Scored; 696 Hits; 147 Doubles; 1 Triple; .283 AVG; .344 OBP; .463 SLG PCT; .807 OPS

### Notable Achievements:

- Has hit more than 20 home runs three times.
- Has knocked in more than 100 runs twice.
- Has surpassed 30 doubles four times, topping 40 two-baggers once (41 in 2014).
- Led NL with 116 RBIs in 2014.
- Has led NL first basemen in: assists once, putouts once, double playsonce, and fielding percentage once.
- Hit three home runs in one game vs. San Diego on April 8, 2015.
- Finished seventh in 2014 NL MVP voting.
- 2014 Gold Glove winner.
- 2014 Silver Slugger winner.
- 2015 NL All-Star.

## 63 – Kirby Higbe (P, 1941-43, 1946-47)

**Dodger Numbers:** 70-38; .648 Win Pct.; 3.29 ERA; 51 CG; 8 Shutouts; 4 Saves; 931 IP; 488 Strikeouts; 1.354 WHIP

### Notable Achievements:

- Won 22 games in 1941.
- Surpassed 16 victories two other times.
- Posted winning percentage in excess of .700 once (.710 in 1941).
- Threw more than 200 innings three times.
- Tossed 19 complete games in 1941.
- Led NL pitchers in wins once and starts once.
- Finished second in NL with .710 winning percentage and 298 pitched in 1941.
- Ranks 10th in Dodgers history with career winning percentage of .648.
- Finished seventh in 1941 NL MVP voting.
- 1946 NL All-Star.
- 1941 NL champion.

Summary and Honorable Mentions

## 64 – Bill Dahlen (SS, 1899-1903, 1910-11)

**Dodger Numbers:** 12 HR; 365 RBIs; 381 Runs Scored; 645 Hits; 97 Doubles; 44 Triples; 137 SB; .266 AVG; .354 OBP; .357 SLG PCT; .711 OPS

### Notable Achievements:

- Finished in double-digits in triples once (11 in 1900).
- Finished second in NL with 82 walks in 1903.
- Led NL shortstops in assists twice and fielding percentage once.
- Two-time NL champion (1899 & 1900).

## 65 – Ralph Branca (P, 1944-53, 1956)

**Dodger Numbers:** 80-58; .580 Win Pct.; 3.70 ERA; 64 CG; 12 Shutouts; 18 Saves; 1,324 IP; 757 Strikeouts; 1.353 WHIP

### Notable Achievements:

- Won 21 games in 1947.
- Posted winning percentage in excess of .700 twice.
- Compiled ERA under 3.00 once (2.67 in 1947).
- Threw more than 200 innings three times.
- Tossed 15 complete games in 1947.
- Led NL pitchers in winning percentage once and games started once.
- Finished second in NL in: wins once, strikeouts once, and innings pitched once.
- 1947 *Sporting News* All-Star selection.
- Three-time NL All-Star (1947, 1948 & 1949).
- Three-time NL champion (1947, 1949 & 1952)

## 66 – Andy Messersmith (P, 1973-75, 1979)

**Dodger Numbers:** 55-34; .618 Win Pct.; 2.67 ERA; 43 CG; 13 Shutouts; 926 IP; 637 Strikeouts; 1.105 WHIP

### Notable Achievements:

- Won 20 games in 1974.
- Won 19 games in 1975.
- Posted winning percentage in excess of .700 once (.769 in 1974).
- Compiled ERA under 3.00 three times, posting mark under 2.50 once (2.29 in 1975).
- Struck out more than 200 batters twice.

– 383 –

- Threw more than 250 innings three times, topping 300 innings once (321⅔ in 1975).
- Tossed 19 complete games in 1975.
- Led NL pitchers in: wins once, shutouts once, complete games once, innings pitched once, WHIP once, and games started once.
- Finished second in NL in: ERA once, strikeouts once, innings pitched once, and WHIP once.
- Ranks among Dodgers career leaders in: ERA (10th), WHIP (fourth), and fewest hits allowed per 9 innings (fifth).
- Finished second in 1974 NL Cy Young voting.
- Two-time Gold Glove winner (1974 & 1975).
- 1974 *Sporting News* All-Star selection.
- Two-time NL All-Star (1974 & 1975).
- 1974 NL champion.

# 67 – Brett Butler (OF, 1991-97)

**Dodger Numbers:** 14 HR; 191 RBIs; 455 Runs Scored; 837 Hits; 75 Doubles; 41 Triples; 179 SB; .298 AVG; .392 OBP; .368 SLG PCT; .760 OPS

**Notable Achievements:**

- Batted over .300 twice.
- Scored more than 100 runs once (112 in 1991).
- Finished in double digits in triples twice.
- Stole more than 30 bases three times, swiping more than 40 bags once (41 in 1992).
- Drew more than 100 bases on balls once (108 in 1991).
- Compiled on-base percentage in excess of .400 three times.
- Led NL in: runs scored once, triples once, walks once, sacrifice hits once, and games played once.
- Finished second in NL in: hits once, triples once, and on-base percentage once.
- Led NL outfielders in: putouts once, fielding percentage twice, and double plays once.
- Tied for 10th all-time on Dodgers with .392 career on-base pct.
- July 1992 NL Player of the Month.
- Finished seventh in 1991 NL MVP voting.
- 1991 NL All-Star.

## 68 – Mike Marshall (P, 1974-76)

**Dodger Numbers:** 28-29; .491 Win Pct.; 3.01 ERA; 42 Saves; 380⅓ IP; 246 Strikeouts; 1.244 WHIP

### Notable Achievements:

- Won 15 games in 1974.
- Saved more than 20 games once (21 in 1974).
- Compiled ERA under 3.00 once (2.42 in 1974).
- Threw more than 200 innings once (208⅓ in 1974).
- Led NL in saves (21), pitching appearances (106), and games finished (83) in 1974.
- Holds Dodgers single-season records for most pitching appearances (106 in 1974) and most games finished (83 in 1974).
- Finished third in 1974 NL MVP voting.
- 1974 NL Cy Young Award winner.
- 1974 *Sporting News* NL Pitcher of the Year.
- 1974 *Sporting News* NL Fireman of the Year.
- Two-time NL All-Star (1974 & 1975).
- 1974 NL champion.

## 69 – Van Lingle Mungo (P, 1931-41)

**Dodger Numbers:** 102-99; .507 Win Pct.; 3.41 ERA; 114 CG; 16 Shutouts; 14 Saves; 1,739⅓ IP; 1,031 Strikeouts; 1.331 WHIP

### Notable Achievements:

- Surpassed 16 victories four times.
- Compiled ERA under 3.00 four times.
- Struck out more than 200 batters once (238 in 1936).
- Threw more than 200 innings five times, topping 300 innings twice.
- Tossed more than 20 complete games twice.
- Led NL pitchers in: strikeouts once, shutouts once, innings pitched once, and games started twice.
- Finished second in NL in strikeouts once and innings pitched once.
- Three-time NL All-Star (1934, 1936 & 1937).
- 1941 NL champion.

## 70 – Frank Howard (OF, 1B, 1958-64)

**Dodger Numbers:** 123 HR; 382 RBIs; 293 Runs Scored; 567 Hits; 80 Doubles; 14 Triples;

3 SB; .269 AVG; .326 OBP; .495 SLG PCT; .822 OPS

**Notable Achievements:**

- Hit more than 20 home runs four times, topping 30 homers once (31 in 1962).
- Knocked in more than 100 runs once (119 in 1962).
- Posted slugging percentage in excess of .500 three times.
- July 1962 NL Player of the Month.
- 1960 NL Rookie of the Year.
- 1963 NL champion.
- 1963 world champion.

## 71 – Kenley Jansen (P, 2010-2016)

**Dodger Numbers:** Record: 19-13; .594 Win Pct.; 2.20 ERA; 189 Saves; 408⅔ IP; 632 Strikeouts; 0.893 WHIP

**Notable Achievements:**

- Has saved more than 40 games twice, topping 20 saves three other times.
- Has compiled ERA below 3.00 seven times, finishing with mark under 2.00 on three occasions.
- Has posted WHIP under 1.000 four times.
- Has recorded more than 100 strikeouts three times.
- Has recorded more strikeouts than innings pitched each season.
- Finished second in NL with 47 saves in 2016.
- Finished third in NL with 44 saves in 2014.
- Holds Dodgers all-time record for most career saves (189).
- Ranks sixth in Dodgers history in pitching appearances (409).
- 2016 NL All-Star.

## 72 – Eddie Stanky (2B, SS, 1944-47)

**Dodger Numbers:** 14 HR; 191 RBIs; 455 Runs Scored; 837 Hits; 75 Doubles; 41 Triples; 179 SB; .298 AVG; .392 OBP; .368 SLG PCT; .760 OPS

**Notable Achievements:**

- Scored more than 100 runs once (128 in 1945).
- Drew more than 100 bases on balls three times.
- Compiled on-base percentage in excess of .400 twice.
- Led NL in: runs scored once, walks twice, on-base percentage once, and sacrifice hits once.
- Led NL second basemen in fielding percentage once and double plays three times.
- Ranks fifth in Dodgers history with career on-base percentage of .405.
- Finished seventh in 1946 NL MVP voting.
- 1947 NL All-Star.
- 1947 NL champion.

## 73 – Charlie Neal (2B, SS, 3B, 1956-61)

**Dodger Numbers:** 73 HR; 312 RBIs; 374 Runs Scored; 659 Hits; 86 Doubles; 28 Triples; 45 SB; .265 AVG; .334 OBP; .409 SLG PCT; .743 OPS

**Notable Achievements:**

- Hit more than 20 home runs once (22 in 1958).
- Scored more than 100 runs once (103 in 1959).
- Finished in double-digits in triples once (11 in 1959).
- Surpassed 30 doubles once (30 in 1959).
- Led NL in triples once and sacrifice hits once.
- Led NL second basemen in: putouts once, fielding percentage once, double plays twice.
- Finished eighth in 1959 NL MVP voting.
- 1959 Gold Glove winner.
- Two-time NL All-Star (1959 & 1960).
- Two-time NL champion (1956 & 1959).
- 1959 world champion.

## 74 – James Loney (1B, 2006-2012)

**Dodger Numbers:** 71 HR; 451 RBIs; 355 Runs Scored; 872 Hits; 173 Doubles; 20 Triples; 29 SB; .284 AVG; .341 OBP; .423 SLG PCT; .764 OPS

**Notable Achievements:**

- Batted over .300 once (.331 in 2007).
- Surpassed 30 doubles three times, topping 40 two-baggers once (41 in 2010).
- Posted slugging percentage in excess of .500 twice.
- Tied single-game franchise record with 9 RBIs vs. Colorado on
- September 28, 2006.
- September 2007 NL Rookie of the Month.

# 75 – John Roseboro (C, 1957-67)

**Dodger Numbers:** 92 HR; 471 RBIs; 441 Runs Scored; 1,009 Hits; 162 Doubles; 44 Triples; 59 SB; .251 AVG; .327 OBP; .382 SLG PCT; .709 OPS

**Notable Achievements:**

- Led NL catchers in: putouts four times, double plays twice, and caught-stealing percentage twice.
- Two-time Gold Glove winner (1961 & 1966).
- Three-time NL All-Star (1958, 1961 & 1962).
- Four-time NL champion (1959, 1963, 1965 & 1966).
- Three-time world champion (1959, 1963 & 1965).

# GLOSSARY

## Abbreviations and Statistical Terms

**AVG.** Batting average. The number of hits divided by the number of at-bats.

**CG.** Complete games pitched.

**CL.** Closer.

**ERA.** Earned run average. The number of earned runs a pitcher gives up, per nine innings. This does not include runs that scored as a result of errors made in the field and is calculated by dividing the number of runs given up, by the number of innings pitched, and multiplying the result by 9.

**HITS.** Base hits. Awarded when a runner safely reaches at least first base upon a batted ball, if no error is recorded.

**HR.** Home runs. Fair ball hit over the fence, or one hit to a spot that allows the batter to circle the bases before the ball is returned to home plate.

**IP.** Innings pitched.

**MVP.** Most Valuable Player

**NL.** National League

**NLCS.** National League Championship Series

**NLDS.** National League Division Series

**OBP.** On-base percentage. Hits plus walks plus hit-by-pitches, divided by plate appearance.

**OPS.** On-base plus slugging

**RBI**. Runs batted in. Awarded to the batter when a runner scores upon a safely batted ball, a sacrifice or a walk.

**RUNS.** Runs scored by a player.

**SB.** Stolen bases.

**SLG.** Slugging percentage. The number of total bases earned by all singles, doubles, triples and home runs, divided by the total number of at-bats.

**SO.** Strikeouts.

**SP.** Starting pitcher.

**SU.** Set-up reliever.

**WIN PCT.** Winning percentage. A pitcher's number of wins divided by his number of total decisions (i.e. wins plus losses).

# BIBLIOGRAPHY

## Books:

DeMarco, Tony, et al., *The Sporting News Selects 50 Greatest Sluggers.* St. Louis: The Sporting News, a division of Times Mirror Magazines, Inc., 2000.

Shalin, Mike, and Neil Shalin, *Out by a Step: The 100 Best Players Not in the Baseball Hall of Fame.* Lanham, MD: Diamond Communications, Inc., 2002.

Thorn, John, and Palmer, Pete, eds., with Michael Gershman, *Total Baseball*. New York: HarperCollins Pub., Inc., 1993.

Williams, Ted, with Jim Prime, *Ted Williams' Hit List*. Indianapolis, IN: Masters Press, 1996.

## Videos:

Ritter, Lawrence and Bud Greenspan. *The Glory of their Times*. Cappy Productions, Inc., 1985.

*The Sporting News' 100 Greatest Baseball Players*. National Broadcasting Co., 1999.

## Internet Websites:

BaseballLibrary.com. *The Ballplayers*. http://www.baseballlibrary.com/baseballlibrary/ballplayers.

Society for American Baseball Research. "SABR Baseball Biography Project." Last modified November 12, 2016. http://sabr.org/bioproject.

MLB Advanced Media. "Historical Stats." Last modified January 20, 2016. http://www.mlb.com/stats.historical/individual.

Baseball Almanac, Inc. "The Ballplayers: A Baseball Player Encyclopedia." http://www.baseball-almanac.com/players/ballplayers.shtml.

Sports Reference LLC. "Players." Last modified December 20, 2016. http://www.baseball-reference.com/players.

Retrosheet.org. "The Players." http://www.retrosheet.org/boxesetc/index. html#players.

Sports Reference LLC. "Teams." Last modified December 20, 2016. http://www.baseball-reference.com/teams.

BaseballChronology.com. "TSN-All-Stars." Last modified 2005. http:// www.baseballchronology.com/Baseball/Awards/TSN-AllStars.asp.